Startups and Crisis Management

Drawing on a mixture of theory, cases, and interviews, *Startups and Crisis Management* provides a valuable overview of how new ventures fared in the wake of the COVID-19 pandemic. It then considers the wider lessons for startups operating in times of crisis and adjusting to the 'new normal'.

The macroeconomic shocks of rising unemployment, lockdowns, and remote working have impacted the entrepreneurial ecosystem and raised questions about how startups can survive, adjust, and thrive once more. This book analyses the reciprocal relationship between startups and their ecosystems, using theoretical lenses such as push and pull factors, necessity entrepreneurship, networking, and embeddedness. Each chapter contains case studies based on interviews with individuals from startups around the world, exploring how real-life firms reacted to the coronavirus crisis.

This illuminating text will be a useful resource for modules exploring startups during times of crisis, and courses on entrepreneurship and crisis management more broadly.

Dafna Kariv is full-time faculty member at the Adelson School of Entrepreneurship, Reichman University, Herzliya, the Head of the Dual Degree Entrepreneurship-Business Administration, and the Chair of the School's research Committee. Professor Kariv is also an Affiliate Professor at HEC, Montreal, Canada.

Kariv is the author of seven academic books, and numerous published papers focusing on international entrepreneurship, entrepreneurial performance, female entrepreneurship and psychological aspects of entrepreneurs. She is a recipient of several prized funds, the Ambassador at GINSUM (German Israeli Network of Startups & Mittelstand) and involved in various academic boards.

Startups and Crisis Management

Dafna Kariv

LONDON AND NEW YORK

Cover image: Getty Images

First published 2023
by Routledge
4 Park Square, Milton Park, Abingdon, Oxon OX14 4RN

and by Routledge
605 Third Avenue, New York, NY 10158

Routledge is an imprint of the Taylor & Francis Group, an informa business

British Library Cataloguing-in-Publication Data
A catalogue record for this book is available from the British Library

Library of Congress Cataloging-in-Publication Data
Names: Kariv, Dafna, author.
Title: Startups and crisis management / Dafna Kariv.
Description: 1 Edition. | New York, NY : Routledge, 2023. | Includes bibliographical references and index.
Identifiers: LCCN 2022018466 | ISBN 9781032003580 (hardback) | ISBN 9781032001043 (paperback) | ISBN 9781003173809 (ebook)
Subjects: LCSH: New business enterprises—Management. | Crisis management.
Classification: LCC HD62.5 .K357 2023 | DDC 658.11—dcundefined
LC record available at https://lccn.loc.gov/2022018466

ISBN: 9781032003580 (hbk)
ISBN: 9781032001043 (pbk)
ISBN: 9781003173809 (ebk)

DOI: 10.4324/9781003173809

Typeset in Univers
by codeMantra

Contents

Acknowledgements

I was about to go out for my morning jog when a lockdown was announced in Israel due to the worldwide coronavirus pandemic. It was March 19, 2020. We were told not to leave our homes unless absolutely necessary and that anyone who violated this directive could be fined. I renounced my jogging routine. In fact, I felt much more protected staying at home with my family. I imagined that any encounter outside, even at a distance, posed a real threat of contamination. While unexpected and somehow shocking, the formal announcement of this first lockdown in Israel was a powerful and enlightening moment for me; I recognized the emergence of a new reality and understood that everything that we deemed 'normal' was about to change. Yet, while previous crisis episodes that I had tackled felt like they couldn't be controlled or managed, with the outbreak of COVID-19, I felt an urge to act, contribute, and 'save the world', albeit from home via my computer; I thought to contribute to entrepreneurs, as this is my expertise. Consequently, I eagerly developed a virtual workshop entitled 'Startups Navigating in COVID-19' that focused on the different avenues and practices entrepreneurs could pursue to effectively navigate their startups through the COVID-19 pandemic. I have presented this workshop all over the world, through Zoom, free of charge, with great enthusiasm. The workshop provided me with a unique opportunity to closely interact with more than 100 entrepreneurs and players in their entrepreneurial ecosystems, from governmental, corporate, and private associations for entrepreneurs to incubators, accelerators, and academia. I could clearly see how the workshop dynamics resonated each country's atmosphere and accurately told the story of their current state. The remarkable insights gained from the workshops gave me a grasp of the unique ways entrepreneurs navigate disruptive periods. It was then that I realized the potential for a book on the topic. I contacted Terry Clague, Senior Publisher, Business and Management and Andrew Harrison, Editor, Business Textbooks, both from Routledge, Taylor & Francis, UK, whose thoughts and insights on new ideas for publication I greatly respect. They urged me to develop the manuscript by steering some piercing directions and suggested broadening the scope of the book to startups' management of crisis episodes in general, rather than just the COVID-19 pandemic. I am so grateful for this suggestion. Our valuable discussions matured into this book. I was fortunate to obtain additional highly professional, thorough, and responsive support from the team of Routledge: Helena Parkinson, Natalie Tomlinson, and Chloe James. This is the fifth book that I am publishing with Routledge, and I consistently appreciate their high expertise, creativity, and open-mindedness along with a kind and thoughtful approach that has always invigorated my own creativity. I am thankful for this valuable collaboration.

For this book, I interviewed more than 20 founders of startups and stakeholder companies in many countries representing a broad range of industries; these were developed into case studies (Chapter 11) and the 'at-a-glance' cases incorporated into each chapter[1]; I was inspired by the different stories that the entrepreneurs shared during the workshops, and these have also been embedded in the book.

This was a stimulating experience for me. Writing a book as things happen, while also participating and not only observing the sequence of events, captivated me not only intellectually but also emotionally. So many people's encouragement, support, and contributions provided the foundation for this book's fruition.

I am grateful to the inspirational heroes who were interviewed for this book's cases; some have garnered remarkable achievements during this book's writing and inspire us all in proving the power of dedication, creativity, and opportunity exploration in times of crisis. Special thanks go to Eran Ben-Shushan, Eynat Guez, Vered Raviv Schwarz, Marcus Dantus, and many more. Through their stories, unique mindsets, and decision-making junctions leading to ambitious actions, these interviews enabled me to craft models of startups' management of the pandemic and develop new knowledge on startups' responses to disruption. Incredible figures, dedicated to supporting entrepreneurship by creating strategic collaborations and paving the way for startups to thrive in the pandemic, opened their doors to me and introduced me to their ecosystems. My thanks go to highly ranked delegates in the Israeli embassies and consulates in Canada, the United States, Mexico, Germany, Czech Republic, Croatia, India; and to the managing teams in the accelerators, incubators, centers for entrepreneurs, angel investors, and managers of venture capital firms.

During the pandemic, I was extremely privileged to be invited as a full faculty member by one of the leading academic institutions in Israel, Reichman University, to be part of the very professional, creative, engaged, supportive, and kind faculty at the Adelson School of Entrepreneurship led by Dr. Yossi Maaravi and Professor Yair Tauman. The school encourages daring, trying, experiencing, and creating, and celebrates all initiatives and undertakings. I am thankful from the bottom of my heart to Yossi, Yair, Dana, Dafna, Gali, Gail, Revital, Ofir, Adi, Tout, and Sharon. My deepest thanks and appreciation go to Reichman University, which has supported me in so many ways, financially, administratively, and technically.

This book could not have been completed without Camille Vainstein, whose copy-editing refined the manuscript's concepts, and contributed enormously to adding depth to the book by polishing my writing so that it adequately articulates my views. This is the fifth book on which Camille and I have collaborated, and I always feel that I am improving my language skills through Camille's insightful remarks and meticulous work.

Thank you, Noa Rosenberg and Itai Heiman, for your accurate, bright, and incredibly valuable assistance in connecting the dots.

Writing a book is an art! It is an epic roller coaster: there are times when ideas flow and times characterized by writer's block; the latter are typical to disruption when attention and thoughts are preoccupied with concerns derived from a crisis' fallout. Emotional support is therefore crucial in advancing the writing process. I am so privileged and grateful to be embraced by my beloved family, the anchor in my life. Due to the relevance of this book, my family was not only my source of encouragement and inspiration but also eagerly contributed through many discussions and examples that I could convert into insightful concepts in my book.

In particular, with my husband Raanan, when both of us were working from home during lockdowns and enjoying quality time together, we could devote longer hours to discussing the 'situation' from various aspects and analyzing it from multiple views; these inspiring discussions added both depth and new 'color' to my work on the book. It was a unique opportunity to brief Raanan on the book's progress, refine my ideas through his insightful feedback, and gain more energy from his endless belief in me. Tomer, Ofir, and Shir, and Maayan, Shiran, and Ella, my pride and source of inspiration, fuel my life with so much joy; by breathing in their passion for life and drive to fulfill their dreams, I feel stimulated and renewed. I am thankful to my mother, Bianca Barel, for her unflagging emotional support and faith in me.

Dafna Kariv

Note

1 In some cases, entrepreneur or business details were changed, as per the interviewee's request.

An inspirational foreword

I was fortunate to meet Professor Uriel Reichman, Founding President and Chairperson of the Board of Directors of Reichman University (RUNI[1]), for an in-depth discussion on the avenues that he has pursued during the pandemic. Professor Reichman's underlying premise has rested on guaranteeing that RUNI's students, faculty, and staff be shielded from the pandemic's fallout. The strategies used by RUNI to navigate the pandemic exemplify how cutting-edge academia engages in multiple roles to concurrently enable its internal partners to pursue their regular lives, while embarking on innovation and advancing frontline contributions to academia and society. During the pandemic's lockdowns and social distancing, Professor Reichman relayed a three-fold message: "I ensured that students would follow their regular programs, so that they would not be forced to graduate later than planned; I protected the students' and staff's health; and we promised to ensure RUNI's continuity." Professor Reichman, a leading, inspirational figure in Israel and worldwide, took action: the campus was immediately digitally equipped to make the complete switch to remote learning, as well as to allow hybrid learning; the faculty was prepared for this obligatory digital revolution, and the collaboration and dialogue with the students was maintained and even strengthened; as an outcome, computer science students mentored the faculty in areas of technology and digitalization, and various inspiring initiatives and undertakings emerged.

While vigorously orchestrating these developments and continually maintaining an open dialogue with the students to carefully follow their dynamic needs, Professor Reichman's continuing endeavor to be officially announced as the first private university in Israel intensified, along with his effort to establish the first private medical school in Israel; as a result, both of these aims were fulfilled during the pandemic; and his new endeavor to establish a cutting-edge Innovation Center and develop new frontline programs has been invigorated. The combined model advanced by Professor Reichman, which focuses on the 'here and now' while forcefully striving to accomplish the ongoing mission, emerged as an inspirational model for RUNI's students, faculty, and staff during the pandemic. "The university was established for the students, who then graduate and become our alumni. It is a long-term relationship, a lifetime. Therefore, at any time, under any conditions, we are here for our students. They are not clients, or 'children'; rather, they are our partners; they are the core of our activity, and the essence of our vision and mission," explains Professor Reichman. Drawing on this foundation, the strategies employed during the pandemic are discussed and crafted conjointly with the students to accurately delve into their new, emerging needs and to respond to them precisely, in tight alignment with environmental advances. "We educate our students through our motto of freedom and responsibility. We provide them with the tools, skills, and spirit to implement their dreams, but only by guaranteeing responsibility for their surroundings and acting within that framework, in tandem," says Professor Reichman. Accordingly, he continues, "any crisis embodies opportunities. It is our responsibility to be hands-on, while continuing to be a role model for our internal and external partners." RUNI has assembled a remarkable ecosystem encompassing leading figures from all over the world who have a deep trust in Professor Reichman's vision, and an appreciation of, and admiration for RUNI's achievements. This goes back to 1994, when many leading figures left their secure jobs to join Professor Reichman in his first and novel steps toward establishing RUNI. The vision, dedication, and responsibility to the surroundings, followed by actions and achievements, are inspiring and stimulating. In Professor Reichman's words: "We need to advance. Technology forces us to take a good long look beyond the here and now, anticipate the future, and incorporate it into the present. Technology, Biomedicine, Sustainability, Globalization, are only some examples of areas that are no longer elective, to be sporadically taught and researched; they now represent the new reality, and embody the message that the 'future is already here', hence, they must be offered in our programs. As a university, we are responsible for pointing out the new, and for advancing toward it with our partners. Lagging behind is not an option." Professor Reichman concludes: "Our students and alumni look up to us; we are there to enable them to write their own narratives, take risks, develop their self-efficacy. We are therefore responsible for paving the most advanced roads for our students so that they can be successful in any direction taken."

Note

1 RUNI was established by Professor Reichman in 1994, and it is the first private university in Israel. https://www.runi.ac.il/en/about/

Chapter One

Paving the way for the 'new normal'

An introduction to the field

- Takeaways
- Overview
- Theoretical glimpse
- Looking at the emerging 'new normal'
- What does the 'new normal' entail?
- The impetus—COVID-19: an unexpected 'occurrence' in a highly technological era
- The methodology
- Summary
- Reflective questions for class

Never waste a good crisis
Winston Churchill

Takeaways

- Recognizing the role of crises in introducing threats as well as opportunities, contingent on various internal and external factors that should be detected
- Remarking that COVID-19 is a unique crisis, due to its widespread exposure, long duration, and the inability to stop it in its initial stages, changing startup ecosystems dramatically
- Observing the reciprocal relations between startups and crises: startups are one of the main factors managing crises and promoting effective recovery of the start-up's scene; startups also provoke crises
- Understanding the complex association of startups-ecosystems-crises by sorting out the actual versus perceived statuses of each (e.g., the startup is actually equipped with the technologies to cope with the crisis' effects versus the founders perceiving the startup as unprepared to manage the crisis)
- Reviewing the crisis-induced challenges faced by startups through different theoretical conceptualizations; opening the mind to diverse perspectives to resonate the startup's course of action in navigating the crisis

DOI: 10.4324/9781003173809-1

Overview

The COVID-19 pandemic is gradually provoking startups and their ecosystems worldwide by introducing uncertainty and inducing dramatic modifications in almost every aspect of the entrepreneurial realm. The pandemic presents a unique situation that has no documented equivalent in the entrepreneurship literature, despite the experience with other recent virus outbreaks such as Ebola and Zika. COVID-19 took the vast majority of startups by surprise, forcing navigation of the unexpected changes 'on the go' whilst adapting to a 'new normal'. The challenge to startups posed by the pandemic is twofold: they need to develop and introduce innovations as in 'normal' times, while embracing the changes that are emerging as an outcome of COVID-19 (e.g., digitalization, working from home, lower investments); such changes may hinder startup's 'normal' flow of activities, survival, and growth.

The existing ecosystems have consistently benefited from the vigorous entrepreneurship, innovation, and developments created by startups; yet, the pandemic has introduced a number of phenomena, for example, unemployment, lockdowns, social distancing, that affect startups and thus expose a flaw in the startup's alleged omnipotence: they have been less efficient at providing prompt and complete solutions in response to the new challenges. The changes that have been introduced by the pandemic have alarmed the startups and their ecosystems, raising the need for a thorough investigation of the new and changing phenomena encountered by the startups and how they should navigate these new conditions.

Reciprocal relationships

Startups are believed to be an effective vehicle to escape or minimize the effects of crises, and have been recognized as a promising key factor in reviving the economy. Because they are relatively small and more vulnerable businesses, the complexities delivered by crises can be harmful or risky for startups, thereby hindering their effectiveness and responsiveness. Customers have less resources to purchase startup's products and services as these are mainly innovative and more of the 'nice to have' variety. Investors may be more reluctant to support startups, because they are also facing financial and business-related difficulties, and ecosystems may unrealistically expect startups to introduce innovation in response to the rising complexities. As a result, startups will encounter more difficulties in creating solutions and eventually surviving.

Concurrently, and almost 'by definition', startups are born in crises; they face multiple crises along their journey in generating financial sources, developing competitive advantages for their product, or obtaining the best technology for their offerings. Startups navigate more naturally within crises—through their accumulated experience, they are equipped with the mindsets, tools, and strategies to cope with crises by exploiting opportunities, using more agile and proactive strategies, or engaging in disruptive innovations.

Startups are also the vehicle that enflames crises; their viability and sustainability rely on disruptive innovation, challenging the prevailing offerings, and recurrently pushing their ecosystem 'out of its comfort zone' by reciprocally adapting their new developments.

Overall, startups under crisis are reliant on the components laid out in Table 1.1, which describes the conditions required for a startup to manage a crisis, and emphasize factors that can be controlled or managed by the startup. While general knowledge would indicate higher levels of all included components, that is, high levels of existing financial capital and a supportive ecosystem that is inclined to assist—which is too idealistic in most cases, this table refers to the minimum required so that no damage will be done; for example, there is no need to be highly inclined to ask for the ecosystem's assistance, should the startup be equipped for crisis events; it would be more useful for the startup to focus on its internal resources, to adjust and redeploy, to manage the crisis effects or in a normal, non-crisis situation, startups may not strive to adjust the ecosystem so that it is supportive; they may lean on their actual and perpetual resources, as shown in Table 1.1. Figure 1.1 illustrates these relationships.

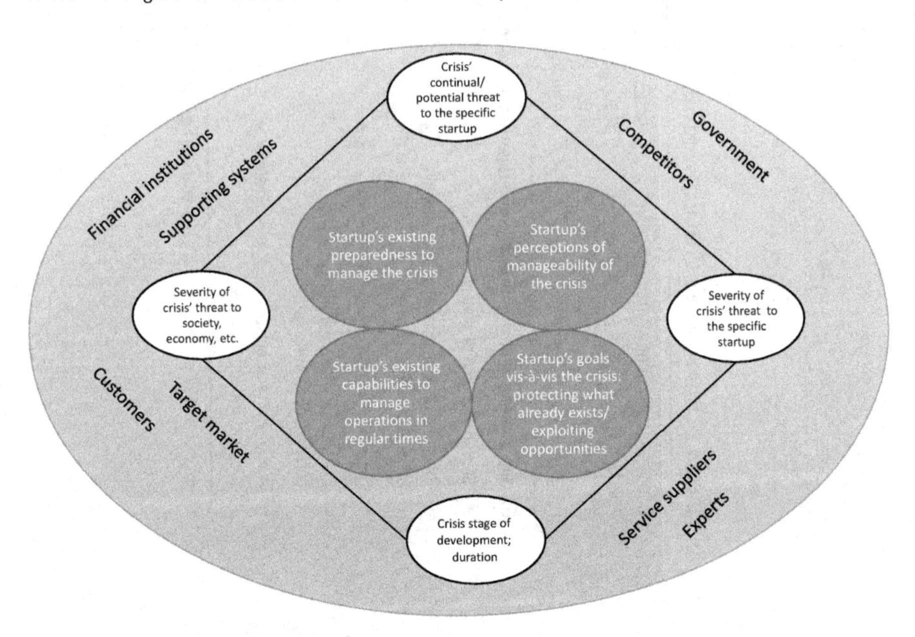

FIGURE 1.1 A multilayered perspective of startups under crises

Overview

TABLE 1.1 The minimum optimal actions required in crisis events

Concurrent conditions when the crisis erupts	Actual resources (e.g., financial, IP, technological)	Perceived resources	Available ecosystem support systems	Startup's willingness to ask for support	Ecosystem's state during the crisis (recession, dynamics)
Startup's management of the crisis with regard to the concurrent crisis conditions[a]					
• Startup's existing resources	+	+	+–	+–	+–
• Startup's robustness to pursue its activities under crisis conditions	+	+	–	+–	–
• Startup's preparedness for crisis events	+–	+–	+	+	+–
• Crisis threat to the startup (e.g., crisis duration, already disrupted)	+	+	+	+	+
• Availability of recognized ways to eliminate the crisis disruption	+	+–	+–	+–	+–

[a] +, very important for managing the crisis; +–, moderately important for managing the crisis; –, not critical (lower importance) for managing the crisis.

Theoretical glimpse

The literature fails to offer a consistent view of startups in times of crisis; moreover, research has almost overlooked the variation in types of crises, the subsequent action taken by startups, and the reciprocal relations between startups and ecosystems that develop in crises. This book takes on those deficiencies and knowledge gaps in the literature and analyzes the challenges introduced by crises through an intertwining of practical and conceptual approaches to understanding the multiplicity of the startup dynamics vis-à-vis crises.

The following theoretical approaches can be employed to construct the theoretical premise of the reciprocal relationships between startup action and activities and crisis dynamics. Table 1.2 provides the implications of the main theoretical perspectives for the crisis framework in which the startup's actions are exhibited. The crisis framework is fueled with uncertainty, with effects that are already hitting the startup, and with competition for resources such as investors' money and customers' attraction to the startup's products. Under such unexpected and unstable conditions, various factors can invigorate or prevent the startup's pursuit of their course of action, including the opportunities they foresee from the crisis' emergence, the strength of networking and their trust in community support, their perceptions as well as resilience in the face of crisis effects on their business, the crisis' actual severity, the startup's preparedness to manage crises, strategies taken to cope with crises, among others. As COVID-19 is still being researched, some parts of the puzzle require deeper attention and exploration.

This book aims to provide some of these missing links by carefully and meticulously analyzing and introducing new insights into information generated from research, practice, and various interviews conducted with entrepreneurs and startup stakeholders worldwide.

TABLE 1.2 Theoretical perspectives and the missing links

Theoretical approach	Implications for startups during crises	The missing links
Dynamic capabilities (e.g., Zahra, Sapienza and Davidsson 2006; Teece 2014)	• Startups develop relevant capabilities which allow them to create new products/services/processes that are aligned to the changing needs in times of crisis, for example • Competitive advantage can be developed through the startup's ability to cope with environmental changes • Dynamic capabilities are change-oriented capabilities that help startups redeploy and reconfigure their existing resources to respond to external changes; crises create an imbalance in the existing resources	• The specific capabilities required to prepare for crises, including those that can be valuable in 'normal' times • The quest to respond to various contrasting changes in the ecosystem by developing new capabilities • The costs of developing dynamic capabilities during crises

(*Continued*)

Overview

Theoretical approach	Implications for startups during crises	The missing links
	• Dynamic capabilities are learned and stable patterns • Dynamic capabilities echo the road forward envisioned by the founder(s) for the 'new normal'	• Whose vision matters? Developing dynamic capabilities though the founders' eyes, the CMO, CTO, etc.
Opportunity exploitation, exploration, discovery (e.g., Shane and Venkataraman 2000; Choi and Shepherd 2004)	• Crises embody opportunities, although they may not always be obvious • Opportunities can be either valuable or risky, in either the short or long term (e.g., by immediately mitigating the disruptive crisis fallout, but risking the startup's future partnerships, investing in a promising project that puts the current cash flow at risk) • There are different stages in addressing an opportunity, from 'simply' identifying it to practicalities, such as activating it	• In times of crisis, startups tend to focus on protecting existing resources • There is still a lack of knowledge on the stimulators that transform the startup's perspective from protecting to investing
Networking Communities Embeddedness (e.g., Chell and Baines 2000; Johannisson 2007) Ecosystems—involvement, support; stakeholders (Stam 2015; Muñoz et al. 2019; Ratten 2020)	• Sharing knowledge, expertise, and action plans is valuable both business-wise and emotionally and socially, especially in situations of lockdowns and social isolation • Resilience and robustness of the startup are contingent on providing the customer with a customized and swift response that can be easily achieved through communities	• Networking while protecting the tangible and intangible resources during turbulent crisis episodes is counterintuitive for startups • More success stories describing the conditions to create this situation are required

Resilience theory (e.g., Roundy, Brockman and Bradshaw 2017; Duchek 2018)	• Resilience theory is important for the psychological aspects when encountering crisis effects; it can be cultivated to fortify startup's ability to bounce back by:
	  • Crafting normalcy
	  • Affirming identity anchors
	  • Making use of communication networks
	  • Putting alternative logic to work
	  • Emphasizing positive feelings while downplaying negative ones
	• Integrated risk management, which is critical in any action taken during a crisis; startups seek to evaluate the risks in all of their activities combined, rather than in isolation
		• Whose resilience should we focus on? That of the startup as a business, the founder(s), the team(s)?
		• Resilient ecosystems are critical in crisis episodes
		• Developing practical resilience-driven methods that work in the crisis management blueprint

Conceptual innovation models	• The main function of an entrepreneur is to introduce innovations, defined by Schumpeter as any new policy that reduces the overall cost of production or increases the demand for products; crises bring opportunities that should be thoroughly assessed for their conversion to innovation
	• Crises can introduce conditions that serve to cultivate the different types of innovation (e.g., incremental, radical, disruptive)
	• Crises embody a great opportunity to innovate internally in marketing and branding; technology; co-creation, etc.
		• Innovation can promote recovery from the disruption as well as inventing the next 'new thing'. Differentiating between the two is imperative
		  • Crises invigorate different types of innovation in different sectors of the startup
		  • Innovation is contingent on location, industry, and crisis characteristics and should be viewed in these contexts

Crisis management models (Fink 1986; Kuckertz et al. 2020)	• Crises consist of stages: prior to the first signs of the crisis outbreak, acute phase, recovery from the damage. Each stage is triggered by different factors. The stages are:
	  • Prodromal
	  • Acute
	  • Chronic
	  • Resolution
	• Proactive, Defensive, and Reactive crisis management refer to the levels of the startup's preparation and acceptance of the crisis as well as of the startup's responsibility to change, contribute, communicate, cooperate, retain transparency and recover, and support the recovery of its stakeholders
		• Research in crisis management should be split into crises that are global, regional, and within the industry
		• There should be a different research approach for the daily crises faced by startups and those with a more widespread effect
		• The avenues taken by startups to cope with crisis effects are crucial
		• The role of the startup in the ecosystem's recovery through collaborations is essential, especially as startups in their initial stages may be more suspicious of collaborations due to IP, fear of imitation, among others

Looking at the emerging 'new normal'

The COVID-19 pandemic is present and global, unleashing changes in every domain of our lives. Experts have already agreed that: "COVID-19 is here to stay. The world is working out how to live with it."[1] Its impact is most powerful, global, and disruptive and above all, beyond any expectations, hitting startups and their ecosystems in unforeseen aspects that should be meticulously screened, learned about, and understood as a platform to sort out strategies to navigate the crisis, to develop innovative—and accurate—responses to current needs (e.g., vaccines, virtual education, or mobile applications for the elderly's safety) and overall to leverage the entrepreneurial ecosystem and in particular startups.

The pandemic has infected millions of people worldwide since its discovery in China in December 2019 and it has forced governments to lock down their populations and businesses, producing manifold changes in the startup's landscape as well as in other areas. The concept of the 'day after' has shifted to one of 'new normal' in seemingly every domain that touches startups, for example, social communication and interactions; vision; business models; innovation; remote work; new meanings of finance, purchasing power, and marketing; and founders' psychological aspects. The implication is that even if the virus is controlled in the future, the changes that have already taken root in the landscape will endure and will require considerable adjustments in the affected domains.

What does the 'new normal' entail?

Under this scenario, academic materials and books should take on the perspective of the 'new normal'. It seems imperative for students, academic staff, and academic course designers as well as stakeholders in the startup ecosystem—for example, investors, government officials, community builders, and accelerator initiators—to both pursue the concurrent building of strategies aligned to the 'new normal' and contribute to shaping or promoting the newly developed ecosystems to foster new startup's development and nurture the existing ones, including those leaving wreckage behind them due to the pandemic.

This book thus offers a pioneering comprehensive overview of startup's actions during the pandemic; it provides an opportunity to capture the multiple aspects of this multifaceted phenomenon facing startups. Its focus is to portray a timely, up-to-date picture of startups and their ecosystems under the COVID-19 crisis and then expand the scope to carefully decipher the reciprocal impacts of startups and crises; identify the strategies of startups engaged in navigating these turbulent times toward preparing for the 'day after', that is, the 'new normal,' and contributing to their ecosystems during and after the crisis. COVID-19 represents a new form of crisis, in that it is 'equally' dispersed throughout the world, affecting startups and forcing changes in various ways. Naturally, no robust research has yet been generated on this pandemic.

This is an essential book, meant to familiarize its readers with the new and emerging reality of startups and encourage them to become involved and proactive in crafting the 'new normal' toward building a better—and perhaps not yet envisioned—world. By providing the foundations for understanding this new phenomenon, startup adjustments to future crises will be easier and more effective.

The impetus—COVID-19: an unexpected 'occurrence' in a highly technological era

In December 2019, reports emerged from Wuhan, China, on the infection of individuals by a highly contagious coronavirus, considered to have evolved from the virus infecting the live animal markets in Wuhan. The Chinese government locked down Wuhan in January 2020. On March 11, 2020, the World Health Organization (WHO) declared the outbreak of Coronavirus disease 2019 (COVID-19), caused by severe acute respiratory syndrome coronavirus 2 (SARS-CoV-2), to be a pandemic encompassing more than 300 million confirmed cases of COVID-19, including 5.4 million deaths globally.

Reports and statistics show the following numbers for January–February 2022[2]:

- Estimated infections are at 95.2 million per day on average
- Hospital census records 1.6 million patients per day on average
- The daily rate of reported deaths due to COVID-19 is greater than four per million in 58 countries
- Around 60% of the world population has received at least one dose of a COVID-19 vaccine
- Globally, 10.35 billion doses have been administered, and 27.13 million doses are administered daily

The pandemic has triggered severe social and economic disruptions around the world, including layoffs, temporary dismissals of employees due to company financial difficulties, and shortages in vaccines, medication, and food. Some business sectors have almost disappeared because they are irrelevant under lockdowns and social distancing, while other sectors have unexpectedly turned into the most robust foundations for communication, workflow, education, and food delivery, among others; yet, not all of these sectors were prestructured and equipped to provide their services and products on such large scales.

While technological advances and digitalization already existed before the pandemic arrived, dependence on these platforms as the main or only option has created chaotic conditions: digital systems collapsed and many companies found themselves 'out of their element' because their digitalization was restricted to specific services; for example, grocery stores digitalized for delivery only, but not for collecting payments for client purchases, or for advertising their products. Moreover, a difference in the sectors, industries, and even locations (e.g., countries or regions within a country) in companies' digitalization and technological expertise was gradually revealed, and these created new realities; for example, people began considering the delivery sector to be more critical than the cultural sector (e.g., entertainment, movies, concerts, tourism). Moreover, when the pandemic broke out, the elderly seemed to be the most vulnerable population, as the rates of infection in their age group were higher than in the rest of the population. When the vaccines were developed, they were first provided to the elderly, reducing their risk of being infected; this resulted in the younger populations, especially children, being more exposed, as vaccines were only developed later for the younger population.

These changes hit entrepreneurship in various ways—in starting new businesses and in operating businesses; some startups went bankrupt or had to close some of their existing operations; some places were deprived of vaccines and treatments and the pandemic's effects were therefore more aggressive. Concurrently, the crisis created opportunities, which some startups might have ignored because they were disturbed by the crisis' effects or because they were focused on protecting the business and took a more cautious approach to managing within the crisis. Other startups went through an initial phase of shock that prevented them from implementing coping activities, but then processed the situation and were organized to manage it. Still others were prepared for crises and employed their crisis management strategies immediately as the COVID-19 pandemic broke out.

The startup's flow of action fluctuated; some started crisis management with full energy, then became alarmed due to the crisis' development, and developed concerns about a severe economic recession or depression in the global economy, or about their business' financial and overall state; yet others went into reactive mode and accelerated the strategies to manage the crisis.

In the case of the COVID-19 crisis, which has been typified by the development of vaccines and treatments that are useful in reducing the spread of the disease and therefore in removing, at least partially, the restrictions of social mobility and closures of schools and workplaces, some startups have been able to 'go back to normal' depending on the local policy, while others still lag behind. These crisis occurrences were unexpected and new to the startup realm. The recognized crisis-related behaviors, mindsets, performance, and coping strategies provided only a partial response to the uncertainty prevailing during the COVID-19 pandemic.

For the first time in history, all countries everywhere encountered the pandemic, and its effects on the startup scene are evident. This situation was instantly resonated in the startup's relationships as they joined together to construct a new reality, in which each startup wins by joining forces with others, hence discarding hostility, and competing by complementing each other's offerings, and by sharing platforms to enable each startup to expand its exposure and presence. These avenues would not be taken under 'normal' conditions (Doern, Williams and Vorley 2019; Alon, Farrell and Li 2020; Brem, Nylund and Viardot 2020; Cortez and Johnston 2020; Harari 2020; Ratten 2020; Winston 2020).

At-a-glance—Seedata.io (https://www.seedata.io/)

Founded in 2021 by Enrico Faccioli and Matt Holland and based in London, Seedata.io develops cybersecurity technology that identifies previously undetected incidents of data leaks, aimed at mitigating the frequency, duration, and impact of security incidents. The technology detects if and when customers' security protection has been compromised and helps customers reduce incident costs as well as fortify the security of their programs. Its success has been announced in the British media (https://tbtech.co/business/cybersecurity-start-up-seedata-io-raises-120000-funding/; https://www.cybsafe.com/); and it was declared the best UK cybersecurity startup of 2021 (https://www.seedata.io/press/beststartup-co-uk-coverage/).

This startup is based on deception technology and it has embarked on an opportunity that is relevant to effects of the COVID-19 crisis—digitalization. More and more companies are operating all of their activities digitally, resulting in a rise of undetected incidents of data leakage. Seedata.io provides trackable records of data within the clients' systems, and monitors and analyzes all events to identify security incidents relevant to the seeds within the clients and alerts the clients of such incidents.

The technology can be employed in various fields; for example, it can detect plagiarism in academia by using existing processes to detect issues with inconsistent results (https://setsquared.exeter.ac.uk/case-studies/helping-identify-plagiarism-with-seedata).

The methodology

To enrich the reader's understanding of startups in times of crisis, the chapters will include mini case studies that exemplify the discussed phenomena. In addition, rich case studies are introduced in the last chapter of the book, all developed exclusively by the

TABLE 1.3 A summative matrix of navigating in times of crisis

Crisis-related difficulties		*Planning for navigation during the crisis*			*Recurring evaluation and implications*
		Focus internally on the business		*Focus on the impact on the ecosystem*	
Sector	Challenges encountered	Aims to be met	Business area	Stakeholders	Assessment measures

author; the premise of such studies lies in engaging many narratives, statistics, figures, and reports derived for stakeholders from various ecosystems. These cases provide a larger overview of the crisis' effects on startups, through an inclusive perspective.

Table 1.3 presents a cumulative approach to managing startups in times of crisis, and can be useful for startup founders to reorder their goals by looking over their plans, resources, and ideas, and restructuring them into the direction to be pursued to manage the crisis.

Summary

Crises—and their effects—are never similar, even those that seem to be in the same category (e.g., health-related crises, environmental crises, terror attacks, or financial recession). There are many components that influence the crisis' effect on the startup. These can be external factors, such as support from the ecosystem, the severity of the crisis, the duration of the crisis, the performance of other businesses in the market, or internal factors. Both external and internal factors echo the startup's existing stability, financial state, liabilities (e.g., to investors, service providers, its employees), and its preparedness for crisis situations. Crises embody uncertainty and are therefore perceived as threats due to the potential deterioration of the situation; these can taper resilience among the startup founders. Due to the threatening aspects of crises, many entrepreneurs aggregate business and personal assets into a defensive, mostly reactive, mode of operation while tackling the crisis. Some startups are prepared to confront crises, but the shock effect of the crisis outbreak pivots their action to a spontaneous reaction rather than going through the prepared strategies. These reactions typify businesses that encounter unexpected eruptions of crisis episodes. Often, such reactions are defensive and protective, and they reduce the startup's ability to see the opportunities that the crisis entails. The losses and gains that crises can bring to the same startup are contingent on perceptions of the startup's capabilities and robustness. There are many examples of businesses that are thriving during the pandemic. On June 19, 2020, *The Financial Times* listed the top 100 companies that had prospered during the crisis,[3] with Apple, Microsoft, Tesla, and Netflix considered to have profited from the pandemic, while Alibaba, AT&T, Boeing, and ExxonMobil, among others, were losers.[4] *The New York Times* addressed this topic on April 30, 2021, in the article "How Big Tech Won the Pandemic," writing,[5] "a year ago, even the tech giants were anxious. Now they have so much money it's awkward." Similarly, startups have lost and gained from the pandemic. According to CNBC,[6] many entrepreneurs feel that:

> the pandemic and its disruptions led many people reassess their lives and consider a different path. 'It made you think about life differently, in a way, when our whole lives were flipped upside down' said Deborah Gladney, who started a business in Wichita, Kansas, with her sister, Angela Muhwezi-Hall, during the pandemic.[7]

To navigate in times of crisis, a holistic perspective is required. Startups need to look around, analyze the situation, detect the changes, and be attentive to the market vibe by examining statistics and trends, such as new business creation or high rates of bankruptcy, and sensing the general atmosphere in their startups and among their stakeholders. Then, they can decide which direction to follow by considering both protection of their existing resources and exploitation of new opportunities that sometimes emerge only through the disruption brought on by a crisis.

Reflective questions for class

1. Ask five to eight people you know about their work-related losses and gains from the COVID-19 pandemic. What are your conclusions? Do they view the pandemic similarly or differently?
2. Search the web for two startups that thrived during the pandemic. Explain their success through the minimum optimal actions required in crisis events (Table 1.1). Which factor(s) prevailed in these startups' success? Explain your findings.

3. Now, search the web for two startups that failed/cut out some of their activities during the pandemic. Explain their failure through the minimum optimal actions required in crisis events (Table 1.1). Which factor(s) prevailed in these startups' collapse? Explain your findings.
4. Explain Zoom or Netflix's success based on two different theoretical perspectives introduced in Table 1.2: Theoretical perspectives and the missing links. What are your main conclusions on their success?
5. Imagine that you are asked to consult a startup in the vaccination industry that is developing an all-inclusive vaccine against all variants of the coronavirus for all ages and health conditions. The founders would like to assess the best time to launch their business. Based on Figure 1.1, a multilayered perspective of startups under crises, list the three most important factors that the founders should consider prior to the launch. Explain your answer.

Notes

1 The Economist, Jul. 4, 2020. https://www.economist.com/international/2020/07/04/covid-19-is-here-to-stay-the-world-is-working-out-how-to-live-with-it

2 See report from the Institute for Health Metrics and Evaluation (IHME) at https://covid19.healthdata.org/global?view=cumulative-deaths&tab=trend ; Oxford "Our World Data" https://ourworldindata.org/covid-vaccinations

3 See https://www.ft.com/content/844ed28c-8074-4856-bde0-20f3bf4cd8f0

4 See https://www.ft.com/content/8075a9c5-3c43-48a5-b507-5b8f5904f443

5 See https://www.nytimes.com/2021/04/30/technology/big-tech-pandemic.html

6 See *Start-Ups Boomed during the Pandemic. Here's How Some Entrepreneurs Found a Niche.* Michelle Fox. May 27, 2021. https://www.cnbc.com/2021/05/27/how-entrepreneurs-found-their-start-up-niche-during-covid-19.html

7 See The *New York Times, Start-Up Boom in the Pandemic Is Growing Stronger.* Ben Casselman. August 19, 2021. https://www.nytimes.com/2021/08/19/business/startup-business-creation-pandemic.html

References

Alon, I., Farrell, M., & Li, S. (2020). Regime type and COVID-19 response. *FIIB Business Review, 9*(3), 152–160.

Brem, A., Nylund, P., & Viardot, E. (2020). The impact of the 2008 financial crisis on innovation: A dominant design perspective. *Journal of Business Research, 110*, 360–369.

Chell, E., & Baines, S. (2000). Networking, entrepreneurship and microbusiness behaviour. *Entrepreneurship & Regional Development, 12*(3), 195–215.

Choi, Y. R., & Shepherd, D. A. (2004). Entrepreneurs' decisions to exploit opportunities. *Journal of Management, 30*(3), 377–395.

Cortez, R. M., & Johnston, W. J. (2020). The Coronavirus crisis in B2B settings: Crisis uniqueness and managerial implications based on social exchange theory. *Industrial Marketing Management, 88*, 125–135.

Doern, R., Williams, N., & Vorley, T. (2019). Special issue on entrepreneurship and crises: Business as usual? An introduction and review of the literature. *Entrepreneurship & Regional Development, 31*(5–6), 400–412.

Duchek, S. (2018). Entrepreneurial resilience: A biographical analysis of successful entrepreneurs. *International Entrepreneurship and Management Journal, 14*(2), 429–455.

Fink, S. (1986). *Crisis management: Planning for the inevitable.* Amacom.

Harari, Y. N. (2020). The world after coronavirus. *Financial Times, 20*(03), 2020.

Johannisson, B. (2007). Enacting local economic development–theoretical and methodological challenges. *Journal of Enterprising Communities: People and Places in the Global Economy.*

Kuckertz, A., Brändle, L., Gaudig, A., Hinderer, S., Reyes, C. A. M., Prochotta, A., Steinbrink, K. M., & Berger, E. S. (2020). Startups in times of crisis–A rapid response to the COVID-19 pandemic. *Journal of Business Venturing Insights, 13*, e00169.

Muñoz, P., Kimmitt, J., Kibler, E., & Farny, S. (2019). Living on the slopes: Entrepreneurial preparedness in a context under continuous threat. *Entrepreneurship & Regional Development, 31*(5–6), 413–434.

Ratten, V. (2020). Coronavirus (covid-19) and entrepreneurship: Changing life and work landscape. *Journal of Small Business & Entrepreneurship, 32*(5), 503–516.

Roundy, P. T., Brockman, B. K., & Bradshaw, M. (2017). The resilience of entrepreneurial ecosystems. *Journal of Business Venturing Insights, 8*, 99–104.

Shane, S., & Venkataraman, S. (2000). The promise of entrepreneurship as a field of research. *Academy of Management Review, 25*(1), 217–226.

Stam, E. (2015). Entrepreneurial ecosystems and regional policy: A sympathetic critique. *European Planning Studies, 23*(9), 1759–1769.

Teece, D. J. (2014). A dynamic capabilities-based entrepreneurial theory of the multinational enterprise. *Journal of International Business Studies, 45*(1), 8–37.

Winston, A. (2020). Is the COVID-19 outbreak a black swan or the new normal. *MIT Sloan Management Review, 16*, 154–173.

Zahra, S. A., Sapienza, H. J., & Davidsson, P. (2006). Entrepreneurship and dynamic capabilities: A review, model and research agenda. *Journal of Management Studies, 43*(4), 917–955.

Chapter Two
Startup dynamics

Takeaways

- Understanding the uniqueness of a startup's dynamics and goals: sustainability, growth, and contribution
- Improving a startup's competitiveness, development of a clear value, competitive advantages, and a constant innovation process
- Introducing and disseminating the startup's offerings—frequently innovative and compounded by new combinations—so that beneficiaries will see the advantage of engaging with the startup
- Examining the external factors that have a substantial impact on the startup—context, ecosystem, environment—thoroughly, transparently, and on a regular basis by being aware of sensemaking rather than only the 'objective facts'
- Analyzing the inner aspects of the startup and identifying the salient processes that determine its core essence—strengthening and improvement
- Identifying opportunities and inhibitors in the external and internal environments of the startup; being aware of their existence and potential and the startup's abilities to manage them

Startup dynamics

This chapter illustrates the dynamic courses of action depicting startup's processes vis-à-vis their external and internal environments and within their context

DOI: 10.4324/9781003173809-2

and ecosystem. The reader will become acquainted with the recurring processes, flow dynamics, and uniqueness of startups and their differentiation from small and medium-sized enterprises (SMEs) or larger companies for a more accurate understanding of the multifaceted, reciprocal relationships between startups and their ecosystems.

By capturing startup's exclusive courses of action, their behavior in the face of crises and disturbances can be better understood; in addition, the core essence of startups—that is, innovation and the introduction of sometimes groundbreaking and controversial offerings, means of production and technology—can lead to disruptive situations that end in crises. Crises do not represent occurrences that should be avoided by startups by all means; crises force startups to try something different or alternatives that may reduce the damaging aspects of the crisis, while maintaining the energetic, stimulating, and creative boosts that are associated with crises.

So, what exactly is a startup? What are its boundaries? Is it a small business with great technology or a big company in its first steps?

Demarcation of a startup

Startups are entrepreneurial businesses in their initial stages of development. They introduce unique, innovative products or services to the market that are contingent on unique, sometimes cutting-edge technologies that either respond to existing deficiencies or dynamics, changing needs, or create an entirely new category of goods and services. The imperative of startups is in turning innovation, inventions, and sophisticated concepts—involving high technology or not—into viable businesses (Goktan and Miles 2011; Trimi and Berbegal-Mirabent 2012). The main essence of startups depends on innovation, thereby disrupting entrenched ways of thinking, producing, and doing business for entire sectors. In Steve Blank's words, "Startups are not a smaller version of a large company" (Blank and Dorf 2020); rather, "Startups are born betting it all"[1] (Blank 2019). They are built on unique models, such as the 'waterfall model'[2] the lean business model (Reis 2011; Maurya 2012; Blank 2013), and Agile (Ghezzi and Cavallo 2020), among others; they are process- and outcome-oriented, including planning, implementation, and validation of innovation, based on a continual learning process aimed at being rapid and sustainable based on a business model that is typical to startups, that is, distinct from SME and large company business models (Osterwalder and Pigneur 2010; Reis 2011; Blank 2013, 2018; Blank and Dorf 2020).

The concept of 'startup' was introduced by *Forbes* Magazine in 1976, in "The unfashionable business of investing in startups in the electronic data processing field," 6/2, August 15, 1976. The term was then further employed by *Forbes* Magazine in 1977[3]:

> The OECD traces the origins of the term, used in its modern sense, back to a 1976 Forbes article, which uses the word as follows: 'The...unfashionable business of investing in startups in the electronic data processing field.' A 1977 Business Week article includes the line, 'An incubator for startup companies, especially in the fast-growth, high-technology fields.'

Despite its roots in the 1970s, the concept is multifaceted, and distinctions between startups and SMEs as well as between startups and 'regular' businesses are sometimes blurred or confusing; this is mainly because startups involve a group of employees who aim to develop, produce, and sell products so as to be profitable and sustainable, and as such they are 'like any other business'. Yet, startups are distinct from both SMEs and 'regular' companies in several aspects; as they are in a relatively early stage of development and constitute an agile culture, they show a flexible mindset with respect to experimenting, trial and error, and changes. These distinctions create a constant crisis arena for startups, in which they are forced to manage the crisis episodes through strategies that require customization, agility, and adaptability, so that imposed challenges are tackled such that the crises' effects can be leveraged for the startup's subsequent development.

According to Kariv (2020), startups are typified by:

Value creation—introduced to their shareholders, that is, customers, users, investors, suppliers, governmental bodies, competitors, communities, and media and that can both affect and be affected by the introduced value. The value can be reflected in the product or service's impact on stakeholders' well-being, wealth, growth, simplicity, innovation, etc.

Competitive advantage—entailing the products, services, process, technology, materials used, infrastructures, marketing methods, etc., which, relative to the existing portfolio of competitors, differentiate the business and are perceived to be more valuable in terms of quality, price, distribution, user-friendliness, environmental friendliness, and business location, among others.

Innovation—mainly considered groundbreaking and revolutionary; embodies rigorous research and development processes affecting all aspects of the startup; and takes on different forms, for example, product-centric, process-based, operation-driven, or unbundling innovation.

Stages of development—startups evolve through sequential stages that echo the startup's development and flow, and are generally considered to start with the first stage of ideation followed by stages of market and ecosystem research and process initiation; the next stages typically refer to analyzing feasibility, profitability, competition; following, exploiting, and exploring existing and potential opportunities for implementation; then iteration, prototype development (minimal viable product [MVP], proof of concept [POC]), a resource-generation and mobilization stage, implementation and reevaluation, and testing for the next iterations. The stages involve acquisition, deployment, mobilization, and creation and undergo multiple iterations to achieve a product-market fit.

The entrepreneur—unlike managers, entrepreneurs are depicted as holding characteristics, mindsets, and approaches that are unique to the startup scene; for example, they are deemed visionary, creative, innovative, more prone to taking high risks, proactive, network-driven, and more likely to be impact-driven. Entrepreneurs' personal and social characteristics are considered to be the backbone of business creation

Startup distinctiveness

Startups are different from other types of businesses. But contrary to the common view, this is not necessarily due to their cutting-edge technological premise; rather, it is because they are an evolving, dynamic structure that is still in its infancy but holds high potential to succeed and sustain.

The main areas that differentiate startups from other businesses refer to the following points embraced by startups (Table 2.1).

Taken together, the components that typify startups combine to challenge the existing settings and structures in the entrepreneurial ecosystem (EE) by introducing disruptive innovation on a large scale and at a rapid pace that can challenge other businesses' operation and outcomes. Consequently, relationships in startups are typified as dynamic, unstable, and volatile, allowing them to prepare for potential crises, as exhibited in Figure 2.1.

TABLE 2.1 The startup's distinctiveness

Innovation and co-creation

a. Creation, from scratch, of *new* technologies, products, settings, and structures, among others. For example, back in 2004, the offer of online social networking services was practically unknown; Facebook[4] innovated by offering its platform (Caers et al. 2013).

b. Embedding innovation in multiple processes and areas within the startup and through upfront, wide exposure, such as in the technology, production, financing the operation, or penetrating new markets, either concurrently, jointly, or separately.

c. Invention, co-innovation, and co-creation are common innovation strategies among startups; these require embracing continual innovation, even if it transforms or pivots the startup's original ideas, to introduce value to its stakeholders (Lee, Olson and Trimi 2012; Ghezzi 2020).

As an example, ABALOBI[5] is an African-based, fisher-driven social mobile app, introducing innovation in its services, social focus, and outreach. This startup created a unique marketplace connecting fisherfolk directly to the restaurants in South Africa that purchase their daily fresh catch, ensuring that they secure fair prices; the outbreak of COVID-19 and subsequent lockdowns forced ABALOBI to renovate; they reoriented their model to allow the fisherfolk to connect directly to consumers' homes. Embedding innovation and substantial changes in its existing logistics system to support the fisherfolk and to remain operational during the pandemic represent natural approaches in startups, although this was simply an extension of ABALOBI's original fundamental principle.

New combinations

a. Creating value by introducing new products, settings, structures, etc. based on existing features that are reorganized into a new configuration and form a unique combination 'package'. Based on the Schumpeterian (1934) concept of 'creative destruction', this approach builds on the type of innovation that combines factors in a new way or provides a new combination; it is pertinent in many startups across its stages of development.

b. The open innovation originates from both the mindsets and operational strategies involving new combinations (Schumpeter 1934, 1939, 1978).

For example, Netflix began as a startup offering online streaming from a library of films and television series; streaming was a known technology and the films and TV series already existed; the innovation lay in combining the two to create a completely new service drawn from existing, well-established ones.

Speed and pace

a. Introducing products and services to the market promptly, thereby profiting from both the position of first-to-market and attracting potential stakeholders through *early adopters*. The prevailing message is that high-speed, continuous development and operation are obligatory for a startup's success.

b. Startups tend to start with the fundamental skeleton of a product termed MVP, which is tested and revised until it is ready to go to market; this process then goes through continuous iterations to improve the product through feedback and usage data.

c. The competitive landscape of startups posits innovation speed and a high pace of product development as key premises to manage the competitive threat, and to confront the actions that can be taken by established businesses with deeper resources and a stable life cycle; therefore, startups rapidly create or improve effective solutions that accommodate these challenges.

d. Startups have to rapidly demonstrate their ability to execute; the 'move fast and break things' attitude is the new reality in startups (Taneja and Chenault 2019).

For example, the company Gusto[6] shares its business' core value: "Don't optimize for the short term. Short-term gains never justify long-term sacrifice. Invest in the future" (Baum et al. 2007; Baum, Schwens and Kabst 2011; Gehrich 2012).

(*Continued*)

Sustainability, growth, and contribution

a. Startups are growth-hacking teams that set strategic principles to grow their business at the outset. These include adaptable long-term strategies and scalable leadership and core values as guidance to achieve their aims in the long term and ensure longevity, while securing their daily operation and success.

b. Vision is a crucial driver in sustaining and growing a business, and it is therefore established in the early stages.

c. The ecosystem has become a prevalent key success factor for startups to steer the company through the early stages. Dynamic and frequent reciprocal connections of the startup with varied stakeholders are very common (Collins and Porras 2005; Freeman and Engel 2007).

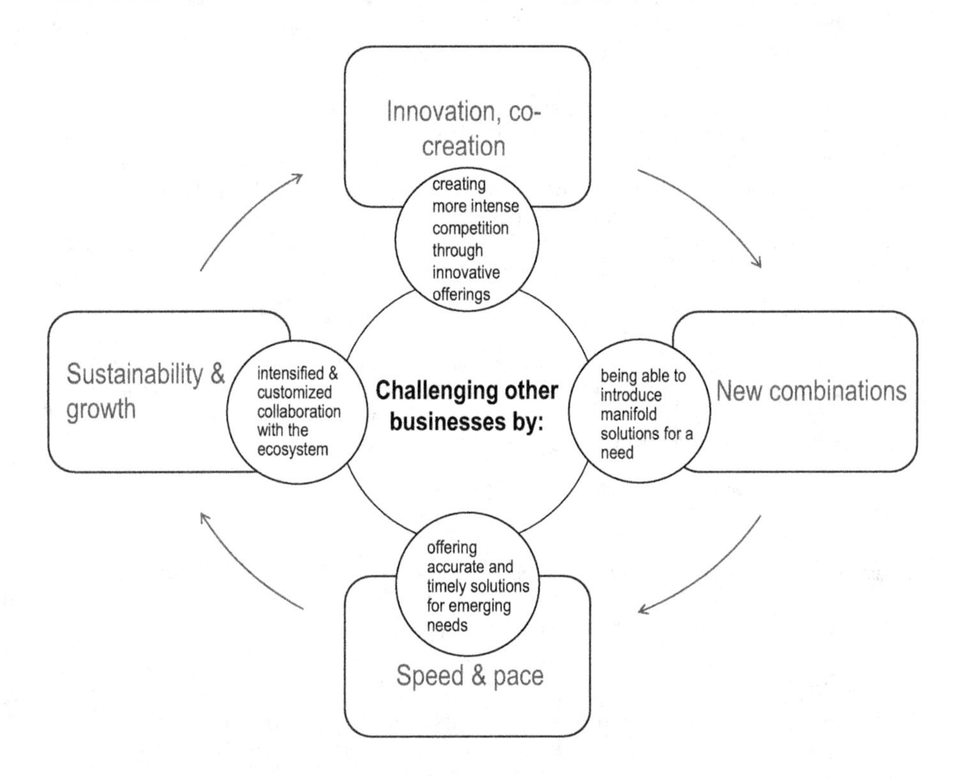

FIGURE 2.1 Startup's imperative 'challenging existing business' settings

The external perspective

A startup's operation draws on the relevant environment. The local environment has a substantial impact on its first steps, representing the immediate area that nurtures the business through easier provision of financial solutions, convenient networking, experts, robust collaborations with leading local companies, and various lucrative regional resources. The global environment is relevant to the growth and expansion of the startup's operational borders, thus extending the startup's market. The virtual environment has become more relevant due to COVID-19 restrictions, including lockdowns and distancing, because it facilitates access to anywhere, anytime, and to anyone, and has fostered a digital economy through e-commerce, e-conferences, and e-meetings as well as digital marketing, thus replicating, in a digital version, each physically activated process and expertise.

Startups and the context

The context in which entrepreneurship develops is garnering more and more attention in research; as it concurrently introduces opportunities for and barriers to entrepreneurial action, it becomes "part of the story" (Zahra and Wright 2011, p. 72), and is broadly documented as the framework that delineates the boundaries for individual opportunities and actions, presenting liabilities or assets for the nature and extent of entrepreneurship. Context comes from the Latin root 'contextus' which means 'a joining together', stressing that the action "is rigorously situated within a sociohistorical and cultural context of meanings and relationships" (Rosnow and Georgoudi 1986, p. 4); individuals are active in constructing contexts, and contexts are not 'out there', they are "part of the act" (p. 6).

Various models have tackled the contextual dimensions, though not necessarily focusing on startups, but more broadly as any contextual dimension or change that affects the startup's action. Contextual models emphasize historical, temporal, institutional, spatial, and social factors, that is, the areas included in the context. Others highlight processes of formal and regulatory frameworks or economic rules and policies that affect the opening, success, and sustainability of startups; yet a different stream emphasizes informal areas, including cultural and social processes, networks, communities, families, and a general embeddedness in the context, such as through ethnic communities or entrepreneurship that is gendered or relates to people of color. Accordingly, the contextual dimensions simultaneously fuel and are molded by people, organizations, and processes.

A fusion of areas and processes was developed by Welter (2011), comprised of four dimensions: institutional, that is, regulatory and normative environment; social, that is, the relations between founders and startup teams; spatial, that is, physical and geographical environment; and a continuum of where entrepreneurship takes place and when this happens.

A different outlook on context was introduced by the Global Competitiveness Report (GCR[7]) (Schwab and Zahidi 2020) published by the World Economic Forum (WEF). It identified contextual dimensions to assess their prevalence across countries and establish a skeleton for comparisons: economic, legal, ethical, technological, educational, infrastructure development, and financial market development. The distribution and combinations of these dimensions create the ground upon which startups act to generate their competitive advantage; as such, differences in the levels of operation and use or effectiveness of factors included in each dimension echo the level of support provided to startups by the context; differences in levels of key performance indicators then arise.

Another conceptual stream identifies context as enacted through symbolic action and communication; entrepreneurs, startup founders, and key stakeholders create the context based on the information gained but following a sensemaking process. Sensemaking refers to interpretations of past events in which entrepreneurs were attentive to the changing cues in their environment to understand ongoing changes in events and their interpretation; these are then shaped into perceptions regarding the development and potential success of the startup.

Startup's key performance indicators consist of alliances, networks, innovation, cutting-edge technology, stable relationships with central stakeholders, reputation, expansion, financial figures, and access to funding as well as constructs such as expertise, inclusion, and sustainability. Contextual constructs contribute to a startup's successful capture of the most valuable, competitive opportunities and resources that can be deployed in the best possible customized way to fit the startup's needs. The wider the scope of the dimensions in the startup's context, the more likely it is that the startup will develop expertise, technology, networks, and alliances (Aldrich and Fiol 1994; Baum 1996; Thornton 1999; Zahra and Wright 2011; Autio et al. 2014; Fried and Tauer 2015; Welter and Gartner 2016; Gaddefors and Anderson 2017; Howe, Desai and Murray 2021).

At-a-glance—digitalization and social orientation during the pandemic

Squatwolf (https://squatwolf.com/) was founded by Wajdan Gul and his wife Anam Khalid in 2016 in Dubai by pursuing a gap in the market for premium and stylish gym wear. In the past two years, Squatwolf has expanded to sell in more than 120 countries and is the largest gym brand in the Middle East. Gul says, "55% of our business is now coming from outside of the GCC. The US is our biggest market outside of the GCC, then the UK, Europe, Canada and Australia."

He adds that "the biggest challenge is to go where our customers are."[1] The two co-founders state that:

> We were a pair of busy corporate professionals from Dubai with a passion for fitness and fashion. As years went by, we became more and more involved in fitness because it was the best release for hectic and stressful routines. We found ourselves frustrated and perplexed by how difficult it was to find the best in class gym wear that could stand up to seriously intense workouts and also give off a prime look.[2]

The two corporate professionals shared a passion for fitness and fashion. Their shared frustrations over not being able to find high-quality gym attire that looked good led them to launch their own business. With the motto "Good things come to those who sweat," Squatwolf was born. With the logistical capabilities of Dubai, the brand has spread beyond the UAE as far as America and Australia. "Every product in our shop has been engineered for active life from fit to stitch to fabric with gym goers in mind, and to fulfill our vision of what gym wear should be," says Gul. "Born in Dubai, we have enlisted loads of UAE trainers and everyday gym goers in our local community to help us design our products, select our fabrics and other materials. And we have loved every minute of it."

During the pandemic, Squatwolf thrived and scaled its business, thanks to the adoption of Meta business tools to harness the power of its data. Using dynamic ads, the company controlled what it was advertising through Facebook and Instagram and saw a 74% increase in return on investment. In addition, the company scaled during the pandemic, thanks to the decision to ramp up its e-commerce offering. "The more data that is shared," says Gul, "the more accurately we can optimize our advertising campaigns and deliver personalized shopping experiences for our visitors."

"When the lockdown started, we decided to go all-in on Meta dynamic ads. We turned off all our other ads and relied on Meta to suggest the right customers – and it just worked," he says. "In the last 12 months, we have grown from a team of 10 to 45. We were not only able to survive but grow as well."[1]

[1] https://squatwolf.com/about/; https://www.euronews.com/2021/12/08/how-is-dubai-s-strategic-location-serving-start-ups

[2] https://www.campaignlive.co.uk/article/activewear-retailer-squatwolf-boosted-roi-74-meta/1733223

Context and crises

Crises are cultivated under conditions of discrepant contexts, as these can reflect an inequality between a startup's performance indicators and its potential success. Moreover, contexts are subject to sensemaking, which reflects an understanding of the context followed by continuous communication and activity; startups engage in action based on how their members construct the meaning of the context. Understanding the context as reinforcing or weakening the startup's goals or as fertile ground for competition, danger, or opportunities will stimulate actions that are 'understood' by the startups as managing the crisis or a potential one. Capturing the startup's reorganization within its context and through multilevel and multidisciplinary perspectives, including the individual, organizational, and institutional levels, can cultivate appropriate crisis-coping strategies and the ability to thrive under potential forthcoming crises; it can enable startups to hone themselves, even or especially under uncertainties and dynamic changes, including creating more resilience to crises and capturing the full essence of sensemaking to create robust ground for managing and coping with crises in collaboration with the context's constituents (Weick 1995; Weick, Sutcliffe and Obstfeld 2005; Bundy et al. 2017; König et al. 2020; Liu 2020; Xing et al. 2020).

A startup's sensemaking of its context operates on cognitive, emotional, and sensory levels and emanates from triggers such as material practices, physical artifacts, cultures, and common knowledge that construct meanings. Startups apply contextual lenses and attach a meaning to or understanding of the 'existing' reality, and subsequently act in different ways—competition, rivalry, collaboration, mutual dependence, and reciprocity, among others. Crises are stimulated by this fused sensing of the existing reality (Stigliani and Ravasi 2012; Schabram and Maitlis 2017; Berthod and Müller-Seitz 2018).

Contexts can be understood through sensemaking as providing stability versus instability; reinforcing versus weakening (e.g., business development, evolution, success); introducing an open-system approach (e.g., in innovation, communication, and collaboration) versus a closed-system approach; and initiating competition, rivalry, responsiveness, or a supportive ground for dominance (Zahra and Wright 2011; Murdock 2012; Spedale and Watson 2013; Watson 2013).

Ecosystems

EEs have been depicted as consisting of players and processes that operate dynamically to encourage and enhance new business creation and further growth; at the same time,

EEs can inhibit business development by introducing intertwined environmental, institutional, or regulatory constraints (Schwab and Zahid 2020) involving the entrepreneurs, significant others, and critical players, such as financial companies, governmental and public organizations, the public sector, universities, and professional and social associations related to entrepreneurship. The concept of EE emerged in the 1980s (Dubini 1989; Spilling 1996); its importance to startup's performance produced a proliferation of definitions of EE (Stam 2015; Najmaei 2016; Motoyama and Knowlton 2017; Cavallo, Ghezzi and Balocco 2019), with a similar core essence that draws a parallel between entrepreneurial and biological ecosystems. As such, similar to the field of biology, the EE embodies an interactive and complex system of living organisms in a physical environment with changing sometimes unpredictable composition and interactions and changes in the elements making up the ecosystem. In a similar vein, Stam (2015, p. 1764) suggested a dynamic approach to the evolution of EE by suggesting its demarcation as "a set of interdependent actors and factors coordinated in such a way that they enable productive entrepreneurship"; the elements that comprise the EE can develop simultaneously and either reinforce or weaken each other over time (Hoskisson et al. 2013; Wright and Stigliani 2013; Autio et al. 2014; Hayter 2016; Stam and Spigel 2016; Borissenko and Boschma 2017; Roundy, Brockman and Bradshaw 2017; Spigel 2017; Cavallo, Ghezzi and Balocco 2019).

Startups hinge on their ecosystems as a support mechanism in which resources, opportunities, information, knowledge, expertise, interactions, and exchanges are embedded, containing everything that startups need in the entrepreneurial process. The startup then processes these elements within the ecosystem into new knowledge, access to key technologies, financial sources, talent, and new opportunities, thus not only facilitating the startup's performance and further success, but also mitigating the existing or potential obstacles faced by the startup in its daily operation (Amin and Cohendet 2000; Garud and Karnøe 2003; Autio et al. 2014; Hayter 2016; Hayter et al. 2018; Kariv, Baldegger and Kashy-Rosenbaum 2022; Kariv et al. forthcoming). Elements composing the EE refer to the entrepreneurial players, organizations (suppliers, customers, venture capitalists, business angels, banks, cooperating partners), institutions (universities, public research organizations, technological centers, sector agencies, financial bodies), and resources (finance, talent, knowledge, and support services) as well as formal networks, and are measured by EE connectivity, diversity, density, and fluidity (Nambisan and Baron 2013; St-Pierre et al. 2015; Stam and Spigel 2016).

The virtual sphere—this enables startups to make use of flexible and Agile business models, modify their products/services in real time in tight alignment with the ecosystem's needs and expectations, and easily and more accurately optimize the search for opportunities and the creation of new ones by incorporating those provided by the digital platforms and ecosystems. Concurrently, quality, effectiveness, efficiency, and profitability are fostered through this 'all-inclusive' sphere that orchestrates technologies, communication analytics, storage, and billing toward a higher, timely, and customized connectedness to the market's needs, attracting higher ecosystem engagement. WalletForAll, a five-year-old European startup, offers virtual personal loans based on blockchain technology; it encountered various difficulties in penetrating the market during its first three years of operation, but continually reworked its MVP for a more customized fit to the market; yet, its customers were hesitant. The specific situation brought on by the COVID-19 pandemic, including people's more intensive use of and dependency on the internet, gave WalletForAll another chance on the potential virtual background, as many people became unemployed 'overnight' and needed loans, along with their enhanced trust in virtual offerings. WalletForAll repackaged and reintroduced its services and figured out that the virtual sphere was most lucrative for their offerings.

Ecosystems and crises

With the changing environment due to the COVID-19 pandemic and the dramatic shift toward a 'new normal' typified by social distancing, borders shutting down, remote communication as the norm rather than the exception, and dramatically higher rates of depression and related psychological distress, the EE has changed structures and operations contingent on the environment and social and cultural realities. When elements of the environment are transformed or become nonexistent, their composition and interactions change; accordingly, the measures of connectivity, diversity, density, and fluidity of the EE become unknown and unexpected and therefore vulnerable (Heaton, Siegel and Teece 2019; Roundy and Fayard 2019; Hsiang et al. 2020; Ratten 2020; Howe, Desai and Murray 2021).

The COVID-19 crisis has accelerated digitalization in communication, education, and online medical consultations; this addition of technology to the EE affects the interrelations of other elements, such as collaborations and partnerships, attracting new, more technologically savvy talent, looking for new financial sources, and developing new business models. As an example, because digitalization has been intensified, startups may turn to crowdsourcing for funding; this was less popular when digitalization was optional, but as the 'new normal' necessitates digitalization, the startup's dependence on traditional funding sources could change. In the long run, a potential follow-up scenario to such changes might be disruption of the relationships between startups and their investors, with startups that are engaged in crowdsourcing leaving venture capitalists, angels, or banks behind. This postulated scenario might cause a dramatic change in the startup ecosystem, based on intensification of digitalization (and not even the introduction of a new element). The new McKinsey Global Survey of executives presented results on managers' reactions to the adoption of digitalization and changes due to the pandemic, stressing the multiple effects of changes in one element of the EE; for example, the need to work and interact with customers remotely called for expertise in data security and moving to the cloud, which required new, unplanned investments. Such technology-related changes are being built now to last in the future and thus require infrastructures that can facilitate sustainable changes.

Similarly, academic research shows that the changing need for digital technologies emphasizes the lack of existing tools to adequately capture these new, emerging needs, hence necessitating new, though still in their infancy, profiles of experts in startups; these experts should be able to fuse a three-dimensional skeleton consisting of thorough expertise in 'big data' and the use of machine learning and algorithms, with an Agile mindset that enables them to learn, try, and iterate and Agile tools to produce products and services that are customized to the new needs; and a new business approach, deriving from the changes in EE elements due to the pandemic's restrictions, such as developing new but still trustworthy and effective *online* communication with customers or a higher awareness of hygiene and health across all production processes (e.g., in areas of food, beverage, medical services, agriculture). Such changes in the EE stem from the crisis and create potentially disruptive episodes of various types; a change in digitalization can create fundamental fluctuations in the funding field (https://www.kauffman.org/entrepreneurship/reports/big-data-directions-research/).

The internal perspective

Startups are presented as multifaceted and complex systems led by non-traditional, innovative dynamics and a unique internal tolerance to changes 'on the go' that enables them to amend, modify, alter, or pivot frequently as opposed to SMEs or larger companies. This agile and flexible approach facilitates their management in the face of crisis effects or alternatively can fortify crisis effects or create new ones. Crises can occur at all stages of the startup's life cycle; due to their disruptive effects, crises can restrict existing activity and further development of the startup's transition to the next stage of its development; since this is a recurrent situation, especially in startups, it is expected to crop up periodically, based on the setting and relationships between the external and internal factors and the nature and approach of the startup's leadership in managing them (Goerres and Walter 2016; Malová and Dolný 2016; Walecka 2016; Tetiana et al. 2018). Different theoretical approaches have investigated startup's dynamics through internal lenses, capturing the relationships of the people and the processes involved, congregated into the unique organizational structures, processes, and flow.

Organizational view

From this perspective, the emphasis is placed on the most salient organizational operations, which lead to substantial outcomes in the startup's performance both concurrently and for the next stages of development. Accordingly, it is important to decipher environmental, ecological, and community-related conditions due to resource dependency and the levels of stability, transparency, and openness allowed by those conditions, which can affect the development of or cutting back on the startup's operations and general performance.

Research stresses the view of startups as open systems for supply and demand of key resources; thus, their development and success are contingent on the dynamic capabilities (Teece 1992; Teece, Pisano and Shuen 1997; Eisenhardt and Martin 2000) of the founders or management, meant to manage the dependence of the startup on external resource providers toward becoming independent (Blau 1964; Pfeffer and Salancik 2003) by endeavoring to generate strategic VRIN[8] resources internally (Aldrich and Auster 1986; Fiegener et al. 2000; Hillman and Dalziel 2003; Lynall, Golden and Hillman 2003; Fiegener 2005; Gabrielsson and Huse 2005).

The relationship of startups with their environments toward obtaining the 'best' resources is inherent to the internal management of existing or potential crises, as direct or indirect competition on resources reflects on the startup's marathonic race to generate or develop the talent, expertise, or material required for the startup. For example, Carsome,[9] one of the largest integrated e-commerce car sales platforms in Southeast Asia, started as a simple platform to sell cars and almost reached unicorn status in Southeast Asia by introducing innovation to the car-selling experience. Such scaling requires rapid adaptation, internally relative to the growing demands and trends of the market and externally by transforming its business into an integrated e-commerce platform for selling used cars within six months by engaging a different approach to integral cloud use. The opportunities arising from the effects of the COVID-19 crisis were captured by shifting their operations to the cloud and leveraging their existing infrastructures, demonstrating a management strategy for crisis effects that consists of obtaining new skills and capabilities and attracting or organizing the financials to enable purchasing the required technological infrastructures.

The generation and deployment of external resources within the startup should align with the startup's goals, culture, and existing strengths; yet by engaging the emerging opportunities from outside to form an agile, dynamic storage of skills and expertise, they embody the relations of the inner perspectives of the startup in the face of crises (e.g., see Kamps and Pólos 1999; Boekerb and Wiltbank 2005; Davis and Cobb 2010; Salamzadeh 2015).

Management aspects

These focus on the relationships among people, teams, and organizational entities who coordinate their efforts toward achieving common goals (Dean and Bowen 1994; Hofstede 1999). Their relevance to startups lies in areas such as strategic management (e.g., see Pettigrew et al. 2001), where people interact to plan, organize, and implement decisions on the startup's current and potential performance, its relationships with the internal and external environments, and its general approach to its vision, potential growth, and business models; human resource and team management, referring to recruitment, selection processes, entering the job, retaining talent, dismissals, which echo the reciprocal relationships between the internal and external environments; and managing the complexity, such as internal relationships, with a special attention to boards of directors, global teams, or inclusion and diversity in the startup (e.g., Kaiser and Müller 2013; Foss and Saebi 2018; González-Cruz, Botella-Carrubi and Martínez-Fuentes 2020).

A process view—opportunities and inhibitors

A process view in the context of startups focuses on the course of action, relations, structures, and settings of internal and external stakeholders, separately or jointly, that embody the startup's actions and performance and consequently its outcomes and success.

Research has tackled the process view with respect to startups through different theoretical approaches; the most salient refers to the capabilities that startups nurture in their pursuit to be sustainable and create a competitive edge that are constantly being updated and embody a good fit to the market and the ecosystem's dynamically changing needs and expectations. The *resource-based view* (RBV) is a forceful theoretical framework applied to explain startup's performance through the business' resources and subsequent competitive value and its VRIN characteristics (Barney 1991). Accordingly, the

RBV stresses that new ventures accrue their internal resources to generate a competitive advantage in the market through financial, human, social, physical, and technological resources that can be either tangible (e.g., machinery, employees, remedies) or intangible (e.g., culture, social capital, expertise). The *dynamic capabilities* (DC) *perspective*, which emerged from the RBV, encapsulates the dynamic outlook in the investigation of startup's performance to delve into how businesses generate and sustain their competitive advantage by considering the vital, unexpected changes in the environment (Teece, Pisano and Shuen 1997; Eisenhardt and Martin 2000); the business' VRIN characteristics to match the changing environment's demands and reconfigure existing capabilities; and the way in which startups alter their internal resources, capabilities, and expertise to adapt to the dynamic, changing environment. A sustainable competitive advantage is engendered by innovation, up-to-date knowledge, accurate information, best matched networks, and most viable opportunities—which can form new, customizable capabilities and thus better align to the environment's changing needs and expectations (Peteraf, Di Stefano and Verona 2013; Arend 2014; Townsend and Busenitz 2015).

Portrayal of startups

Startups are portrayed as unique entities; they embody unique dynamics and related stakeholders; their uniqueness is mainly exhibited in the various avenues of their composition, arrangements, and dynamics. As such, while the elements that comprise the startup's processes are also found in large companies or SMEs, the ways in which they are orchestrated, including the structure, pace of change, and agility, differentiate their internal actions and flow. To illustrate this, professional elements are embedded in any business; they are exhibited in its expertise, knowledge, and accomplishments; and are sorted into professional or expertise-related sections (e.g., departments, sectors, teams). The same *elements*, that is, expertise and knowledge, exist in startups as well, but are differently designed and activated, structurally, functionally, socially, strategically, and with regard to agility, effectiveness, and their endurance. Startups have designed virtual teams, multicultural projects, project-based 'tribes', scrum and large-scale scrum (LeSS) frameworks, and various agile ways to make the most effective use of the knowledge and expertise that already exist in the startup for manifold purposes, such as operating the business, developing innovation, and exploiting and creating opportunities; in addition, startups orchestrate these elements to boost the circulation of the ongoing, developed, and innovative knowledge and constantly enable its intensification. The agile ways in which startups orchestrate their people, processes, actions, and structures constitute the business' potential opportunities and inhibitors in tandem.

TABLE 2.2 Startup's unique internal operation elements as opportunities and inhibitors

Elements	Opportunities	Inhibitors
Expertise, knowledge, knowledge management, dynamic capabilities	• Hiring new employees • Merging with new businesses, departments • Continual organizational learning • Developing a continual platform of (expertise-based) innovation	• Laying off unsuitable expertise • Team conflicts on mastering the 'best' expertise • Competition for talent and hires
Product and technology innovation	• Developing a competitive edge • Introducing new value to customers • Empowering the business • Promoting open innovation • Attracting investments	• Internal aversion to innovation, which can lead to internal disputes, refusal to perform innovative tasks, unwillingness to cooperate • External reluctance in embracing the introduced innovation, leading to customers' unwillingness to buy the startup's offerings, and stakeholders' refusal to collaborate with the startup
New 'rules', work approach, organizational culture	• Opportunity to improve business practices, approaches • Startups introduce innovations in products and technology, and should therefore embrace the process of organizational innovation • Enhancing renovation, as new approaches stimulate novelty • New hires bring new approaches and organizational cultures, which could complement the new rules and approaches	• Disputes over the new definitions of the rules and approaches • Reluctance to follow the new rules and approaches, thereby interrupting the 'work chain' • Internal conflicts between members who are following and those who are not following the rules and approaches • Leadership and management crises, especially in people governance
Tangible and intangible infrastructure, material, equipment, applications	• Improving and updating the existing infrastructure (higher speed, less errors) • Expanding the business' production and related processes • Improving the offerings • Recuperating(Facilitating?) employees' work (by new equipment, applications) • Rising efficacy and efficiency	• Requires more resources or funds • Requires training the personnel to use the new equipment • Employees may demonstrate an inability to adjust to the new equipment's functions, leading to frustration, incapability and misfunctions
Relationships with stakeholders, e.g., the board, investors, partners	• Strengthening trust and collaboration • Stimulating areas for collaboration • Stakeholders request that their networks join them in collaborating with the startup	• The uniqueness of the elements seems risky and distances the stakeholders • Stakeholders warn their networks to stay away from the startup

The Agile approach and methodology in startups respond to their need to react to changes proactively, promptly, and accurately by altering their actions, processes, structures, and strategies, among others, and to be able to constantly respond to the ongoing dynamics in their ecosystems. This requires a constant awareness of external changes and concurrent timely internal responses to those changes, while still fortifying the startup's mastery in its area and while enabling the startup to proceed with its daily operation and future development. As such, startups develop dynamic capabilities, that is, the ability to continuously create and develop tangible and intangible assets (Teece, Pisano and Shuen 1997; Teece 2007), and therefore take different types of risks that can lead to success or failure.

Knowledge management is one of the salient practices supporting the Agile approach; it is reflected in startups through practices of acquiring, applying, and assessing the existing knowledge in the startup and constantly preparing the teams for any potential changes, crises, or disruptions.

The following example demonstrates this notion: HauteC[10] is a three-year-old startup in the food tech industry in Scandinavia that provides solutions for high-end, stylish, vegan food, customized for each guest, by employing a unique fusion of sophisticated technology and chic cuisine; it is led by its co-founders Fiia, a former chef in a Michelin restaurant, and Sohvi, a tech expert with many years of experience in highly influential companies in the areas of machine learning and cyber security. Initially, HauteC attracted various restaurants and catering companies that were impressed by its technology and tasty food; however, with the COVID-19 pandemic, HauteC experienced a severe decrease in orders and sales. Fiia and Sohvi decided to implement the Agile methodology in 2020 and used Scrum to enhance the technology team's commitment to hastening their tasks (called Sprint); in fact, they used elements that were similar to those used in any

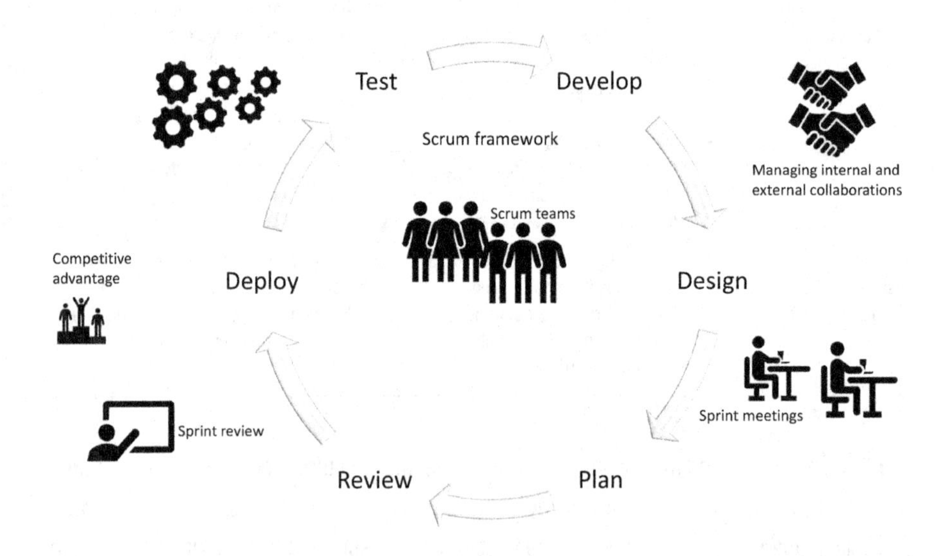

FIGURE 2.2 Use of unique elements in startups: an Agile-driven approach

business, for example, breaking tasks into smaller, more manageable pieces, showcases, presentations of daily accomplishments, and morning team meetings; yet the pace, flow, and dynamics within each team and in relation to other teams were faster and more accurate than in the past. HauteC reported in 2021 that due to the Agile methodology and the newly embedded Agile approach, it doubled its attractiveness to investors; thus, these elements introduced opportunities. However, they did not improve the company's exposure in the marketplace or allow it to outperform its competitors; instead, sales and future orders decreased, indicating inhibition; this emphasizes the dual, contrasting roles of new combinations of basic elements, that is, Agile, Scrum, and Sprint methods, on the startup's subsequent success (Senge and Sterman 1992; Pantiuchina et al. 2017; Teberga and Oliva 2018; Oliva and Kotabe 2019).

Inherent disruptors

"It is in our nature to be pioneers. We are not wired to wait around for a return to normality."[11] This quote encapsulates the spirit of startup founders, and describes their approach to crises, disruptions, or any types of interruptions that require modification or detach the startup's action from its initial plans. In fact, startups evolve through crises and disruptions, and these pop up along all stages of their development and encompass all domains, specialties, and organizational spheres. For many startups, crises are a fertile ground for initiating their activities; examples of startups that were born during the COVID-19 crisis are InSphero[12] and Lemoptix[13]; others have increased their sales and some of them have experienced great success. According to the CBInsights,[14] in July 2021 there were more than 700 unicorns around the world, stressing the 'favorable' premise of some startups thriving during the crisis; others have escaped closures that threatened their businesses prior to the pandemic outbreak. Taken together, such startup successes during the COVID-19 pandemic present a picture that is diametrically opposed to that of SMEs or some large companies in times of crisis. The natural and normal evolution of startups that goes 'hand in hand' with their inherent crises and disruptions, along with their accumulated experience in encountering, managing, and succeeding or failing to cope with those crises, are the drivers to startup's further and sometimes improved performance despite the crisis effects. Startups are used to implementing rapid changes in their actions to pivot or accelerate them toward faster growth; by being relatively small, prone to take risks and oriented to foster innovation, leveraging their offerings virtually, being deeply embedded in digitalization, and using marketing, dissemination, or attracting investors through social networks and innovative methods, startup's strategic planning, decision-making, and implementation are facilitated.

Crises are everywhere in the startup's realm, represented by any adversity or gap tackled, for example, a need for experts in specific areas when there is a shortage of such experts in the ecosystem or alternatively high costs for such experts that the startup cannot afford; a perfect MVP that is unattractive to the target market; a promising collaboration with investors that ultimately fails, leading to liquidity difficulties; regulations that restrict the startup's production process, use of its materials, or dissemination of its offerings; lawsuits; brain drain; and many other disruptive situations that force the startup to reinvent some of its processes or business models (Linnenluecke 2017; Ketchen and Craighead 2020; Kudyba 2020; Priyono, Moin and Putri 2020; Ratten 2020; Soto-Acosta 2020; Bărbulescu et al. 2021; Lee and Trimi 2021; Rodrigues and de Noronha 2021).

Summary

Startups represent a unique entity; they seem to operate like a regular business in the normal business realm, yet their characteristics differentiate them from SMEs and large businesses and largely facilitate their rapid growth and agile operation. This then enables them to be aligned with the ecosystem's needs and introduce a continual, up-to-date competitive advantage. These characteristics need to be deciphered and identified in times of crisis, because they play a role in managing the crisis' effects, in many cases, to the benefit of the startup.

This chapter covered the startup's characteristics by focusing on its demarcation by identifying its borders, including value creation, stages of development, and various combinations of innovative operations, such as through the Agile approach. Yet, like any other businesses, startups function in a context that can mold their features in introducing opportunities for collaboration, exploitation of new technology, joining partnerships, etc.; concurrently, startups form the structure and function of the context as powerful entities that have a substantial impact on their environments.

This chapter further addressed the external and internal aspects of the context that is relevant to startups; their impact on the startup's operation and potential success were discussed, along with their aptness to boost or disrupt or interrupt initial plans. Finally, when startups experience an inherent disruption, they are in their natural arena; they are used to functioning under stress, with gaps and with the need to change, pivot, and improvise on an ongoing basis. As such, a crisis such as the COVID-19 pandemic may signify only one element in the well-known sequence of crises that accompany their flow.

Reflective questions for class

1. Search the internet for two or three startups in your area, and list four or five characteristics that typify them as startups:

   a) Identify the characteristics that differentiate them from SMEs

   b) Identify the characteristics that differentiate them from large companies

2. Address the theoretical concepts introduced in this chapter that are relevant to startup demarcation. Choose *one* of those concepts; identify three to four components that explain how startups can manage the impact of COVID-19 by using/implementing/operating these components.
3. The chapter discusses some unexpected outcomes for startups during the COVID-19 pandemic, such as new launches, unicorns, and new collaborations, among others. Based on startup's characteristics, what would you suggest startups to ADD to their portfolio to guarantee such outcomes in future potential crises. Be specific; for example, in proposing to enhance *new combinations*, provide actual examples of those combinations.
4. Search for a startup that has evolved into a unicorn; analyze its achievement with respect to the components of its context. What are your suggestions for new startups striving to become unicorns with regard to their relations and actions with their context?
5. Discuss the challenges and opportunities in the required transformation of a startup from face-to-face operation to a virtual sphere. What are your main conclusions?

Notes

1 See https://www.nutanix.com/content/dam/nutanix-cxo/pdf/McKinsey's%20Three%20Horizons%20Model%20Defined%20Innovation%20for%20Years.%20Here's%20Why%20It%20No%20Longer%20Applies.pdf

2

The waterfall model has been around since the 1970s and is 'a framework for software development in which development proceeds sequentially through a series of phases'. The progress flows from one phase to another in order, although short feedback loops are allowed. It is possible to move backwards and make modifications based on the feedback...

3 Source: 1977 *Business Week* (Industr. edn) September 5: An incubator for startup companies, especially in the fast-growth, high-technology fields.

4 See https://www.britannica.com/topic/Facebook.

5 See http://abalobi.info/
6 See https://gusto.com/about
7 See https://www.weforum.org/reports/the-global-competitiveness-report-2020
8 See VRIN = valuable, rare, inimitable, and non-substitutable resources.
9 See https://www.carsome.my/
10 Based on an interview of the founders by the author. Some of the startup's details have been changed as per the founders' request.
11 See Interview with BOOM CEO Federico Mattia Dolci; https://www.eu-startups.com/2021/07/it-is-in-our-nature-to-be-pioneers-we-are-not-wired-to-wait-around-for-a-return-to-normality-interview-with-boom-founder-federico-mattia-dolci/
12 See https://www.startup.ch/index.cfm?page=129382&profil_id=448
13 See https://www.startup.ch/lemoptix
14 See https://www.cbinsights.com/research-unicorn-companies. For additional information: https://startupbase.com.br/home/startups?q=&states=all&cities=all&segments=all&targets=all&phases=all&models=all&badges=Unic%C3%B3rnio

References

Aldrich, H., & Auster, E. R. (1986). Even dwarfs started small: Liabilities of age and size and their strategic implications. *Research in Organizational Behavior.*

Aldrich, H. E., & Fiol, C. M. (1994). Fools rush in? The institutional context of industry creation. *Academy of Management Review, 19*(4), 645–670.

Alvedalen, J., & Boschma, R. (2017). A critical review of entrepreneurial ecosystems research: Towards a future research agenda. *European Planning Studies, 25*(6), 887–903.

Amin, A., & Cohendet, P. (2000). Organisational learning and governance through embedded practices. *Journal of Management and Governance, 4*(1), 93–116.

Arend, R. J. (2014). Social and environmental performance at SMEs: Considering motivations, capabilities, and instrumentalism. *Journal of Business Ethics, 125*(4), 541–561.

Autio, E., Kenney, M., Mustar, P., Siegel, D., & Wright, M. (2014). Entrepreneurial innovation: The importance of context. *Research Policy, 43*(7), 1097–1108.

Bărbulescu, O., Tecău, A. S., Munteanu, D., & Constantin, C. P. (2021). Innovation of startups, the key to unlocking post-crisis sustainable growth in Romanian entrepreneurial ecosystem. *Sustainability, 13*(2), 671.

Barney, J. (1991). Competitive advantage. *Journal of Management, 17*(1), 99–120.

Baum, J. R., Frese, M., Baron, R. A., & Katz, J. A. (2007). Entrepreneurship as an area of psychology study: An introduction. *The Psychology of Entrepreneurship, 1*, 18.

Baum, M., Schwens, C., & Kabst, R. (2011). A typology of international new ventures: Empirical evidence from high-technology industries. *Journal of Small Business Management, 49*(3), 305–330.

Berthod, O., & Müller-Seitz, G. (2018). Making sense in pitch darkness: An exploration of the sociomateriality of sensemaking in crises. *Journal of Management Inquiry, 27*(1), 52–68.

Blank, M., Lorion, R., Ferrari, J., & Davidson, W. (2019). *Invitation to participate in an analysis of our published literature.* American Psychological Association (APA). 10.1037/e628622012-089

Blank, S. (2013). Why the lean start-up changes everything. *Harvard Business Review, 91*(5), 63–72.

Blank, S. (2018). Startups are not a smaller version of a large company. In *The GuruBook* (pp. 130–133). Productivity Press.

Blank, S., & Dorf, B. (2020). *The startup owner's manual: The step-by-step guide for building a great company.* John Wiley & Sons.

Boeker, W., & Wiltbank, R. (2005). New venture evolution and managerial capabilities. *Organization Science, 16*(2), 123–133.

Bundy, J., Pfarrer, M. D., Short, C. E., & Coombs, W. T. (2017). Crises and crisis management: Integration, interpretation, and research development. *Journal of Management, 43*(6), 1661–1692.

Caers, R., De Feyter, T., De Couck, M., Stough, T., Vigna, C., & Du Bois, C. (2013). Facebook: A literature review. *New Media & Society, 15*(6), 982–1002.

Cavallo, A., Ghezzi, A., & Balocco, R. (2019). Entrepreneurial ecosystem research: Present debates and future directions. *International Entrepreneurship and Management Journal, 15*(4), 1291–1321.

Collins, J. C., Porras, J. I., & Porras, J. (2005). *Built to last: Successful habits of visionary companies.* Random House.

Davis, G. F., & Cobb, J. A. (2010). Resource dependence theory: Past and future. In *Stanford's organization theory renaissance, 1970–2000.*

Dean, J. W., & Bowen, D. E. (1994). Management theory and total quality: Improving research and practice through theory development. *Amr, 19*(3), 392–418. 10.5465/amr.1994.9412271803

Dubini, P. (1989). The influence of motivations and environment on business start-ups: Some hints for public policies. *Journal of Business Venturing, 4*(1), 11–26.

Eisenhardt, K. M., & Martin, J. A. (2000). Dynamic capabilities: What are they? *Strategic Management Journal, 21*(10–11), 1105–1121.

Fiegener, M. K. (2005). Determinants of board participation in the strategic decisions of small corporations. *Entrepreneurship Theory and Practice, 29*(5), 627–650.

Fiegener, M. K., Brown, B. M., Dreux, D. R., & Dennis Jr, W. J. (2000). The adoption of outside boards by small private US firms. *Entrepreneurship & Regional Development, 12*(4), 291–309.

Foss, N. J., & Saebi, T. (2018). Business models and business model innovation: Between wicked and paradigmatic problems. *Long Range Planning, 51*(1), 9–21.

Freeman, J., & Engel, J. S. (2007). Models of innovation: Startups and mature corporations. *California Management Review, 50*(1), 94–119.

Fried, H. O., & Tauer, L. W. (2015). An entrepreneur performance index. *Journal of Productivity Analysis, 44*(1), 69–77.

Gabrielsson, J., & Huse, M. (2005). "Outside" directors in SME boards: A call for theoretical reflections. *Corporate Board Role Duties and Composition, 1*(1), 28–37. 10.22495/cbv1i1art3

Gaddefors, J., & Anderson, A. R. (2017). Entrepreneursheep and context: When entrepreneurship is greater than entrepreneurs. *International Journal of Entrepreneurial Behavior & Research.*

Garud, R., & Karnøe, P. (2003). Bricolage versus breakthrough: Distributed and embedded agency in technology entrepreneurship. *Research Policy, 32*(2), 277–300.

Gehrich, G. (2012). *Build it like a startup: Lean product innovation.* Greg Gehrich.

Ghezzi, A. (2020). How entrepreneurs make sense of lean startup approaches: Business models as cognitive lenses to generate fast and frugal Heuristics. *Technological Forecasting and Social Change, 161*, 120324.

Ghezzi, A., & Cavallo, A. (2020). Agile business model innovation in digital entrepreneurship: Lean startup approaches. *Journal of Business Research, 110*, 519–537.

Goerres, A., & Walter, S. (2016). The political consequences of national crisis management: Micro-level evidence from German voters during the 2008/09 global economic crisis. *German Politics, 25*(1), 131–153.

Goktan, A. B., & Miles, G. (2011). Innovation speed and radicalness: Are they inversely related? *Management Decision.*

González-Cruz, T. F., Botella-Carrubi, D., & Martínez-Fuentes, C. M. (2020). The effect of firm complexity and founding team size on agile internal communication in startups. *International Entrepreneurship and Management Journal, 16*(3), 1101–1121.

Hayter, C. S. (2016). A trajectory of early-stage spinoff success: The role of knowledge intermediaries within an entrepreneurial university ecosystem. *Small Business Economics, 47*(3), 633–656.

Hayter, C. S., Nelson, A. J., Zayed, S., & O'Connor, A. C. (2018). Conceptualizing academic entrepreneurship ecosystems: A review, analysis and extension of the literature. *The Journal of Technology Transfer, 43*(4), 1039–1082.

Heaton, S., Siegel, D. S., & Teece, D. J. (2019). Universities and innovation ecosystems: A dynamic capabilities perspective. *Industrial and Corporate Change, 28*(4), 921–939.

Hillman, A. J., & Dalziel, T. (2003). Boards of directors and firm performance: Integrating agency and resource dependence perspectives. *Academy of Management Review, 28*(3), 383–396.

Hofstede, G. (1999). Problems remain, but theories will change: The universal and the specific in 21st century global management. *Organizational Dynamics, 27*(1), 34.

Hoskisson, R. E., Wright, M., Filatotchev, I., & Peng, M. W. (2013). Emerging multinationals from mid-range economies: The influence of institutions and factor markets. *Journal of Management Studies, 50*(7), 1295–1321.

Howe, B. T., Desai, S., & Murray, H. (2021). 2020 New employer business indicators in the United States: National and state trends. Available at SSRN 3897027.

Hsiang, S., Allen, D., Annan-Phan, S., Bell, K., Bolliger, I., Chong, T., Druckenmiller, H., Huang, L. Y., Hultgren, A., & Krasovich, E. (2020). The effect of large-scale anti-contagion policies on the COVID-19 pandemic. *Nature, 584*(7820), 262–267.

Kaiser, U., & Müller, B. (2013). Team heterogeneity in startups and its development over time. *ZEW-Centre for European Economic Research Discussion Paper,* 13-058.

Kamps, J., & Pólos, L. (1999). Reducing uncertainty: A formal theory of organizations in action. *American Journal of Sociology, 104*(6), 1776–1812.

Kariv, D. (2020) Start-up and small business life. In Carayannis, E.G. (Eds.), *Encyclopedia of creativity, invention, innovation and entrepreneurship.* Springer. DOI: https://doi.org/10.1007/978-3-319-15347-6_466

file:///C:/Users/user/Downloads/Kariv2013_ReferenceWorkEntry_Start-UpAndSmallBusinessLife.pdf (Encyclopedia - https://link.springer.com/referencework/10.1007/978-3-319-15347-6

Kariv, D., Baldegger, R. J., & Kashy-Rosenbaum, G. (2022). 'All you need is... entrepreneurial attitudes': A deeper look into the propensity to start a business during the COVID-19 through a gender comparison (GEM data). *World Review of Entrepreneurship, Management and Sustainable Development, 18*(1–2), 195–226.

Kariv, D., Kaplan, O., Ibanescu, M., & Cisneros, L. (Accepted, forthcoming). From perceptions to performance to business intentions: What do women and men entrepreneurs really see? *International Journal of Entrepreneurship and Small Business (IJESB).* DOI: 10.1504/IJESB.2020.10034846.

Ketchen Jr, D. J., & Craighead, C. W. (2020). Research at the intersection of entrepreneurship, supply chain management, and strategic management: Opportunities highlighted by COVID-19. *Journal of Management, 46*(8), 1330–1341.

Klock, M., Baum, C. F., & Thies, C. F. (1996). Tobin's Q, intangible capital, and financial policy. *Journal of Economics and Business, 48*(4), 387–400.

König, A., Graf-Vlachy, L., Bundy, J., & Little, L. M. (2020). A blessing and a curse: How CEOs' trait empathy affects their management of organizational crises. *Academy of Management Review, 45*(1), 130–153.

Kudyba, S. (2020). COVID-19 and the acceleration of digital transformation and the future of work. *Information Systems Management, 37*(4), 284–287.

Lee, S. M., Olson, D. L., & Trimi, S. (2012). Co-innovation: Convergenomics, collaboration, and co-creation for organizational values. *Management Decision.*

Lee, S. M., & Trimi, S. (2021). Convergence innovation in the digital age and in the COVID-19 pandemic crisis. *Journal of Business Research, 123,* 14–22.

Linnenluecke, M. K. (2017). Resilience in business and management research: A review of influential publications and a research agenda. *International Journal of Management Reviews, 19*(1), 4–30.

Liu, Y. (2020). The micro-foundations of global business incubation: Stakeholder engagement and strategic entrepreneurial partnerships. *Technological Forecasting and Social Change, 161,* 120294.

Lynall, M. D., Golden, B. R., & Hillman, A. J. (2003). Board composition from adolescence to maturity: A multitheoretic view. *The Academy of Management Review, 28*(3), 416–431. 10.5465/amr.2003.10196743

Malová, D., & Dolný, B. (2016). Economy and democracy in Slovakia during the crisis: From a laggard to the EU core. *Problems of Post-Communism, 63*(5–6), 300–312.

Maurya, A. (2012). *Running lean: Iterate from plan a to a plan that works.* Lean.

Motoyama, Y., & Knowlton, K. (2017). Examining the connections within the startup ecosystem: A case study of St. Louis. *Entrepreneurship Research Journal, 7*(1).

Murdock, K. A. (2012). Entrepreneurship policy: Trade-offs and impact in the EU. *Entrepreneurship & Regional Development, 24*(9–10), 879–893.

Najmaei, A. (2016). How do entrepreneurs develop business models in small high-tech ventures? An exploratory model from Australian IT firms. *Entrepreneurship Research Journal, 6*(3), 297–343.

Nambisan, S., & Baron, R. A. (2013). Entrepreneurship in innovation ecosystems: Entrepreneurs' self–regulatory processes and their implications for new venture success. *Entrepreneurship Theory and Practice, 37*(5), 1071–1097.

Oliva, F. L., & Kotabe, M. (2019). Barriers, practices, methods and knowledge management tools in startups. *Journal of Knowledge Management.*

Osterwalder, A., & Pigneur, Y. (2010). *Business model generation: A handbook for visionaries, game changers, and challengers.* John Wiley & Sons.

Pantiuchina, J., Mondini, M., Khanna, D., Wang, X., & Abrahamsson, P. (2017). Are software startups applying agile practices? The state of the practice from a large survey. Paper presented at the *International Conference on Agile Software Development,* 167–183.

Peteraf, M., Di Stefano, G., & Verona, G. (2013). The elephant in the room of dynamic capabilities: Bringing two diverging conversations together. *Strategic Management Journal, 34*(12), 1389–1410.

Pettigrew, A., Starkey, K., & Hambrick, D. (2001). Power and change: Andrew Pettigrew on strategy and change [and commentary]. *The Academy of Management Executive (1993–2005),* 45–47.

Pfeffer, J., & Salancik, G. R. (2003). *The external control of organizations: A resource dependence perspective.* Stanford University Press.

Priyono, A., Moin, A., & Putri, V. N. A. O. (2020). Identifying digital transformation paths in the business model of SMEs during the COVID-19 pandemic. *Journal of Open Innovation: Technology, Market, and Complexity, 6*(4), 104.

Ratten, V. (2020). Coronavirus (Covid-19) and entrepreneurship: Cultural, lifestyle and societal changes. *Journal of Entrepreneurship in Emerging Economies.*

Reis, E. (2011). The lean startup. *New York: Crown Business, 27,* 2016–2020.

Rodrigues, C. D., & de Noronha, Matheus Eurico Soares. (2021). What companies can learn from unicorn startups to overcome the COVID-19 crisis. *Innovation & Management Review.*

Rosnow, R. L., & Georgoudi, M. (1986). The spirit of contextualism. *Contextualism and Understanding in Behavioral Science: Implications for Research and Theory,* 3–22.

Roundy, P. T., Brockman, B. K., & Bradshaw, M. (2017). The resilience of entrepreneurial ecosystems. *Journal of Business Venturing Insights, 8,* 99–104.

Roundy, P. T., & Fayard, D. (2019). Dynamic capabilities and entrepreneurial ecosystems: The micro-foundations of regional entrepreneurship. *The Journal of Entrepreneurship, 28*(1), 94–120.

Salamzadeh, A. (2015). New venture creation: Controversial perspectives and theories. *Economic Analysis, 48*(3–4), 101–109.

Schabram, K., & Maitlis, S. (2017). Negotiating the challenges of a calling: Emotion and enacted sensemaking in animal shelter work. *Academy of Management Journal, 60*(2), 584–609.

Schumpeter, J. (1934). *The theory of economic development.* Harvard University Press.

Schumpeter, J. A. (1939). *Business cycles.* McGraw-Hill.

Schumpeter, J. A., & Lekachman, R. L. (1978). *Can capitalism survive?* Harper & Row.

Schwab, K., & Zahidi, S. (2020). Global competitiveness report: Special edition 2020. Paper presented at the

Senge, P. M., & Sterman, J. D. (1992). Systems thinking and organizational learning: Acting locally and thinking globally in the organization of the future. *European Journal of Operational Research, 59*(1), 137–150.

Silva, D. S., Ghezzi, A., de Aguiar, R. B., Cortimiglia, M. N., & ten Caten, C. S. (2020). Lean Startup, Agile Methodologies and customer development for business model innovation: A systematic review and research agenda. *International Journal of Entrepreneurial Behavior & Research.*

Soto-Acosta, P. (2020). COVID-19 pandemic: Shifting digital transformation to a high-speed gear. *Information Systems Management, 37*(4), 260–266.

Spigel, B. (2017). The relational organization of entrepreneurial ecosystems. *Entrepreneurship Theory and Practice, 41*(1), 49–72.

Spilling, O. R. (1996). The entrepreneurial system: On entrepreneurship in the context of a mega-event. *Journal of Business Research, 36*(1), 91–103.

Stam, E. (2015). Entrepreneurial ecosystems and regional policy: A sympathetic critique. *European Planning Studies, 23*(9), 1759–1769.

Stam, E., & Spigel, B. (2016). *Entrepreneurial ecosystems.* USE Discussion paper series, 16(13).

Stigliani, I., & Ravasi, D. (2012). Organizing thoughts and connecting brains: Material practices and the transition from individual to group-level prospective sensemaking. *Academy of Management Journal, 55*(5), 1232–1259.

St-Pierre, J., Foleu, L., Abdulnour, G., Nomo, S., & Fouda, M. (2015). SME development challenges in Cameroon: An entrepreneurial ecosystem perspective. *Transnational Corporations Review, 7*(4), 441–462.

Taneja, H., & Chenault, K. (2019). Building a startup that will last. *Harvard Business Review, 7,* 23–27.

Teberga, P. M. F., & Oliva, F. L. (2018). Identification, analysis and treatment of risks in the introduction of new technologies by start-ups. *Benchmarking: An International Journal.*

Teece, D. J. (1992). Competition, cooperation, and innovation: Organizational arrangements for regimes of rapid technological progress. *Journal of Economic Behavior & Organization, 18*(1), 1–25.

Teece, D. J. (2007). Explicating dynamic capabilities: The nature and microfoundations of (sustainable) enterprise performance. *Strategic Management Journal, 28*(13), 1319–1350.

Teece, D. J., Pisano, G., & Shuen, A. (1997). Dynamic capabilities and strategic management. *Strategic Management Journal, 18*(7), 509–533.

Tetiana, H., Maryna, C., Lidiia, K., Michail, M., & Svetlana, D. (2018). Innovative model of enterprises personnel incentives evaluation. *Academy of Strategic Management Journal, 17*(3), 1–6.

Thornton, P. H. (1999). The sociology of entrepreneurship. *Annual Review of Sociology, 25*(1), 19–46.

Townsend, D. M., & Busenitz, L. W. (2015). Turning water into wine? Exploring the role of dynamic capabilities in early-stage capitalization processes. *Journal of Business Venturing, 30*(2), 292–306.

Trimi, S., & Berbegal-Mirabent, J. (2012). Business model innovation in entrepreneurship. *International Entrepreneurship and Management Journal, 8*(4), 449–465.

Walecka, A. (2016). Determinants of managers' behaviour in a crisis situation in an enterprise-an attempt at model construction. *Management, 20*(1), 58–70.

Watson, T. J. (2013). Entrepreneurship in action: Bringing together the individual, organizational and institutional dimensions of entrepreneurial action. *Entrepreneurship & Regional Development, 25*(5–6), 404–422.

Weick, K. E. (1995). *Sensemaking in organizations.* Sage.

Weick, K. E., Sutcliffe, K. M., & Obstfeld, D. (2005). Organizing and the process of sensemaking. *Organization Science, 16*(4), 409–421.

Welter, F. (2011). Contextualizing entrepreneurship—conceptual challenges and ways forward. *Entrepreneurship Theory and Practice, 35*(1), 165–184.

Welter, F., & Gartner, W. B. (2016). *A research agenda for entrepreneurship and context.* Edward Elgar Publishing.

Wright, M., & Stigliani, I. (2013). Entrepreneurship and growth. *International Small Business Journal, 31*(1), 3–22.

Xing, Y., Liu, Y., Boojihawon, D. K., & Tarba, S. (2020). Entrepreneurial team and strategic agility: A conceptual framework and research agenda. *Human Resource Management Review, 30*(1), 100696.

Zahra, S. A., & Wright, M. (2011). Entrepreneurship's next act. *Academy of Management Perspectives, 25*(4), 67–83.

Chapter Three

Types of crises

- Takeaways
- Introduction
- Crisis portfolio
- Demarcating crises
- Indicators of disruptive events
- Crisis dimensions
- Crisis core topic
- How does the event topic affect the startup?
- Sequential crisis events
- Generation of 'other indicators'
- COVID-19 and the new wave of crises
- Summary
- Reflective questions for class

Takeaways

- Noting that not all disruptive and disastrous events turn into crises, a set of indicators need to converge and interact in ways that will stimulate an outbreak
- Recognizing that intertwined measures, even of a same event, can mold various crisis profiles; and startups react to the concurrent crisis profile rather than automatically reacting to a crisis based on previous experience (e.g., COVID-19 originated from SARS, yet due to intertwined relations, evolved differently)
- Reviewing the different dimensions of a crisis to be employed as valid tools for constant validation of the startup's product-market fit in light of the specific crisis (e.g., a touristic App would be the best device for tourists, but during the pandemic, tourism stopped and then changed dramatically, such that the App is no longer useful; yet it could have been most useful during crises of war and violence)
- Acknowledging that crises have primary and secondary (potential) effects on startups; first on the core business of the startup, especially if the crisis topics or other indicators align with the business' product/services, and second by the impact of the crisis on the general market and ecosystem, that is echoed in attracting talent,

DOI: 10.4324/9781003173809-3

cross-border collaborations (under travel restrictions) or the power of purchase of the startup's products/services

- Spotting the impact of the 'other indicators' to detect the startup's view of each indicator's significance to its strategy and action; some indicators entail opportunities that should be quickly exploited

Introduction

This chapter focuses on the identification and demarcation of crises through multidimensional lenses; it does not discuss ways of managing or coping with the crises, as these are thoroughly debated in Chapter 8. The literature in entrepreneurship research probing crises in the entrepreneurial landscape is vast, focusing mainly on managing and coping with these crises. This chapter delves into the previous stage and aims to shed more light on the factual and perceptual directions that demarcate an event as a crisis. Consequently, it endeavors to provide more insight on the quest to define the impact on a startup prior to the activity taken to handle the situation.

History is replete with situations, episodes, and phenomena that are considered sources of disasters and crises, encompassing the negative consequences during and after their occurrence. Concurrently, considerable developments were introduced thanks to such crises, proving that crises encapsulate negative and positive effects, along with negative and positive perceptions of the crisis' potential effects. Moreover, a crisis can have both positive and negative effects on entrepreneurship. It may trigger a decline in the desire for a business' products or services, in investors' interest in the business, and in the business' volume and profitability, risking the startup's survival, and have negative effects on the personal psychological perceptions and attitudes of entrepreneurs. However, a crisis can also provide the impetus to scout for new opportunities and resources and to develop products, services, or business-related operations that can respond, either directly or indirectly, to the crisis' hazards and effects. Moreover, crises can serve as turning points, where businesses that faced difficulties leverage the crisis to recover. For example, R-Pur[1] has been making anti-pollution masks since 2015 using a sophisticated technology that filters out various types of toxins and purifies air; the COVID-19 pandemic enabled it to scale up its business. According to Flavien Hello, the founder and CEO of R-Pur: "We managed a 700% increase. We multiplied our production by 7 in 2020, but of course, demand was so high, we couldn't meet all of it."[2]

In fact, the dual meaning or connotation of a crisis is rooted in the languages; according to Wikipedia,[3] the Chinese word for 'crisis' is composed of two Chinese characters signifying 'danger' (wēi, 危) and 'opportunity' or 'change point' (jī, 机; 機), and 'krisis' in ancient Greek[4] signified the preference of one alternative over another, exemplifying its multifaceted nature; in Hebrew,[5] 'mashber' (רבשמ) refers to something broken; it can also be understood as something that induces distress, thus associated with its negative angle; this is similar to its negative connotation in Arabic (قبيصم) (Zamoum and Gorpe 2018), leading scholars such as Coombs to define a crisis as the perception of an unexpected and unpredictable threatening occurrence that can generate great hardship to multiple stakeholders, hence emphasizing perceptions rather than 'an objective situation' and its negative effects.

Crisis portfolio

Vast research has been dedicated to defining and delineating crises and to determining which negative occurrences might be considered outside the scope of crises. Unexpected epidemics, tsunamis, floods, fires, or earthquakes have a severe, immediate, and visible destructive impact on different areas, such as casualties, living conditions, the environment; and an additional ongoing impact, after the negative episode is solved, on the economy, employment, and psychological outcomes. Such natural hazards are perceived as unpredictable and uncontrollable or semi-controllable due to their source, that is, nature. However, throughout history, other threats have also been recognized, such as wars, terrorism, situations of violence or conflict, and nuclear and biological threats, which can be either physical or virtual, as violence and crime are prevalent on the internet. These occurrences may or may not have an immediate or visible effect and the severity of their impact may be revealed only gradually, so that when they emerge, the gravity of these occurrences is still unknown. While in each of these cases the episode is associated with a negative, disagreeable, and acute disruption of the routine, not all negative disruptions evolve into crises and not all negative episodes require an intervention that draws from the crisis management protocol. It is therefore crucial to categorize the types of occurrences that evolve into crises, outline them, and decode the measures that can provide a reliable basis for classifying an episode as a crisis or not. For example, would official announcements be appropriate for considering a situation as a crisis or media coverage, rumors by word of mouth, or massive traction in social media?

The literature in entrepreneurship that focuses on crises has dedicated extensive attention to crisis management but has neglected defining the crisis, thereby creating a void in delineating a crisis, as not each negative episode warrants crisis management intervention. Through the entrepreneurship framework, this chapter attempts to trace the nature of crises along with their conceptual definitions and demarcation, to shed light on the intertwined existence of startups and crises and their reciprocal impact. This chapter offers models, insights, and examples of crises that have evolved outside of the business and that have affected an entire industry, a geographical locale, or a local economy. Organizational crises are beyond the scope of this chapter and of this book's focus (Irvine and Anderson 2004; Boin and McConnell 2007; Brünjes and Revilla-Diez 2013; Doern 2016, 2017; Linnenluecke and McKnight 2017; Grube and Storr 2018).

Demarcating crises

Crises are broadly defined as unexpected, high-impact events that create high levels of threat to many people and encompass chaotic conditions and uncertainty. Not all such events turn into crises. The three critical components that 'transform' an event into a crisis are when the event is actually or is perceived as *a disruption* (e.g., surprising, uncontrollable), *a major threat* (e.g., harming people, damaging property, or disrupting life's normal course), and *contingent on time pressure.*

One of the most comprehensive inventories of crises was compiled by Mitroff (1988), who listed various topics, areas, and contents of crises at the business level, external and internal, while focusing on crises, such as natural disasters, terrorism, boycotts, large-scale system failures; however, she failed to illustrate the major impact of crises on the environment, the ecosystem, and then reciprocally on the startup. Yet, the 'objective' components, even of events that are definitely catastrophic, may not develop into a crisis. For example, forest fires affect many people in different ways—food, water, housing, employment, but these catastrophes are not considered crises; however, a political incident involving a few people could erupt into international conflicts and regional violence. 'Objective' characteristics are reinforced by the subjective perceptions that individuals embrace in understanding the event. A bulk of research in psychology offers more consideration of subjective indicators along with the objective ones in defining crises, such as *sensing* a threat, *perceiving* the probability of loss/harm, or *feeling* insecure, especially when these are expressed by a large number of people who have been exposed to the same situation. The perceptual aspect has become a forceful measure in delineating the concept (Ansell, Boin and Keller 2010; Herbane 2010; Buchanan and Denyer 2013; Dutta 2017; Xu et al. 2021).

Overall, an event is considered a crisis according to the balance of the nexus of objective components (e.g., disasters, hardship) and subjective perspectives (e.g., perceptions, attitudes, worries, fears), as demonstrated in Figure 3.1.

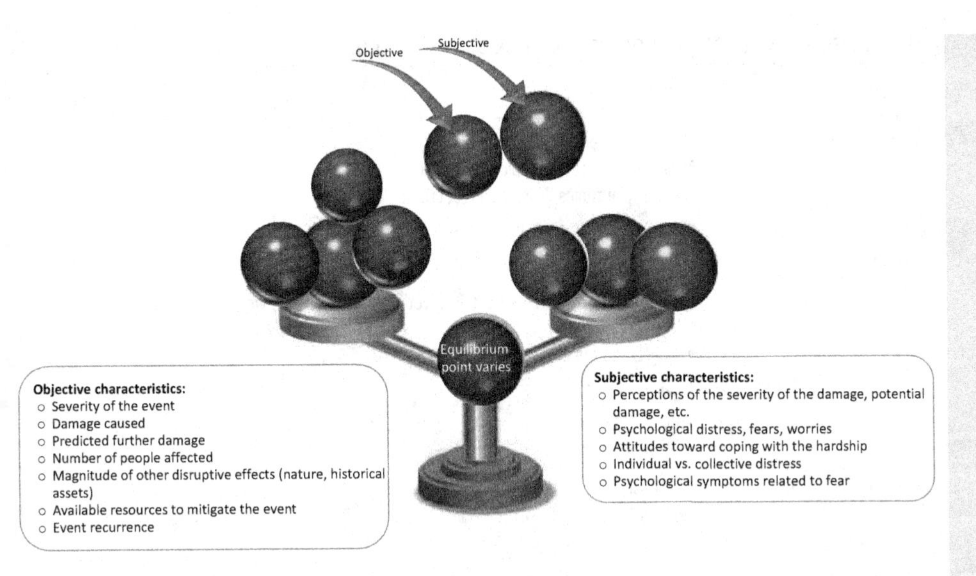

FIGURE 3.1 The nexus of objective and subjective components of a crisis

Indicators of disruptive events

What is it that turns an event into a crisis? The following measures provide some insight into the evolution of some events into crises. History presents many examples of similar events that, under different triggers, either turned into a crisis or were treated as 'just' a troublesome event.

Intertwined measures of the same event or of different events can trigger the emergence of crises; in addition, changes in one or more of these measures can create different types of crises, with different effects and extents, involving different related impacts. For example, Sudan[6] is a country facing conflict and violence (i.e., first disruptive event), high inflation (second disruptive event), a refugee crisis (third disruptive event), and COVID-19 (fourth disruptive event). This multiplicity of harmful events has prompted multiple crises in Sudan, resulting in crisis consequences such as food insecurity, displacement, and financial difficulties, with millions of innocent people affected. To understand the dynamics of the events' evolution into a crisis, we might imagine some measures of Sudan's events occurring in, for example, a European country or with a different timing, for example, after the 9/11 crisis; these changes, among many other combinations, would probably dramatically change the profile of Sudan's crises, even though similar events triggered them.

The measures that can prompt the outbreak of a crisis are:

Measures	Measures' angles
Topic	• Originating from nature, human • New and unexpected topics for a crisis • Hierarchy of topics, from the most critical

Who is affected by the event?	• People
	  • >> Innocent individuals
	  • >> Individuals intentionally involved in the event (*war, violence, financial crises*)
	  • >> Countries
	  • >> Large regions
	• Animals
	• Natural resources
	• Political damage

Power of the affected people	• Financially • Politically • Socially
Multiple crises at a time	• Troublesome events associated with more than one topic that are related or unrelated, affecting a specific region • More than one troublesome event associated with the same topic affecting a specific region • Troublesome events associated with the same topic affecting different regions
Timing	• Periodically • In fragile times (after disasters, instability, migrations, etc.)
Areas affected	• Affluence/poverty • Regional resilience • Potential recovery
Media coverage	
Governments' involvement	
International associations' involvement	
International assistance	

The transformation of events into a crisis is therefore not automatic, and is contingent on different measures or characteristics of those events. Changes in these characteristics, including time, duration, magnitude, or severity, can alter the profile of the crisis and its consequent dimensions; these changes may also lead to or avoid the outbreak of a crisis.

Crisis dimensions

Crisis dimensions are based on worldwide continual research conducted by different associations and aimed at tracking crises and characterizing them: the ways in which they are coped with and managed, their immediate and long-term impact, among others. Accordingly, indexes and statistics have been developed. INFORM[7] *assesses the severity of a crisis which is calculated as impact × condition of affected people + complexity*; the Organization for World Peace (OWP)[8] traces the key players involved in a crisis and the timeline by region; the United Nations Development Program (UNDP)[9] disaster index is an informational tool describing four hazards—drought, cyclones, earthquakes, and floods—through quantitative data (not human perception); the International Disaster Database (EM-DAT),[10] supported by the World Health Organization (WHO) and the Belgian government, contains essential core data on mass disasters around the world from 1900 and an updated section on 'disasters of the week' stemming from various sources, including United Nations (UN) agencies, non-governmental organizations, insurance companies, research institutes, and press agencies; official agencies such as the WHO[11] collect data on their respective core topics; the World Bank maps crises from various perspectives, their characteristics, effects, etc., including climate change disasters, clean water, poverty, and health, among others; other associations monitor and frame their core actions using data and information on crises, such as the Joint Monitoring Programme (JMP) on Water Supply, Sanitation and Hygiene (WASH), the United Nations Children's Fund (UNICEF), and many others. These sources must track crises and assess their severity, to be able to manage them once they have already erupted as well as to explore pre-crisis events and disruptive events' dynamics for prediction, preparation, and monitoring.

For startups, such indications are critical for concurrent and future situations; they constitute an important tool for the constant validation of their product-market fit associated with the crisis impact; in addition, they provide a practical strategy to prepare for managing hardship, that is, coping with the threat, and scouting for new and emerging needs, that is, exploiting opportunities.

At-a-Glance—from crisis to startup

Hassan Hassan is the founder of a cybersecurity startup operating in Germany and Austria. Hassan came from an area that faced frequent violent crises, and he and his family were forcibly displaced to Europe. Hassan's dedication contributed to his participation in an international program, in which he started the cybersecurity business. Hassan describes the crises that he went through as his great fortune:

> when you are part of a crisis, wars, terror, lack of food, death in the family, and your regular routine no longer exists, you are forced to 're-start' your life, starting from re-checking and validating anything that you do,

> to ensure that it is the most appropriate thing to do, under the specific conditions.

says Hassan.

Accordingly, after almost a decade, during which Hassan established his startup, completed his academic studies, and raised a family, he was well-equipped with the required strategies to manage the COVID-19 pandemic.

> "When the pandemic started, I instructed all of our employees to focus on new needs that can arise due to this specific virus, I urged them to be creative, even imaginative, and pinpoint new opportunities. Our marketing department 'discovered' a new need, which was associated with a smart tool to trace offensive vocabulary on the internet, which has increased dramatically during the pandemic,"

said Hassan. He and his team thoroughly examined the pandemic's measures and its different potential avenues and impact to scout for new opportunities, including new conduct (rise in violence on internet), thus creating new needs.

> I remember myself in a shelter back then, reading any news I could come across to plan my next step, and leave the shelter for an independent and better life. This strategy promoted me to my older life as the founder of a successful startup

concludes Hassan.

Disruptive events are potential direct or indirect sources for a crisis outbreak. According to the World Bank[12] and other sources, crises can be categorized based on several dimensions.

Crisis core topic

Crises fall into different core topics and subcategories, as shown in the following list. Most crises are typified by more than one topic, or subtopic, concurrently; with the COVID-19 pandemic, the crisis originated from the topic of physical health, and due to lockdowns—to mental health, educational inequality (virtual education is enjoyed by those who have computers at home, access to high-quality internet, etc.), inequality in employment (some employees were asked to leave), financial-related issues (some owners of SMEs were more severely affected by the lockdowns, etc.), showing that the topics associated to the pandemic are health—physical and mental, social inequality (in education) and job insecurity. The multiplicity of topics can emerge in different ways, as described in Figure 3.2 and in the following.

1. The crisis originates from more than one source (representing more than one topic)—the crisis encompasses two or more topics, which are related and expected (e.g., drought and hunger)
2. The crisis originates from one source and concurrently triggers another source—the crisis encompasses two or more topics concurrently, which are related (e.g., hunger >>> children's health problems)
3. The crisis originates from one source, and the longer it lasts, the more likely that it will trigger another source—the crisis encompasses two or more related topics sequentially (e.g., hunger >>> inequality in education)

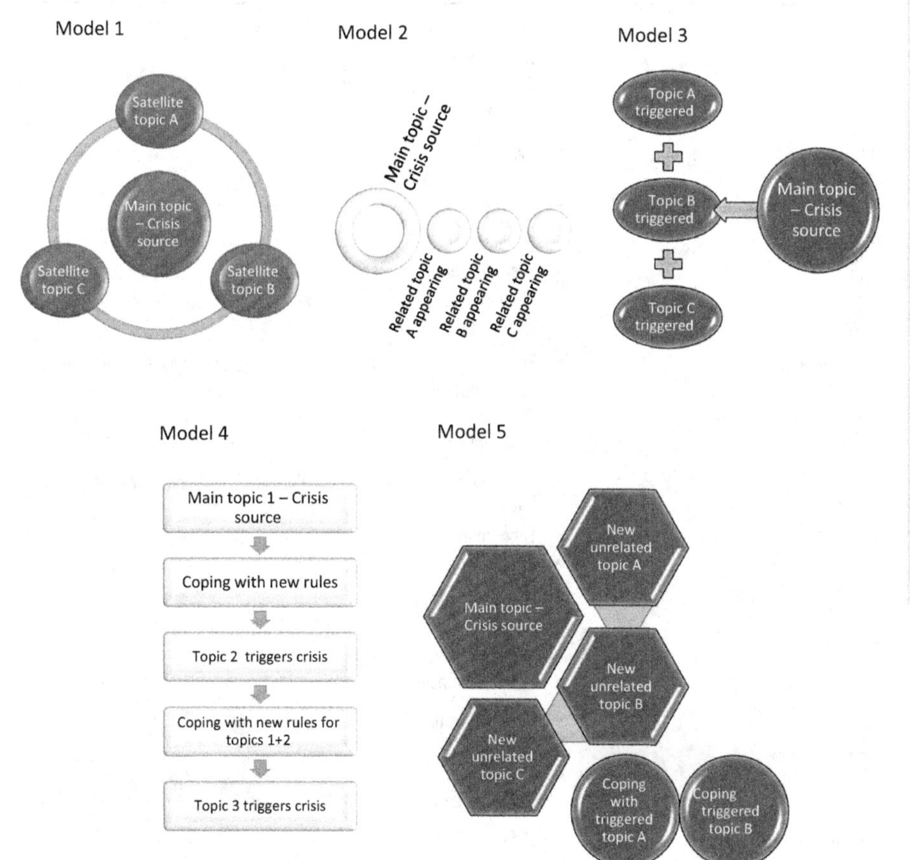

FIGURE 3.2 Models of relationships among crisis topics

4. The crisis originates from one source and the avenues to managing the crisis create different sources—one topic, management/coping, and more topics for the crisis arise; these topics are semi-related (health problem >>> *lockdowns to avoid contagion [management of the crisis]* >>> national financial crisis)
5. Subsequent to model 4, each topic is broken up into various topics and subtopics, which are unrelated and unexpected (e.g., terror attack such as in 9/11 >< splits into national discrimination, social inequality >< splits into financial segregation toward people of ethnic groups >< splits into inequality in education, etc.)

Drawing on 62 categories of research directions found in a recently published bibliometric review (Xu et al. 2021), crises are associated primarily with business economics and finance-related sources and consequences (i.e., their main source); then other categories appear, reinforcing the notion that crises are multitopic phenomena.

Topics and areas	**Subtopics**
Health	• Infectious diseases • Nutrition • Pandemic preparedness and COVID-19 • Vaccines
Education	• Inequality in education • Lack of education • Girls' education
Environment	• Biodiversity • Marine plastic pollution • Natural capital • Reduction in gas flaring
Finance-related issues	• Financial stability: global, regional, local, sectorial, gender-based, discriminatory • Financial inclusion • Financial integrity
Inequality	• Social protection: jobs and development, pensions, safety nets, cash transfers • Labor markets • Infrastructure
Fragility, conflict, and violence	• Regions in conflict • Refugees • International displacement, deportations • Conflict intensity
Regional integration	• Protecting cities • Security • Employment • Urban development
Social inclusion	• Disability inclusion • Indigenous peoples • People with special needs

Food security	• Famine • Refugees and food supply • Conflicts in food/agriculture areas
Natural factors	• Drought • Earthquake • Flood • Fire
Water	• Sanitation • Water resources

There are different categorizations and no clear-cut associations between topics, such as the climate change crisis affecting sanitation: these are two different phenomena, which may or may not be announced as crises, but they are directly related through two other crises, that is, global warming and clean-water shortages; these latter crises trigger other phenomena that can further enhance climate change and sanitation; the other phenomena could be related to a higher demand for air-conditioning systems due to climate change and global warming, and we would therefore expect increased production of air-conditioning systems, with growth in the rates of industry production and activity potentially affecting the soil, water, and pollution, and eventually 'interfering' in environmental factors. These may increase the effects associated with climate change and sanitation. A focal startup might thus be affected by these two crises—climate change and sanitation—even when its main activity is in a different sector (see example in Figure 3.3).

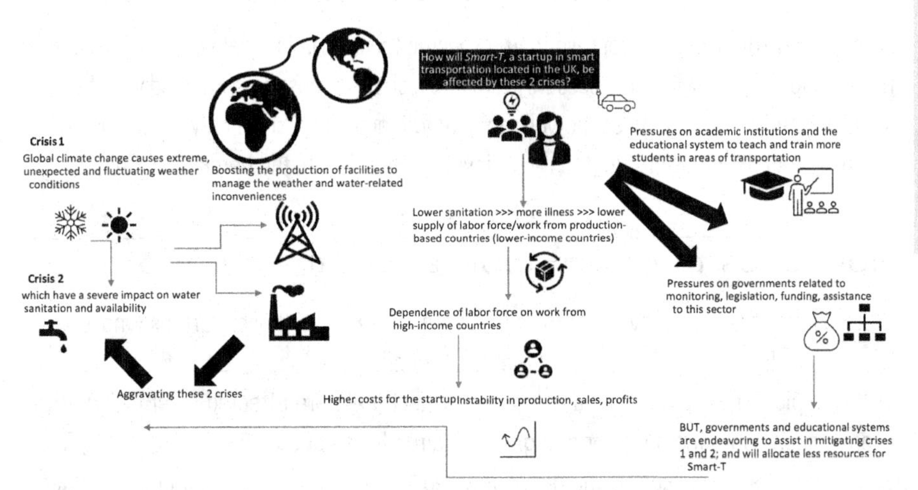

FIGURE 3.3 Crises' indirect effects on a startup

Some studies tend to connect event topics and the probability their evolving into a crisis as a function of several factors: $\sum$ topics x f(regional perspective/industry/political power/recurrence/culture/timing and focus) = crisis outbreak.

Regional perspective	Depending on the region's experiences with such events or the resources available to mitigate them; for example, conflicts in agricultural areas can be disruptive events that stimulate a food crisis in regions that are suffering from food-related difficulties (famine, irrigation problems, currency difficulties) such as Sudan, Yemen, Ethiopia[13], but may not explode into a crisis in more affluent regions, and such conflicts may be local, limited to groups, tribes, etc.
Industry	Threatening events occurring in industries that are either critical or alternatively sought after will be more apt to stimulate a crisis; for example, major threatening events in health, water, and food are considered to endanger the survival of people and animals, whereas events threatening areas of inequality, education, or the environment are considered less critical. Similarly, some industries have gained interest and traction, such as internet, cybersecurity, and threats to those 'powerful' industries can trigger a crisis, such as the Y2K bug crisis.
Political power of the 'event' participants	A crisis is disseminated by people and therefore troublesome events that involve politically influential people will be announced more promptly and loudly. Similar events may turn into a crisis or not, depending on the *if* and the *how* people spread it.
Recurrence of the same 'event'	Disruptive events that are recurrent, such as drought, floods, natural forest fires, etc., can be harmful and potentially cause damage in the long run, yet not necessarily be declared crises, as they may be expected. This is relevant to violence, terror, and other human-based events that are recognized to recur. The emergence of a repeated event results in a sort of resilience.
Culture	Some cultures emphasize values such as independence and self-provision, like the North American culture (Hofseded 1980, 1998), and would consider events related to unemployment or financial stability as severe events that can potentially activate crises.
Timing and focus	Regions, sectors, and industries may be implicated in various foci and engaged in different endeavors, so that the emergence of a disruptive event can garner different levels of attention from the people involved; for example, under threats of terror attacks, events related to unemployment will garner only a marginal focus as compared to times with no terror-related threats.

As such, a disruptive event representing a specific topic (e.g., inequality, financial insecurity, unemployment) will not necessarily turn into a crisis; it must be entangled with factors such as location, timing, focus, power, etc. that will activate a crisis only when combined and will mold the crisis profile (the topics involved, the length, the hardship it creates).

How does the event topic affect the startup?

Startups are affected by events' topics in several ways. First, those startups whose core business is directly related to a topic that is under crisis are influenced by the fluctuation of that topic; for example, startups in the agro-tech field are affected by any disruptive events, such as floods, fires, or drought, that directly affect anything related to agriculture. Second, startups can be indirectly affected by crises with topics that do not reflect their core business. For example, disruptive events such as floods, fires, or drought can influence startups in fintech as well, because these events and subsequent crises influence the regional or national financial and monetary situation; these can also have a sequential impact on startups in consumption, culture, or recreation that are affected by the financial situation in a country, being hedonistic commodities rather than utilitarian needs, and such crises will affect purchase power and traction of such commodities.

A secondary impact relates to changes created by crises in social, cultural, and financial conditions, which can affect various components or processes in the startup, including, for example, attracting investments, which can be challenging when the national financial state worsens; or collaborating with stakeholders in the ecosystem or attracting the best experts, who may relocate to other regions/countries once they encounter multiple crises.

A tertiary impact stems from the national mood, resilience, and creativity, echoed in the startup's robustness, innovativeness, and overall the attention allocated to creativity, risk-taking, and vigorous activity. During crisis episodes, individuals possess less ability to monitor and regulate their thoughts and behaviors, including their stress and anxiety, and they are less inclined to raise new ideas or employ creativity in their work; this then affects the startup's ability to expand its innovation, and further on, its competitive advantage (Lyubomirsky and Nolen-Hoeksema 1995; Brown, Rocha and Cowling 2020; Kuckertz et al. 2020; Wang et al. 2020).

Sequential crisis events

Crises are comprised of varied components that tend to stimulate other components, hence potentially other crises which will be revealed sequentially. These components have to do with topics as well as length, timing (seasonal, once in a decade, etc.), recurrence, severity, and expectancy of the crisis arising, among others. Compounded crisis events that surface one after the other exhaust the ability to manage, monitor, or control the hardship, as resources, expertise, and human engagement, energy, and time exploited to manage the situation(s) are not infinite; more accidents and mistakes arise when crises are active and unstoppable; in addition, adjustment to changes and the new rules implemented to cope with one or more of the disruptive events can be difficult, resulting in refutation or denial (e.g., refusal to vaccinate against COVID-19[14]) and subsequent conflicts between the ones affected by the crises and public officials and the media, among others. These, in turn, affect the entrepreneur and the startup in various ways. As opposed to encountering a single crisis, the consequences of sequential crises are more strongly echoed in the startup's performance, for the following reasons:

Single crisis	**Sequential crises**
• Easier to detect	• Involving different topics, factors (e.g., timing, location, focus), which require different, sometimes opposite, ways of tackling them
• Swifter demarcation of the crisis' main characteristics	• Uncertainty of the boundaries of each crisis due to the intertwined relationships between their components
• Enables more accurate benchmarking to learn about the crisis' flow and dynamics	• There are multiple combinations of sequential crisis events, impeding any insight on a particular combination
• Ability to understand how the crisis affects each of the employees[15] in their work and life	• Each crisis or disruptive event has a unique effect on the employees
• Preparation for the next crisis is possible	• Preparing to manage or avoid sequential crises is unrealistic due to the multiplc variations and combinations

Sequential crisis events have different types of impact on the startup, which can be categorized into direct and indirect:

Direct effect—defined as a first-tier impact on the startup's core business, product or service, or the business' dynamics (e.g., technology, marketing, human capital).

Indirect effect—regarded as having a similar impact on the business' dynamics (compared to the direct effect), but generated by factors that have been affected by the crisis and not directly by the crisis dimensions.

Direct and indirect impacts of a crisis are central to the startup's understanding of and preparation to tackle the crisis. Direct effects usually occur more quickly and are unexpected, yet they tend to affect the ecosystem in a relatively similar way; for example, a lockdown addresses almost all startups; when competitors are similarly affected, the long-run consequences of the crisis on the specific startup seem less harmful. The indirect effect allows analyzing the crisis situation and predicting its secondary effects, hence making room for some preparation, either practical or psychological; yet the impact is more 'customized' to the specific startup, as it does not hit all ecosystem participants equally.

Multiple crises—the emergence of several crisis events in parallel; these events are not necessarily connected to each other, but they arise at the same time (not sequentially), and their occurrence does not seem to be a direct or indirect response to either the outbreak of or the coping strategy for a prior crisis. Multiple appearance can be represented in dual or triple disruptions, which spread faster and to an amplified extent, resulting in fierce damaging effects. Multiple crises can start by hitting specific regions or sectors or breaking out among specific groups; yet, due to the concurrent emergence of events, they tend to either directly or indirectly affect other groups, which were not the original targets of the crises (e.g., Arezki and Nguyen 2020; Baldwin and Di Mauro 2020).

Generation of 'other indicators'

Crises introduce new models that require a shift in the known equations regarding the components that enhance their harshness, such as a longer duration of negative episodes being more harmful or a wider spread of such episodes inducing more serious damage. The contribution of each indicator to the crisis profile is not automatically echoed in the crisis' severity or in its consequences on the surrounding environment; rather, the crisis indicators depict the crisis content, structure, and dynamics, which are helpful in predicting the changing clusters of ongoing crises, to better understand their sources and impact and to prepare to either avoid them or challenge them.

The following indicators are known:

Other indicators	Specification of indicators
• Duration	• Minutes, hours, days, months
• Timing	• During specific conditions (regional, international) • While other crises are active
• Recurrence, 'waves'	• Seasonal • Following specific conditions
• Location	• Restricted to one region or spread out • Regionally or internationally disseminated • Affluence of the region of the outbreak in resources, money, expertise • Regions affected by political power
• Crisis dynamics	• Pace (rapid, medium, or slow occurrence) • Intensification with time
• Extent of people affected	• Versus those not affected by the same stimulus • Versus potential damage of the crisis
• Other damage (not people)	• Nature (animals, forestry, natural resources) • Historic, heritage sites • Property, buildings, people's possessions
• Severity of hardship—survival	• During the crisis outbreak • In the short run • In the long run
• Severity of hardship—disruption in normal living conditions	• During the crisis outbreak • In the short run • In the long run
• Uniqueness of the damaged resources	• Historical • Natural assets • Rare animals

(Continued)

Other indicators	Specification of indicators
• Preparatory stage to manage the crisis	• Immediate • In the short run • In the long run
• Preparatory stage to manage crisis recurrence	
• Government protection, official international protection	
• Exhaustion of resources needed to handle the crisis	
• Dependence on others to manage the crisis	

Examples of health-related crises that have severely affected populations can illustrate their unpredictable flow, for example, the 2009 avian flu (N1H1), the severe acute respiratory syndrome (SARS) virus in 2003, or the Ebola virus disease (EVD), with waves of outbreaks from 1976 in the Democratic Republic of Congo and Sudan, then in 2014–2016 in West Africa, then another outbreak in 2018–2019 in the eastern Democratic Republic of Congo, and AIDS, with the first reported cases in 1981 which gradually rose, where restrictions imposed on sexual encounters and the production of a cocktail of medications enabled managing the epidemic. While emerging from the same 'topic' (health), their length, duration, recurrence/waves, regional versus international spread of the infection, the political power of the infected, and other indicators create different profiles for these crises. Despite emanating from the topic of health, their impact on startups varied greatly due to the other indicators that were attached exclusively to each crisis (Maguire, Hardy and Lawrence 2004; Lo, Cheung and Law 2006; Levy and Scully 2007; Papaoikonomou, Segarra and Li 2012).

The startup's view—not all startups in affected regions experience a substantial direct impact from a health crisis situation; the routine course of life is not dramatically altered, except for those employees who have experienced illness or death in the family, requiring their absence from work, or sick employees directly affecting their startup's performance. Maintaining the regular routine, including going to work, keeping customers and connections, attracting new collaborations, for some people, their startups are an escape from the disruptive situation. Concurrently, health-related crises are typified as spreading uncertainty among startups; the dynamics of the crisis is unpredictable, as there is no 'partner' to negotiate with (as opposed to negotiating with other governments, international associations, banks, etc.). Such uncertainty negatively affects innovation, profitability, and engagement in customer satisfaction in the startup and can indirectly affect the mood, engagement, and trust in startups during crises regarding their future. Moreover, crisis length and recurrence can also intensify the feeling of uncertainty, along with suspicion, increased pessimism and decreased hope, and loss of the general joy and energy to initiate, innovate, and succeed, hence indirectly negatively affecting the startup's activity and performance. In practice, longer or recurrent crises exhaust the resources needed to tackle the crisis and to prepare for managing it, as reflected in the startup's actions: removing some projects, rejecting new ones, and avoiding new initiatives, because handling a crisis on an ongoing basis drains the startups' means, funds, and assets. COVID-19 stemmed from the topic of health; yet, unlike the crises presented above and other health-related crises, it has a unique profile. As such, COVID-19 entails both threats and opportunities; by impeding the regular course of action through which startups shut down or suspend their activities, the pandemic urges quick adaptation, and therefore encourages startups to initiate and pivot to respond to the dramatic new, rapid, and constantly changing needs that the pandemic has created. Eventually, these startups can benefit from the outbreak through change and innovation.[16]

COVID-19 and the new wave of crises

COVID-19 encapsulates several indicators, as demonstrated in the following list, as well as sequential and multiple crisis occurrences in tandem, along with visible direct and indirect fallout, which is unfamiliar and unexpected. The pandemic broke out in a general atmosphere of scientific omnipotence and the concurrent, gradually improving technology and expertise required beating any adversity in the fastest and highest-quality way. Moreover, the pandemic was expected to be restricted geographically, especially because the virus was deemed a 'simple' one. The abrupt understanding that the human coronavirus is not as 'simple' as expected—it is relatively large for viruses that use RNA to replicate, can infect many cell types, mainly causes respiratory infections, mutates successfully, and can infect and actively reproduce in the upper respiratory tract—was something of a surprise, which subsequently created doubts and disagreements among scientists and medical experts.

As a consequence, the COVID-19 pandemic has increasingly fostered mistrust of the people involved in the crisis, in medicine and science, mainly as a result of the non-definitive messages from experts and officials. The COVID-19 pandemic can be analyzed through the crisis indicators as follows:

Duration	Unknown
• Timing	Quite close to other health-related crises
	Quite close to various crises in the different regions
• Recurrence, 'waves'	There are waves
	What stimulates the viral spurts in each region is unclear
• Location	Around the world

(Continued)

Duration	Unknown
• Crisis dynamics	Contagious, thus typified by escalation (i.e., more and more people become infected) Indirect effects on markets, finance, and startups escalate in association with infection intensification
• Extent of people affected	High rates around the world (illness and mortality) High indirect effects—job loss, unemployment, mental disturbances due to social distancing, distress for the elderly Regional differences in the rates of affected people
• Other damage (not people)	Indirect effect on nature (though not necessarily damage), for example, animals exploring urban areas that have become isolated due to lockdowns, reduced traffic on roads and decreased noise disturbance impacts wildlife
• Severity of hardship—survival	Direct effect of the virus on individuals' and their family members' sickness or mortality
• Severity of hardship—disruption in normal living conditions	Social distancing New rules, for example, masks, presentation of a 'green pass', uncertainty about mobility Restricted travel Startups have been harmed due to temporary encumbrances on investments, strategic collaborations Deepening mental health symptoms Effects on working conditions (virtual work, pivoting of projects, absence of employees)
• Uniqueness *of* the damaged resources	Human lives
• Preparatory stage to manage the crisis	Deluded assessment of the health community's preparation for such crises Vaccine and medication development at a swift pace with best quality expected
• Preparatory stage to manage crisis recurrence	Misconceptions originating from prior experiences with health crises
• Government protection, official international protection	Governments and international offices are proactively seeking solutions
• Exhaustion of resources needed to handle the crisis	Crisis intensification seems to stimulate medical, biological, and health-related developments Mental exhaustion in handling aspects of social restrictions
• Dependence on others to manage the crisis	Large dependence on healthcare personnel, medical staff, hospital capacity Large dependence on the development of a 'cure' Large dependence on the public complying with the new rules, including getting vaccinated

(Alon, Farrell and Li 2020; He and Harris 2020; Kirk and Rifkin 2020; Maritz et al. 2020; Ratten 2020).

Summary

This chapter delved into the different dimensions of crisis events which can turn, sometimes unexpectedly, into a crisis or sequential/multiple crises. Delineating the boundaries of crisis events is a forceful avenue to decoding the crisis phenomenon, especially as history has proven that some disaster events that affected many people passed almost unnoticed, whereas some 'simpler' events, with less casualties, turned into major crises. This chapter starts by introducing the crisis portfolio, following its demarcation by elucidating the difference between a disruptive event and a crisis, and emphasizing the three critical components that 'transform' an event into a crisis: disruption, a major threat, and contingent on time pressure.

The indicators of disruptive events are portrayed in this chapter, for example, the event topic, who is affected by the event, the power of the affected people, multiple crises at a time and timing, followed by a more in-depth list of the core topics attached to crises: health, education, environment, finance-related issues, and conflicts, among others. The intertwined relationships of these topics and their subtopics and the direct and indirect effects of such occurrences on the startup's course of action are discussed to show how startups experience crisis episodes and the practical and perceptual fallout of crises.

Sequential and multiple crises are delineated to illustrate the complexity of these types of 'crisis packages' for startups. Finally, crisis indicators are assembled from research into a 'package of indicators' that may seem general and unconnected, yet embedding these indicators within the crisis dimensions can create different crisis portfolios, including 'turning' some disruptive events into crises while mitigating the crisis in other cases. The following indicators are included: duration, timing, recurrence, location, dynamics, extent and severity of the hardship on affected people, and other damage. By generating the discussed concepts and analyzing the COVID-19 pandemic in light of those concepts, the exclusiveness of the pandemic is illustrated.

Reflective questions for class

1. Find two different ongoing crises. Discuss the differences between the two crises based on your analysis of the nexus of objective and subjective components of a crisis (Figure 3.1). What are three to four main conclusions from your analysis?
2. Address the nutrition crisis worldwide by generating information and data on its evolution in the last five to seven years. Using three different 'other indicators', explain the severity of this crisis and share your prediction of its future impact.

3. "The International Rescue Committee (IRC) has released its 2021 Emergency Watchlist, a global list of humanitarian crises that are expected to deteriorate the most over the coming year. The triple threat of conflict, climate change and COVID-19 is driving the crises in nearly all Emergency Watchlist countries, threatening famine in several in 2021."[17] List the crises included in the IRC report and explain, through direct and indirect effects (Figure 3.3), why these specific crises are considered the most threatening.
4. Discuss which of the models introduced in Figure 3.2 *Models of relationships among crisis topics* applies to the COVID-19 crisis. Explain your answer.
5. The Rapids (https://www.therapids.co/) is a startup that has pivoted due to COVID-19 from 'Field Trip' workshops to 'Remote Field Trips' to help businesses seize opportunities, deliver mission-critical change, and ride these rapids. Explain this pivot using at least five concepts/models discussed in this chapter. What is your conclusion regarding the pivot? Was it worthwhile?

Notes

1 See https://www.r-pur.com/

2 See https://www.euronews.com/2021/04/02/the-top-gadgets-to-come-out-of-the-covid-19-pandemic

3 See https://en.wikipedia.org/wiki/Chinese_word_for_%22crisis%22

4 See https://www.bbc.com/news/blogs-magazine-monitor-34154767

5 The author is a native Hebrew speaker; רבשמ could originate from רבשנ/רובשל broken or a sense of distress רבש; it can also signify something that is not complete, a fraction of the whole picture.

6 See https://reliefweb.int/report/sudan/2021-humanitarian-response-plan-sudan-january-december-2021;https://www.wfp.org/countries/Sudan?utm_source=google&utm_medium=cpc&utm_campaign=12269583315&utm_content=125607295369&gclid=CjwKCAiAnO2MB-hApEiwA8q0HYYIIEynFMzrTqv_hv8oN5hvA9rCOYtXm1gay4xdPEAI1tZ7goPVvZRoCnoc-QAvD_BwE&gclsrc=aw.ds

7 INFORM is a collaboration of the Inter-Agency Standing Committee Reference Group on Risk, Early Warning and Preparedness and the European Commission. See https://drmkc.jrc.ec.europa.eu/inform-index/INFORM-Severity/Methodology

8 See https://theowp.org/

9 See https://www.humanitarianlibrary.org/resource/undp-disaster-index

10 See https://www.emdat.be/

11 See https://www.who.int/data/collections

12 See https://www.worldbank.org/en/who-we-are

13 See https://www.fsinplatform.org/sites/default/files/resources/files/GRFC%202021%20050521%20med.pdf

14 See By the Numbers: Who's Refusing Covid Vaccinations—and Why. Robert Hart, *Forbes*, September 5, 2021, 06.30 am EDT. https://www.forbes.com/sites/roberthart/2021/09/05/by-the-numbers-whos-refusing-covid-vaccinations-and-why/?sh=1bc6959f52ea

15 Employees and the teams in a startup are the ones managing and coping with crises.

16 See https://www.maddyness.com/uk/2020/03/31/19-businesses-pivoting-in-response-to-covid-19/; https://research.qut.edu.au/ace/2020/04/30/covid19-pandemic-as-external-enabler-of-entrepreneurship/

17 See 2021 Emergency Watchlist
The top ten crises the world should be watching in 2021; https://www.rescue.org/article/top-10-crises-world-should-be-watching-2021

References

Alon, I., Farrell, M., & Li, S. (2020). Regime type and COVID-19 response. *FIIB Business Review, 9*(3), 152–160.

Ansell, C., Boin, A., & Keller, A. (2010). Managing transboundary crises: Identifying the building blocks of an effective response system. *Journal of Contingencies and Crisis Management, 18*(4), 195–207.

Arezki, R., & Nguyen, H. (2020). Novel coronavirus hurts the Middle East and North Africa through many channels. *Economics in the Time of COVID-19,* 53.

Baldwin, R., & Di Mauro, B. W. (2020). Economics in the time of COVID-19: A new eBook. *VOX CEPR Policy Portal,* 2–3.

Boin, A., & McConnell, A. (2007). Preparing for critical infrastructure breakdowns: The limits of crisis management and the need for resilience. *Journal of Contingencies and Crisis Management, 15*(1), 50–59.

Brown, R., Rocha, A., & Cowling, M. (2020). Financing entrepreneurship in times of crisis: Exploring the impact of COVID-19 on the market for entrepreneurial finance in the United Kingdom. *International Small Business Journal, 38*(5), 380–390.

Brünjes, J., & Diez, J. R. (2013). 'Recession push' and 'prosperity pull' entrepreneurship in a rural developing context. *Entrepreneurship & Regional Development, 25*(3–4), 251–271.

Buchanan, D. A., & Denyer, D. (2013). Researching tomorrow's crisis: Methodological innovations and wider implications. *International Journal of Management Reviews, 15*(2), 205–224.

Doern, R. (2016). Entrepreneurship and crisis management: The experiences of small businesses during the London 2011 riots. *International Small Business Journal, 34*(3), 276–302.

Dutta, S., Lanvin, B., & Wunsch-Vincent, S. (2017). *Global innovation index 2017.* Cornell University.

Grube, L. E., & Storr, V. H. (2018). Embedded entrepreneurs and post-disaster community recovery. *Entrepreneurship & Regional Development, 30*(7–8), 800–821.

He, H., & Harris, L. (2020). The impact of Covid-19 pandemic on corporate social responsibility and marketing philosophy. *Journal of Business Research, 116,* 176–182.

Herbane, B. (2010). Small business research: Time for a crisis-based view. *International Small Business Journal, 28*(1), 43–64.

Hofstede, G. (1980). Culture and organizations. *International Studies of Management & Organization, 10*(4), 15–41.

Hofstede, G. (1998). Attitudes, values and organizational culture: Disentangling the concepts. *Organization Studies, 19*(3), 477–493.

Irvine, W., & Anderson, A. R. (2004). Small tourist firms in rural areas: Agility, vulnerability and survival in the face of crisis. *International Journal of Entrepreneurial Behavior & Research.*

Kirk, C. P., & Rifkin, L. S. (2020). I'll trade you diamonds for toilet paper: Consumer reacting, coping and adapting behaviors in the COVID-19 pandemic. *Journal of Business Research, 117,* 124–131.

Kuckertz, A., Brändle, L., Gaudig, A., Hinderer, S., Reyes, C. A. M., Prochotta, A., Steinbrink, K. M., & Berger, E. S. (2020). Startups in times of crisis–A rapid response to the COVID-19 pandemic. *Journal of Business Venturing Insights, 13,* e00169.

Levy, D., & Scully, M. (2007). The institutional entrepreneur as modern prince: The strategic face of power in contested fields. *Organization Studies, 28*(7), 971–991.

Linnenluecke, M. K., & McKnight, B. (2017). Community resilience to natural disasters: The role of disaster entrepreneurship. *Journal of Enterprising Communities: People and Places in the Global Economy, 11*(1), 166–185.

Lo, A., Cheung, C., & Law, R. (2006). The survival of hotels during disaster: A case study of Hong Kong in 2003. *Asia Pacific Journal of Tourism Research, 11*(1), 65–80.

Lyubomirsky, S., & Nolen-Hoeksema, S. (1995). Effects of self-focused rumination on negative thinking and interpersonal problem solving. *Journal of Personality and Social Psychology, 69*(1), 176.

Maguire, S., Hardy, C., & Lawrence, T. B. (2004). Institutional entrepreneurship in emerging fields: HIV/AIDS treatment advocacy in Canada. *Academy of Management Journal, 47*(5), 657–679.

Maritz, A., Perenyi, A., De Waal, G., & Buck, C. (2020). Entrepreneurship as the unsung hero during the current COVID-19 economic crisis: Australian perspectives. *Sustainability, 12*(11), 4612.

Mitroff, I. I. (1988). Crisis management: Cutting through the confusion. *MIT Sloan Management Review, 29*(2), 15.

Papaoikonomou, E., Segarra, P., & Li, X. (2012). Entrepreneurship in the context of crisis: Identifying barriers and proposing strategies. *International Advances in Economic Research, 18*(1), 111–119.

Ratten, V. (2020). Coronavirus (Covid-19) and entrepreneurship: Cultural, lifestyle and societal changes. *Journal of Entrepreneurship in Emerging Economies.*

Wang, C., Pan, R., Wan, X., Tan, Y., Xu, L., McIntyre, R. S., Choo, F. N., Tran, B., Ho, R., & Sharma, V. K. (2020). A longitudinal study on the mental health of general population during the COVID-19 epidemic in China. *Brain, Behavior, and Immunity, 87,* 40–48.

Xu, Z., Wang, X., Wang, X., & Skare, M. (2021). A comprehensive bibliometric analysis of entrepreneurship and crisis literature published from 1984 to 2020. *Journal of Business Research, 135,* 304–318.

Zamoum, K., & Gorpe, T. S. (2018). Crisis management: A historical and conceptual approach for a better understanding of today's crises. In *Crisis management-theory and practice.* IntechOpen.`

Chapter Four

Born into crises

Takeaways

- Noting that startups encounter crises frequently and manage them; the occurrence of more dominant or severe adversities should still be viewed by the entrepreneur as one of multiple crises faced, hence the routine rather than the exception
- Understanding that a crisis is delineated by the entrepreneur's perceptions as threatening or not, as an opportunity or not, etc.; and that it is the entrepreneur's responsibility to identify the crisis, outline it and operationalize it, prior to acting on it
- Being aware of the different perceptual approaches to tackling a crisis and their possible effects. Each approach then leads to practices that are relevant to responding to the concurrent crisis events as well as to preparing for future crises
- Acknowledging that information is a major asset held by entrepreneurs during crises; it should be employed in a customized way to control its circulation and flow, along with the relevant content, to the stakeholders
- Recognizing the evolution of a crisis and its varied outcomes for the business

DOI: 10.4324/9781003173809-4

- Identifying the entrepreneurial abilities, skills, and strengths that entrepreneurs possess and can use to mold the employees' views and engagement in the business' ability to manage the crisis

Born into crises

This chapter addresses crises encountered by startups along their entrepreneurial journey by building upon the crises' components and the consequent actions taken by startups and exploring concepts typifying startups in the era of COVID-19. The focus here is on the initial phases of crisis management; the strategies to manage the crisis are not delineated; rather, this chapter is aimed at elucidating the areas that need to be acknowledged prior to the act of coping with the crises' effects. The material introduced in this chapter is compiled from typical crises encountered by startups on a 'regular' basis and the discussion then expands to worldwide crises, such as recessions, economic and financial crises, and environmental and social crises. It does not, however, delve into organizational or internal crises; the focus is on external crises that affect the entrepreneurial ecosystem and therefore specific startups.

This chapter crystallizes the conceptualization of the new challenges and complexities brought on by crises, including the COVID-19 pandemic, and delves into the ways in which entrepreneurs and startups tackle them. We cross-examine the challenges tackled by startups in 'common' crises and the actions taken to cope with them, and the 'new' challenges posed by the COVID-19 crisis. Various areas are covered, ranging from startups that are exposed to greater hardship and risk through their introduction of innovation, the latter often rejected by existing businesses and customers, to their perceptions and views of the crisis, and the ways in which they demarcate it, circulate it, communicate it, and decide upon the avenues to be taken to respond to it. This chapter's main assumption is that the way crises are perceived by the entrepreneur will determine the startup's image, its attractiveness and the trust placed by internal and external stakeholders in it, and therefore must be deciphered (Alesch et al. 2001; Rosenthal, Boin and Comfort 2001; Roser et al. 2020; Rozell and Wilcox 2020; Rudan 2020).

Conceptual models of startups under crises

Startups are more prone to crises due to their natural entrepreneurial journey, which is fueled by emergencies and 'ups and downs'. The literature in entrepreneurship tackles the area of crises through three main elements: (a) a challenge to the enterprise, (b) the factor of uncertainty, and (c) a limited decision time; and startups, relative to any small or large business, tend to perceive the crisis as potentially detrimental and damaging, while they tend to consider their professional, psychological, and organizational capital as extremely relevant to managing the crisis, so that both the stress related to the crisis and coping perceptions are extremely high. Startups' basic perceptions of their coping abilities are contingent on several factors:

1. Strong management (trustworthy, stable, managing daily crises effectively)
2. Vision, hope, and self and team efficacy
3. Shared and well-embedded values (aligned with the startup's practices)
4. Team trust (in the management, their peers, their abilities)
5. An ongoing learning culture (curiosity about new areas, constant personal and team enrichment)

The role of perception

Startups perceive a crisis as a threat and opportunity, in tandem. They are therefore in no hurry to eliminate the crisis' sources or effects, as these may entail business opportunities for the startup. In times of crisis, gaps and needs surface and are more easily identified. Perceptions of a crisis as an occurrence that should be immediately versus more easily dealt with, to either mitigate its effects or pivot those effects for the startup's interests, will determine the startup's practices and coping strategies.

Perceptions resonate four parameters: entrepreneurial culture, entrepreneurial ecosystem, perceived stakeholder support, and economic context. Research has shown that cultural factors play a key role in entrepreneurs' initial perceptions of a crisis as an immediate threat versus an opportunity (i.e., threats that are manageable and worthwhile). The ecosystem's structure, plentifulness, and dynamics can also mold perceptions of the crisis' severity; in a similar vein, the perceived support provided by stakeholders versus their hostility affect entrepreneurs' perceptions, including the impact of conflictual versus calmer ecosystems, stakeholders' dynamics, or a cultural aptness to assist where startups are struggling versus a more distant, cultural approach of 'to each their own'. Finally, the economic context is recognized to determine entrepreneurs' perceptions about the crisis, apparently as a function of entrepreneurs' confidence in, and hope of a full recovery and expanded opportunities.

Seymour and Moore (2000) introduced two concepts to illustrate crises: the Python, that is, a crisis that occurs gradually or periodically, and the Cobra, which occurs suddenly and has impactful consequences. While these types seem to be clear-cut and self-evident, their categorization also seems to be dependent on the entrepreneur's perceptions based on the four parameters (culture, ecosystem, perceived stakeholder support, and economic context); it is imperative to recognize this, because the practices and subsequent actions taken by entrepreneurs will be tightly associated with their perceptions of the crisis' harshness. For example, a startup that perceives a recession as a Python will allocate time, resources, and expertise to prevent or best practices to manage crisis situations; however, a startup that considers the same recession as a Cobra, that is, unexpected and not aligned with the economic or political forecasts and analyses, will respond to it through a series of unplanned, impulsive, and sporadic actions, referred to in research as defensive responses. While there is no clear model for responding to crises, and both sets of actions can bring more adversity or opportunities, perception of the crisis matters. Treating crises as Python enables maintaining more cohesion, trust, and hope at the team level, and is therefore imperative for the startup's psychological capital and its energy to cope with the crisis events (Seeger, Sellnow and Ulmer 1998; Seymour and Moore 2000; Evans and Elphick 2005; Latham 2009; Herbane 2013).

Startups' views of crises

There are two conceptual approaches to crisis demarcation. First, the preventive approach, which builds on methodical preparation and an initial forecast of the crisis event, so that efforts, resources, plans and expertise are allocated to 'crisis management, prior to its appearance'; this approach assumes that the crisis will never materialize. Second, the constructive approach alleges that in normal, non-crisis times, preparations for a potential crisis are unnecessary, leading to a futile waste of resources; it is only when a crisis occurs that the startups will push to mitigate the hardship associated with it; accordingly, the startup's management embraces practical tactics to both decipher the crisis' flow and circulate that information to its internal and external stakeholders.

Here is a closer look at the two approaches in deciphering a crisis:

Preventive approaches	
Escaping	• Preventing the crisis from occurring by closely observing the environment and detecting 'signs' that could indicate an emerging crisis • Preparing various scenarios and the resources that will be needed for any type of potential crisis • Constantly allocating resources, time, energy, and expertise for possible occurrence • Requiring thorough and continuous internal communications to engage the team toward this goal • When 'signs' are detected, the startup can easily split its activities into those assigned to manage the crisis and its regular ones
Solving	• Identifying the sources, characteristics, and potential effects of an emerging crisis • Acting in time to solve the situation • Taking all of the conditions of the situation into account to create a solution • Taking a strategic look to connect the best solution to managing a crisis with its future effects on the business • Continually aggregating and filtering information to craft the best solution to cope with the crisis

Constructive approaches	
Interactive	• Incorporating planning, monitoring, and acting upon a current or potential crisis before, during, and after the crisis occurs • This involves continuous learning and training of all startup employees and periodic updating and modification of the created plans • Each member of the startup needs to engage in a 'crisis role', connected to their normal roles and expertise in the business • Implementing an agile communication strategy to circulate information internally and externally • Allocating resources in advance to create and sustain such a strategy
Proactive	• This involves continuous training of the startup's employees and periodical updating of the plans to manage the crisis • An in-depth benchmarking of ways to communicate the crisis and accordingly to act upon it • The management is open to its employees' ideas and suggestions on avenues to tackle the crisis

Circulating the news—refers to the avenues taken to inform the stakeholders about the emergence of a crisis and its concurrent and potential effects. Startups need to control the information flow, content, and bulk, especially in today's era of fake news, disinformation, hoaxes, misbehavior, rumors, and gossip that can be intentionally or unintentionally misleading and are based on factitiousness or self-interpretations that easily and almost uncontrollably flood the virtual realm, and are powerful in forming a startup's image, even when the facts tell a different story (Cardoso Durier da Silva, Vieira and Garcia 2019; Egelhofer and Lecheler 2019; Carlson 2020). It is not only fake news that spreads uncontrollably; 'regular' news can also impact impressions of the startup, thus requiring more intense monitoring of the news flow.

Crisis effects can both allude to the internal resilience of the startup and increase or decrease this resilience; for example, the impact of uncontrollable news (i.e., news that the management would not announce) may harm the team's cohesiveness, depending on its concurrent resilience and unity; hence, it is imperative that the entrepreneurs/startup managers make a strategic decision on the circulation of information, to monitor and act whenever information affects any internal processes or dynamics. Similarly, crises affect the portrayal of the startup's image to its external stakeholders and collaborators, and the startup's control of the circulation of information can be critical. The components that should be considered in controlling information flow in times of crisis are:

1. Consistency—the information should be clear, simple, and reliable
2. Body language and tone—along with the conveyed information, other signals are transmitted and should be aligned with the content of the information to create trust and confidence

3. Bad news—should be gently but clearly communicated and should be accompanied by clarifications based on facts; then the vision should be (re)announced
4. Vision—the vision is stable, while the strategies and avenues to reach it may change based on crisis effects; the vision embodies the target point; as long as it is constant and firm and does not change due to the crisis situation, it reflects the startup's robustness
5. So, what's next?—it is the entrepreneur's obligation to disseminate the strategy and practices for the next steps, including the risks and opportunities and the chances of recovery. These steps should be sharply and clearly articulated and address each employee's role in the mission of overcoming the crisis (Pauchant, Mitroff and Ventolo 1992; Clarke and Varma 1999; Santana 2004; Sahin, Ulubeyli and Kazaza 2015).

The critical factors for startups to consider in a crisis, which determine how the crisis will be perceived, are:

Individual (entrepreneur)—the entrepreneur will have an emotional response to the emerging crisis, usually after a shock, involving a breakthrough in realizing the truth that the situation must be tackled. At this point, the entrepreneur comprehends the situation, though not necessarily realistically, and may enact a flight response, namely refuse to think or worry about the situation, reframing it, renaming it, converting it into a different context, etc.

Organizational—the startup as a unit will usually identify the significance of the crisis differently from the entrepreneur (founder), contingent on measures that differ from those involved in the entrepreneur's views. The understanding of the crisis is more diffuse as it refers to the unique concerns of each member of the startup related to the crisis. Accordingly, various ideas for solutions can arise. In this context, the atmosphere, the general vibe, and the organizational approach to demarcating the crisis are all most important for organizational resilience. To gain such resilience, the values associated with the vision and trustworthy management are critical.

Ecosystem—while the entrepreneur (individual) and the startup (organization) represent the internal stakeholders involved in the process of crisis management, the ecosystem consists of stakeholders who are external to the startup. These stakeholders are varied, as are their perceptions of the crisis, which reflect their interests, in terms of both the effects of the crisis on their own course of action and on their views of how the crisis will impact a specific startup and how this compounded impact will affect the stakeholder. For example, a bank, representing a key stakeholder, will hold views on how a specific crisis will affect its business as well as on how the crisis will affect startups that are connected to this bank. During crisis events, it is the startup's responsibility and interest to control the view held by stakeholders on the situation. It therefore needs to present healthy and vigorous activity, avoid acts or processes that can provide the 'wrong' image (e.g., dismissals of employees, bankruptcy, lawsuits).

A different outlook into how startups perceive and therefore circulate information on a crisis involves the following factors:

- WOW crisis—unexpected, terrifying, and perceived as threatening; yet, the entrepreneur feels equipped with the knowledge, resources, networks, and resilience, among others, which will enable coping with the crisis and recovering
- Short-term crisis—not as dramatic as the WOW crisis, but a threating situation nevertheless, which is recognized and expected to be solved in the short term (e.g., an unexpected local decline in traction/interest in the startup's products)
- Long-term crisis—enduring crisis occurrences, either serial, gradual, or continual, which may not be massively threatening, yet due to duration, exploit resources and therefore risk the startup's activity
- Long-term effect of the crisis—unexpected aftereffects of a crisis that has already passed, such as employees' resignations, decrease in customer trust in the startup products and services. The sources of such aftereffects can be difficult to determine, and may not be directly related to the startup but to changes in the environment (e.g., higher demand for employees in the marketplace, higher competition for similar products), thus preparations for aftereffects are difficult to implement.

Chronicle of a crisis foretold

Startups are born into crises and concurrently they create crises. A crisis is mainly an unexpected, uncontrollable, and undesirable situation, event, episode, or occurrence that can be temporary or permanent and that threatens or is perceived to threaten the stability of the startup. It can either originate internally or can be brought on by external influences; in both cases, the crisis 'happens' whenever the business escalates to the point at which the crisis event is out of the startup's control or is perceived as being unresolvable; if left unaddressed, it could damage the startup permanently. Hence, the crisis episode poses an imminent threat to the organization; the situation involves surprise; and due to the severity of the problem, as well as its unexpected nature, the disruptive situation puts pressure on the startup to make timely and effective decisions, to enable its survival or at least minimize potential damage.

In the context of startups, crises are unavoidable. In fact, some models consider the emergence of crises as an imperative means to grow by adopting crisis management methods and enabling the business to advance its processes and activities regardless of crises that can pop up at any time.

In the startups' realm, the main archetypes of crisis situations are categorized into *internal* and *external*, and *consensus* and *conflict*. Internal refers to conflicts, misunderstandings, an inability to produce the offerings, frustration or disappointment with internal capability or performance and intellectual property pitfalls, among others. External crisis episodes cover conflicts with stakeholders outside the business, inability to attract funds, clients' rejection of the offerings, competition from other startups, cybercrime, inability to obtain the rights to use inventions, technologies, designs or other trademarks, etc. Consensus situations include natural disasters (e.g., hurricanes, floods) and technological disasters (e.g., explosions, accidents); conflict situations include man-made crises (e.g., civil disturbances, wars, terrorism, and violence).

The frequent emergence of crisis situations in the startup's journey allows it to be more resistant to the 'next crisis', as the crisis is considered a systematic link in the chain that is expected, although its content, duration, severity, etc., may be indefinite.

Startups' resistance to crisis episodes is reflected in the following:

- The startup's mindset—adopting the approach that crises are inherent to the entrepreneurial process and are sometimes the engine that enables pushing forward. Crises are not considered failures; they are neither avoided nor intentionally induced.
- Team dynamics—startups' teams are resistant to conflicts, disappointments, or the inability to accomplish their plans. They are equipped with the mental and emotional capital to pursue and work together during and after crises; they are directed to implement their goals, as they 'know' that crises exist and are an ongoing process and will therefore arise in the future and should be managed.
- Organizational structures—the startup's structure enables it to carry out its goals even in disruptive situations; for example, many startups are simultaneously fragmented by expertise and unified in their know-how; other startups place their subdivisions in different locations (e.g., marketing in Europe, R&D in the United

States, production in China); these examples, among others, attest to the startup's agility mainly due to its alertness to disturbances and being prepared to continue despite the crises.

- Organizational processes—automation, innovation, unique recruitment processes, exclusive ways to maintain 'talent', and legislative issues are among the startup's practices that are meant to protect it from frequently encountered turbulence. For example, innovation enables recovering from damage in existing projects due to crises as innovative projects are on board; retaining the best talent allows the startup to recuperate by using this talent to manage the damage and so on.
- Technology—the large scope of technology, from use of cutting-edge technology for product development to digitalizing 'regular' processes (e.g., payment, advertising), enables the startup to escape some crises' damaging effects on the startup's pursuit. For example, startups that rapidly digitalized their delivery, marketing, or payment processes with the outbreak of COVID-19 could proceed with their regular activities uninterrupted.
- Networking capabilities—sharing, asking for support, assisting, and absorbing the ecosystem's knowledge are imperative avenues to increasing resilience and obtaining practical assistance in times of crises (Shepherd 2003; Herbane 2013; Schrank et al. 2013; Doern 2016; Sozinova, Fokina and Fufacheva 2017; Alves et al. 2020).

Startups expect, even appreciate, crises. Moreover, entrepreneurs would be wary if vulnerable stages or situations in the startup's flow were crisis-free; they might suspect that 'something is wrong', for example, the crisis is 'there' but they overlooked it.

In addition, many startups triumph through crises, even when ineffectively managed; being in the 'eye of the storm' is an alleged imperative in the startup's journey. Startups are expected to undergo a challenging, difficult journey, and crises embody such challenging experiences, which cannot be ignored as they put the business' survival at risk. Accordingly, the COVID-19 pandemic has been perceived among several startups as an 'ordinary' link in their chain of actions and not as an adversity that cannot be handled. Startups have tended to pursue their course of action while 'ignoring' the pandemic's effects, such that work in the startups has continued normally, with the addition of local/national restrictions. Such an approach has led to two different consequences:

a. Startups that prepared for the worst assigned resources to provide more adequate responses to the new needs introduced by the crisis, both within and outside the business. Thus, the startup continued its regular work, but adjusted it by putting some projects on hold, prioritizing some unplanned projects (e.g., maintaining clients' engagement virtually, transforming to a digitalized system), managing the staff who work from home during lockdowns differently, etc.

b. Startups that trusted that nothing will change did not adjust their priorities, resource allocation, or any other activity; when restrictions required adaptations, the startups improvised and reacted ad hoc, thus took the risk of making impulsive decisions, including being less careful about financial effects. The startups' belief that they can survive the situation, and that they need to act as if this is a usual occurrence in their course of action, dictated their conduct.

A closer look at crises: the when, why, and what

The impact of crises in the startup's life depends on the compounded matrix of the different stages of the crisis' evolution and those of the startup's development (see Figure 4.1). This combination can explain the perceptions of degree of crisis severity for the business, deriving from measures related to the crisis, such as duration, already existing damage to the business or to other businesses, the essence of the threat (e.g., medical, loss of money, food shortage, violence), and how they are perceived by entrepreneurs in relation to the crisis stage; concurrently, severity is a function of entrepreneurs' perceptions of their coping resources, strategies, funds obtained from investors, networking, etc., which are also based on the stage of development of the startup.

	Pre-crisis (the first occurrence) The emergence of a crisis is only assumed, yet the first occurrence(s) have already damaged some businesses, and fear is rising	**Immediate period of the crisis** The crisis event is intense and threatening; there is damage everywhere. Information is spreading unchecked, creating rumors and fear	**Post-crisis** The crisis event is under control, and its impact is either no longer apparent or is also under control. Yet, the consequences of the crisis are still to come for business and financial aspects
Pre-startup phase (bootstrap; personal and team debts; ideation phase, the product is in its alpha phase)	Low. Entrepreneurs are still visionary and omnipotent; they do not have much to lose.	Intermediate. While damage is apparent, the entrepreneurs believe that they can adjust their technology and profit from the crisis. They are ready to pivot.	High. The startup's entrepreneurs cannot predict the clients' financial purchase power, needs and preferences after the crisis; nor can they predict the competitors' accomplishments and new offerings at this stage.
Initial stages (pre-seed funds; the product has been developed and is attracting interest, there are some sales; investors are interested)	Low. Entrepreneurs depend on their agility; they are encouraged by their achievements.	High. The entrepreneurs experience the threats and damage of the crisis event; adjusting and pivoting are costly and risky.	High. Resources have been spent on ad-hoc needs; concurrently, the product is not definitively developed, thus is not attracting clients or investors, especially post-crisis when everyone is still vigilant with their resources.
More developed stages (1st and 2nd rounds of investments; the product is developed, marketing is developed, international relations are developed; competition is high)	Intermediate. Entrepreneurs believe in their offerings, but they are also accountable to their investors.	High. Damage is substantial; investors are concerned and urge the startup's entrepreneurs to reach their goals and stand by their obligations to them.	Intermediate. Things are going back to normal, the startup has developed products and marketers; the startup has solid ground to pursue its projects. Yet, clients' purchase power and investors' activity are still vague.

FIGURE 4.1 Evolution of crisis and startup stages—perceptions of crisis severity

Crisis life cycles and characteristics

Crises develop in a certain manner and follow a cycle, a nonlinear process that can advance, regress, or 'skip' a stage. There are different models to categorize the life cycle of a crisis; these are the most well-established stages:

- Prodromal stage—identifying the looming crisis through an incident or case that might be an indicator of crisis development, though it often arises prior to official confirmation of the crisis' emergence. This stage involves initiating preventive measures to prepare for the indefinite outcomes of the crisis.
- Acute stage—the actual crisis has broken out and its negative effects are visible and evident; in addition, many news and fake news items have surfaced, aggravating the fear and worry attached to the situation. Startups need to manage the acute situation promptly to protect their employees (e.g., health, security, keeping their jobs), resources (e.g., property, financial assets, their investors, their talent), and achievements (e.g., their offerings, signed contracts, existing loyal clients) as well as to constantly advance their activity, as competitors who are more agile or more resourceful can exploit the crisis and benefit from its effects, thereby becoming stronger from the risk and damage incurred by the startup.
- Chronic stage—the crisis seems to have run its course but its lingering effects are still evident; concurrently, there are massive coping efforts by governments to eliminate the sources of the crisis and manage its disruptive effects. This time seems to introduce hope and disappointment as the crisis may appear to be 'under control', but its threats are still active. Startups, being agile in nature, adjust to the new situation and can easily adapt to frequent, unexpected changes.
- Resolution stage—this is the end of the crisis event but not the end of its life cycle, as consequences can appear later on (Fink 1986; Nunamaker, Weber and Chen 1989; Boin, Stern and Sundelius 2005; Howell and Miller 2006; Liou 2015; Phan and Narayan 2020).

Startups gather information on crises from many sources. The reliability, frequency, and biases of these sources fluctuate; for example, the COVID-19 pandemic has brought with it a large amount of misleading or even false information; fake news and conspiracy theories on the virus' effects have proliferated on social media; even the World Health Organization (WHO) warns of an overabundance of misinformation during epidemics. Entrepreneurs have found it difficult to rely on formerly trusted information that is crucial for their activity. Moreover, recent studies have shown that the effects of this misinformation have led many people to reject information from expert authorities.

In the case of startups, which are typified as holding a high propensity for rebelliousness and dissent and as tending to resist instructions and rules, the chaotic situation of information and misinformation would not be considered disturbing or disorienting, since entrepreneurs absorb information from the outside but process it independently, then mold their sensemaking of the magnitude of the crisis' effects on their business. They plan a crisis management strategy relative to the perceived threat or damage entailed by the crisis. The Organisation for Economic Co-operation and Development (OECD) shows that while the pandemic has negatively affected startups, with the rate of business entries declining in most OECD countries, industries, and sectors, the number of bankruptcies is moderate; this indicates effective management of the crisis (Habersaat et al. 2020; Uscinski et al. 2020; World Health Organization 2020; Zarocostas 2020).

Research shows that crisis-related preparations in startups include signal detection; preparing preventive measures, such as forming and training crisis teams; damage control, which is aimed at localizing the crisis' perceived effects on the business; recovery, which refers to prioritizing the operations required to restore the business to normalcy; and learning, which is an investigation of the business' performance under the crisis and improvement of those operations and activities that are being poorly performed.

According to Shrivastava's (1993) model, crises are treated and perceived through the four Cs: Causes, Consequences, Caution, and Coping. This model, although formulated

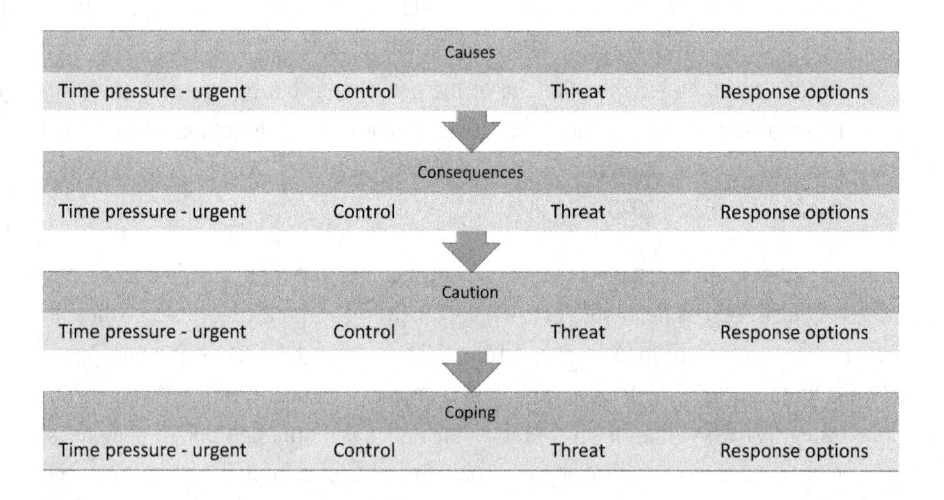

FIGURE 4.2 Entrepreneurs born into crises: a new look at crisis perceptions

for the corporate world, is still relevant to new crises and ways of managing them; startups might operationalize the four Cs by incorporating the following: time, control, threat, and response options; thus, a refined model based on the seminal works of Shrivastava and Mitroff (e.g., Shrivastava et al. 1988) as well as others is introduced (Figure 4.2) (Pauchant, Mitroff and Ventolo 1992; Shrivastava 1993; Stern and Sundelius 2002; Elliott, Harris and Baron 2005; Pearson and Mitroff 2019; Vašíčková 2019).

Accordingly, an analysis of each facet of the crisis, namely each of the four Cs, refers to time pressure, that is, the urgency of identifying the causes, consequences, caution, and coping; the degree of control of each of those facets; the severity of the threat and its effect on each of those factors; and the response options and their association to each of the C factor. The following example illustrates this: in 2000, the technological Millennium Bug was threatening to 'shut down' people's lives by destroying all digitally based systems, including electricity, computers, banks, airplanes, resulting in a catastrophic disaster. The crisis perception model, introduced in Figure 4.2, explains how the Y2K crisis was mitigated, having relatively minimal disastrous effects, as all four Cs were tackled in advance through multidisciplinary work by collaborators from different disciplines and expertise in different companies around the world, in an effort to predict any cause or consequence that might cause Y2K to explode, diagramming multiple optional worst-case scenarios; then, dedicated teams from around the world were assigned to create plans for caution and coping strategies; correspondingly, the factors of time pressure (urgent), control, threat, and response options were monitored and hypothetically manipulated, thus providing a solid ground to simulate a variety of potential situations and setups in case everything did shut down.

The distinctiveness of the COVID-19 pandemic crisis

The dramatic fallout of the COVID-19 pandemic has had a unique impact on startups, which differs from that of previous crises. Due to the global and widespread emergence of the pandemic and its effects everywhere, startups have reacted with relatively prompt proactivity. First, lockdowns and quarantines dramatically slowed down and sometimes completely halted startups' activities, then, through hasty redeployment of their existing resources, many took action by either perusing their planned activities, pivoting, starting something from scratch, or addressing and improving internal processes 'until things go back to normal'. These actions were made possible by the startup's unique characteristics, that is, the entrepreneur, the team, and the business, recapped in Figure 4.3.

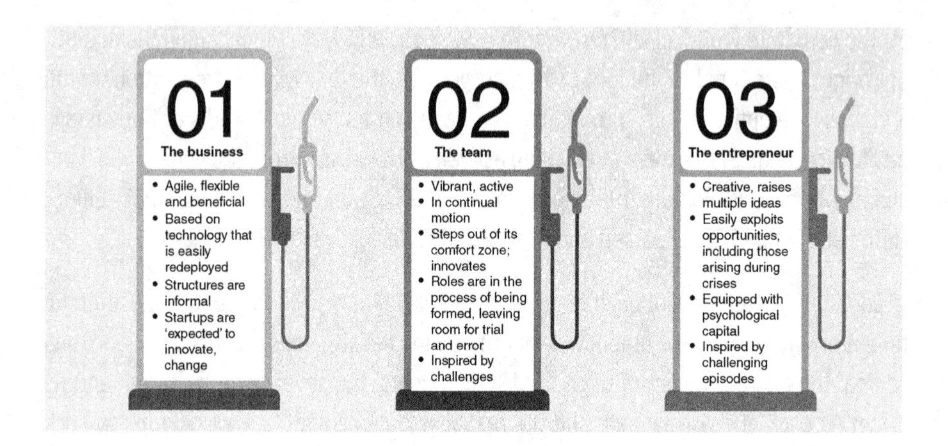

FIGURE 4.3 Startup features as enablers of crisis management

The specific characteristics of the COVID-19 pandemic, its global and wide-ranging array of effects—negative and positive—in each industry and sector, and governments' lack of preparedness for this type of catastrophe challenged entrepreneurs with a new type of disturbance in their daily activities. Since entrepreneurs are used to tackling disturbances and COVID-19 was in essence just one of many 'regular disrupting occurrences', it entailed a higher proportion of vagueness than any regular crisis. Specifically, crises are triggered by different sources and emerge from various external and internal forces, which create vulnerabilities within the startup. The source of the COVID-19 crisis is mainly health-related, yet its consequent disruptive effect can be felt in the startup's financial, marketing, or technological aspects. Facing such a massive crisis, startups found it more complicated to anticipate the kinds of adversity that it might introduce, and subsequently found it difficult to take action to mitigate the crisis' effects due to their multifaceted nature. This can be also explained by the high levels of intensity in each of the four crisis conditions: *low probability*, reflected in the surprise generated by COVID-19's outbreak and in the initial ineptness of governmental and business entities to respond to it, using existing technologies, vaccinations, or medical care systems; *ambiguity*, echoed in the inability to predict when and how the pandemic will end; *high consequence*, reflected in the destruction that it has already caused (e.g., mortality, interruption in business activities, unemployment); and *decision-making time pressure*—rapid changes were imperative in working from home, digitalizing many processes in the business, embracing new strategies to communicate, retaining loyal clients, etc. (Pearson and Clair 1998; Irvine and Anderson 2004; Runyan 2006; Herbane 2010).

Research has identified several barriers to recovery during the COVID-19 pandemic: access to capital, liquidity difficulties, the need to become familiar with new ways of communicating, leading to inconsistencies in communication; for example, in areas with internet, communication persisted, whereas in the other areas, startups were isolated from the world with no means of communication, especially during lockdowns and quarantines. Some businesses were able or allowed to re-open more quickly than others based on local regulations, and were able to generate increased sales due to limited competition and a heightened desire of the population to 'return to normal', while other businesses stayed closed. In their article "Remembering the startups we lost in 2020: a look back at startups large and small that didn't make it through hell year," TechCrunch put together a list of startups that the pandemic damaged so drastically that they had to close down. One example is HubHaus, a long-term housing rental platform, targeting working professionals in cities; it had raised money, but by WeWork's failed IPO investors who lost interest in HubHaus. When the coronavirus pandemic reached the United States, it severely damaged the rental market and the business closed. In the case of Rubica, which offered tools that were more advanced than antivirus software while still remaining accessible to individuals and small businesses, customers curtailed their expenditures during the pandemic, and the company failed to convince investors that there was a business there.

Startups create crises

Startups are known to be disruptive by questioning the known and established and introducing innovative, sometimes revolutionary, developments, while defying the existing systems, structures, technologies, etc. Most introduced innovations create a crisis in the market by rendering existing companies and their products useless. Entrepreneurs are known to be innovative and restless and to be constantly advancing to the next development, initiative, or trend. As entrepreneurs are less sensitive than incumbents to pivots, that is, modifications and changes 'on the go', crises can stimulate their impetus to innovate; they can promptly and easily identify the opportunities introduced by crises, the new needs and the 'to-be-developed' products and services that can respond to those needs. CNBC listed 50 disruptive companies emerging from the pandemic "whose breakthroughs are influencing business and market competition at an accelerated pace" and that represent the future in areas such as food supply, health, and ways of studying, communicating, paying, and shopping. These include the US company Zipline, which uses drone technology to deliver medical supplies, including vaccines, to Rwanda and Ghana, revolutionizing the transmission and delivery of goods to different places around the world; GoPuff, which disrupted the convenience store industry by introducing an app in which a user places an order from over 3,000 listed items and, for a flat $1.95 delivery fee, has their selections delivered in under 30 minutes; and UiPath, which makes robotic process automation software based on artificial intelligence for robots that will enable companies to automate back office, repetitive, and time-consuming tasks.

Abilities and skills—enablers or inhibitors in deciphering crises?

The reciprocal relationship between crisis situations and founders' characteristics is visibly demonstrated in the avenues taken to respond to the new challenges introduced by a crisis. Research in entrepreneurship has shown entrepreneurs' unique abilities that create leadership performance which can be aligned with the crisis effects.

The main areas that are critical for founders in times of crisis include:

- Information flow—targeted to the founders/leaders and to the startup teams
- Preparation—formulating various alternative avenues to tackle different scenarios of complexities under obscure and unexpected situations and dynamics
- Trust—the entrepreneur and the startup should strive to communicate trustworthy conduct to the startup's teams and external stakeholders
- Influence—the entrepreneur and the startup need to lead, to stay on top of things, and to manage emergency situations
- Communication—should be continual, clear, and simple; a gap in information flow, a vagueness or reluctance in real, open communication (not just transmitting news) can create distrust and suspicion both inside and outside the business
- Authenticity and accuracy—the 'name of the game' is reliability, conveying the message authentically and accurately, to sustainably gain the trust of employees, stakeholders, and interest groups

These areas demand integrity, vision, risk-taking, proactivity, charisma, and sensemaking, all of which typify entrepreneurs as well as the ability to organize, strictly prepare, and exhibit analytical capacity that is then echoed in the business' management—characteristics which do not typify entrepreneurs. As such, during crises, founders need to identify the strengths that can leverage their ability to demarcate the crisis situation and paint the precise picture that they wish to disseminate of their startup during the crisis. Moreover, the various combinations of these abilities, for example, a taking-charge approach, strategic thinking, and seeking team acceptance, among many others, form the leadership styles that are also important during crisis events.

At-a-Glance—Social, technological startup

Imani and Hibo are two Kenyan women entrepreneurs who established a virtual learning center for delinquent juveniles throughout Africa for the purpose of securing these young people's future; they attracted large funds from investors in the United States and Europe and were about to expand their activity to the United States. The COVID-19 pandemic severely curbed their activity; potential support was withdrawn due to the investor's difficulties during the pandemic; the contracts in Africa were nearly up and new contracts with delinquent juvenile associations did not materialize because the market had ceased to support non-virus-related initiatives. The two women ran out of money and were asked by their financial supporters to hold their business activities until the pandemic had run its course. But they were determined to keep the business in motion. In June 2020, they published a 'call for action' on social media in an effort to attract university students who were in lockdown to contribute voluntarily to their initiative through virtual lectures, chats, and talks with the young people and some technological contributions. As they did not get any reply, the founders decided to direct their call to countries outside Kenya. It took more than one month to receive the first response, from Hakim, a student from France whose parents were originally from Kenya. He started to work with Imani and Hibo, and they documented his work and communicated it on social media. Then, two other students from Europe joined the startup as volunteers; after six months, the startup had attracted six students, all from outside Africa. Imani and Hibo's dedication and leadership enabled them to proceed with their vision even in the direst of situations when it seemed that there was no hope for their startup. In June 2021, the two received a European prize in the category of social, technological startups.

Leadership styles in depicting crises

The vast literature in entrepreneurship on leadership styles that apply to the crisis depiction stage, prior to planning crisis management strategies, group these styles into the following categories.

The *directive leader* is characterized as strong and decisive, adopts a take-charge approach, has well-defined expectations, communicates clearly, and typically expects people to follow the dictum without questioning it too deeply. This 'do what I say' approach can be very effective in an internal crisis or when working with problem employees. However, this leadership style may inhibit initiatives in crisis situations that require organizational flexibility or innovative action.

The *transformational leader* is described as self-assured, adaptable, and logical. He/she consults with subordinates and seeks input to make consensus decisions. This type of leader thinks strategically, is detail-oriented yet able to see the big picture, and is capable of drawing from diverse experiences to connect the dots using cause-and-effect logic. This type of leader may not be the most appropriate in the case of an extreme time crunch, if only because it takes time to build consensus.

The *transactional leader* can be thought of as a dot the i's and cross the t's kind of leader. This leader focuses on a small set of individual details, is intelligent, follows the rules, and gets the job done. The transactional leader is bound by rules and regulations, making him/her ill-suited to managing the dynamics of most emerging crisis situations.

The *cognitive leader* is perceptive and imaginative. Characteristics include knowledge leadership, expertise in a specific area, 'big picture' thinking, strategic thinking, and participative decision-making. While the cognitive leader is often perceived as lacking sufficient empathy and the interpersonal skills to manage a serious external crisis successfully, he/she may be quite effective in leading an internal crisis in collaboration with his/her experienced, seasoned staff to coordinate communication and provide managerial insight, infrastructure, and support (Schoenberg 2005; Wang 2008; Wooten and James 2008; Veil, Buehner and Palenchar 2011; Bowers, Hall and Srinivasan 2017).

Summary

The typical course of action for startups is fueled by crisis events; startups are recognized as being 'born into crises', representing their unique 'essence', namely by effectively tackling and subsequently managing difficulties and barriers, such as in attracting investors and funding, creating a perfect product-market fit that also entails innovation, or scouting and identifying the best technology for their products, among others. Startups 'pass' the most important trial run of their business' development.

While crises in the startup's evolution represent a *chronicle of known occurrences foretold*, the entrepreneurs need to establish a position of being on top of things. This chapter sheds light on new angles of the entrepreneurs and their startups under crisis by delineating the areas where one 'needs to be on top of things' for the purpose of leading the startup toward a 'new normal' where it can recuperate its condition and position. Entrepreneurs' perceptions of a crisis shape their consequent set of actions and practices in the business vis-à-vis the crisis; this is contingent on the initial strengths of the business, for example, trusted management, a shared vision, and values aligned with the vision and daily practices, among others. The crisis can be perceived as either a threat or an opportunity, requiring immediate action or a full range of resources or not. By refining perceptions of a crisis into a more detailed strategic and practical understanding of what the crisis demands and consists of, entrepreneurs can develop a straightforward approach to tackling the concurrent and future crises. The preventive and constructive approaches discussed in this chapter can be operationalized into business practices that mirror the robustness of the startup to its internal and external stakeholders. It is not only practices that are relevant to the startup's 'return to normal'-driven strategies, but also the way in which information is circulated by the startup and external interest groups. Different stakeholders develop different views on the effects of a crisis on a specific startup; see, for example, startups in the tourism sector during the COVID-19 pandemic, which have been harmed by the pandemic; while it will be automatically assumed that the startup has been severely affected, the picture can change through information flow and content, which are controlled by the entrepreneur.

Crisis effects are diverse and fluctuate across the individuals and organizational bodies associated with the startup, that is, WOW effect crisis, short-term crisis, long-term crisis, and long-term effect of the crisis. Hypothetically, when the crisis has passed, the entrepreneur and some external stakeholders may still consider the continued crisis effects on the startup and be reluctant to collaborate with that startup.

Entrepreneurs' skills and abilities as well as their leadership styles are imperative assets in monitoring, controlling, and shaping the image of the startup in times of crisis, including its strengths and struggles in the face of the crisis. When information is well disseminated in a reliable way and under a robust leadership, the startup can leverage the hardship into new opportunities.

Reflective questions for class

1. Yoni and Adi are the founders of an automotive startup located in Israel, which develops a powerful connectivity inside and outside the car. The journey to developing the best technology was very difficult, fraught with barriers and unexpected crises; for example, two experts that were recruited for R&D and were specialists

in this area left the startup without warning, and a competing product was developed by a powerful and established company (that produces different products) and was launched two months before the planned launch of their product; yet, Yoni and Adi managed to handle these barriers. The outbreak of COVID-19 introduced another barrier: in attracting investments. Based on the startup's history, and drawing on this chapter's foci, list three to four avenues that Yoni and Adi should follow to set the groundwork for coping with the pandemic's effects on their efforts to attract funds. Explain your answer.

2. Search the internet for two startups that have been affected by the pandemic; provide the links to their websites, posts, and other material specifying these startups' situation. Compare these two startups' management of the crisis situation by employing the concepts described in Figure 4.3: Startup features as enablers of crisis management. What are the main differences between those startups' conduct, mindsets, and perceptions with regard to the pandemic? Explain those differences explicitly for the business, the team, and the entrepreneur.
3. Search https://www.cnbc.com/2020/05/15/these-companies-have-filed-for-bankruptcy-since-the-coronavirus-pandemic.html for a company that went bankrupt during the COVID-19 pandemic. Provide a half-page description of the company based on additional internet searches. Suppose you had met the founders three months before their liquidation and you could still 'save' the situation, and based on the chapter section "Chronicle of a crisis foretold," how would you advise them to manage the situation? Explain your answer.
4. Search for Akara (https://www.akara.ai/) from Dublin, which develops robots for hospitals that decontaminate spaces and are therefore relevant to the COVID-19 pandemic. To leverage its offerings and view the pandemic as an opportunity for Akara (as people and companies concerned with contamination), list the most important skills, abilities, and leadership styles that you would recommend its founders employ to scale up during the COVID-19 pandemic and after the virus has been controlled. Explain your answer.
5. Five founders of a startup, SOS-AR, which develops augmented reality devices for emergency team training, are asking for your advice on how to manage the complex situation that they are facing: lack of funds and financial support and a dispute among the founders regarding closing the startup. This startup was founded five years ago; three of the founders developed the technology and two others leveraged it into the marketplace. Various bodies expressed interest and the startup

gained traction; then, the three founders who developed the technology launched a new startup (that turned out to be very successful) while still being involved in SOS-AR; this created conflicts and lack of trust among the five founders, which were then echoed in the business' atmosphere and employees' engagement and dedication to SOS-AR. The five founders decided to keep SOS-AR in its initial form and to 'give it another chance'; then, when COVID-19 emerged, the founders could not attract financial support, and ran out of money and resources. While the business ran into a bad situation, the three founders who launched the other startup did not feel the pandemic's effects. The differences in the founders' perceptions of the crisis' severity spurred more conflicts among the founders and then in the business as a whole. As their advisor, analyze the complex situation based on the model introduced in Figure 4.2: Entrepreneurs born into crises: a new look at crisis perceptions.

What are your recommendations?

References

Alesch, D. J., Holly, J. N., Mittler, E., & Nagy, R. (2001). Organizations at risk: What happens when small businesses and not-for-profits encounter natural disasters.

Alves, J. C., Lok, T. C., Luo, Y., & Hao, W. (2020). Crisis management for small business during the COVID-19 outbreak: Survival, resilience and renewal strategies of firms in Macau.

Boin, A., Hart, P., Stern, E., & Sundelius, B. (2005). The politics of crisis management: Understanding public leadership when it matters most.

Bowers, M. R., Hall, J. R., & Srinivasan, M. M. (2017). Organizational culture and leadership style: The missing combination for selecting the right leader for effective crisis management. *Business Horizons, 60*(4), 551–563.

Cardoso Durier da Silva, Fernando, Vieira, R., & Garcia, A. C. (2019). Can machines learn to detect fake news? a survey focused on social media. Paper presented at the *Proceedings of the 52nd Hawaii International Conference on System Sciences.*

Carlson, M. (2020). Fake news as an informational moral panic: the symbolic deviancy of social media during the 2016 US presidential election. *Information, Communication & Society, 23*(3), 374–388.

Clarke, C. J., & Varma, S. (1999). Strategic risk management: the new competitive edge. *Long Range Planning, 32*(4), 414–424.

Doern, R. (2016). Entrepreneurship and crisis management: The experiences of small businesses during the London 2011 riots. *International Small Business Journal, 34*(3), 276–302.

Egelhofer, J. L., & Lecheler, S. (2019). Fake news as a two-dimensional phenomenon: A framework and research agenda. *Annals of the International Communication Association, 43*(2), 97–116.

Elliott, D., Harris, K., & Baron, S. (2005). Crisis management and services marketing. *Journal of Services Marketing.*

Evans, N., & Elphick, S. (2005). Models of crisis management: An evaluation of their value for strategic planning in the international travel industry. *International Journal of Tourism Research, 7*(3), 135–150.

Habersaat, K. B., Betsch, C., Danchin, M., Sunstein, C. R., Böhm, R., Falk, A., … & Butler, R. (2020). Ten considerations for effectively managing the COVID-19 transition. *Nature Human Behaviour, 4*(7), 677–687.

Herbane, B. (2010). Small business research: Time for a crisis-based view. *International Small Business Journal, 28*(1), 43–64.

Herbane, B. (2013). Exploring crisis management in UK small-and medium-sized enterprises. *Journal of Contingencies and Crisis Management, 21*(2), 82–95.

Howell, G., & Miller, R. (2006). How the relationship between the crisis life cycle and mass media content can better inform crisis communication. *PRism, 4*(1), 1–14.

Irvine, W., & Anderson, A. R. (2004). Small tourist firms in rural areas: agility, vulnerability and survival in the face of crisis. *International Journal of Entrepreneurial Behavior & Research.*

Latham, S. (2009). Contrasting strategic response to economic recession in start-up versus established software firms. *Journal of Small Business Management, 47*(2), 180–201.

Liou, Y. (2015). School crisis management: A model of dynamic responsiveness to crisis life cycle. *Educational Administration Quarterly, 51*(2), 247–289.

Nunamaker Jr, J. F., Weber, E. S., & Chen, M. (1989). Organizational crisis management systems: planning for intelligent action. *Journal of Management Information Systems, 5*(4), 7–32.

Pauchant, T. C., Mitroff, I. I., & Ventolo, G. F. (1992). The dial tone does not come from God! How a crisis can challenge dangerous strategic assumptions made about high technologies: The case of the Hinsdale telecommunication outage. *Academy of Management Perspectives, 6*(3), 66–79.

Pearson, C. M., & Clair, J. A. (1998). Reframing crisis management. *Academy of Management Review, 23*(1), 59–76.

Pearson, C. M., & Mitroff, I. I. (2019). *From crisis prone to crisis prepared: A framework for crisis management.* Routledge.

Phan, D. H. B., & Narayan, P. K. (2020). Country responses and the reaction of the stock market to COVID-19—A preliminary exposition. *Emerging Markets Finance and Trade, 56*(10), 2138–2150.

Rosenthal, U., Boin, A., & Comfort, L. K. (2001). *Managing crises: Threats, dilemmas, opportunities.* Charles C Thomas Publisher.

Roser, M., Ritchie, H., Ortiz-Ospina, E., & Hasell, J. (2020). Coronavirus disease (COVID-19)–statistics and research. *Our world in data, 4.*

Rozell, M. J., & Wilcox, C. (2020). Federalism in a time of plague: How federal systems cope with pandemic. *The American Review of Public Administration, 50*(6–7), 519–525.

Rudan, I. (2020). A cascade of causes that led to the COVID-19 tragedy in Italy and in other European Union countries. *Journal of Global Health, 10*(1).

Runyan, R. C. (2006). Small business in the face of crisis: identifying barriers to recovery from a natural disaster 1. *Journal of Contingencies and Crisis Management, 14*(1), 12–26.

Sahin, S., Ulubeyli, S., & Kazaza, A. (2015). Innovative crisis management in construction: Approaches and the process. *Procedia-Social and Behavioral Sciences, 195*, 2298–2305.

Santana, G. (2004). Crisis management and tourism: Beyond the rhetoric. *Journal of Travel & Tourism Marketing, 15*(4), 299–321.

Schoenberg, A. (2005). Do crisis plans matter? A new perspective on leading during a crisis. *Public Relations Quarterly, 50*(1), 2.

Schrank, H. L., Marshall, M. I., Hall-Phillips, A., Wiatt, R. F., & Jones, N. E. (2013). Small-business demise and recovery after Katrina: rate of survival and demise. *Natural Hazards, 65*(3), 2353–2374.

Seeger, M. W., Sellnow, T. L., & Ulmer, R. R. (1998). Communication, organization, and crisis. *Annals of the International Communication Association, 21*(1), 231–276.

Seymour, M., & Moore, S. (2000). *Effective crisis management: Worldwide principles and practice.* Cassell.

Shepherd, D. A. (2003). Learning from business failure: Propositions of grief recovery for the self-employed. *Academy of Management Review, 28*(2), 318–328.

Shrivastava, P. (1993). Crisis theory/practice: Towards a sustainable future. *Industrial & Environmental Crisis Quarterly, 7*(1), 23–42.

Shrivastava, P., Mitroff, I. I., Miller, D., & Miclani, A. (1988). Understanding industrial crises. *Journal of Management Studies, 25*(4), 285–303.

Sozinova, A. A., Fokina, O. V., & Fufacheva, L. A. (2017). Reorganization of entrepreneurial structures within global crisis management: Problems and perspectives. In *Overcoming uncertainty of institutional environment as a tool of global crisis management* (pp. 3–8). Springer.

Stern, E., Sundelius, B., Nohrstedt, D., Hansén, D., Newlove, L., & Hart, P. (2002). Crisis management in transitional democracies: The Baltic experience. *Government and Opposition, 37*(4), 524–550.

Uscinski, J. E., Enders, A. M., Klofstad, C., Seelig, M., Funchion, J., Everett, C., Wuchty, S., Premaratne, K., & Murthi, M. (2020). Why do people believe COVID-19 conspiracy theories? *Harvard Kennedy School Misinformation Review, 1*(3)

Vašíčková, V. (2019). Crisis management process-a literature review and a conceptual integration. *Acta Oeconomica Pragensia, 27*(3–4), 61–77.

Veil, S. R., Buehner, T., & Palenchar, M. J. (2011). A work-in-process literature review: Incorporating social media in risk and crisis communication. *Journal of Contingencies and Crisis Management, 19*(2), 110–122.

Wang, J. (2008). Developing organizational learning capacity in crisis management. *Advances in Developing Human Resources, 10*(3), 425–445.

Wooten, L. P., & James, E. H. (2008). Linking crisis management and leadership competencies: The role of human resource development. *Advances in Developing Human Resources, 10*(3), 352–379.

World Health Organization. (2020). *Getting your workplace ready for COVID-19: How COVID-19 spreads, 19 March 2020* (No. WHO/2019-nCov/workplace/2020.2). World Health Organization.

Zarocostas, J. (2020). How to fight an infodemic. *The Lancet, 395*(10225), 676.

Chapter Five
External effects of crises

- Takeaways
- Introduction
- The outward impact of crises
- Main external concerns
- Effects across sectors
- External systems affect ecosystems
- Summary
- Reflective questions for class

Takeaways

- Acknowledging that crisis effects on external systems can substantially affect the startup's course of action, through direct and indirect (first and second) tiers, by disrupting the startup's supply chain
- Tracking the crisis' external effects bottom-up and top-down, to determine the subsequent focus on managing the crisis: either through internal adaptation of the startup that by gaining more attention will penetrate other entities in the ecosystem (bottom-up), or by focusing effort on changing regional regulations, financial compensation for startups, etc., which will affect the startup (top-down)
- Delving into the relationships between the startup and the ecosystem while considering the types of crisis disruptions (poverty, inequality, safety issues, living conditions, deprivation of education) to detect the contribution that startups can bring to the ecosystem and vice versa
- Assessing sectorial challenges in times of crisis, so that startups in specific sectors can find new avenues to use their existing achievements differently, in alignment with the crisis conditions and constraints. The tourism sector is discussed to exemplify the challenges
- Outlining the ecosystem components: organizations, processes, and capabilities, and the ecosystem's vitality, assessed by its connectivity, diversity, density, and fluidity. By spotting these characteristics, startups can more accurately obtain what they need from the ecosystem to survive or even thrive during times of crisis

DOI: 10.4324/9781003173809-5

(e.g., obtaining more networks from ecosystems with higher levels of connectivity among organizations). Similarly, startups can promote the ecosystem characteristics that are disrupted by the crisis through their processes

- Recognizing the role of stakeholders' feedback as a 'compass' that can lead startups to accurately manage the crisis (which is creating chaotic conditions within the startups)

Introduction

Crises have an impact on external systems and processes in organizations, regions, societies, and markets, among others. These effects can range from inaccessibility of raw material due to a natural disaster, national bankruptcy due to a financial crisis, or unavailability of knowledge or expertise to repair the damage caused by the crisis, such as with the outbreak of COVID-19. Such external effects are echoed in the startup's internal functions, processes, and overall performance through interconnected operations; for example, natural disasters such as floods or earthquakes that cause regional damage to infrastructures (e.g., roads, buildings, human injuries and fatalities) impair the startup's ability to function, due to its dependence on these external systems. In turn, the changes in the startup's internal functions and processes further affect the external systems through the supply chain and interconnected operations; for instance, when startups decrease their production of a specific product because they cannot produce it when the external infrastructure is damaged (roads, buildings), the lack of that specific product is then felt externally. According to a report issued by the McKinsey Global Institute, the COVID-19 pandemic has disrupted household consumption; while expenditures for products increased dramatically in the initial stages of the COVID-19 outbreak, their production, sales, new related products, and innovations in the production process all decreased, leading to a void in external functions, while concurrently the demand for new household products increased. A *New York Times* article entitled "How the World Ran Out of Everything" states that "global shortages of many goods reflect the disruption of the pandemic combined with decades of companies limiting their inventories." This portrays the crisis effect as the 'supply chain running amok', because the pandemic has hampered business operations, spread chaos, and created vast supply chain shortages, which are reflected in the startups' operation and then back in the external systems' operations. Thus, disruption of the supply chain by crises can be direct or indirect, termed first and second tier, respectively, and illustrated in Figures 5.1 and 5.2.

The first tier reflects the changes imposed by the crisis on organizations, bodies, structures, and processes that can directly affect the startup's functions, structures, plans, and outcomes; in turn, fallout from the startups can trigger changes in the external factors, with the startups' effects contingent on the rate and magnitude of their changes. For example, during the COVID-19 lockdown, travel was restricted, including travel to the workplace; this regulation (represented in Figures 5.1 and 5.2 by puzzle piece no. 5) affected startups' financial dynamics, because many routine functions had to be converted to virtual ones, thereby slowing down the workflow, and those that could not be performed virtually had to be eliminated. These conversions were effected through trial and error, costing money, time, etc. Because they were spending more money, the startups had to dismiss some employees, representing the macro impact on the startup. Dismissal of the more skilled employees had a rebound effect on customer loyalty, sometimes resulting in desertion (puzzle piece no. 1 in Figure 5.1), showing that the startups' changes are echoed in and sometimes drive changes in external factors.

Aggregation of these reciprocal interactions between external and internal (i.e., startup) impacts—shown as the first tier—ensues, as more startups encounter similar interactions with the external changes, which, in turn, can trigger large-scale, cultural, social, and market effects, as presented in Figure 5.2. For example, health-related crises accelerate the development of new areas in research and practice, such as vaccination, decontamination, illness prevention, etc., and these developments then prompt changes in the educational system—schools' and higher education's curricula, new programs, budgets assigned for the development of laboratories and experimentation; such developments can advance regulations on the use of vaccinations or restrictions to avoid contamination. Natural disasters (e.g., the 2010 earthquake in Haiti, Hurricane Katrina in 2005, the 2011 tsunami in Japan, or the tornado in Kentucky in 2021) are followed by waves of population movement and immigration and breed employment fluxes in

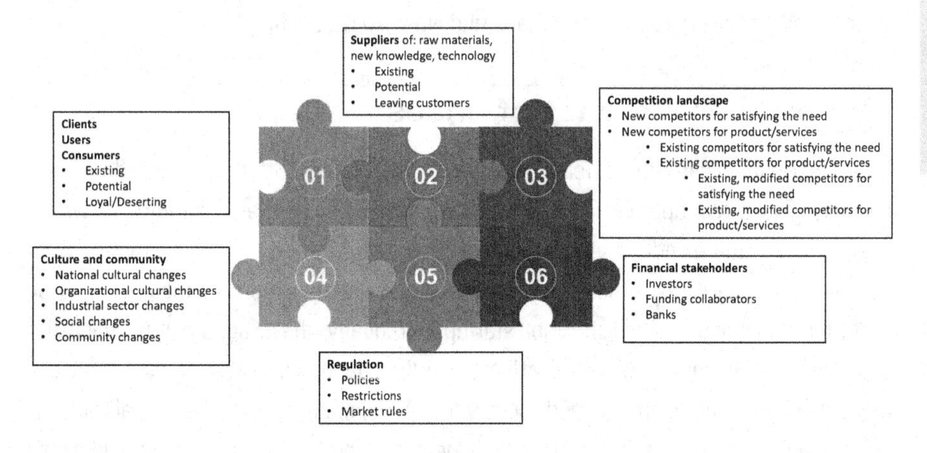

FIGURE 5.1 Reciprocal relationships between external forces and startups—first tier

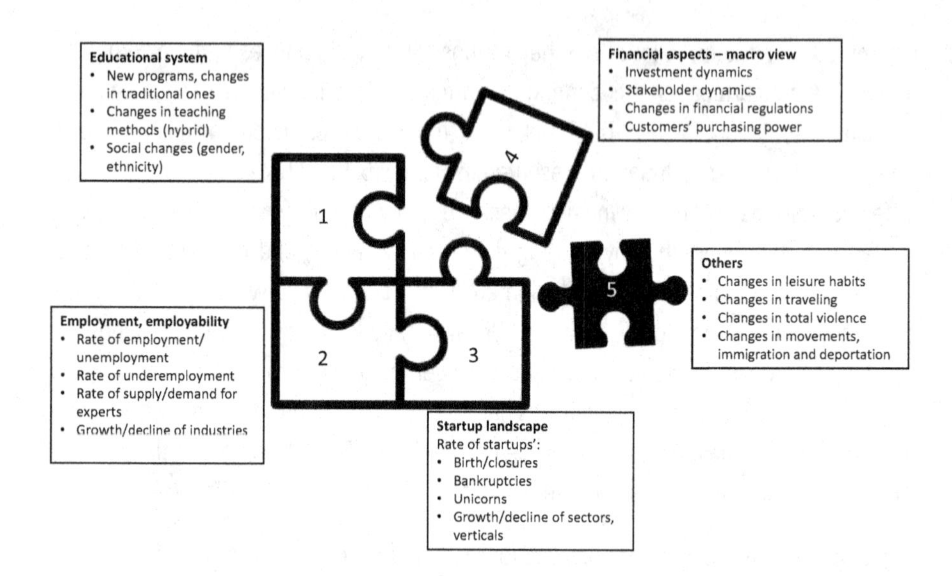

FIGURE 5.2 Reciprocal relationships between external forces and startups—second tier

the origin and destination countries. Financial crises (e.g., the Great Depression of the 1930s, the 2008 global financial crisis subsequent to the bankruptcy of Lehman Brothers, 'Brexit') cause wide-ranging, global-level changes to the competitive landscape and financial structures and processes.

This chapter aims to portray the shock effect engendered by crises across external organizations and processes that provoke changes in startups' dynamics by identifying the main external forces that are affected by crises and examining their reciprocal relationships with startups, focusing mainly on the first tier of influence (Klapper and Love 2011; Peris-Ortiz, Fuster-Estruch and Devece-Carañana 2014; Skandalis and Ghazzawi 2014; Vegetti and Adăscăliţei 2017; Hausmann and Nedelkoska 2018).

The outward impact of crises

Crises' external and internal effects can be examined from a bottom-up or top-down perspective. These two approaches are differentiated mainly by the assignation of where crisis effects initiate and subsequently the direction of the crisis' flow. A bottom-up view assumes that the crisis effects and the consequent management of those effects by a startup will trigger action in other startups; gradually, these actions will reach the startups' stakeholders who can be affected by the changes in the startups, such as in production pace and quantity, need for raw materials, modified use of external technology and money, or fluctuations in employee demand. The top-down approach addresses the large-scale external changes caused by crises to crucial systems, such as financial, educational, or health systems, which shake up the startup's routines, and force it to take internal action.

Bottom-up perspective—an inductive approach, in which generalizations are formed based on the startup's unique experience in the face of an event; startups in the tourism sector, for example, have faced a dramatic decrease in sales during the COVID-19 pandemic due to travel restrictions; by accumulating evidence from similar startups in the tourism sector, a general conclusion of a severe impact of the pandemic's restrictions is then established (e.g., disseminated through the media, social media, by word of mouth). Accordingly, external systems react; for instance, investors and strategic partners will be more reluctant to create or maintain connections with tourism startups; customers may be more cautious in purchasing tourism services or be worried about the sector's possible collapse, which would affect their purchase; employees in this sector will feel at risk of losing their jobs, and since their expertise is in tourism, it may no longer be applicable, hence they might be unemployed; novice startups in this area may pivot into other sectors. Different external movements will then influence the crisis' impact on the startup, and obviously such changes will bounce back on the startup.

Top-down perspective—a deductive approach that identifies the large-scale external dynamics as the initiators of the startup's course of action. For example, the crisis linked to detection of the HIV virus was associated with widespread stigmatization of groups of people who were considered to be a source of the contamination and therefore had severe difficulties finding employment (e.g., Castro and Farmer 2005; Surgevil and Akyol 2011; Shepherd and Patzelt 2015); these external changes in the employment system then penetrated the individual or business sphere, resulting in homosexuals choosing to start businesses in which the work environment and space were aligned with their values and beliefs, thereby escaping the hardship of stigmatization or unemployment; alternatively, a startup would hire more experts, as some had become unemployed simply for being gay.

It is important to detect these approaches as each derives from a distinct origin, thus bringing about different implications for the crisis effect, as demonstrated in Figure 5.3. Accordingly, crises spawn both higher and lower rates of startup initiation. Due to the collective nature of businesses and markets, as reflected in imitation, benchmarking, competition, customer-supplier relationships, networks, etc., a startup's conduct in times of crisis has a substantial impact on other startups and in the long run on the entire market and ecosystem; hence, the contrasting 'facts' on changes in startup initiation

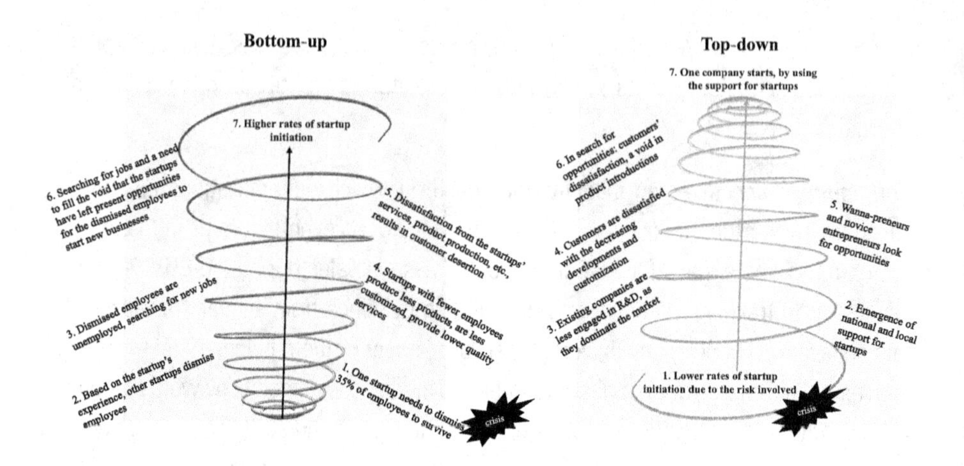

FIGURE 5.3 Crisis effects through bottom-up and top-down views

rates can increase mistrust and panic among entrepreneurs. However, by distinguishing the 'facts' and identifying the approach used to reach them, these inconsistencies can raise new ideas and open new avenues for startups' conduct during a crisis. As such, the startup is open to drilling down and following the forces and processes that produced those 'facts' to extract the related opportunities and avoid the included threats. For example, rather than accepting that crises produce a dearth of experts for recruitment, as more people are engaged in crisis-related activity (e.g., people are infected/sick, have lost their homes, are taking care of family members in need), the entrepreneur can look for experts by locating employees who have been dismissed from other startups due to the crisis.

Main external concerns

To cover the various aspects associated with external systems and processes that are affected in times of crisis, the United Nation's Sustainable Development Goals (SDGs) will be used in this section. SDGs are considered areas in which the world can be shaped to be sustainable, just, and truthful, and are at the forefront of global decision-makers' debates. The goals are: no poverty; zero hunger; good health and well-being; quality education; gender equality; clean water and sanitation; affordable and clean energy; decent work and economic growth; industry, innovation, and infrastructure; reduced inequalities; sustainable cities and communities; responsible consumption and production; climate action; life below water; life on land; peace, justice, and strong institutions; and goal-oriented partnerships.

Crises change the structures and processes of various external areas, which can be encapsulated in the SDGs. According to the Sustainable Development Goals Report 2020 issued by the United Nations, the forecast for each of the goal areas indicates deterioration, which will be reflected in higher rates of poverty, especially among vulnerable populations and in less developed countries that have historically been disproportionately affected by disasters; energy, infrastructure and clean water are lacking and becoming even more scarce; the supply of fair work and employment will dramatically decrease; severe disruptions in construction, manufacturing, and transport industries will show intensified effects along their value chains, leading to worsening poverty, unemployment, and inequalities in labor markets, especially among those for which construction and manufacturing are the leading sources of income (Caligiuri et al. 2020; Chakraborty and Maity 2020; Davison 2020; Coccia 2021). While crisis outbreaks indisputably shake up each of these areas, the effects are portrayed differently in relationships with startups, as shown in Table 5.1.

TABLE 5.1 Reciprocal relationships between external areas and startups: a SDG perspective

SDG areas[a]	How crises in SDGs affect startups (SUs)	How startups (SUs) affect SDGs
• Living conditions: 1. End poverty 2. Zero hunger	• Low purchasing power of customers, both financially and due to general hopelessness • Customers buy only the basics >> SUs experience decreased sales and traction, and future interest in their product is questionable; governments anticipate the starting of new businesses to fill the void; a global expectation of innovation and responding to the need	• Provide a source of employment • Activate a full range of suppliers from the ecosystem, hence contributing to economic recovery • Innovate! SUs can mitigate hunger, etc. • SUs' modeling gives hope
• Employability: 3. Good health and well-being 4. Quality education 5. Gender equality 6. Decent work and economic growth 7. Reduced inequalities	• Decreased supply of qualified human capital • Deepened inequalities and lack of decent work • Deficiencies in total well-being • Blocked economic growth >> SUs suffer from unqualified applicants and entrants; innovation is at risk; a general expectation of change that can arise from SUs; unemployed, uneducated, or workforce suffering inequality can be driven to improve capabilities, to be employable in SUs	• Offer employment, mitigate inequalities in the labor market, and increase well-being • Put pressure on the educational system to educate and train the population to respond to the SUs' needs
• Infrastructure resilience: 8. Sustainable cities and communities	• Hardship in cities, with infrastructure, production, etc., • The robustness/resilience of cities and institutions decreases	• Build up the resilience of cities and promote sustainable communities • Stimulate partnerships, innovation, and a vital industry dynamics

9. Industry, innovation, and infrastructure	>> The hardship is exhibited in the SU's low-quality infrastructure, decreased production, and weakened innovation; disrupting the external supplier chains; SUs moving away from areas of adversity; more conflict and disputes revealed in SUs; cities, industries, partners are keen to see more innovation and entrepreneurship and will support SUs' initiation	• Reduce conflicts through engagement in the SU's mission • Production and consumption are improved due to SUs' demands and needs; the operational cycle is strengthened
10. Responsible consumption and production		
11. Peace, justice, and strong institutions		
12. Partnerships for the goals		
• Basic needs for survival: 13. Affordable and clean energy 14. Clean water and sanitation 15. Climate action 16. Life below water 17. Life on land	• Lack of basic needs • Loss of resources, heritage • Rise in diseases, death • Influence on education, employment >> Lower propensity to start a business under **such conditions; lower probability of SU survival and success;** *SUs that do survive can address the conditions as 'beta sites' to test their innovation, and improve people's lives*	• Innovation provides solutions to needs • Green and sustainable processes are a model for the industry, hence promoting decreased resource usage

[a]In bold: the threats; in italics: the opportunities.

External systems that are affected by crisis events produce a fertile ground for startups to innovate and supply the new needs and to exploit new opportunities that embody the crisis effects mirrored in each area.

Effects across sectors

Crises expose different sectors to new and varied challenges, often unlike any that they have experienced before, such that the sectors' known sensitivity to the economic, organizational, and business cycles takes on different forms under crises. This sensitivity is first echoed in customers' dependence on or loyalty to a sector; for example, customers will always consume food, resulting in lower sensitivity of the food sector to crises, whereas sensitivity of the automobile sector may be higher, because people tend to hesitate before purchasing a new car during crises. A sector's sensitivity to a crisis will then be reflected in investors' engagement with those sectors; for example, in the case of a health crisis, the ecosystem will tend to offer resources to health-related sectors to combat the crisis' effects. Finally, sector sensitivity will be mirrored in the government's support, which combines crisis effects with local or national agendas.

In general, while some sectors can survive hardships of any frequency or extent, others experience instability stemming from unknown changes in the supply and demand fluxes. Nevertheless, the common view that the basic needs for survival and safety, such as food, health, shelter, and mobility, will determine sector sensitivity and consequent stability, is debatable; specifically, the crisis' characteristics, for example, the already evident impact, severity of outcomes, availability of coping measures, elicit fluctuations in sensitivity, which are then seen as changes in the startup's course of action (e.g., sales, traction, costs, and revenues).

The specific needs induced by a crisis, for example, mitigating an illness, supporting people that have suffered severe, unexpected disruptions in their standard of living (money, employment), providing shelter for people who have lost their houses, or feeding people in a famine, determine which sectors are essential in a specific crisis and therefore their sensitivity to the crisis' effects. These essential sectors are often supported by national or regional funds, to enable their continued functioning, so that restrictions will not apply to these sectors' businesses; on the contrary, these businesses will be further maintained by support from the public, media, social media, and general discourse. For example, after the 9/11 tragedy and the following crisis, firemen were highly praised. A recent article on crisis management in the Harvard Business Review discusses changes in the Fire Department of New York (FDNY) in the context of that tragedy:

> In the last 20 years, the FDNY has moved from a highly effective yet dated firefighting force to a modern emergency management and response organization. In 2015, it was ranked as the top government employer and the 17th overall best employer in the U.S. by *Forbes*.

This example demonstrates the uniqueness of different types of crises and the traces they posit in the various sectors.

A glimpse into COVID-19

The COVID-19 pandemic has changed the rules of the game. Traditionally, the 'secure' sectors, such as the food industry and travel, thrive during crises. With respect to food, this is not only because it is a basic need, but also because purchasing prepared food or going out to restaurants provide substantial time-saving avenues (rather than having to cook during disasters or terror incidents) or routes for escape (restaurants). Travel embodies safety, providing the ability to leave regions at risk for safer or calmer ones. Other sectors, such as delivery and virtual communication, are considered 'nice to have', but not absolutely necessary. However, the International Labor Organization (ILO) has published reports on the sectors' statuses during the COVID-19 pandemic, and these stress the role of new factors in determining how critical a sector is. Their main insights show that sectors that have evolved during the pandemic are those that:

- directly and promptly fight the virus—health care, including the development of vaccines and medication;
- facilitate the requirement for social distancing, for example, delivery, virtual communication;
- develop protective measures against contamination, such as masks, disinfection products, shifting functions to distant/virtual arenas;
- take care of emerging second tier problems, such as in children's education (by enabling remote learning) and isolation and loneliness of the elderly (by creating safety devices for this segment of the population).

Sectors that are not directly linked to mitigating or managing the pandemic yet cover the basics in society have devoted this pandemic time to strengthening their foundations, such as construction, roads, automobiles, agriculture, textiles. These sectors have not experienced dramatic dips as their projects are often supported by state budgets.

Sectors in which most of the work can be executed while maintaining a safe, hygienic, and secure environment have also been able to maintain their regular activity, for example, any work in the open air, such as jobs in construction, ports, forests, agriculture; virtual work, such as high-tech companies; and work that is traditionally performed remotely by service providers (e.g., designers, developers). However, sectors that are based on sharing and crowds, as in sharing economy, have undergone extreme changes, so that co-working and cohabitation places have diminished due to the transmissibility of the virus through coughing, sneezing, or simply breathing or even touching objects. The shared economy has therefore moved to the virtual realm.

The instructions for hygiene during the COVID-19 pandemic—only gathering in small groups, social distancing, banning most public transportation, and halting avoidable outdoor activities, among others—have led to swift and considerable changes in trends, echoed in the sectors of, for example, travel, tourism, entertainment, air transportation, and airports. People have renounced the 'nice to have' activities and strengthened their home- and family related activities; as such, sectors such as gaming, home cooking, and home entertainment have thrived. One example of exploiting a sector's vulnerability can be found in a pivoted startup founded by two Israelis who developed a smart pill container for the elderly that is designed to alert a contact or responsible family member(s) if a pill is not taken at the appropriate time (Feast and Bretag 2005; Bjørkdahl and Carlsen 2019; Aassve et al. 2020; Aloi et al. 2020; Gössling, Scott and Hall 2020; Xiong et al. 2021).

Tourism—a unique case

During the COVID-19 pandemic, countries closed their borders, imposed travel restrictions, and declared quarantine periods for travelers; these restrictions were immediately felt in the tourism sector, including international and domestic travel and visits, flights, public transport, accommodations, cruises, restaurants, and professional and cultural events, such as conferences, concerts, musicals, shows, sports events, festivals, museums, and movies.

The impact of event cancellations and travelers' avoidance of restaurants, hotels, and cruises has affected the entire supply chain, for example, tour guides, sports club instructors, and services provided to hotels and restaurants (including food, catering, laundry, spa, and entertainment, among others), leaving many people jobless and uncertain as to when or how their expertise will be relevant once the COVID-19 crisis has passed. Startups have exploited the void in this area by developing sophisticated products that enable maintaining routines without breaking the restrictions or risking contamination through virtual tourism, streamed concerts and shows, and remote museum visits (e.g., Chang, McAleer and Wong 2020; Gretzel et al. 2020; Higgins-Desbiolles 2020; Sigala 2020; Travel and Council 2020; Fotiadis, Polyzos and Huan 2021).

External systems affect ecosystems

As we have seen in previous chapters, entrepreneurial ecosystems are comprised of organizations and processes that interact dynamically and reciprocally, forming conducive environments for startups. Drawing on the leading conceptual model in entrepreneurship research, this consists of organizations, processes, and capabilities, as demonstrated below, which can be changed by crises' effects on the external systems.

Ecosystems consist of:

Organizations	**Processes**	**Capabilities**
• Higher education infrastructures • Labor market • Financial • Public sector • Private sector	• Policy • Culture • Networks • Market dynamics • Research and Development (R&D) • Communication and media • Competition • Rivalry and conflicts versus shared processes	• Supporting programs • Financial support • Professional support • Individual capabilities • Entrepreneurial attitudes, orientations, intentions

Since entrepreneurial ecosystems are based on external factors, any changes in these factors are reflected in this ecosystem's components. Entrepreneurial ecosystems' vitality is predominantly measured by their connectivity (e.g., program connectivity, spin-off rate, deal-making networks), diversity (e.g., multiple economic specializations, mobility, equality of opportunities, immigrants), density (e.g., new and young firms, share of employment in new and young firms, sector density, especially with respect to high-tech), and fluidity (e.g., population flux, labor market reallocation, high-growth firms), so that severe external effects will be reflected in each of the ecosystem's components. As entrepreneurial ecosystems embody the space that nurtures startups and fosters their development, they will 'naturally' adjust their vitality to enable startups to thrive.

The intertwined relationships of the crisis' external effects, the ecosystem components, and the ecosystem's measures of viability, as displayed in Table 5.2, exhibit the complex compounded dynamics of external effect impositions on the ecosystem. Entrepreneurial ecosystems aim at nurturing startups. Accordingly, these ecosystems are expected to demonstrate a high level of resilience through their participants in different avenues, such as adapting themselves to the external effects, striving to change any effects that can threaten the startups nurtured within the ecosystem, removing hurdles, including organizations or processes that can risk the ecosystem's stakeholders, and adding new entrants, among others.

Entrepreneurial ecosystems are 'programmed' to manage crises, so that their standard efforts are directed to detecting areas (e.g., geographical, social, technological, business, mindset) that can pose risks for the ecosystem's stakeholders and its processes, while adjusting its components to facilitate startups and other stakeholders' operation and development. For example, the International Trade Center illustrates the ecosystem's key role in the digital transition in African nations in the following examples of self-sustainable tech hubs that strive to make a profit while responding to the African market's needs during the pandemic: Joseph Mwanyika, executive director of Ennovate HUB in Tanzania, holds a generalized view, stressing that "technology is our new reality," and it needs to be advanced by pushing startups forward through the ecosystem's joint efforts; Simunza Muyangana, co-founder and director of entrepreneurship at BongoHive in Zambia, takes a sectoral approach by seeking out opportunities for technology to address the challenges in those sectors and supporting new startups in those sectors. Both as well as other emerging entities see the critical role of the ecosystem, especially in times of crisis, and look for different avenues to connect startups, sometimes even pre-startup

TABLE 5.2 Ecosystem components and viability in the face of crises' external effects—a crisis management perspective

	Ecosystem components											
	Organizations				**Processes**				**Capabilities**			
Ecosystem viability												
External effects of crises—categories:	**Con.**[a]	**Div.**	**Den.**	**Flui.**	**Con.**	**Div.**	**Den.**	**Flui.**	**Con.**	**Div.**	**Den.**	**Flui.**
Deprived living conditions				Maintain/ encourage existing firms that are tackling needs				Fund R&D of existing startups that are tackling needs				Relocate experts in areas of specific needs to work in existing startups
Employability		Facilitate new female-led entrants				Funding for example, invest in, endow new female-led startups				a) Target technology education in schools to girls		

(*Continued*)

	Ecosystem components											
	Organizations				Processes				Capabilities			
Ecosystem viability												
External effects of crises—categories:	Con.[a]	Div.	Den.	Flui.	Con.	Div.	Den.	Flui.	Con.	Div.	Den.	Flui.
Infrastructure resilience			Facilitate new entrants in areas that have been severely disrupted by the crisis				Create links between leading businesses and new startups in disrupted areas				Train, mentor, support startup founders in disrupted areas	
Basic needs for survival	Encourage spinoffs (SOs) of startups in green economy				Create robust networks for nurturing the SOs				Train, mentor, support SOs			

a *Con.*, Connectivity; *Div.*, diversity; *Den.*, density; *Flui.*, fluidity teams, to established, corporate stakeholders, thereby smoothing the first steps for entrepreneurs by providing a safety net, especially in risky times of crisis (Suresh and Ramraj 2012; Nambisan and Baron 2013; Colombo et al. 2019; Heaton, Siegel and Teece 2019; Roundy and Fayard 2019).

Yet, the dependence of the startups included in an entrepreneurial ecosystem fluctuates, based on their unique needs during crisis events, for example, funds, training, mentoring, networks, publicity, and niche penetration, among many others. Ideally, customized measures are required to respond to the needs of the startup that arise in a crisis, but in the absence of such customized processes in the ecosystem, the stakeholders and connectors strive to introduce the following:

- Robust networking processes between established and nascent businesses, including periodical (e)meetings, joint activities, and projects (e.g., Malecki 2011; Cavallo, Ghezzi and Balocco 2019; Cavallo, Ghezzi and Sanasi 2021)
- Diverse vertical representation of a wide scope of environmental and social needs that have emerged due to the crisis and should be addressed rather than focusing only on the highly ranked vertical, such as high-tech, health, or space (e.g., Maroufkhani, Wagner and Ismail 2018; Audretsch et al. 2019)
- A diversity of entities included in the ecosystem, with fair representation of the genders, ethnicity, age, social economic status, physical and mental needs, etc., to operate an ecosystem built on equality and trust and to introduce a model for new entrants (e.g., Acs et al. 2017; Welter et al. 2017; Maritz et al. 2020)
- Connectors—entrepreneurial employees in large established firms can act as ecosystem connectors on a global scale, connecting distinct regional entrepreneurial ecosystems in their role as knowledge integrators (e.g., Malecki 2011; Stam 2018; Stam and Van de Ven 2021)
- Dynamic and agile embracing of change and entrepreneurial ecosystem entities that are structured such that they can take on different roles, to provide new ways to support or share various resources (e.g., Auerswald 2015; Malecki 2018)

To protect startups from the effects of a crisis, entrepreneurial ecosystems not only engage their heterogeneous stakeholders to take on specific roles and carry out their responsibilities, but also strive to obtain prolific interactions between the entities comprising the ecosystem (e.g., investors with banks and government representatives with academia) by creating open boundaries between them, to exchange resources, expertise, and information, and strengthen the entrepreneurial dynamics in times of crisis.

Stakeholders' feedback—a fertile ground for crisis management

Entrepreneurial ecosystem entities exhibit positive, negative, and mixed feedback loops, offering startups a clear reflection of their direction and achievements; as such, they are of great value for startups' crisis management.

This feedback is offered through the ecosystem processes and dynamics; positive feedback is reflected in stakeholders' support of a startup, based on its products, technology, growth, or specific cause (fighting inequality in the labor market by recruiting diverse individuals; promoting the environment by using green processes). Such support serves as a signal for startups that they are acting in accordance with the ecosystem's principles and expectations with regards to innovation, contribution, etc.; this support is therefore most valuable for startups to underpin their crisis management activity. Negative feedback is echoed in a hesitant relationship between the ecosystem's stakeholders and the startup in terms of funding, strategic collaboration or referring the startup to other entities, customers, etc. Startups often ignore this signal rather than relating it to their performance; instead, they attribute it to 'difficult times' or 'overall reduced market activity due to the crisis'—this, despite the fact that some startups thrive during crises. Accordingly, the compounded effect of the crisis and the ecosystem's reluctance to approach the startup will aggravate the latter's situation. Mixed feedback involves support of some of the startup's functions or processes while ignoring others, thereby leading to disproportionally fortified functions and drying up of the functions that did not attract the ecosystem's support; this, in turn, results in changes in the startup's essence. For example, a promising startup in France developed a smart conversational bot for businesses; it is programmed for specific conversational scenarios with women, men, people of different ages or educational level, etc. During the COVID-19 pandemic, the startup began to face 'lack of interest' from potential customers, which the founders related to disruptions caused by the pandemic. Yet, this did not seem to be an adequate explanation for the customers' reluctance, because at the same time, a direct competitor raised large investments. A deeper analysis revealed that some leading global companies were interested in the unique bot technology (it embeds a visual dialog chatbot that can interpret images), but not in the product itself. This mixed feedback provided a significant clue as to the direction this startup should pursue to regain its competitive edge in the ecosystem in times of crisis (Cohen 2006; Muldoon, Bauman and Lucy 2018; Beech and Anseel 2020; Carniel and Dalle 2020; Haarhaus, Strunk and Liening 2020; Tatoglu et al. 2020).

At-a-Glance—creating a community in times of crisis

Bav (originally Bhavna) Patel is a 29-year-old co-founder of the TecKhet* community from the UK. Bav started her undertaking six months ago, when her startup ceased to attract more needed funds and was put on hold for at least a year. Bav was raised in Bihar, India, born to a family of farmers who suffered from unemployment and poverty; she studied at an international school far from her home, where she won a grant for her outstanding science project, which sent her on a summer program to the UK. In this program, Bav initiated a project for 'smart farms' that won another prize; and with the assistance of bilateral agencies, Bav relocated to the UK and started her academic studies in Agricultural Engineering at the university. There, she met Andrew and Ru (originally Ruwaihim from Pakistan) and the three co-founded TecKhet, a startup developing smart solutions for farms in rural areas. They started with an agribot, and the R&D process advanced very smoothly; the co-founders won a prize from the university's accelerator that enabled them to hasten the bot's technological development; government agencies from India and Pakistan expressed their interest in partnering with TecKhet for further technological developments. However, when COVID-19 broke out, these agencies became occupied with crisis events in India and Pakistan, and broke their connection with TecKhet. At that time, Andrew was infected by the Coronavirus, hospitalized, and underwent a long rehabilitation process, and was therefore absent, de facto, from TecKhet. Bav and Ru realized during the course of their intensive search for funding that many people were intrigued by smart farming, technology, and agriculture; they decided to initiate the TecKhet community, based in university accelerators; they have assembled a gradually growing number of entities, including public and private companies, startups, mentors, and service providers in technology, finance, and law. The co-founders have further visions and goals for the community and see its value to the entire ecosystem in this area.

**Khet is the Indian word for farm.*

A chaos perspective

According to the chaos theory, some disruptive events trigger startups to follow disordered, random, cumbersome, and unpredictable dynamics, mainly based on a sense of urgency in disruptive times that prompts businesses to act immediately and forcefully.

Such random performance, when exhibited across the startup's functions, is often riddled with errors and suffused with actions that may seem relevant for tackling the crisis but could be damaging in the long run; for example, dismissing highly paid employees when sales decrease due to a crisis, but in the long run, the highly paid employees might have been able to extract the startup from the crisis' effects. A chaotic course of action is known to slow down the actual performance of a business and impair its ability to achieve stability over time. According to Levy, the ecosystem's robustness entails the "fundamental order and structure behind complex events" (p. 169) and can act as a compass; through feedback from the ecosystem, startups can aim their functions and processes to a point where the ecosystem's signals and the startup's vision converge. From this perspective, one avenue to mitigate crisis effects and manage crisis corollaries is to generate feedback from the ecosystem; specifically, startups should spot the functions that have become 'chaotic', for example, are operated sporadically and in disorganized fashion due to the crisis, such as marketing, sales, layoffs, and recruitment of workers, and challenge them with the stakeholders' feedback by either proactively asking for insights from investors, corporate representatives, accelerator leaders, etc., or by just being very attentive to any comments from customers, competitors, suppliers, etc., that can then be inspected by the startup. Enlightening ideas can be obtained by generating the ecosystem's feedback, and the startup can more accurately regain its equilibrium (as opposed to chaos) and improve its practices.

Summary

The effect of crises on startups is twofold: a direct effect on the startup's internal functions, termed the first tier, and an indirect effect that influences the startup through changes emerging in external systems, termed the 2nd tier. These are not stand-alone effects. They create unique reciprocal relationships between the startup and its connected external systems.

These relationships can be investigated using a bottom-up perspective, considering a startup's action vis-à-vis the crisis, and the origin of the stakeholders' action that is contingent on and aligned with the startup's moves; or a top-down perspective, which considers the large-scale external changes forcing the startup to take internal action. In either case, crisis outcomes (e.g., poverty, well-being, education, sustainable cities and communities, clean water and sanitation, climate change) can be viewed and assessed by the reciprocal changes, that is, the damages and opportunities that they introduce into the external systems, which then affect startups and vice versa.

Crises are also central in the sectorial landscape. Startups in different sectors are differently affected by crises. Those that benefit from crises are often those that provide products/services that directly fight the crisis damage, assist in developing coping measures, or respond to new second tier problems that have arisen due to the crisis.

The ecosystem is an external force that embodies the vibrant foundation of the startup's crisis management activity; it is composed of startups and their stakeholders and aims to facilitate these entities' operations by prominently nurturing startups through various dynamic measures and with stakeholders. Nurtured startups then 'give back' with their inventions, innovation, updated knowledge, cutting-edge technology, etc., to the ecosystem and subsequently to the society, the environment, and the marketplace. Therefore, the ecosystem's structure and processes are designed to place startups in a paramount position at the outset and protect them from any disturbances by adjusting the ecosystem dynamics to the startup's needs and constraints imposed by the crisis. The role of feedback obtained from the stakeholders is thus crucial in modulating startups' performance in times of crisis and is reflected in the stakeholders' willingness to fund, mentor, consult, or partner with a startup. The ecosystem stakeholders become the startups' 'compass', enabling them to regulate their crisis-related actions, regain an organized and routine course, and mitigate the chaos to which they have been subjected.

Reflective questions for class

Pick two financial crises from the following list or elsewhere. Questions 1–3 address your two selected financial crises:

United States' housing bubble, 2003–2011; automotive industry crisis, 2008–2010 (United States); Icelandic financial crisis, 2008–2012; Spanish financial crisis, 2008–2016; European sovereign debt crisis, 2009–2019; Greek government's debt crisis, 2009–2019; Portuguese financial crisis, 2010–2014; crisis in Venezuela, 2012; Ukrainian crisis, 2013–2014; Brazilian economic crisis, 2014–2017; Chinese stock market crash, 2015; and Brexit.

1. Briefly describe each of the two crises that you chose (up to five lines); then list the three main external forces that were most affected by each of these crises (based on Figure 5.2: Reciprocal relationships between external forces and startups—second tier. What are the similarities and differences between these crises with respect to external forces? Explain your findings.

2. Pick one of the portfolio companies at TechStars https://www.techstars.com/portfolio?category=companies+in+program; describe it (up to five lines). Suppose it had started during one of the crises that you chose. Analyze the startup and external force relationships from bottom-up and top-down perspectives (based on Figure 5.3: Crisis effects through bottom-up and top-down views).
3. Suppose you are invited to advise the government on the directions new startups should take to succeed in the face of one the crises that you chose. Which sector(s) would you recommend that the startups focus on? Use an illustration (e.g., pie diagram, histogram) to demonstrate the distribution of the sectors. Explain your answer.
4. What is your recommendation to ecosystem developers and connectors for leveraging the ecosystem to manage the COVID-19 pandemic? Fill in the relevant cells of Table 5.2: Ecosystem components and viability in the face of crises' external effects—a crisis management perspective, with regard to the COVID-19 pandemic in the region in which you currently reside.
5. Choose one startup that failed during the COVID-19 pandemic. You may use the lists of TechCrunch, Forbes, or any other list. Describe the startup (up to five lines) and the causes for its failure (up to five lines). Based on the chapter's models and concepts, discuss how the ecosystem might have assisted the startup and prevented its failure.

References

Aassve, A., Cavalli, N., Mencarini, L., Plach, S., & Livi Bacci, M. (2020). The COVID-19 pandemic and human fertility. *Science, 369*(6502), 370–371.

Acs, Z. J., Stam, E., Audretsch, D. B., & O'Connor, A. (2017). The lineages of the entrepreneurial ecosystem approach. *Small Business Economics, 49*(1), 1–10.

Aloi, A., Alonso, B., Benavente, J., Cordera, R., Echániz, E., González, F., … & Sañudo, R. (2020). Effects of the COVID-19 lockdown on urban mobility: Empirical evidence from the city of Santander (Spain). *Sustainability, 12*(9), 3870.

Audretsch, D. B., Cunningham, J. A., Kuratko, D. F., Lehmann, E. E., & Menter, M. (2019). Entrepreneurial ecosystems: Economic, technological, and societal impacts. *The Journal of Technology Transfer, 44*(2), 313–325.

Auerswald, P. P. (2015). *Enabling entrepreneurial ecosystems.* Ewing Marion Kauffman Foundation.

Beech, N., & Anseel, F. (2020). COVID-19 and its impact on management research and education: Threats, opportunities and a manifesto. *British Journal of Management, 31*(3), 447.

Bjørkdahl, K., & Carlsen, B. (2019). Introduction: Pandemics, publics, and politics—staging responses to public health crises. In *Pandemics, publics, and politics* (pp. 1–9). Springer.

Caligiuri, P., De Cieri, H., Minbaeva, D., Verbeke, A., & Zimmermann, A. (2020). International HRM insights for navigating the COVID-19 pandemic: Implications for future research and practice. *Journal of International Business Studies, 51*(5), 697–713.

Carniel, T., & Dalle, J. (2020). Towards entrepreneurial ecosystem indicators: Speed and acceleration. arXiv Preprint arXiv:2006.14313.

Castro, A., & Farmer, P. (2005). Understanding and addressing AIDS-related stigma: From anthropological theory to clinical practice in Haiti. *American Journal of Public Health, 95*(1), 53–59.

Cavallo, A., Ghezzi, A., & Balocco, R. (2019). Entrepreneurial ecosystem research: Present debates and future directions. *International Entrepreneurship and Management Journal, 15*(4), 1291–1321.

Cavallo, A., Ghezzi, A., & Sanasi, S. (2021). Assessing entrepreneurial ecosystems through a strategic value network approach: Evidence from the San Francisco Area. *Journal of Small Business and Enterprise Development,*

Chakraborty, I., & Maity, P. (2020). COVID-19 outbreak: Migration, effects on society, global environment and prevention. *Science of the Total Environment, 728*, 138882.

Chang, C., McAleer, M., & Wong, W. (2020). Risk and financial management of COVID-19 in business, economics and finance. *Journal of Risk and Financial Management, 13*(5), 102.

Coccia, M. (2021). The relation between length of lockdown, numbers of infected people and deaths of Covid-19, and economic growth of countries: Lessons learned to cope with future pandemics similar to Covid-19 and to constrain the deterioration of economic system. *Science of the Total Environment, 775*, 145801.

Cohen, B. (2006). Sustainable valley entrepreneurial ecosystems. *Business Strategy and the Environment, 15*(1), 1–14.

Colombo, M. G., Dagnino, G. B., Lehmann, E. E., & Salmador, M. (2019). The governance of entrepreneurial ecosystems. *Small Business Economics, 52*(2), 419–428.

Davison, R. M. (2020). The transformative potential of disruptions: A viewpoint. *International Journal of Information Management, 55*, 102149.

Feast, V., & Bretag, T. (2005). Responding to crises in transnational education: New challenges for higher education. *Higher Education Research & Development, 24*(1), 63–78.

Fotiadis, A., Polyzos, S., & Huan, T. T. (2021). The good, the bad and the ugly on COVID-19 tourism recovery. *Annals of Tourism Research, 87*, 103117.

Gössling, S., Scott, D., & Hall, C. M. (2020). Pandemics, tourism and global change: A rapid assessment of COVID-19. *Journal of Sustainable Tourism, 29*(1), 1–20.

Gretzel, U., Fuchs, M., Baggio, R., Hoepken, W., Law, R., Neidhardt, J., Pesonen, J., Zanker, M., & Xiang, Z. (2020). e-Tourism beyond COVID-19: A call for transformative research. *Information Technology & Tourism, 22*(2), 187–203.

Haarhaus, T., Strunk, G., & Liening, A. (2020). Assessing the complex dynamics of entrepreneurial ecosystems: A nonstationary approach. *Journal of Business Venturing Insights, 14*, e00194.

Hausmann, R., & Nedelkoska, L. (2018). Welcome home in a crisis: Effects of return migration on the non-migrants' wages and employment. *European Economic Review, 101*, 101–132.

Heaton, S., Siegel, D. S., & Teece, D. J. (2019). Universities and innovation ecosystems: A dynamic capabilities perspective. *Industrial and Corporate Change, 28*(4), 921–939.

Higgins-Desbiolles, F. (2020). Socialising tourism for social and ecological justice after COVID-19. *Tourism Geographies, 22*(3), 610–623.

Klapper, L., & Love, I. (2011). The impact of the financial crisis on new firm registration. *Economics Letters, 113*(1), 1–4.

Malecki, E. J. (2011). Connecting local entrepreneurial ecosystems to global innovation networks: Open innovation, double networks and knowledge integration. *International Journal of Entrepreneurship and Innovation Management, 14*(1), 36–59.

Malecki, E. J. (2018). Entrepreneurship and entrepreneurial ecosystems. *Geography Compass, 12*(3), e12359.

Maritz, A., Perenyi, A., De Waal, G., & Buck, C. (2020). Entrepreneurship as the unsung hero during the current COVID-19 economic crisis: Australian perspectives. *Sustainability, 12*(11), 4612.

Maroufkhani, P., Wagner, R., & Ismail, W. K. W. (2018). Entrepreneurial ecosystems: A systematic review. *Journal of Enterprising Communities: People and Places in the Global Economy.*

Muldoon, J., Bauman, A., & Lucy, C. (2018). Entrepreneurial ecosystem: Do you trust or distrust? *Journal of Enterprising Communities: People and Places in the Global Economy,*

Nambisan, S., & Baron, R. A. (2013). Entrepreneurship in innovation ecosystems: Entrepreneurs' self–regulatory processes and their implications for new venture success. *Entrepreneurship Theory and Practice, 37*(5), 1071–1097.

Peris-Ortiz, M., Fuster-Estruch, V., & Devece-Carañana, C. (2014). Entrepreneurship and innovation in a context of crisis. In *Entrepreneurship, innovation and economic crisis* (pp. 1–10). Springer.

Roundy, P. T., & Fayard, D. (2019). Dynamic capabilities and entrepreneurial ecosystems: The micro-foundations of regional entrepreneurship. *The Journal of Entrepreneurship, 28*(1), 94–120.

Shepherd, D. A., & Patzelt, H. (2015). Harsh evaluations of entrepreneurs who fail: The role of sexual orientation, use of environmentally friendly technologies, and observers' perspective taking. *Journal of Management Studies, 52*(2), 253–284.

Sigala, M. (2020). Tourism and COVID-19: Impacts and implications for advancing and resetting industry and research. *Journal of Business Research, 117*, 312–321.

Skandalis, K. S., & Ghazzawi, I. A. (2014). Immigration and entrepreneurship in Greece: Factors influencing and shaping entrepreneurship establishments by immigrants. *International Journal of Entrepreneurship, 18*, 77.

Stam, E. (2018). Measuring entrepreneurial ecosystems. In *Entrepreneurial ecosystems* (pp. 173–197). Springer.

Stam, E., & Van de Ven, A. (2021). Entrepreneurial ecosystem elements. *Small Business Economics, 56*(2), 809–832.

Suresh, J., & Ramraj, R. (2012). Entrepreneurial ecosystem: Case study on the influence of environmental factors on entrepreneurial success. *European Journal of Business and Management, 4*(16), 95–101.

Surgevil, O., & Akyol, E. M. (2011). Discrimination against people living with HIV/AIDS in the workplace: Turkey context. *Equality, Diversity and Inclusion: An International Journal.*

Tatoglu, E., Frynas, J. G., Bayraktar, E., Demirbag, M., Sahadev, S., Doh, J., & Koh, S. L. (2020). Why do emerging market firms engage in voluntary environmental management practices? A strategic choice perspective. *British Journal of Management, 31*(1), 80–100.

Travel, W., & Council, T. (2020). Economic impact reports. *World Travel and Tourism Council.*

Vegetti, F., & Adăscăliţei, D. (2017). The impact of the economic crisis on latent and early entrepreneurship in Europe. *International Entrepreneurship and Management Journal, 13*(4), 1289–1314.

Welter, F., Baker, T., Audretsch, D. B., & Gartner, W. B. (2017). Everyday entrepreneurship—a call for entrepreneurship research to embrace entrepreneurial diversity. *Entrepreneurship Theory and Practice, 41*(3), 311–321.

Xiong, J., Wang, K., Yan, J., Xu, L., & Huang, H. (2021). The window of opportunity brought by the COVID-19 pandemic: An ill wind blows for digitalisation leapfrogging. *Technology Analysis & Strategic Management*, 1–13.

Chapter Six

Effects of crises on startups—a micro-perspective

- Takeaways
- Micro-perspective—an inward look
- Process/business innovation
- The 'new normal' in the business
- Being prepared for the 'new normal'
- Making the exception routine
- The digitalized entrepreneur
- Summary
- Reflective questions for class

Takeaways

- Tracking the effects of the COVID-19 pandemic on the startup's inner processes
- Delving into the crisis' impact on the 'formation' of the digitalized entrepreneur
- Assessing crises' effects on changes in business models
- Evaluating the opportunities and threats of remote work
- Outlining the new, creative developments in the startups as a function of crises' restrictions
- Embracing agility and openness to new formats and processes developed by the startups' teams vis-à-vis crises' impact

Micro-perspective—an inward look

This chapter is dedicated to the internal dynamics of the startup in times of crisis. It delves into the startup 'black box' by examining the changes in a large array of activities, processes, and relationships inside the business as well as in the attitudes and mindset of the founders and their teams. The vision, strategy, and management, along with social, organizational, and psychological, aspects of startups during a crisis are analyzed through the outlook of businesses' changes and innovation by elucidating the opportunities and threats envisioned in light of the crisis. Examples are provided of startups around the world (e.g., Hausman and Johnston 2014; Giones et al. 2020).

DOI: 10.4324/9781003173809-6

Crises create a 'new normal' that forces the addition of new formats within the known ones due to the crisis' specific conditions; yet, while the proportion of known formats is usually larger than that of the new ones, the COVID-19 pandemic has transformed this balance, such that in some industries, the proportion of new formats has surpassed that of the former known ones, such as in education, communication, and payment, for example, which have changed dramatically due to social distancing.

Embedding the new into the known, be it in technology, organizational structure, or business models, stimulates innovation by either inventing 'something from scratch' or improving the standard and known; it is a typical case of stepping out of one's comfort zone. Many examples prove the impact of crises and the subsequent conditions they create economically, socially, and environmentally, which force companies to redeploy their resources, knowledge, expertise, and business setup to manage the changes or respond to new emerging needs. For example, tea bags were invented before World War I in 1908, when the tea and coffee importer Thomas Sullivan sent customers silk bags of tea as a marketing gimmick. After the war, the modern tea bag was introduced de facto, as it had been intended for easy transfer to soldiers at the front line. The tea example demonstrates the powerful impact of disruptive times in introducing a product: prewar, the gimmick did not evolve into a sought-after product, yet the war triggered its popularity. In addition, the war's push echoes a series of internal changes and improvements taken at the business level to introduce tea bags as a marketable product—changes in vision, production, and marketing as well as engaging the teams to produce new products and change their known work habits or convince them of the inevitability of tea bags entering markets beyond the soldiers' needs to enable the product's application.

Crises and disruptive conditions shake up existing mindsets, customs, norms, and individuals' priorities, and therefore affect market needs, tastes, expectations, and overall, the readiness to either stick with the 'regular and known' or adopt the 'innovative and unknown'. As an example, it was only when HIV had spread in 2001 to more than 28 million people in the world that the landscape entirely changed. HIV was discovered in the Democratic Republic of Congo in around 1920. In the 1980s, it rapidly spread and became a global pandemic; here, mindsets, needs, and openness to new concepts, along with renouncing some traditional views of love and marriage, among others, were pertinent.

Such changes that appear from the outside have both an immediate and continuing impact on the startup's products and services as well as on its internal processes, presenting as both opportunities and threats to the startup's activity; threats, however, do not necessarily result in damage; they can trigger improvements, innovation, and a letting go of the usual or known. Outside changes, especially deriving from situations that are considered disrupting and troublesome, are enforced, unpredictable, and uncontrollable; these have a negative impact on perceptions of other aspects of the startup and overall, on the external world; concurrently, such situations can promote creativity, opportunity exploitation, exploration, and proactivity, exhibited in entrepreneurs' initiatives and actions aimed at managing the situation (Baron 2008; Tang, Kacmar and Busenitz 2012; Dew et al. 2015; Davidsson, Recker and von Briel 2020).

The sources of changes stemming from disruptive effects and the consequent opportunities and threats attached to those changes are exhibited in Table 6.1.

TABLE 6.1 Emerging changes—opportunities and threats

	Opportunity	Threat
New market's needs (e.g., solutions during shutdowns for: older people, students in schools)	• Develop acute solutions • Develop needed, untapped niches • Create new needs, aligned with those articulated by the market	• Confusion between the startup's needs and the customers' needs • Startup's inability to respond/ adequately respond to the needs
New market's expectations (e.g., prompt delivery of goods, more supportive and customized service) since people are tense under crisis	• Develop sustainable, long-lasting products aligned with expectations • Develop service formats that are aligned with expectations • Use various avenues (e.g., online, machine learning, prompt and timely 'push') to satisfy expectations	• Frustration with inability to respond to expectations • Customers' disloyalty/ desertion
Customers' purchasing power decreases; priorities change (e.g., job loss, business closures, health-related costs)	• Produce creative methodologies to monitor the dynamic priorities • Embed web-based use, to reach out to and engage market niches that cannot purchase, but remain engaged with the startup	• Customers purchase only the basics • Prioritization of buying fluctuates and is unexpected • Definitions of necessity and 'nice to have' are blurred
Changes in economic, environmental, social conditions (e.g., unavailability of environmental resources, economic crises, more illness and mortality)	• Seek new technologies, raw material, infrastructures that can be profitable • Scout for new partners who become accessible as conditions change (e.g., celebrities who are no longer working due to shutdowns and cancellation of entertainment events)	• Potential lack of available resources • Competition over resources • Complicated to forecast decisions and plans, as changes are still ongoing

(*Continued*)

	Opportunity	Threat
The inevitability of withdrawing from known habits (e.g., studying in crowded classes, kissing/hugging as a form of greeting)	• Develop substitute products and services, and enlarge the scope of offerings • Leverage the substitute products for new uses and new markets	• Frustration, leading to a negative psychological projection on the startup (e.g., blaming, accusations, mistrust) • Clinging to habits (that must be discarded), thus reluctant to use new products/services
More time to think (e.g., in shelters, hospitals, quarantine)	• Leave the 'comfort zone' to find other avenues for the business, respond with acute solutions, start to study • Entrepreneurship as a new avenue to pursue	• Thoughts can be negative and damaging, and lead to negative emotions
Values change (e.g., doing good, community values, people of color, MeToo movement)	• Values that lead to new mindsets and to the development of products and new mature offerings, to meet the change in values • Market's openness to embracing the new values	• Insufficient market maturation to embrace values associated with doing good • In times of crisis, people can be self-centered and preoccupied with their own problems

Process/business innovation

This innovation, which stems from the disrupted conditions' effects, can be seen in the creation of changes and improvements in the startup's products or services known as the primary activities of their value chain. It can also be seen in the practices, methods, or expertise in the business, which are then revealed in the startup's functions, such as production, manufacturing, UI/UX design, marketing, delivery, and advertising; these are considered secondary activities in the value chain involving process innovation, as these further develop the primary activities. Both products/services and process innovation are manifested in the startup's activity, success, and sustainability. According to Porter's model (1980, 1985), these activities include procurement—the acquisition of resources and material (e.g., prices, suppliers and vendors, inbound logistics), human resource management, attracting the best-suited talent, managing employees effectively, infrastructure, the business' support systems which maintain daily operations, and technology, including equipment, hardware, software, procedures, and technical knowledge. As such, the inner changes can result from a need to support product or service innovation emanating from crises. These changes can then be adopted and serve various uses—not only for applying product/service innovation (Porter 1980, 1985, 1990; Senge 1980).

The history of Kleenex exemplifies inner changes that are secondary activities triggered by a crisis to resolve gaps in needs, expectations, and purchase power. The product Kleenex was visualized during World War I by Kimberly-Clark, a manufacturer that developed crepe paper for use as a gas mask filter; in 1929, this paper was introduced for use as a handkerchief during allergy season, and then colored Kleenex tissues were introduced, followed a year later by printed tissues. In 1932, pocket packs of Kleenex were introduced. That same year, the Kleenex company came up with the phrase "The handkerchief you can throw away!" to use in their advertisements. The case of Kleenex represents full operational and value chain changes to apply an idea derived from the needs associated with war to mass production and delivery. Specifically, crises signify a critical point for decisions at the startup level on embedding innovation in both products/services and processes. In other cases, process innovation is scarcely connected, if at all, to the product/service innovation, standing by itself as an opportunity to be embraced; for example, working from home is an implementation of process innovation that stemmed from COVID-19 restrictions, and it is spreading, even though it was not directly aimed at supporting primary activities.

Implementing changes and innovation is risky, specifically in startups where the offerings are relevant and marketable despite the crisis. Any conversion of a function in the startup's activities, even in the secondary activities or in those considered marginal, can activate a chain reaction and cause unexpected damage to the products/services and to the final offering, resulting in higher than expected costs or internal reluctance to adopt the imposed changes. For example, for startups that scout for innovative solutions to product-related challenges using a 'hands-on' strategy, which requires experimentation and the creation of prototypes, transitioning to artificial intelligence (AI) as a process-related solution for social distancing restrictions can put the product at risk, because procuring information from AI may provide different data quality, a different pace, or different inspected aspects; these, in turn, can increase frustration with the experts in charge, who may then decide not to use the AI, but rather return to prototyping; this will ultimately result in higher-than-expected costs for the startup, as it has paid for the purchase and maintenance of the AI, as well as for the experts' work on these experiments.

Enforced changes brought about by crises can be considered an opportunity or a threat, depending on the viewpoint (Valikangas and Gibbert 2005; Loon, Otaye-Ebede and Stewart 2020; Muñoz, Kimmitt and Dimov 2020; Sohl, Vroom and McCann 2020). To leverage these changes, exposed as either opportunities or threats, internal process development can be activated, as demonstrated in Table 6.2.

TABLE 6.2 Leveraging the changes caused by crises

	Opportunity and threat	Process developments
Procurement		
Opportunity	• Panicked suppliers and vendors are willing to be flexible in negotiations • Need for innovative logistics	• Collaborations and partnerships with rivals • Mergers of suppliers and vendors into the same business (a one-stop shop structure) • Robotics in systems, logistics, machinery, etc., to produce more and cheaper material (which is scarce during crises) • Digitalizing operations
Threat	• Material is scarce and expensive • Aggressive competition for materials and resources	
Human resources		
Opportunity	• Talented people are searching for jobs • Applicants are flexible with respect to work conditions • People are willing to work in distant locations	• New educational and training programs • On-the-job training • Flexible work conditions (payment, working from home, commuting) • Mix of expertise • New roles, new jobs • Governmental and public programs for the unemployed • Working remotely • Recognition of work-life balance concepts
Threat	• Conditions call for letting employees go • Lack of talent (e.g., those who are infected, have lost their homes, are at the front in war situations, have quit their job to take care of their family)	
Infrastructure		
Opportunity	• Support systems need renovating • The ecosystem 'shares' the same problems	• Establish collaborations and partnerships with the ecosystem to share infrastructure • Use virtual means for delivery and financing • Leverage the conditions to renovate and upgrade the infrastructure
Threat	• Mobility and transportation are restricted (i.e., due to quarantine; border closings) • The regular finance system does not apply due to social distancing restrictions	
Technology		
Opportunity	• New technologies emerge • Multiple functions can be digitalized • There is growth in the number of graduates and students in technology	• Offering talented employees the opportunity to gain more technology literacy • Easier to attract talent • Opportunity to reorganize the cyber-related system in the startup
Threat	• Talented employees may feel irrelevant if they are not technologically savvy • Security and privacy are at risk.	

The 'new normal' in the business

Unlike other crises, the sizable impact of the COVID-19 pandemic has created a 'new normal', where the proportion of new working forms has surpassed that of the regular and known ones, unlike crises that preceded it. This 'new normal' has been and still is developing to enable businesses' operation, and is assumed to be a temporary arrangement. However, as the COVID-19 pandemic continues with the emergence of more and more variants, these 'temporary' arrangements are becoming a central and inherent part of the working format. Examples of these arrangements include a higher dependency on delivery for almost any goods and purchases or online payment. World experts predict that some of these 'temporary' arrangements stemming from the pandemic will craft the 'new normal', such that things will never go back to the 'old normal'.

The 'new normal' is a response to global restrictions, mainly social distancing and its effects, although the pandemic has also enforced other restrictions, for example, concerning hygiene, which have not affected the 'new normal' as markedly. Social distancing has created various changes that seemingly occurred 'overnight' and with no preparation. For example, some businesses—and even sectors—were hastily and almost completely eliminated, such as travel, restaurants, the entertainment sector, sporting events, and other businesses in which people gathering together was the core offered experience; at the same time, some business and sectors became compulsory 'overnight', although they had not been prepared for the pace and amount of rising expectations and demand and could not respond to them in a timely and high-quality fashion, such as the delivery sector, online services (e.g., medical counseling, psychological treatment, home sports). In addition, social isolation and distancing deepened the need for internet exposure and operation of almost all of the startups' functions, from attracting clients to recruiting employees online, selling online, and collecting bills virtually.

Digitalization has become a central backbone of the 'new normal'. For most startups, it has become a compulsory sphere of communication as well as of multiple activities and functions. Many startups, drawing on their own technological capabilities, have developed digital tools and applications internally for communication, monitoring, updating, calculating, evaluating, and other functions that provide solutions in times of shutdowns. As a side effect, new opportunities have arisen, for example, connecting with people from other locations and time zones on a regular basis, recording the meetings, and 'daring' to approach the 'unapproachable' people due to open-access digitalization; studies show that celebrities in the pandemic situation, who have been confined to their homes with no prospect of work for some time and harboring fears on how to stay relevant, have started to proactively reach out to their audience, offer their support, help, skills, etc., to keep their presence alive. Vanessa Hudgens, actor and singer, launched a soft drink that contains cactus juice during the pandemic and was quoted as saying: "The situation made us have more of a push and focus on the direct-to-consumer/e-commerce world..."; the singer Rihanna created the Fenty Skin line that supports environmentally friendly packaging and is marketed as gender neutral; actress Cameron Diaz launched a wine label, Avaline; and others have performed acts of kindness for businesses, showing that celebrities are more accessible and have more in common with entrepreneurs.

The 'new normal' has also changed the known occupational stratification. Due to the pandemic fallout, millions of people across the globe have been dismissed from their jobs or have closed their businesses, temporarily or permanently, resulting in a new way of categorizing 'essential' and 'non-essential' jobs and occupations, turning the known and established occupational prestige stratification upside down. Some workers have been deemed 'essential' and others 'redundant', based on the new conditions governed by viral contamination; as such, employees in grocery stores, on garbage trucks, and working as cleaners in hospitals, along with medical doctors, nurses, and scientists in pharmaceutics, have all been labeled 'essential', while university professors, athletes, and some government officials have become 'non-essential' and have been instructed to stay home. Workers in some of the 'unnecessary' jobs and occupations, such as chef, actor, or tour guide, have had to reinvent themselves, as prospects of returning to their old jobs and occupations seem slim. The new categorization is still in progress and does not yet rely on any solid criteria, making it complicated to predict the skills that will be required in the future or labor demand. One putative criterion is a compounded measure of human interactions and physical proximity, for example, medical care, personal care, onsite customer service, leisure, and travel. Occupations that are ranked higher in this compounded measure are the most 'problematic' ones, as the pandemic has reduced both human interactions and physical proximity; these occupations require a dramatic transformation for the 'new normal'. Startups are tackling such transformations through three main points: (a) new products/services for external use—this is an opportunity to develop a marketable 'substitute' for these occupations through technology, new business settings, and creative deployment of resources, among others, as new products/services based on the startup's technology and infrastructure; (b) new products/services for internal use—develop alternatives for the startup's operations and activities that minimize human interactions and maximize physical distance; and (c) creating new businesses as new opportunities emerge.

Being prepared for the 'new normal'

Severe situations allow reevaluating the existing business and working models by inspecting those organizational processes that, through the years, have been operated almost 'automatically', such as the startup's management practices, business models, financial strategies, or marketing approaches and practices while endeavoring to adjust these processes to a new and still threatening reality. The 'new normal' is not a generic concept; practices that have changed or are about to change due to the pandemic's effects will probably not be equally effective for all startups; rather, the 'new normal' refers to the unique practices, strategies, and even mindsets that each startup is adjusting to, hence echoing the startup's unique ecosystem, culture, sector, business development, embedded technology, and many other components. Once a 'matrix' of measures is generated for the 'new normal' in a specific startup, then it can be disseminated to other businesses with similar characteristics with some adaptations.

Making the exception routine

The flow of the COVID-19 pandemic is typified by frequent scenarios of variant outbreaks in different locations worldwide, followed by relatively quiet times when the number of infected is mitigated regionally by the use of newly developed vaccines and medications and restrictions involving social distancing and mask-wearing; this flow gives value to embracing the exception as a way of life. Startups are used to an unstable, erratic life course; yet, the pandemic has exposed entrepreneurs to a different type of instability that is not directly associated to their startup's activity, yet affects its achievements, profits, and prospects in various aspects; these can be resonated in the product's relevance to its stakeholders, including customers, users, supporters, etc., in the marketing strategies or in the avenues taken to recruit experts. For example, a startup located in London, UK, is in the midst of developing a secure way to communicate virtually through a unique, smart technology; it is mainly aimed for psychologists, consultants, and therapists to give them and their clients a protected space where services can be provided in times of closures and quarantines. While the demand for such virtual services during the pandemic is on the rise, it is not known whether the need will endure; in the case of a complete cure for COVID-19, patients may favor returning to face-to-face sessions, and the relevance of the product will decrease. In such cases, the customary tools, such as market research, feasibility tests, or analyses of current trends, may be useless in the face of the pandemic's erratic flow. Making the exception routine would mean preparing for different scenarios in the startup's operations, such as technology use, or in the target users; these preparations would be conducted while developing the technology for its original use, in tandem. In normal times, the prevailing business models (e.g., Osterwalder et al. 2011; Reis 2011; Maurya 2012; Blank 2013; Blank and Euchner 2018) would lead entrepreneurs to operate the business following a lean model: to focus on and be engaged in a goal and to accomplish it.

Crises change business models, plans, and routines. But while most of the business' preparedness is geared toward 'returning to normal', the COVID-19 pandemic has exposed businesses to a need to prepare for an ever-changing environment and a seemingly infinite sequence of crises. As such, strategies seeking to curtail exposure to potential deviations from normal business operations once the crisis has hit or strategies aimed at pinpointing the business activities that can be saved from the crisis' damage are only part of the preparation needed to face the pandemic's flow (Ritchie 2004; Clauss 2017; Foss and Saebi 2017; Clauss et al. 2019; Kraus et al. 2020; Pedersen, Ritter and Di Benedetto 2020; Ritter and Pedersen 2020).

Application of business models in a startup enforces identification of the value proposition and the creation of a valid value for any situation, including in crises. However, as crises are unpredictable and develop in unexpected stages, the value creation can be puzzling. Constantly changing the business model will prevent the business from evolving properly, as it will be more engaged in changing than in developing and evolving. Hence, in times of crisis, the changes aimed at creating the business' value will be made to some of the business model's components or to finding alternative ways to tie them together so as to constantly create value while adapting to the crisis' changes; for example, digitalizing the marketing efforts (i.e., one component) or linking the marketing activities to technology (i.e., an alternative link between components). A complex change during a crisis of the entire architecture of the business model would be risky and resource consuming. Changes in components of a business model stem from tackling the environmental challenges; concurrently, any changes at the business level can create a sequence of dynamic changes in the environment (e.g., Chesbrough 2007, 2010; Giesen et al. 2010; Wirtz, Schilke and Ullrich 2010; Lee, Olson and Trimi 2012; De Reuver, Bouwman and Haaker 2013; Foss and Saebi 2017). The COVID-19 pandemic posed new challenges in this respect, as the business models changed from the "...architecture for product, service and information flows, including a description of the various business actors and their roles" (Timmers 1998, p. 4) to "...a set of expectations about how the business will be successful in its environment" (Downing 2005, p. 186), and then to a new conceptualization that combines questioning their own expectations' relevance and significance to the changing environment with new mindsets of agility and acceptance to starting over at any stage of the business (Battiliana et al. 2012; Lahindah et al. 2020; Rodrigues and de Noronha 2021).

At-a-Glance—Carb-Free*

Isla, Esme, and Graham, co-founders of a startup in the UK, exploited the opportunities introduced by the COVID-19 crisis and engaged in "re-calculating and changing our startup's processes," according to Isla. The three young co-founders started a project in an accelerator in the UK to measure carbon emissions through smart techniques, such as big data and real-time data ingestion for analytical processing and to enable businesses to make timely operational decisions based on their tracked emissions. Their technology and offerings attracted the interest of various companies. "Then COVID-19 came, and our partners had more crucial topics to take care of," said Isla, yet, the interest was still there and the customers reassured Carb-Free that they would use their products. The co-founders decided to 'make the best' of this disrupted situation; they inserted chatbots to respond to basic customer queries. "It was Esme's idea. She pushed us to take advantage of the thriving of AI during the pandemic, to try in our internal processes; then we may embed it in our products," said Isla. As a result, Carb-Free could sustain its relationships with existing customers and attract some others with the help of the chatbots; it was also 'fun' for the employees who worked at home during lockdowns to develop scenarios for the chatbot.

The digitalized entrepreneur

Digitalization is considered a valuable option for harmonizing with regular face-to-face settings; the pandemic switched conditions by turning the non-usual formats and processes into the main ones, sometimes as the only alternative to keeping the startup's wheels in motion. Digitalization was traditionally employed to shorten time and distance spans; then, as the web introduced common applications free of charge, it became a means of saving costs, for example, connections through e-mails or video calls were less expensive than travel or using landline telephones; digital payments reduced the costs associated with waiting in long lines or parking problems; and marketing online reduced the regular marketing- and advertising-related costs. Yet, until the COVID-19 pandemic, digitalization was recognized as a supplement to the startup's full range of activities, as it provided only a partial experience, compressed into unidimensional, screen-based vision and hearing. The digital experience ignored the other senses, as technology could not yet embed them in its new developments (the sense of smell, touch or taste, for example), thus leaving those functions that require using the ignored senses behind. As an example, introducing a new taste, such as umami, was impossible in crises involving isolation and working from home, as the technology could not capture the function of taste digitally. In addition, even sight and hearing were restricted by the technology's capacity; for example, using the improved cloud-based video conferencing services for virtual meetings enabled seeing the participants from specific angles with a few moves and gestures and the quality of the voice could fluctuate, among others. Digitalization was optional and an add-on to the real, full experience of communication, meeting, socializing, learning in face-to-face physical encounters. The digitalized entrepreneur has to 'squeeze' the startup's experiences, activities, and processes to fit the screen.

In times of crises such as the COVID-19 pandemic, digitalization has enabled the startup to keep its operations in motion. In many countries, and for a long time during the pandemic, digitalization was, in fact, the only means of doing so. Digitalization has spread into various areas (see Figure 6.1).

As demonstrated in Figure 6.1, the digitalized entrepreneur operates a complex, compounded matrix comprised of an array of performances/activities (e.g., communication,

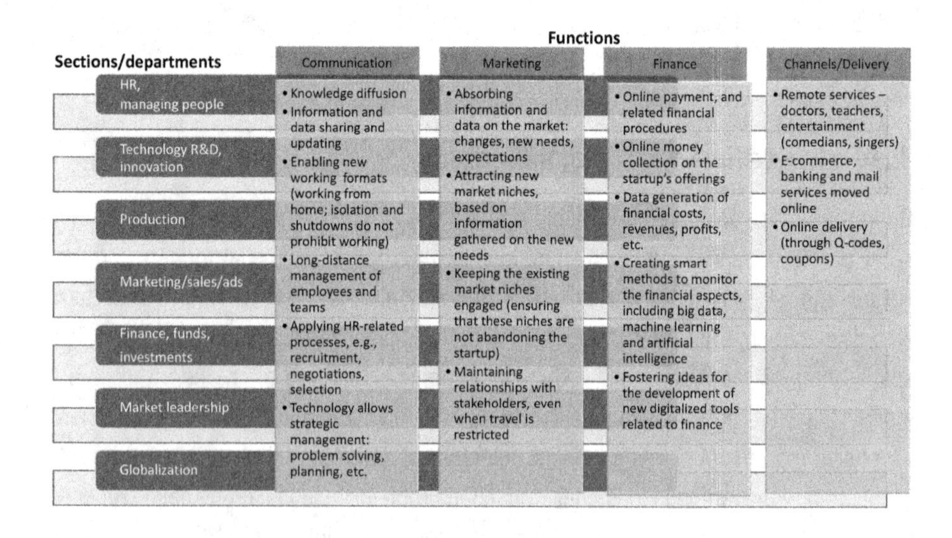

FIGURE 6.1 The digitalized startup: functions and sections

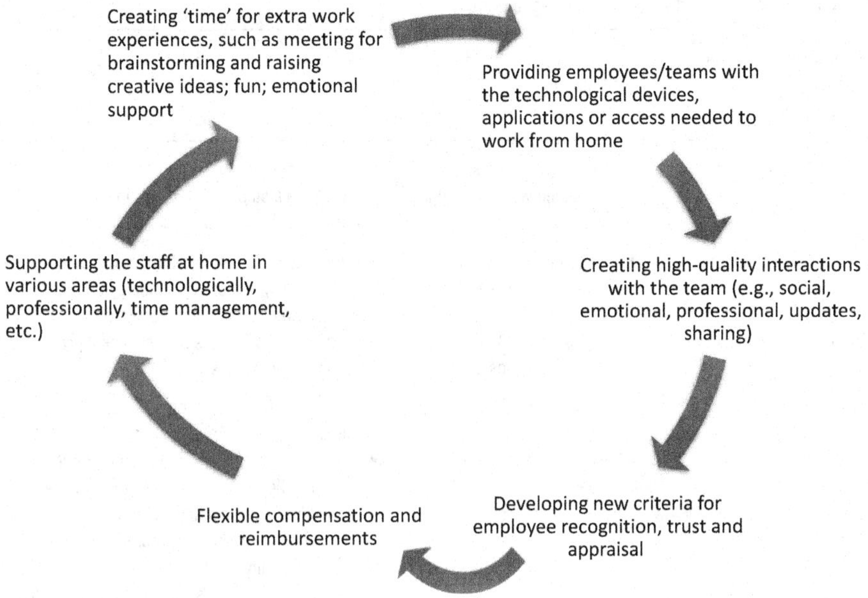

Creating 'time' for extra work experiences, such as meeting for brainstorming and raising creative ideas; fun; emotional support

Providing employees/teams with the technological devices, applications or access needed to work from home

Creating high-quality interactions with the team (e.g., social, emotional, professional, updates, sharing)

Developing new criteria for employee recognition, trust and appraisal

Flexible compensation and reimbursements

Supporting the staff at home in various areas (technologically, professionally, time management, etc.)

FIGURE 6.2 Enablers of hybrid work arrangements

marketing, finance) combined with an array of the startup's functions/departments (e.g., managing people, technology, production), which are consequently broken down into multiple business activities, business models' expertise, and operational processes. It is therefore imperative to detect the enablers of hybrid work arrangements (Figure 6.2).

Operating digitalized processes in a large range of the startup's spheres requires different efforts, recapitulated in Table 6.3.

Digitalization can evolve into positive or negative outcomes for the startup in either its offerings or its daily operation; it can stimulate innovation, new ways of tackling challenges, cheaper operation, expanded globalization and dissemination, and more prompt, cheaper, or clear-cut procedures for production, delivery, or payment; in short, it can produce higher effectiveness coupled with lower costs and larger dissemination and exposure.

The internet has created *affordability*: the perception of a 'here and now' and the complementary applications enabling immediate purchase, delivery, and communicating the acquisition are all available free of charge, thus providing an illusion that anything can be had just by sitting at the computer. Reciprocally, startups have gained from their digitalized behavior by capturing markets that have fueled them and pushed them into

TABLE 6.3 Managing the crisis through digitalization

Processes (e.g., functions, activities, departments, expertise)	Technology to enable process digitalization	Efforts required by the startup
Existing processes	• Existing processes are sustained with no change	• No change • Keeping a stable, firm 'place' in the dynamically changing startup
Adjusting existing processes	• Existing processes are crucial, but the existing technology is unable to support them; thus, changes in the processes are required	• Adjustments in the startup's processes • Planning of further adjustments in associated or contingent activities • Agility and openness to change and pivoting from original plans
Creating new processes	• Existing technology is unable to transfer the value of existing processes	• Innovate! Developing new processes, functions, activities, etc. • Securing resources, expertise, infrastructure, etc. for the development of new processes • Convincing internal and external stakeholders of these new processes' value or inevitability • Training the startup's stakeholders in how to operate the new processes • Using existing material, infrastructure, machinery, to create new processes • Reorganizing existing processes to create new ones
Renouncing existing processes	• Existing technology cannot support existing processes, or requires too many resources to adjust the existing processes or technology	• Resilience – in 'letting go' of processes that can no longer be operated • Deployment of resources to compensate for the loss of existing processes

superpowerful startups, evolving into companies such as Facebook, Apple, and Amazon; these companies have become extremely influential, eliminating the competition and producing innovation and regulations. As digitalization becomes more substantial in times of crisis, both the perception or illusion of affordability and the emergence of putative superpower startups increase. These avenues may lead to some negative effects of the dependence on digitalization, both technology- and non-technology-based. Possible effects of the enhanced digital presence on the startup are summarized in Table 6.4 (Tarafdar et al. 2007; Galluch, Grover and Thatcher 2015; Maier et al. 2015; Nambisan 2017; Fossen and Sorgner 2021; Gimpel and Schmied 2019; Vasilev et al. 2020).

TABLE 6.4 Negative and positive effects of digitalization on various levels of the startup

Positive effects			Negative effects		
Individual	Team	Organization	Individual	Team	Organization
Feeling a connection while isolated/in quarantine, or distant from other people at work	Better teamwork communication and more frequent updates	Gaining more data; transforming data to big data, and gaining profound insights on various aspects	Use of shorthand in language; compact communication; use of signs, emojis instead of words to express feelings, and to compensate for language differences	Getting used to a 'robotic' style of teamwork; no emotions, feelings or 'small talk' in the team's virtual dynamics	Technology-related effects: spam, malware, hacking, violation of digital property rights
New ways of communicating with internal and external stakeholders		Enhancing the visibility of the startup (e.g., sales channels)	Superficial communication; fewer deep and detailed brainstorming sessions through digital tools		Non-technological, malicious use of the internet: online theft, cyberbullying, supporting delinquents; making it easier to commit crimes
A sense of self-accomplishment and higher resilience in operating technological tools and applications	Closer proximity to the customer (e.g., engagement, prompt adjustments, constant improvements)		Distress due to lack of human contact; mounting rates of depression; addiction	Complex algorithms that are beyond human understanding and control can cause damage; information's sources are unknown, there is a lack of accountability	
Improved work conditions; enabling a work-life balance	Encouraging innovation! Development of new products and services; making use of technology for higher effectiveness		Privacy of individuals and teams is negatively affected; personal attacks		Hostile effects on the interactions among organizations, as startups that use more machine learning have more information on competitors and can eliminate them
Opportunity to gain digital skills and functional literacy to use electronic devices and applications	Providing stakeholders with affordable and widespread access to the startup's activity and offerings				

Summary

Pandemics as well as other types of crises impose new realities on businesses. In the case of startups, which are used to changing, dynamic, and unexpected scenarios at the outset, such new realities are deemed ordinary and expected. Startups embrace agility, tolerance, and acceptance of change, and more naturally pivot and alter internal processes compared to other types of businesses. Yet, the COVID-19 pandemic introduced a dynamic that confronted startup founders with new challenges, calling for a fresh look to identify, demarcate, and then plan how to manage them. These included reevaluating the market's needs, such as marketing or purchase during shutdowns; the market's expectations, such as being prepared for prompt delivery of goods or for a more supportive and customized service; and the 'known habits', for example, businesses that were contingent on getting together physically needed to reorganize their processes and activity. Values changed, which required startups to embed or strengthen new concepts of 'doing good' or community values. Startups turned some of those dramatic changes into opportunities; yet, each such potential opportunity, which could result in failure and was therefore deemed risky, compelled restructuring the inner business' processes and activities and redeploying resources to manage the changes.

One of the most substantial adaptations was the move to digitalization for each of the business' aspects, that is, communication, marketing, finance, channeling, delivery, and more, across all sections and departments; necessitating management of the existing processes by sustaining, adjusting, or renouncing processes as well as creating new ones, all requiring a substantial learning and assimilation period.

The 'new normal' is starting to be recognized as a customized rather than generic concept. It does not encompass a 'template' of the dos and don'ts; instead, it is a conceptual skeleton that *enables* continual change through planned arrangements at the business level due to crisis scenarios, now and in the future.

Reflective questions for class

1. A new startup in clean tech that saves energy for lighting, cooling/heating, etc., was gaining attention from governmental associations until the pandemic broke out. Then the founders noticed that gradually the teams were becoming distressed due to lack of human contact; there was hostility in the interactions with partners and there was malicious technology and malware.

   a. Explain the new 'phenomena' based on the chapter's content.
   b. Provide two to three recommendations to the founders on how to manage the situation.

2. A startup using augmented reality (AR) to improve brands' product visualization was located in a country that was frequently declared a 'Red Zone', and therefore the activity was adjusted so that the work could be done from home. The core activity of this startup is based on creativity, ideation, and the 'extra vibe' that is sparked through interactions between the teams at work; digitalization is extinguishing this spark, and the competitive advantage of the startup lies in its creativity. Provide three to four suggestions on how to manage this challenge.
3. Three co-workers of an international company quit their jobs to start a new business dealing with a breakthrough in homomorphic encryption that enables sharing confidential data with privacy and security. Due to the crisis situation, they are wondering 'what they should take into consideration' in starting their business for the best fit with the exceptional situation where everything is constantly changing. Suggest two to three ways to start a business in this field to guarantee their success.
4. Search the internet for an entrepreneurial business that is *not* technological and seems to make only light use of digitalization. Describe the business and its surroundings (e.g., country, sector, competition). List three to four statements on the benefits of digitalization for this business in times of crisis. Explain your answer.
5. Maria and Doreen are scientists who have developed a platform for building decentralized applications for peer-to-peer connectivity in dataset sharing for academic research. Based on the emerging changes—opportunities and threats—introduced in this chapter (Table 6.1), list two to three opportunities and two to three threats relevant to their business. Explain your answer.

References

Baron, R. A. (2008). The role of affect in the entrepreneurial process. *Academy of Management Review, 33*(2), 328–340.

Battiliana, J., Lee, M., Walker, J., & Dorsey, C. (2012). In search of the hybrid ideal.

Blank, S. (2013). Why the lean start-up changes everything. *Harvard Business Review, 91*(5), 63–72.

Blank, S., & Euchner, J. (2018). The genesis and future of Lean Startup: An interview with Steve Blank. *Research-Technology Management, 61*(5), 15–21.

Chesbrough, H. (2010). Business model innovation: Opportunities and barriers. *Long Range Planning, 43*(2–3), 354–363.

Clauss, T. (2017). Measuring business model innovation: Conceptualization, scale development, and proof of performance. *R&D Management, 47*(3), 385–403.

Clauss, T., Abebe, M., Tangpong, C., & Hock, M. (2019). Strategic agility, business model innovation, and firm performance: An empirical investigation. *IEEE Transactions on Engineering Management, 68*(3), 767–784.

Davidsson, P., Recker, J., & von Briel, F. (2020). External enablement of new venture creation: A framework. *Academy of Management Perspectives, 34*(3), 311–332.

De Reuver, M., Bouwman, H., & Haaker, T. (2013). Business model roadmapping: A practical approach to come from an existing to a desired business model. *International Journal of Innovation Management, 17*(01), 1340006.

Dew, N., Grichnik, D., Mayer-Haug, K., Read, S., & Brinckmann, J. (2015). Situated entrepreneurial cognition. *International Journal of Management Reviews, 17*(2), 143–164.

Downing, S. (2005). The social construction of entrepreneurship: Narrative and dramatic processes in the coproduction of organizations and identities. *Entrepreneurship Theory and Practice, 29*(2), 185–204.

Foss, N. J., & Saebi, T. (2017). Fifteen years of research on business model innovation: How far have we come, and where should we go? *Journal of Management, 43*(1), 200–227.

Fossen, F. M., & Sorgner, A. (2021). Digitalization of work and entry into entrepreneurship. *Journal of Business Research, 125*, 548–563.

Galluch, P. S., Grover, V., & Thatcher, J. B. (2015). Interrupting the workplace: Examining stressors in an information technology context. *Journal of the Association for Information Systems, 16*(1), 2.

Gibbert, M. (2005). Boundary-setting strategies for escaping innovation traps. *MIT Sloan Management Review, 46*(3), 58.

Giesen, E., Riddleberger, E., Christner, R., & Bell, R. (2010). When and how to innovate your business model. *Strategy & Leadership.*

Gimpel, H., & Schmied, F. (2019). Risks and side effects of digitalization: A multi-level taxonomy of the adverse effects of using digital technologies and media.

Giones, F., Brem, A., Pollack, J. M., Michaelis, T. L., Klyver, K., & Brinckmann, J. (2020). Revising entrepreneurial action in response to exogenous shocks: Considering the COVID-19 pandemic. *Journal of Business Venturing Insights, 14*, e00186.

Hausman, A., & Johnston, W. J. (2014). The role of innovation in driving the economy: Lessons from the global financial crisis. *Journal of Business Research, 67*(1), 2720–2726.

Kimmitt, J., & Dimov, D. (2020). The recursive interplay of capabilities and constraints amongst microfinance entrepreneurs. *International Journal of Entrepreneurial Behavior & Research.*

Kraus, S., Clauss, T., Breier, M., Gast, J., Zardini, A., & Tiberius, V. (2020). The economics of COVID-19: Initial empirical evidence on how family firms in five European countries cope with the corona crisis. *International Journal of Entrepreneurial Behavior & Research.*

Lahindah, L., Sudirman, I., Bahri, R., & Rahmatillah, I. (2020). Facing the new normal by increasing company performance with orientation on innovation, entrepreneurship and creativity. *Management Science Letters, 10*(16), 4033–4038.

Lee, S. M., Olson, D. L., & Trimi, S. (2012). Co-innovation: Convergenomics, collaboration, and co-creation for organizational values. *Management Decision.*

Loon, M., Otaye-Ebede, L., & Stewart, J. (2020). Thriving in the new normal: The HR microfoundations of capabilities for business model innovation. An integrated literature review. *Journal of Management Studies, 57*(3), 698–726.

Maier, C., Laumer, S., Weinert, C., & Weitzel, T. (2015). The effects of technostress and switching stress on discontinued use of social networking services: A study of Facebook use. *Information Systems Journal, 25*(3), 275–308.

Maurya, A. (2012). *Running lean: Iterate from plan A to a plan that works.* Lean.

Nambisan, S. (2017). Digital entrepreneurship: Toward a digital technology perspective of entrepreneurship. *Entrepreneurship Theory and Practice, 41*(6), 1029–1055.

Osterwalder, A., Pigneur, Y., Oliveira, M. A. Y., & Ferreira, J. J. P. (2011). Business model generation: A handbook for visionaries, game changers and challengers. *African Journal of Business Management, 5*(7), 22–30.

Pedersen, C. L., Ritter, T., & Di Benedetto, C. A. (2020). Managing through a crisis: Managerial implications for business-to-business firms. *Industrial Marketing Management, 88*, 314.

Porter, M. E. (1980). Industry structure and competitive strategy: Keys to profitability. *Financial Analysts Journal, 36*(4), 30–41.

Porter, M. E. (1990). The competitive advonioge of notions. *Harvard Business Review, 73*, 91.

Porter, M. E., & Millar, V. E. (1985). *How information gives you competitive advantage.*

Reis, E. (2011). The lean startup. *New York: Crown Business, 27*, 2016–2020.

Ritchie, B. W. (2004). Chaos, crises and disasters: A strategic approach to crisis management in the tourism industry. *Tourism Management, 25*(6), 669–683.

Ritter, T., & Pedersen, C. L. (2020). Analyzing the impact of the coronavirus crisis on business models. *Industrial Marketing Management, 88*, 214–224.

Rodrigues, C. D., & de Noronha, Matheus Eurico Soares. (2021). What companies can learn from unicorn startups to overcome the COVID-19 crisis. *Innovation & Management Review.*

Senge, P. M. (1980). A system dynamics approach to investment-function formulation and testing. *Socio-Economic Planning Sciences, 14*(6), 269–280.

Sohl, T., McCann, B. T., & Vroom, G. (2020). The transmission of economic shocks in multidivisional firms: A capabilities-based view. Paper presented at the *Academy of Management Proceedings, 2020*(1) 16591.

Tang, J., Kacmar, K. M. M., & Busenitz, L. (2012). Entrepreneurial alertness in the pursuit of new opportunities. *Journal of Business Venturing, 27*(1), 77–94.

Tarafdar, M., Tu, Q., Ragu-Nathan, B. S., & Ragu-Nathan, T. S. (2007). The impact of technostress on role stress and productivity. *Journal of Management Information Systems, 24*(1), 301–328.

Timmers, P. (1998). Business models for electronic markets. *Electronic Markets, 8*(2), 3–8.

Vasilev, V. L., Gapsalamov, A. R., Akhmetshin, E. M., Bochkareva, T. N., Yumashev, A. V., & Anisimova, T. I. (2020). Digitalization peculiarities of organizations: A case study. *Entrepreneurship and Sustainability Issues, 7*(4), 3173.

Wirtz, B. W., Schilke, O., & Ullrich, S. (2010). Strategic development of business models: Implications of the Web 2.0 for creating value on the internet. *Long Range Planning, 43*(2–3), 272–290.

Chapter Seven
Strategy, preparation, and design

- Takeaways
- Introduction
- Startups design the action in the face of crises
- Startup management's assessment of the situation
- Cognitive heuristics
- Designing the strategy
- The focus of preparation
- Decision-making in times of crisis
- Crisis preparedness
- Designing the required capabilities
- Summary
- Reflective questions for class

Takeaways

- Understanding the importance of preparing and designing a crisis management strategy; entrepreneurs tend to consider themselves 'natural experts' in crisis management due to startups' normal development through crises, but they are accustomed to specific crises
- Acknowledging that crisis situations are differently interpreted by entrepreneurs depending on their approach to the crisis as a stressful situation, a threat or opportunity, and the perspective of time
- Identifying the stakeholders' expectations from the startup to be included in the design for a crisis management strategy; customizing the design accordingly
- Gearing up the capabilities required to design the framework of the crisis management strategy
- Being attentive to cognitive heuristics and biases, being open to other interpretations of the situation, and being prepared to let go of these heuristics, especially the ones risking the startup in disruptive times

DOI: 10.4324/9781003173809-7

- Being clear and up-front in designing the framework of the crisis management strategy so that the employees know, accept, and are trained for their responsibilities in the crisis
- Continually analyzing, adjusting, and refining the designed crisis management strategy, with concomitant internal communication to keep the team updated

Introduction

Between the outbreak of a disruptive, external event and the startup's coping strategies, there is a 'valley' replete with different approaches, attitudes, and subsequent actions, which should be more thoroughly decoded because they are important to the startup's effective management and coping with the disruption. Generally, the startup's senior management—the founders, CEO, members of the board of directors—recognizes and identifies conditions, situations, or even an episode that may interrupt regular activity in the environment, market, or ecosystem in ways that will markedly affect the specific startup's activity and that will need to be tackled and managed to mitigate or avoid the consequent potential difficulties.

Although startups evolve in crises, those crises tend to be 'tailored' to the specific startup's business models (e.g., competition, difficulties in attracting investments, difficulties in recruiting the best experts). External crises, however, are more generic in nature and more widespread (e.g., health-related situations that affect many people, natural disasters that affect innocent people, or financial crises that create hardship for the market as a whole). With external crises, the startup needs to pivot its crisis management strategy to a new one that will address the unfamiliar crisis. Any unfamiliar situation creates a 'valley' of mixed information, news, rumors, and narratives with fluctuating levels of validity and reliability, which are then translated by the startup's management into a call for action.

This chapter probes this 'valley' to identify the dynamics in the startup when the crisis is 'out there' affecting the startup's routines and threatening to keep on impeding the startup's course of action, and discusses the avenues taken by startups to structure their strategies and preparations to manage such crises.

Startups design the action in the face of crises

When events are recognized as crises, their economic, social, and political impact on the market has already been revealed regionally, nationally, or globally and the repercussions of the crisis are known. In such cases, the startup has several alternative avenues to tackle the situation, as shown in Table 7.1. The startup's founders react emotionally

TABLE 7.1 Startups' approaches to disruptive events

	Less stressful	*More stressful*
Maintaining the routine	Business as usual	Embrace the routine[1]
Strategies for adjusting to the crisis	Misery likes company[2]	Stay awake, remain vigilant[3]

in two dimensions: the personal dimension, embodying personal stress, worries, fear of the potential threats, and nervousness; and the 'parental' dimension, referring to entrepreneurs' eagerness to protect the business, the employees, and the processes. These dimensions lead to two different approaches to tackling the crisis: first, by locating it on the line between a temporary difficult episode and a long and most disruptive situation; and second, by choosing strategies that range from sticking to the routine to revising and reordering the business' focus to manage the crisis.

- Business as usual—a crisis is a crisis de facto when it is treated as a crisis; some entrepreneurs may either ignore the disruptive situation or decide to reframe it as a temporary inconvenience, making it less stressful; accordingly, they do not see any reason to change their business' course of action from the planned and already activated. Embracing this approach allows the startup to gain a competitive advantage, as resources and projects are targeted to continue with the business' plans, while most of their competitors are probably pivoting from their regular activity to respond to the crisis' effects. In addition, following this approach enables entrepreneurs to show the image of a resilient startup to both inside and outside stakeholders, and affirms the customers', investors', and employees' loyalty when 'things go back to normal', based on their trust that this is a healthy and trustworthy startup.
- Misery likes company—some entrepreneurs do not place much weight on the adversity brought about by a crisis and they do not deem the situation to be stressful; yet, they are aware of its complex, unpredictable flow, prompting the ecosystem around them to respond to the crisis in various ways that can change the rules of the game. Under this approach, though not stressed by the situation, entrepreneurs will engage in a crisis management strategy and reassemble their resources, expertise, technology, etc., toward responding to the crisis, both to be prepared once the changes implemented in the ecosystem do affect their startup and to fit in, be part of the situation, rather than be considered outsiders that are unaware of the fallout or are overconfident as regards the crisis' impact.
- Embrace the routine—entrepreneurs may experience high levels of stress due to the encountered crisis and manage it by carrying on with their startup's activity

and embracing the routine. This approach can signify a kind of a 'transitional situation'[4] represented by sticking with the well recognized and known, including known people, projects, organizational processes, and business practices. Aligned with the attachment theory (Winnicott 1986), following known situations provides a source of comfort and enables processing anxieties and concerns, and moving on to action rather than distrusting the situation, that is, the crisis effects and consequently freezing.

- Stay awake, remain vigilant—high stress levels can accompany entrepreneurs' enhanced action of 'arming themselves' with strategies that can respond to the encountered adversity. In practice, this approach pushes entrepreneurs to allocate resources, expertise, and time to develop coping strategies, which are beyond the business' scope of actions. Adopting this approach may produce a feeling of being prepared; yet, these coping strategies are not necessarily the most adequate for managing the crisis being faced. Crises frequently entail different characteristics and require different strategies to manage their subsequent impact.

Startups also react to a disruptive situation by focusing on a point along the line that ranges from negative effects—referring to interruptions in projects and collaborations, financial damage, and dismissal of employees, among others, to positive effects—alluding to opportunities, better positioning, a timely response to new needs, etc.; and along a time period perspective that ranges from defining the situation in the here and now to considering the long term, that is, 1–15 years in the future (Table 7.2).

- Close to the vest—startup entrepreneurs threatened by a disruptive situation may limit their perspective to the here and now while disregarding the opportunities that crises may entail in the long run. They keep their 'cards' close and avoid collaborations, exchanges, or interactions that require sharing or imparting information as well as plans or even feelings regarding the crisis effects.
- Innovating and initiating—some startup entrepreneurs are excited by a crisis and see the opportunity that it brings; yet they may focus on the opportunities

TABLE 7.2 Exploiting the crisis from a startup's point of view

	Here and now	*In the long run*
Threat	Close to the vest	Lower engagement
Opportunity	Innovating and initiating	Vision to scale

exhibited in the here and now. It is important to ensure that they can foresee the next step in these opportunities' dynamics, as some may be beneficial in the short term but not in the long run.

- Lower engagement—the longer the threat, or perception of a threat lasts, the more damaging its potential effects, and the situation can escalate. Startup managements under threat exhaust their energy and can lose confidence and feel hopeless in managing the hardship. As a result, their engagement with the startup's vision, goals, and processes as well as with their colleagues, partners, and employees decreases. It is important to detect this outlook, as it can be most damaging for the startup.
- Vision to scale—some startup managements are enthused by the long-run opportunities that crisis episodes present and can already 'see' how to upgrade their startup's activity. While this approach is positive and scalable, it is important to ensure that it aligns with concurrent resources and with the expectations of the internal and external stakeholders to avoid unexpected fallout induced by the 'big plans'.

Startup managements can use the template in Figure 7.1 to assess their own approach to defining and demarcating a crisis, at the time of the crisis and in the long run, to prioritize the activities and projects that will be sustained along with new activities and projects to be developed to manage the crisis. The template can be filled in by the startup management and employees and can be used as a joint and shared platform for further preparation for the crisis' effects.

Name of respondent ________ Role in startup ________	*Here & now*		*In the long run*		
	Threat	Opportunity	Threat	Opportunity	
Current activities/projects:					
For example: *(during COVID-19) opening a new market for a sports app targeting elderly people*	• *Elderly people are less likely to use apps* • *During a health crisis, they may be even more reluctant*	• *Many elderly people feel alone* • *Many elderly people avoid outdoor sports* • *People consider sports to be essential*	• *Competitors can also target the elderly, and older people can be overwhelmed with 'too much innovation'*	*More elderly people will get used to the technology, and the app's services can extend to a marketplace for sporting goods, virtual coaches, equipment*	Maintaining the elderly project
New activities/projects: crisis strategies					
For example: *Ensuring that the startup's climate is relaxed, trusting and engaged*	• *Employees face personal health difficulties* • *The overall mood (lockdowns, continual contamination) is depressed*	• *'Going to work' is escapism* • *Life is boring with restrictions in traveling, social and cultural activities; work is interesting*	• *Employees will be depressed, quit their job, be unengaged, etc.* • *People will feel more and more alone, isolated*	• *People will look for places where they feel that they belong, as a family* • *Communities will thrive*	Building a community

FIGURE 7.1 Template for assessing crisis effects on a startup

Startup management's assessment of the situation

The responsibility of the management to its internal and external stakeholders is a key factor in a startup's preparation to manage a crisis. This responsibility is dispersed and multifunctional, as it involves different stakeholders who have various contingencies for the startup. Management needs to secure the staff workplace and avoid dismissals, guarantee the well-being of the employees, and the safety of the teams, that is, internal stakeholders, along with promising continued offering of their products and services with minimal interruptions, assuring their accountability to their strategic partners and maintaining their contracts with investors, that is, external stakeholders. Each individual stakeholder expects the startup to maintain a different function (e.g., production, profitability, personal safety of the employees); hence, the management is required to encapsulate various elements to provide the best solution for each stakeholder that suits its own goals and draws on concurrent resources or even optimizes the resources. The interaction of these elements can result in counterproductive fallout; for example, in financial crises, ensuring staff employment can risk the startup resources allocated for putting out its products, hence endangering its accountability to the external stakeholders. Figure 7.2 illustrates this.

In this context, the resource-based theory (Barney 1991; Alvarez and Busenitz 2001; Chae, Koh and Prybutok 2014), an influential approach in strategic management, can be applied as a managerial framework to determine the concurrent and most critical assets and resources that a startup should maintain and fortify to achieve sustained performance and a competitive advantage in disruptive situations. Examples of business resources

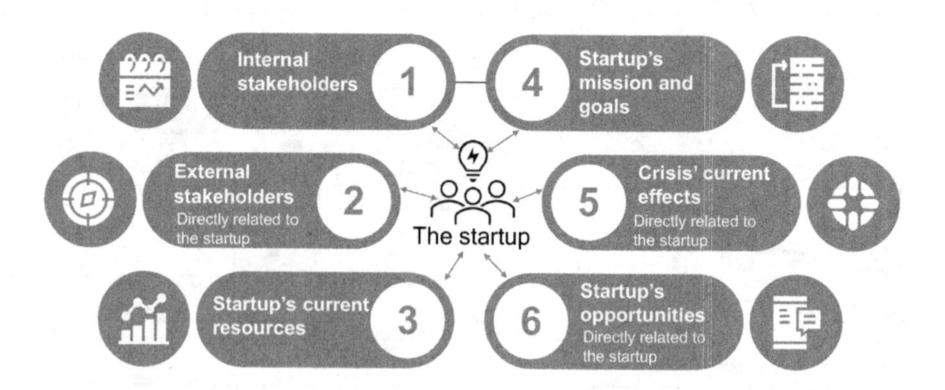

FIGURE 7.2 Startups' pre-mobilization in a crisis

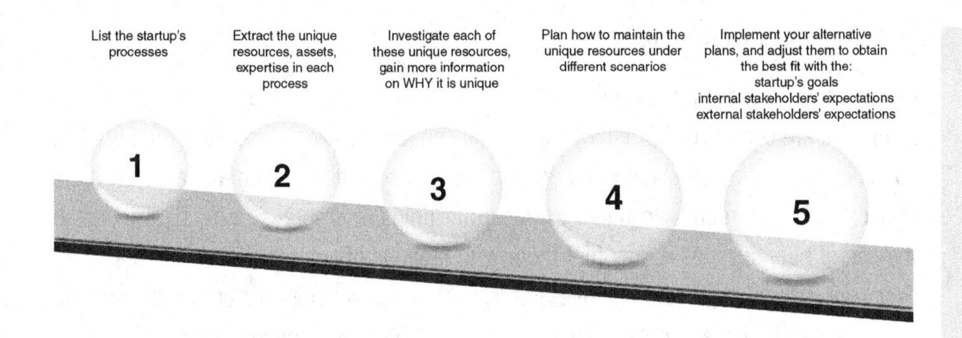

FIGURE 7.3 Startups' preparation to maintain their resources—a roadmap

include information systems, expertise, and networks, among others. The startup is seen through resource-based theory as a 'bundle of resources' that are combined and can interact, change, stimulate other resources, and other capabilities, and are therefore relevant to the preparation of a startup's crisis management plan. By performing an in-depth investigating of the startup's inventory of assets and resources, managements can prepare alternative plans, as illustrated in Figure 7.3.

The role of the startup's management in orchestrating resources and stakeholders to maintain concurrent activity, while both securing the crisis' unique assets and exploiting its opportunities, is demanding, multilayered, and complex, as some components can oppose each other and exhaust each other's resources. It is therefore important to design the response rather than automatically acting to mitigate the crisis' impact; in some cases, the approach of 'waiting for the storm to pass' is more valuable for the startup.

Cognitive heuristics

Preparing for a disruption means turning the hypothetical idea of a potential crisis into a concrete one, that is, it 'becomes real', as actions and projects are activated to manage the crisis even if only for a 'just in case' scenario. Preparing for a potential crisis is an awakening insight, but while it forces entrepreneurs to rescind their denial of the crisis' emergence and take action, it does not necessarily lead to a thorough understanding of the situation, which could be misinterpreted as overly good or overly bad. Often, limited knowledge and strong emotions trigger embroidered or even flawed perceptions of the crisis fallout vis-à-vis the entrepreneur's perceived control in managing it, which may result in entrepreneurs' reluctance to prepare a crisis management strategy, thus warranting an in-depth look.

Heuristics and biases

Perceptions are biased, especially in crisis situations which are typified by uncertainty. Heuristics are cognitive shortcuts that are individually created by people to simplify and speed up their judgments about a target attribute by replacing it with a related attribute that comes more readily to mind. In uncertain times, entrepreneurs tend to increase the use of heuristics, as it may fuel them with feelings of control, protection, and over-optimism, which shape the positive emotions that are valuable for entrepreneurs and their startups in times of crisis; however, this could be risky if these biases affect entrepreneurs' judgment: they may avoid taking action to protect their startups or alternatively take dangerous action, both deemed suitable to manage the (misjudged) situation. While its role in simplification may have some validity, an absolute dependence on heuristics may lead to under- or overestimating the situation and to misinterpretations, that is, cognitive biases. Such biases are embodied in the entrepreneurial realm in different forms, such as the illusion of having control of the crisis, which may then lead to the perception that crisis management preparation is futile. For example, the use of heuristics in 'judging' the COVID-19 crisis as disruptive only to the tourism sector may lead to misconceptions for entrepreneurs in other sectors, fueling them with a feeling that they are protected and that their decision to prepare for a crisis may be misaligned with the crisis-related market's dynamics, hence risking their startup. This is an example of representativeness heuristics, that is, a shortcut pushing entrepreneurs to make judgments based on attributes that resemble or are similar to the target attribute; however, there are various fallacies that lead to an incorrect and unrealistic understating of the situation, which can trigger inadequate or deficient preparations that put the startup at risk (Tversky and Kahneman 1973; Simon, Houghton and Aquino 2000; Keh, Der Foo and Lim 2002; Simon and Houghton 2003; Cassar and Craig 2009; Hayward et al. 2010; Bingham and Eisenhardt 2014).

Designing the strategy

Design of a startup's crisis management strategy should consider both the existing regular strategy and its related projects and activities, which the startup advances in its daily routine, and a corresponding strategy that should be related to the startup's original and leading strategy, in addition to a new one that manages practices in response to the crisis. For example, a leading strategy to prevent crisis effects involves special team development and training to manage the worst-case scenario; this consumes time and money and redirects the people assigned to the special team to a different activity rather than advancing their originally assigned projects. The decision to apply such a strategy is associated with the context, including timing (e.g., critical stages of the startup, advancement of competitors), costs (e.g., the startup's financial state, potential revenues, cash flow), employees' engagement (e.g., redirecting employees to a special team might upset them or put them in task conflict). In addition, the designed strategy, though aimed at managing the crisis, should be aligned with the original strategy, that is, it should be designed to support and advance the original strategy rather than 'just' mitigating the crisis' negative outcomes.

This compounded design requires strategies that:

- Effectively mitigate the crisis' damaging effects on the startup
- Endure (when the crisis is extended)
- Include activities that are customized to each of the startup's projects, departments, or functions
- Enable maintaining and supporting the usual projects and activities (rather than draining them by transferring their resources to developing new strategies)
- Be based on an accountable business and financial plan
- Create acceptance of rather than resistance or reluctance to adopting the strategies
- Make use of the existing expertise in the startup (e.g., employees' specialties, technology)
- Stimulate opportunity exploitation and exploration
- Stimulate innovation

Figure 7.4 demonstrates the preparations needed to design the coping strategies; it includes the startup functions such as technology, production, finance, and HR that are restructured in a crisis event; for example, times of crisis are characterized by reduced sales that consequently cut into the startup's cash flow, and these dynamics influence the financial function, production (due to decreased demand for the product and costly storage of unpurchased products), and technology (converting many functions to digital operation). Rather than implementing crisis-related strategies during or after the startup's functions have been changed 'by the crisis', managements can pre-design these functions by tailoring alternative strategies for each of them; this will enable controlling and managing the crisis situation while maintaining the robustness of each function during the crisis.

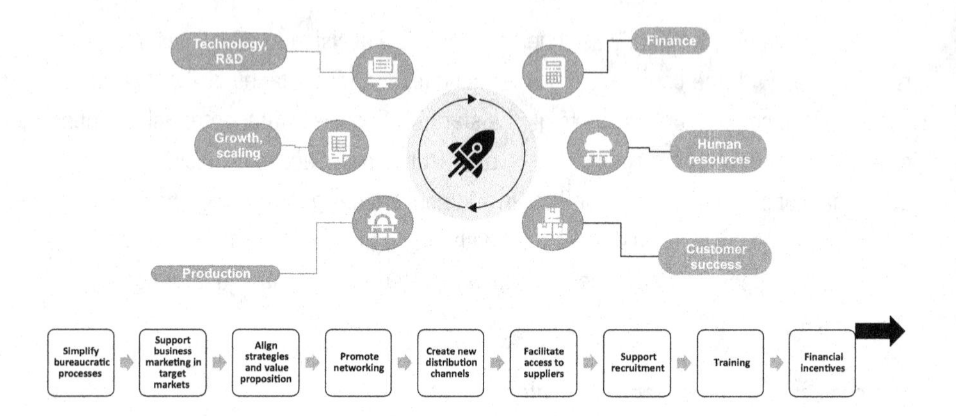

FIGURE 7.4 Designing the coping strategy: functions and strategies

Strategies designed for crisis management include simplifying bureaucratic processes, supporting business marketing in target markets, promoting networking, and training for the new trends, among others. Not all strategies are relevant to the startup's functions; some crisis episodes trigger a specific strategy that applies to several different functions, for example training or recruitment, which can apply to any department/function; other crisis events may prompt specific strategies for each department/function; yet other events may elicit dynamic strategies for each department/function, which change as the crisis continues. The variety, customization, and management of the strategies developed for managing a crisis are reflected in the time and money consumed; a leading general strategy that applies to all departments/functions will be less costly than a variety of strategies that require customization for each function.

Designing strategies requires exceptional decision-making capabilities, as in crisis events: decision-making should be prompt, accurate, coherent (to avoid improvisation and randomness), and communicated in such a way that the relevant people will follow the decision. While in the daily course of action, the startup's employees are more confident and trusting in the management's decisions, in crisis events, there is a substantial gap between the employees' expectations that the management's decisions will provide the best solutions to managing the crisis effects and the management's ability to formulate the best solutions, which is hampered by time constraints, lack of information, and emotional stress. This situation, in turn, affects the employees' confidence in the startup's management, and this decrease in confidence can last even when things go back to normal.

The focus of preparation

The multiple avenues used by startups to address a crisis are classified in research into several main categories:

- Prevention—measures to either avoid the crisis episode or its specific effects on the startup
- Mitigation—measures to reduce the potential crisis damage to the startup's course of action
- Preparedness—measures to develop a conjoint ability to effectively respond to the new needs that arise when the crisis breaks out
- Response—actions carried out immediately before, during, and immediately after a hazard's impact, as the activation of emergency operations
- Recovery—measures to 'bring things back to normal'

The startup's management designs crisis management strategies by considering measures from some of these categories based on the startup's critical need; in other words, the most precious asset(s) that the startup needs to protect.

Only developed, prosperous, and highly successful startups can afford to design strategies for multiple scenarios for each project that address all response categories; this is a megaproject that would be very costly. Moreover, designing crisis strategies devotes time and resources to a potential scenario that may not happen at all or manifest differently. The decision to design crisis strategies draws on the startup management's perceptual balance between leaving the regular work prior to the occurrence of a disruptive event or while it happens. The premise of such a decision can be the expected damage or the expected profit. Expected damage refers to the negative effects of either the crisis, in the case of a startup that has not designed a crisis management tool to respond to such negative effects, or of damages introduced by the actual act of developing special crisis management activities, which involves taking the startup's resources away from their original mission; for example, transforming the resources from the marketing department to the development of a task team to mitigate crisis effects may harm concurrent marketing efforts (Betts, Huzey and Vicari 2012; Kuckertz et al. 2020).

Decision-making in times of crisis

The decision-making process is complex in regular times; when compounded with the risks, insufficient information, uncertainties, and potential damage typifying crises, it becomes even more complex.

The three most prominent decision-making processes in the entrepreneurship literature are:

(a) the rational process, which stems from cognitive models of entrepreneurial behavior; it emphasizes the role of thinking prior to deciding and involves stages such as definition, diagnosis, and design in a rigorous platform for decision-taking; these processes draw on reliable data, numbers, and facts, and advocate preparation and planning prior to an occurrence. The rational process is therefore relevant to crisis events; however, when facts are inaccurate and information is fake, and this is not necessarily recognized by the entrepreneurs, they may use a rational decision-making process that is biased and potentially damaging to the business; (b) the intuitive process, which draws on visions, ideas, and interpreting the information; it does not rely on facts; rather, it fills the gap between the known, existing, and conscious and the unknown, salient, and unconscious. This process orchestrates various signals to craft the decision-making, known in research as evolving by preparation, incubation, illumination, and verification. Its relevance to startups in crises is evident, as information is scarce and uncertainty plentiful; by combining the startup's vision with signals that the entrepreneurs receive from what they 'see, sense, and feel' rather than what they 'think and analyze', this process of decision-making can be beneficial for retaining the vision and goals and designing the crisis strategies;

(c) the improvisational process emphasizes 'doing' through enactment, selection, and retention. Improvisation hinges on experiences and what has been learned from those experiences and is therefore relevant to entrepreneurs in crises who can act while taking decisions, especially when the situation is characterized by confusion and time constraints (Bird 1988; Allinson, Chell and Hayes 2000; Khatri and Ng 2000; Mintzberg and Westley 2001; Baker, Miner and Eesley 2003; Ireland, Hitt and Sirmon 2003; Miller and Ireland 2005; Pina 2007).

Along with these processes, research sorts the areas of decision-making into programmed versus non-programmed, tactical versus operational, routine versus strategic, and organizational versus personal, among others. To simplify the decisions that need to be taken during a crisis, the Eisenhower Decision Matrix[5] can be applied, as it assists in classifying and planning decisions based on their urgency and their importance in four descending priorities, from important and urgent decisions to those that are not important or urgent. To apply this matrix, the decision-making process follows several main steps: defining the problem and determining the kind of knowledge and information sought; structuring the matrix accordingly; breaking down the decision goals into small pieces, to be able to craft alternatives for each 'piece'; using past experiences for comparison, learning, and refining the decision; using intuition to configure each decision's barriers and opportunities; and then designing the decision. For example, a startup that had developed a smart, customized, and location-based technology for short-term rentals of professional working spaces, including the relevant equipment (e.g., painting studios, carpentries, sewing spaces, clinics for psychologists or dentists), when the owners are away had to make some significant decisions when the COVID-19 crisis erupted. With social distancing and lockdowns, many people began to work from home, threatening the very essence of this startup. To take a responsible decision, the entrepreneurs and the management began by defining the problem: unwillingness to work outside the home, thus weakening the perceived value of short-term rentals; a special team was created to validate this definition of the problem by interviewing (virtually) different professionals who are independent workers and, on occasion, need a working space. The team then sorted the more than 1,000 responses into their major themes, such as "I would like to have the option of working outside my home," "the most important thing is the level of hygiene in this space," and so on. The team designed a solution for each theme, and then determined the capabilities and resources at hand that could be immediately employed for developing these solutions and which solutions were most needed. These analyses enabled the special team to acquire a more thoughtful understanding of the startup's capabilities and resources and to start developing "something from nothing", referring to existing resources; this had a relief effect for the entrepreneurs and management, who felt more protected against the crisis. Finally, this startup decided to expand its offerings to different professionals, as the owners of the professional spaces became strategic partners who wished to rent out those spaces. This methodical and systematic decision-making process, which combined logical, intuitive, and improvisational perspectives, enabled taking this decision.

Crisis preparedness

One of the most widespread models for preparing to manage a crisis includes the following areas:

- Risk mapping and analyses of current and potential risks; visible and latent fallout (e.g., hacking into the startup's confidential records versus an increase in employees' feelings of uncertainty due to the economic situation)
- Response responsibility plan: every individual in the startup knows their responsibilities, roles, and range of operation (e.g., professionally, managerially, business-wise, geographically) in advance
- The 'Go!': decisions about the specific time, event, consequences, etc., that will necessitate activation of the crisis strategies
- Communication deliverables: first internally, then external to the startup; collectively or individually; use/no use of specific terms; timing—before versus during the crisis event
- Emergency contacts: reliable people, companies, and associations that will support and speed up the response process
- 'Hands-on': ongoing triad assessment—the feasibility of operating the above protocol, including the components that are well managed and those that are not; the consequences of the applied crisis strategies; the resilience of those who are directly related to the applied strategies; and to verify how long and how far they are willing to endure the crisis response (e.g., startup employees, clients, stakeholders, investors)

At-a-Glance—MyCity managing in pandemic

MyCity is an American startup founded 3.5 years ago by five ex-military commanders, aimed at preventing/reducing crime and violence in cities. They are developing a face recognition product that is embedded in cities' existing sensors for surveillance; the technology uses biometrics to map facial muscle dynamics of anyone passing in the street; and through artificial intelligence (AI) tools, automatically analyzes and detects the immediate likelihood of that individual performing a violent act. Test runs in 12 cities in Central and South America reduced local violence during the testing period by 75% (compared to rates of violence in corresponding cities and during the same period in previous years). Being ex-military commanders, the founders planned and continually maintained a thorough crisis protocol, which turned out to be advantageous in 2020 when more than 120 cities in Central and South America, whose participation in MyCity's next round of testing had already been secured, renounced their commitment due to the pandemic. Adelmo Morales, MyCity's first employee, in charge of marketing in Latin America as well as of emergency preparedness, said: "everything was prepared and set military-style, as if a catastrophe was about to burst 'tomorrow'." Adelmo worked with professionals around the world to create the best crisis management strategies, and it paid off:

> When COVID-19 started to show damaging signs, and gradually, more and more cities were backing out of taking part in our tests, James, our COO, announced an emergency event, and we changed the protocol of MyCity overnight; everybody was already trained, the systems that needed to be operated had been tested on a quarterly basis and were well-maintained, so their operation was smooth; there was no confusion among the staff, and the atmosphere was goal-oriented and straightforward.

Marketing was transferred from government to the public sector and funding shifted to governmental grants and allowances; both shifts exhibited successful results, and MyCity has not experienced any losses during the pandemic.

> While I was the person who explored crisis strategies and formed the most customized plan for MyCity, I was still surprised to see how compliant our staff was, and how immediately each one embraced their emergency responsibilities. MyCity's preparation built its resilience and has been proven in its 'numbers',

concludes Adelmo.

Preparing the startup requires planning a protocol for each area mentioned above, by establishing alternatives for the different crisis profiles, then testing those alternatives through simulations, to decide upon the best one; this is followed by arranging personal meetings with the startup staff who are involved or are expected to be involved during the crisis, and if required, training them for their 'crisis roles'. Concurrently, the startup should prepare its internal staff, who will not have 'emergency responsibilities' in a potential crisis, by setting alternative organizational processes, training, and psychological care, among others, if or when a crisis breaks out.

The external stakeholders are a crucial factor in the startup's preparation for a crisis, and should therefore be told of the startup's strategies to manage potential crises, using a balanced message that will reinforce the stakeholders' confidence in the startup's robustness and elevate their trust in its values of sharing, transparency, and sincerity. Yet, the stakeholders should also be alerted to the risks involved in collaborating with the specific startup during a crisis. For example, a startup located in the United States that developed a smart device to aggregate health-based data from COVID-19 over-the-counter home tests, using an add-on accessory, is in the midst of fund raising to scale up the marketing. A major section in their investor negotiations is dedicated to the 'next crisis', including their crisis management strategies and current preparations for the next hardship.

Continual preparedness is a standard routine dedicated to analyzing, planning, monitoring, and training for 'exceptional events' that will either damage or advance the business. It hinges on several practices, including a continual diagnosis of scenarios and the problems they might entail; obtaining data and available information on potential scenarios and the proposed solution(s) in past occurrences; and studying the advantages, disadvantages, and results of each. The information may be qualitative, such as reports, interviews, opinions, facts, or experiences, or quantitative, for example, numbers and statistics, among others, but should enable reaching an appropriate solution to the problem. By discussing the alternatives and offering ideas and previous experiences with them, the staff becomes familiar with the advantages and disadvantages of the solutions and will be more engaged and resilient during the crisis.

Comprehensive preparation is built on one leading decision or on a set of decisions that are straightforward and clear, based on the concept that in an actual crisis, time is a major asset and prompt management of the situation guarantees less harm to the business. Dry runs are performed to validate the crisis preparation, followed by evaluations and continuing adjustments and readjustments of plans.

Designing the required capabilities

Managing a crisis can be exciting and stimulating, even though it can entail threats, while preparing plans for managing a crisis can be boring and repetitive work. Many entrepreneurs tend to neglect such planning, especially those who are confident in their crisis- management capabilities. Designing crisis management preparation strategies requires: *cognitive* abilities of analysis, composition, evaluation, and critical thinking; *creative* abilities, which are seen in entrepreneurs' resourcefulness in developing new, sometimes unconventional, alternatives as possible solutions to a crisis; this, in turn, enables them to gain a competitive advantage through their management of the disruptive situation, as most of the competitors will have used traditional methods; and *communication* abilities to well disseminate the plan through avenues that maintain trust in the startup's strength, while concurrently clarifying the strategies to be taken if a crisis emerges. The image of a startup drawing on ethical values of honesty, reliability, and consistency is imperative, as it could guarantee the stakeholders' loyalty during and after the crisis event (Parashevas 2006; Santella, Steinberg and Parks 2009; Al-Dabbagh 2020).

The role of founders' decision-making in crisis management is critical to the startup's effective management of and recovery from the crisis effects. As such, a robust design for the strategies is required to create the best match to the startup's needs while acknowledging the context. Since preparations relate to future crises, the whole design is dynamic and is adjusted to the changing context, for example, designing a plan when the startup is in a bootstrap, but activating it (i.e., when the crisis starts) after one or more funding rounds from external investors, effecting changes in the planned strategies as the startup now has return of investment liability; such contextual changes require congruent adjustments in the design of the crisis management strategies. To ascertain that efforts are well directed to responding to the potential crisis by concurrently tracking the evolution of the startup and its environment, some measures can be valuable: establishing a crisis management operations room; creating 'emergency work teams' consisting of the startup's staff and of specialists and experts; delegating roles and responsibilities; creating an efficient communication system to transfer information quickly, accurately, and decisively; learning from experience and mistakes; and treating the preparation as a routine that can be fun and contribute to the startup's cohesiveness and commitment.

Summary

There is an undefined, blurry 'space' termed 'valley' in this chapter, between the emergence of information about a crisis and the action taken by entrepreneurs. This 'valley' encompasses the external perspective, referring to anything happening outside of the startup that is transmitted to the entrepreneur through information, personal or others' experiences, and the overall market dynamics during the initial stages of the crisis event or even prior to its emergence; and an internal perspective, delving into entrepreneurs' processes of defining, deciding, preparing, and designing the strategy to manage the crisis situation. The 'valley' is influenced by these external and internal powers, which are dynamic and changing, so that some situations may be perceived by different entrepreneurs as more or less stressful or be contingent on emotions associated with current or future consequences of the crisis, which may not accurately reflect the actual crisis effects.

In this chapter, we discussed the main dissonance tackled by startups between their 'crisis routine' mode—drawing on their development through crises and generating strategies and mindsets that facilitate their coping with any 'additional' crisis, and their confusion and bewilderment when facing crises emerging outside of the startup that can affect or potentially affect it. Startups seem to be used to 'tailored' disruptions, which they manage with agility and creativity, whereas crises consisting of such components as natural disasters, infection and illness, or famine, for example, are unfamiliar to the startups, hamper their routines, and thus reduce the entrepreneurs' feeling of control and enhance their feelings of uncertainty and threat. Research shows that prior to a disruptive situation or in its initial stages, uncertainty is at its highest, followed by stress and confusion. By recognizing these feelings and classifying them into stressful or non-stressful situations, threats or opportunities, concurrent or long-term effects, and the interaction of those components, the design of the preparation for a crisis can be more accurate and more customized to the startup's departments, functions, and projects.

Startups need to prepare simultaneously for both preventing the materialization of perceived threats into real, disruptive effects and gearing up to exploit the opportunities involved in the crisis. In addition, the preparation needs to be modified for the internal and external stakeholders. Because this complex design addresses only the preparation, that is, prior to, and not in the face of a concrete threat, it involves various heuristics, biases, and difficulties in the decision-making process.

The 'valley' should be considered a moratorium in which crises can be prepared for, where the difficulties in designing crisis management strategies that encompass the described complexity can be tackled and the strategies customized to the stakeholders. The framework should therefore include developing a template for risk mapping analyses, planning a responsible strategy, formatting the communication deliverables, and deciding on emergency contacts, among others.

Reflective questions for class

1. Read: "Engaging Startups in COVID-19 Crisis Response. How COVID-19 Startups Can Boost the Economy Further"[6] at https://startupgenome.com/articles/engaging-startups-covid-crisis-response and address the three points indicated in the article and given below using the model of startups' pre-mobilization in a crisis (Figure 7.2). There is no need to respond to each of the following points separately. What are your main conclusions and insights?

   Bearing in mind the potential of startups to fix current issues and future economies, let's take a look into:

   I. *The set of problems we must solve as a local, national and global startup ecosystem*

   II. *Examples of communities that are activating startups to solve COVID-19 related issues*

   III. *How the government can support this process*

2. Interview two entrepreneurs on their approaches to a crisis in the initial stages of crisis emergence, based on Table 7.1: Startups' approaches to disruptive events, and Table 7.2: Exploiting the crisis from a startup's point of view. Compare the entrepreneurs' approaches by listing their similarities and differences. Explain your findings.
3. Search for information on BrewDog (at https://www.brewdog.com/uk/) from various sources. Apply the model of preparation based on Figure 7.3: Startups' preparation to maintain their resources—a roadmap, for the next potential crisis. List four to five main implications for other startups in the food and beverage sector.
4. Julia and Antoni are co-founders of JustHere, a startup located in Poland that develops a smart navigation system for smart cities. They are in the midst of a dispute on the need to design a crisis management strategy for a hypothetical crisis. Julia favors avoiding any cost or time investment in such preparations and advancing the technological development of JustHere to gain a competitive advantage over competitors; she says that "in the worst scenario, if and when we tackle a crisis unprepared, we can pivot the technology to another product that is not in navigation. But we need to complete the technology development." Antoni invested the seed money in JustHere from his former startup's success, and he is unwilling to take risks by ignoring potential crises, including the COVID-19 pandemic which he thinks can evolve in new directions. List three to four points

strengthening Julia's point of view and three to four points supporting Antoni's view. What is your conclusion? Explain.

5. Read the Bloomberg article "The Covid Bankruptcies: Guitar Center to Youfit"[7] at https://www.bloomberg.com/graphics/2020-us-bankruptcies-coronavirus/. You are asked to publish a commentary of half a page on this article that shows how startups can avoid bankruptcy by applying the concepts presented in this chapter.

Notes

1 Inspired by the saying of Steve Jobs "Don't let the noise of others' opinions drown out your own inner voice."

2 See the source at https://en-academic.com/dic.nsf/enwiki/2234638

3 Inspired by Martin Luther King Jr., who said: "Our very survival depends on our ability to stay awake, to adjust to new ideas, to remain vigilant and to face the challenge of change."

4 'Transitional object' is a mental representation of something perceived to be part of the external world or it may be the mental representation of another person existing independently of the self. Accordingly, a plausible behavioral explanation for sticking with the routine is that transitional objects (that could refer to a specific routine procedure at work, for example) provide comfort and security by reducing separation anxiety, even if unrealistic. In the case of entrepreneurs during crises, separation would refer to the well known that no longer exists, such as business routines or people who have been dismissed due to the situation; and the routine provides a feeling, though not necessarily realistic, that there has not been any separation (Winnicott 1986).

5 See https://luxafor.com/the-eisenhower-matrix/ ; https://www.youtube.com/watch?v=DX4LStJGny4

6 See Startup Genome by Laís de Oliveira, May 21, 2020.

7 By Davide Scigliuzzo, Josh Saul, Shannon D. Harrington, Claire Boston, and Demetrios Pogkas. Published July 9, 2020. Updated January 1, 2021.

References

Al-Dabbagh, Z. S. (2020). The role of decision-maker in crisis management: A qualitative study using grounded theory (COVID-19 pandemic crisis as a model). *Journal of Public Affairs, 20*(4), e2186.

Allinson, C. W., Chell, E., & Hayes, J. (2000). Intuition and entrepreneurial behaviour. *European Journal of Work and Organizational Psychology, 9*(1), 31–43.

Alvarez, S. A., & Busenitz, L. W. (2001). The entrepreneurship of resource-based theory. *Journal of Management, 27*(6), 755–775.

Baker, T., Miner, A. S., & Eesley, D. T. (2003). Improvising firms: Bricolage, account giving and improvisational competencies in the founding process. *Research Policy, 32*(2), 255–276.

Barney, J. (1991). Firm resources and sustained competitive advantage. *Journal of Management, 17*(1), 99–120.

Betts, S. C., Huzey, D., & Vicari, V. (2012). Crisis management for small business: Advice for before, during and after a crisis. *Journal of International Management Studies, 12*(4)

Bingham, C. B., & Eisenhardt, K. M. (2014). Response to Vuori and Vuori's commentary on "Heuristics in the strategy context". *Strategic Management Journal, 35*(11), 1698–1702.

Bird, B. (1988). Implementing entrepreneurial ideas: The case for intention. *Academy of Management Review, 13*(3), 442–453.

Cassar, G., & Craig, J. (2009). An investigation of hindsight bias in nascent venture activity. *Journal of Business Venturing, 24*(2), 149–164.

Chae, H., Koh, C. E., & Prybutok, V. R. (2014). Information technology capability and firm performance: Contradictory findings and their possible causes. *MIS Quarterly, 38*(1), 305–326.

Hayward, M. L., Forster, W. R., Sarasvathy, S. D., & Fredrickson, B. L. (2010). Beyond hubris: How highly confident entrepreneurs rebound to venture again. *Journal of Business Venturing, 25*(6), 569–578.

Ireland, R. D., Hitt, M. A., & Sirmon, D. G. (2003). A model of strategic entrepreneurship: The construct and its dimensions. *Journal of Management, 29*(6), 963–989.

Keh, H. T., Der Foo, M., & Lim, B. C. (2002). Opportunity evaluation under risky conditions: The cognitive processes of entrepreneurs. *Entrepreneurship Theory and Practice, 27*(2), 125–148.

Khatri, N., & Ng, H. A. (2000). The role of intuition in strategic decision making. *Human Relations, 53*(1), 57–86.

Kuckertz, A., Brändle, L., Gaudig, A., Hinderer, S., Reyes, C. A. M., Prochotta, A., ... Berger, E. S. (2020). Startups in times of crisis–A rapid response to the COVID-19 pandemic. *Journal of Business Venturing Insights, 13*, e00169.

Miller, C. C., & Ireland, R. D. (2005). Intuition in strategic decision making: Friend or foe in the fast-paced 21st century? *Academy of Management Perspectives, 19*(1), 19–30.

Mintzberg, H., & Westley, F. (2001). *It's not what you think.*

Paraskevas, A. (2006). Crisis management or crisis response system? A complexity science approach to organizational crises. *Management Decision.*

Pina E Cunha, M. (2007). Entrepreneurship as decision making: Rational, intuitive and improvisational approaches. *Journal of Enterprising Culture, 15*(01), 1–20.

Santella, N., Steinberg, L. J., & Parks, K. (2009). Decision making for extreme events: Modeling critical infrastructure interdependencies to aid mitigation and response planning. *Review of Policy Research, 26*(4), 409–422.

Simon, M., & Houghton, S. M. (2003). The relationship between overconfidence and the introduction of risky products: Evidence from a field study. *Academy of Management Journal, 46*(2), 139–149.

Simon, M., Houghton, S. M., & Aquino, K. (2000). Cognitive biases, risk perception, and venture formation: How individuals decide to start companies. *Journal of Business Venturing, 15*(2), 113–134.

Tversky, A., & Kahneman, D. (1973). Availability: A heuristic for judging frequency and probability. *Cognitive Psychology, 5*(2), 207–232.

Winnicott, D. W. (1986). The theory of the parent-infant relationship. *Essential Papers on Object Relations*, 233–253.

Chapter Eight
Managing crises

- Takeaways
- Introduction
- Fight or flight?
- The effective crisis management plan
- Implementing the crisis management protocol
- Shared coping action
- Response strategies
- The entrepreneur's dilemma
- Coping with crises using innovative strategies
- Reviewing business models
- Summary
- Reflective questions for class

Takeaways

- Choosing a strategy/practice to manage a crisis is a complex process that requires a multifaceted analysis of the business' capabilities, the crisis' severity, and the founder(s)' commitment, abilities, and priorities with regards to the coping process
- Coping with a crisis requires thinking about both the short- and long-term consequences of the response strategies, offensive and defensive approaches to crisis management, and internal and external stakeholders' engagement in crisis management
- Elimination or mitigation of the severe crisis fallout can hasten the emergence of new challenges that have not been anticipated, and therefore requires a concurrent perspective on investing and maintaining strategic plans during crises
- Discovering and exploring opportunities is a key crisis management strategy, though it is perceived as risky or as hindering the goal of protecting the business in times of crisis; it requires adopting a new and open mindset
- Maps and blueprints of crisis management strategies, practices, and tools are useful for choosing, on the spot, the most feasible, valuable, and opportunity-driven processes to cope with the crisis' effects. They necessitate agility and tolerance

DOI: 10.4324/9781003173809-8

to change as the crisis evolves and changes the anticipated conditions and the consequent crisis management tools

Introduction

This chapter focuses on managing disruptions while they are happening. In practice, this 'time period' covers different points in time because the emergence and course of a crisis are identified differently by different startups depending on the magnitude of the effects/potential effects on that startup. Nevertheless, once the startup detects the active disruption, it acts, as this point in time is perceived by the startup's founders as the acute time to cope with the crisis' effects. In reality, there is no one single point in time that defines the immediate, acute, or urgent time to act; moreover, once the founders consider the occurrence as acute, the subsequent action is inevitable. Several academic models have tackled the 'timing' of the response through a crisis event sequence model (Buchanan and Denyer 2013; Doern, Williams and Vorley 2019), demonstrated through a six-phase event sequence: the first segment of the sequence focuses on pre-crisis planning; the second phase consists of precipitating toward the disruptive occurrence; the third looks at measures to control the crisis; the fourth investigates the reasons why the crisis emerged; the fifth focuses on learning from the experience; and the sixth centers on implementing the lesson learnt (Smallbone et al. 2012; Bullough, Renko and Myatt 2014; Simón-Moya, Revuelto-Taboada and Ribeiro-Soriano 2016; Williams and Shepherd 2016a, b; Martinelli, Tagliazucchi and Marchi 2018).

Despite this sequence, the actual responding action aimed at managing the crisis is a matter of the entrepreneur's perceptions of when exactly that action is required; this is not necessarily when the crisis emerges (segment 2). The two following examples portray the relevance of crisis interpretation in the actual response. In the summer of 2019, Russel and Chloe from the UK launched a location-based, AI service for jewelry to be worn at luxury occasions, which went viral and gained massive traction until the first lockdown in the UK. "The pandemic was out there, but we felt secure, and 'untouchable' due to our rolling success, and we kept the business as usual," says Chloe. During the lockdown, people were still visiting the website, so the founders did not consider the pandemic to be a crisis; they even hired some interns to help them with the UX/UI. "When we figured out that the crisis is hitting us, in June 2020, we both panicked; we decided to collaborate with a jewelry chain, owned by family members, to join forces, to navigate in these crazy times," says Chloe. In the case of Nathalie and her team from Canada, the response to the pandemic was immediate. Nathalie had been a victim of sexual violence, and she launched a unique and smart technology-based service with three co-founders, all female victims of sexual violence, that enables young girls and women to walk safely and freely in the streets. The startup received funds from family and friends and from the government in 2018, and was partially operated in Canada and the United States through the mediation of municipalities. When the COVID-19 pandemic erupted and some countries went into lockdown, Nathalie sensed the threat to the startup—even though the pandemic had not yet reached North America—because during lockdowns the streets would be empty; she approached her strategic partners to change the focus of the service to domestic violence. Nathalie and her team thus reacted prior to the actual occurrence of the crisis (segment 1).

Fight or flight?

Research shows that the act of crisis management often involves a fight or flight response to the disruption. From this perspective, early preparation for the potential disruption can moderate these impulsive fight or flight reactions.

However, the fight or flight response is not a stand-alone phenomenon. The model in Figure 8.1 traces the fight or flight perspective in the face of a crisis. The first instinctive detection and interpretation of a disruption is an internal response, drawing on perceptions, fears, interpretations, and rumors, but not on factual events per se; it is based on the following aspects:

(a) Is the occurrence relevant or irrelevant to the startup? Is it 'factual' or hypothetical, that is, threatening but not yet hitting (e.g., 'already hitting the startup' versus 'no real threat to the startup')?

(b) Is the disruption affecting the startup directly or indirectly? For example, financial crises can disrupt the financial state of the startup's suppliers, which, in turn, may affect the startup's standard supply chain.

(c) Is the effect general or local (i.e., 'already partially hitting the startup')?

Where the disruption is partial, such as affecting a specific department or function, it can be bypassed through other functions. The second phase centers on a comparative look, focusing on 'me' versus 'others' in the acute event and ranging from 'only others are affected by the crisis, whereas our startup is untouchable', to a victimized approach referring to 'why me/us?'. The last phase is affected by the two previous phases, which can be intertwined and have a proliferating effect on the interpretation of the crisis (e.g., severity, threatening, magnitude); it refers to the people or institutions that are or should be involved in the act of responding, aimed at managing the crisis, for example, only the

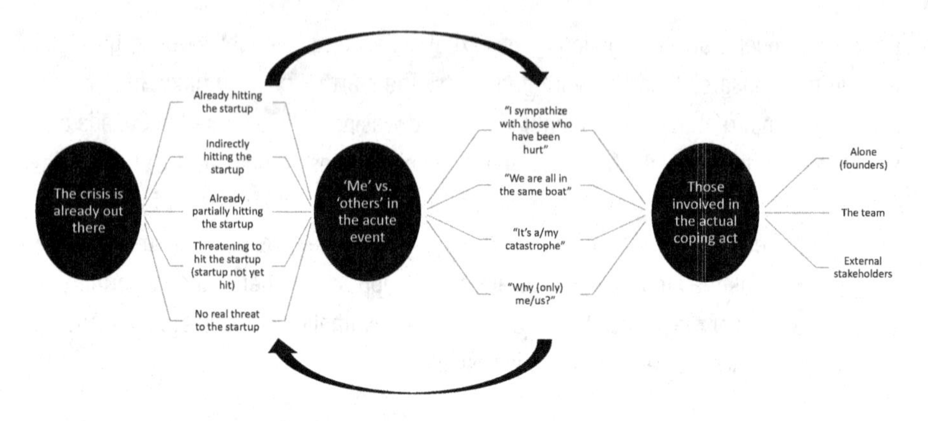

FIGURE 8.1 When does acute coping happen?

founders/leaders, the teams (all teams, management teams, local/professional teams), or collaborators and strategic partners from the ecosystem.

The subsequent action taken to manage the disruption relies on a three-faceted practical blueprint that maps the preparedness of the startup to the crisis, encompassing the following points:

- Startup's capacity:
  - A command center for times of crisis; chain of command in the team during a crisis
  - Backup resources and being able to swiftly obtain the backup material
  - Up-to-date training and plans for crisis episodes
  - Procedures for assessing the severity of an event and its impact
- The founders' approach to crisis management:
  - Preemptive approach—seeking to prevent a crisis at the earliest signs
  - Proactive approach—referring to initiating an action early in the crisis' emergence, aimed at shaping or controlling the occurrence/severity/pace, etc. of the crisis events
  - Responsive approach—responding to a crisis situation upon detecting its earliest signs by an action that seems to lead to effective action that accounts for long- and short-term results
  - Reactive approach—a defensive course of action when crisis signs emerge

- External and internal stakeholders—referring to the role assigned to stakeholders in combating the crisis. The following categorization echoes the relevance of the stakeholders in the crisis context:
    - *Proactive approach*—internal and external stakeholders that could potentially be affected participate in crisis preparation, play a role in coping with the crisis, and embark on actions and processes aimed at recovery
    - *Accommodative approach*—recognition of a possible crisis and involvement of some internal and external stakeholders in preparation and coping strategies
    - *Defensive approach*—decision to address only crises with high expected costs and involving internal and external stakeholders only if required by law
    - *Reactive approach*—denial of a potential crisis, whereby the startup rejects any role, responsibility, or cooperation designed to manage the crisis.

The effective crisis management plan

The concept of change

The effective plan is contingent on the entrepreneurs', teams', and stakeholders' willingness to embrace it, as plans do not automatically manage disruptive situations; even a meticulous plan, which includes the full range of aspects of the business' needs under potential crises, may be less or not at all effective if the entrepreneurs are hesitant regarding its implementation or outcomes. One main reason for reluctance in preparing and then implementing crisis management plans is a fear of change. Change is an underlying factor and mindset in crisis management. Crises change the conditions, businesses change, people involved in the crisis change, and consequently uncertainty and insecurity diffuse into all aspects of the startup. The change becomes the 'new normal', and therefore, any negative connotation of change impedes successful implementation of a crisis management program. Drawing on Kotter's book *A Sense of Urgency*, startups need to cultivate a positive outlook on change, so that internal and external stakeholders can more easily engage in change, and dedicate efforts to practicing change on an ongoing basis, so that in times of crisis, change is regarded as one of the basic 'ingredients' that a startup confronts, uses, and implements, and indeed, toward which it moves. It is only by embracing the concept of change along with the associated mindset and strategies that a startup can implement crisis management programs.

Kotter's eight-step model for engaging in change includes: creating a sense of urgency by presenting the change's intriguing aspects and positive potential; building a coalition of active change agents to guide, coordinate, and encourage others on the implementation of the company's desired changes; communicating the reasons behind the initiatives for change and the expected final result; ensuring that everyone is on the same page, forming support teams and reducing anxiety; removing barriers to change implementation; generating short-term wins to track progress and to encourage moving forward; monitoring the change implementation; and anchoring the changes in the corporate culture.

Startups equipped with change-driven strategies are expected to develop both change-driven mindsets and more agile approaches to the work being done, and combining these increases the startups' ability to embrace change and effectively respond to a crisis' fallout.

Reframing the concept of acute

'Acute' is a word that is commonly associated with gravity or severity combined with a sense of immediacy and it is mainly associated with serious illness or traumatic injury; it therefore carries the connotation of something that has highly damaging consequences, and that is the result of 'negligence' or careless analysis, preparation or planning of a situation; this stems from the common but erroneous notion that by being well prepared, startups are guaranteed to avoid acute, that is, severe situations. This common notion is not categorically accurate. Many examples illustrate startups, organizations, and even governmental bodies that prepared for a crisis but misjudged the situation or erred in implementing a plan that fit the acute conditions. In contrast, an acute response—typified by intuitive decisions, chaotic management, and impulsive strategy implementation—often results in more profitable outcomes. The cases of Periscope and Zoom demonstrate this. Twitter bought Periscope in 2015 for $100 million; in 2021, it announced that it would be phasing out the app due to declining use (from the Twitter help center: "Periscope apps are no longer live as of March 31, 2021").[1] In other words, the acute pandemic situation did not allow Periscope to survive, even though the leadership might have had a plan for crisis management. Zoom, however, embraced the sudden exponential growth in the use of their product, though it posed many challenges to operations, security, and fee collection, among others. Zoom's unplanned, responsive, and maybe even impulsive response to its growing customers—removal of the 40-minute time limit on the free version of the product for educational institutions—provided the message that it had carefully detected the acute situation and was providing the most accurate response to it, even though it might not have been a prepared one.

A new view of 'acuteness' as an enabling concept should be embraced, where it can open the way to vast opportunities as well as threats. It should not be seen as a synonym for providing 'first aid' or as an automatic sign of the startup's imprudence or recklessness, but rather, as an avenue to involve the wider entrepreneurial ecosystem and long-term activities to ensure rapid recovery and growth.

Implementing the crisis management protocol

Facing a crisis or a disaster is always unexpected, even if its emergence has been accurately predicted; this initial reaction is always followed by uncertainty and feelings of urgency and immense pressure. Of the various models drawing from different disciplines, four main approaches are encapsulated in this section, as presented in Figure 8.2.

These approaches enable delving into the set of resources, actions, processes, and networks, among others, that entrepreneurs generate to cope directly with the crisis' effects. The first approach refers to *fighting the damage* by endeavoring to stop the direct disruptive source from targeting the startup, taking care of those who are affected, and recuperating the damage, for example, repairing internet-related damage from the 9/11 catastrophe as it was occurring or protecting employees and their families who were injured by the floods in Chennai, India, in 2015.[2] The second approach, *retrenchment*, is more calculated than the first, as it aims to cope, immediately and in the short term, by reducing costs while retaining the basics. For example, in January 2019, François Levy and his team launched a dating app that uses machine learning technology and began to gain traction by physically visiting academic institutions and operating 'dating

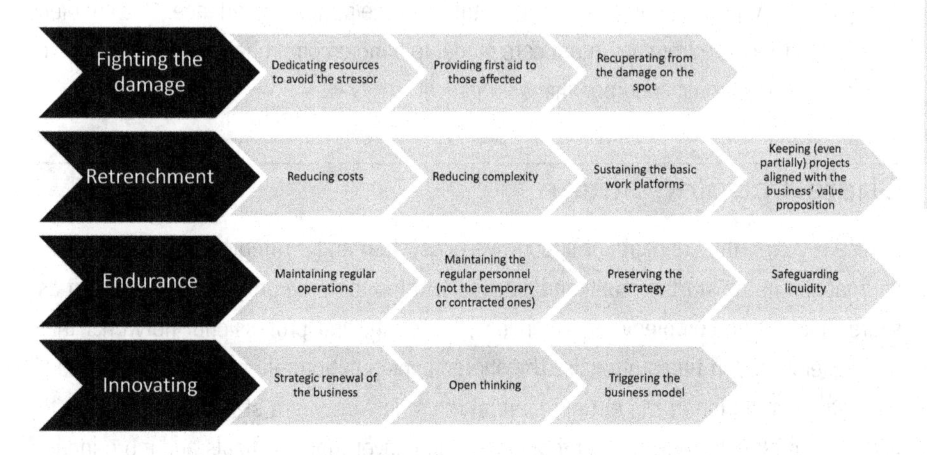

FIGURE 8.2 Approaches to managing an existing crisis

festivals' on campuses; then COVID-19 appeared. François immediately transformed the physical festivals into virtual ones, and then kept them virtual even when students were allowed to return to campus. He was determined to ensure low costs while retaining the essence of the startup, that is, the dating festivals. The third approach, *endurance*, is more strategic; it aims to maintain the operations, projects, personnel, collaborations, etc., that work by allocating the resources to those operations that are fruitful and will not endanger the business, safeguarding their existence. This approach was adopted by a team of three founders of a relatively new startup (2018) developing online educational games that target the Latin American educational market. The emergence of COVID-19 forced the team to reexamine its processes and decide on the best blueprint to follow; the founders decided to stick to their course of action and strategy, align the activities and projects with their vision, which included looking for new collaborations and opportunities, while at the same time adopting a more vigilant policy, whereby new projects were meticulously verified before taking them on. This approach is intricate, as it may be interpreted by the startup's employees and external collaborators as indicating that the startup, showing 'business as usual', is unaffected by the crisis; nevertheless, the core reason for deciding upon this approach involves a damage minimization attitude, because the startup is under threat. Finally, some startups cope with the crisis by taking an innovative albeit risky approach, on the premise that the situation is risky (due to the crisis) and therefore offers an opportunity to leverage the conditions and innovate. The following case exemplifies this approach. Michelle Davey established Wheel, a health-care platform that helps staff clinical workforces by creating an infrastructure for hybrid medical workforces. The COVID-19 pandemic provided Wheel with an innovative albeit risky opportunity to involve new players, such as insurers or very large retailers such as Walmart and Amazon, through a refragmentation of the patient experience. This enabled the startup to evolve from an urgent care model to a more comprehensive platform, from primary care to chronic condition management.[3]

Shared coping action

In recent years, the concepts of supportive ecosystem and strategic partnerships have bourgeoned in the startup realm and have penetrated the area of crisis management as shared platforms, complementary services, bartering, and professional networks that are implemented in times of crisis. The shared coping action relies on the premise that the optimal situation in the entrepreneurial realm is win-win; a startup's failure due to the crisis implies further failures that spread and cover more verticals and more industries, and that either directly or indirectly, generally or partially, affect each player in the

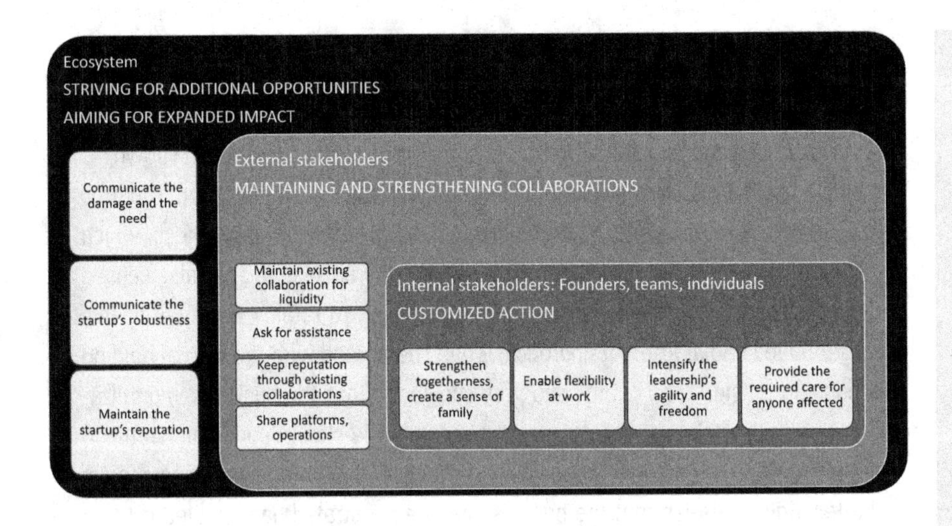

FIGURE 8.3 Startup's comprehensive view in coping with an acute crisis

ecosystem. The model demonstrated in Figure 8.3 tracks the decisions to spread the coping action from internal stakeholders to external stakeholders and then to the ecosystem.

The ability to more accurately tackle and control the disruptive situation can be achieved by involving only the internal stakeholders, but the impact will be limited and temporary; to join forces, maintain existing collaborations and endeavor to reach a win-win situation, the involvement of external stakeholders is required. To have a larger impact, exploit new opportunities of mutual interest and lead in managing the crisis, joint action with the ecosystem is needed. For example, during the COVID-19 pandemic, startup founders have had to decide when, how much, and in which way to enable employees to work from home in a way that suits the startup's needs (i.e., internal stakeholders); to maintain the relationship with their strategic partners, startups are coordinating their internal setting of working from home with their external partners (i.e., external stakeholders); and to gain a higher impact, such as compensation for working from home, startups are coordinating their coping activities with the ecosystem.

At-a-Glance—crisis management in a digitalized meat shop

Saana joined her older brothers Albertus and Serafin in their meat shop, restaurant and butchery, after graduating from university and introducing a digital application aimed at preserving customers through AI technology. The new device was of great value and the business ran well and expanded from Nordic Europe to other countries in Europe; one of the leading plans, which was expected to be the most profitable, was to franchise the meat shop. With the outbreak of COVID-19 and lockdowns, the founders of the meat shop experienced a severe slowdown, as clients stopped visiting the restaurant, which was their main attraction. Albertus and Serafin reacted swiftly to these changes by protecting the business, which included terminating all future plans to expand and franchise it. They also ceased digitalization of the business; they found no reason to retain customers at this stage. Saana had a different approach; while she agreed with the idea of holding expansion outside the country, she was convinced that the business' digitalization was crucial. Saana was determined to retain the shop's leadership status in the market and to preserve the existing strategic collaborations with companies; the technological leap that the business had demonstrated had enabled it to be competitive. Many new collaborations were formed due to the general perception in the ecosystem of this business' progress. Assistance from one of the leading mentors in the Nordic ecosystem enabled the meat shop to reconfigure its capacity and resources and rearrange its financials so that it could maintain and develop the AI application. This proactive coping strategy turned out to be most successful; in fact, the business began generating higher profits than before the pandemic due to its steadiness in times of crisis, which strengthened the stakeholders' trust in it.

Response strategies

Research has introduced a range of strategies adopted by startups during crisis events, which can be roughly categorized into defensive strategies—focused on the short term and based on adopting measures aimed at maintaining efficiency and guaranteeing the survival of the business; these include restructuring and resizing strategies—through cost-cutting, selling of non-strategic assets and reducing personnel costs. These strategies mainly focus on holding one's ground and finding a foothold during a challenging situation by contemplating the business processes that keep the startup from losing more money, while maintaining the concurrent client base and providing a more stable context to make complex decisions without threatening the startup's competitive advantage; and offensive strategies, which are adopted for the medium and long term and are realized through new investments and an innovation process to maintain and strengthen the competitive advantage, by seizing the opportunities that the crisis has revealed and moving forward to secure new businesses, make new sales, and capitalize on the convoluted market. Such strategies are exhibited in the introduction of new products and processes, penetration of new markets, and growing the business (e.g., spin-offs, geographical expansion). Entrepreneurs who follow such strategies are not ignoring or failing to accurately analyze the situation; rather, the 'transformation' of threats into opportunities is more obvious to them at this point in time.

In addition, studies show that startups follow either externally directed or internally directed strategies. The former refers to market-oriented strategies, pricing strategies, and an international orientation, and the latter to the startup's structures, processes, systems, and resources (Chattopadhyay, Glick and Huber 2001; Latham 2009; Sternad 2012; Fairlie 2013; Bennett and Nikolaev 2021; McDonald and Eisenhardt 2020). The main strategies are:

- *Restructuring strategies*—internally directed actions that involve cutting costs to improve efficiency. Such strategies relate to traditional product/market combinations and do not involve significant dimensional variations. Firms try to improve efficiency by improving productivity and reducing expenditure on a wide range of activities; these strategies are defensive in nature.
- *Resizing strategies*—externally directed actions, also defensive in nature, oriented to refocusing the core business and avoiding any investment in any non-core processes; these can involve ceasing investments in products/product lines, withdrawal from markets, selling the business or some parts of it, and closure of plants and production sites, among others.
- *Downsizing strategies*—actions taken to improve efficiency and reduce operating costs by optimizing asset utilization and divesting itself of marginal and less profitable activities. These may result in cost and asset cuts decreasing the business' competitiveness on the spot and lower its ability to successfully recover from the crisis' effects.

The next two strategies align with Penrose, who considers disrupted times as follows: "depression is sometimes looked on as a good time to expand: costs are low, plants can be constructed and equipment bought cheaply" (Penrose 1995, p. 244), and presenting "opportunities to invest, innovate and expand into new markets in order to achieve or extend a competitive advantage during the recession and beyond" (Kitching et al. 2009).

- *Innovation and development strategies*—planning and investing in technological innovation, process, and product innovation as well as in the recruitment of experts who can fuel the business with more innovation, so that the startup can equip itself with innovations while the competitors are facing disruptive times, and may be more engaged in defensive strategies. Startups that favor these strategies are often also encountering the same threats as their competitors, yet they consider the risks in developing innovation at this point in time to be less risky than protecting their startup by resizing or downsizing it.

- *Reorganization strategies*—these are internally directed offensive actions, focused on improving organizational aspects, requalifying the firm, and strengthening its business-based structure; they can be manifested as redefining responsibilities, enhancing information system controls, investing in human resources, and so on. Such strategies are useful to maintaining commitment and engagement in the business as well as a feeling of concern and caring (Deans 2009; Kitching et al. 2009; Latham 2009; Thompson 2009; Papaoikonomou, Segarra and Li 2012; Sternad 2012).

The entrepreneur's dilemma

The decision on which strategy should be taken to manage the crisis is multifaceted and requires a deep understanding of possible consequences, which may bring about a large array of outcomes, some of which may be disruptive in the short or long term.

From the entrepreneur's point of view, the conditions that will determine the strategy to be employed are related to the following points, and are considered by deciphering both the concurrent conditions and the predicted change in conditions in the mid and long term:

The business

- Who decides on the crisis management strategies—how many people, is it easy to reach them, do they share similar views on the startup's goals, directions?
- Who implements the decided-upon crisis management strategies?
- Who monitors the implementation—performance quality, results, the business' state after the implementation?
- What is the current financial situation of the startup?
- What is the general atmosphere in the startup? Are employees engaged and loyal, are they afraid, are they doing their utmost to overcome the crisis?
- Is there pressure from external stakeholders to embrace a specific strategy to manage the crisis; are there contrasting pressures?
- Are there processes/practices/employees in the startups that did not fit well despite the crisis and should have been reassessed? Would it be a suitable time to reconfigure them?
- Is there an expectation in the startup that 'something should change' despite the crisis and it would be a suitable point in time to make that change?
- Is there an opportunity that seemed 'out of reach' but the crisis enabled reconsidering/exploiting it?

The crisis

- What type of disruption has the crisis already produced? What and who are the most affected in the business by the disruption? How severe is the crisis' effect?
- Are competitors affected similarly by the crisis?
- How are strategic collaborators 'treating' the crisis, by being more reluctant to engage in new collaborations or sustain the existing ones, by pushing the startup to cut costs, etc.?
- Is the crisis unique or recurrent? Unexpected or anticipated?
- What types of opportunities has the crisis introduced? Who is seizing the opportunities so far and what are the outcomes of opportunity exploitation by others around them?
- Is the crisis' severity increasing with time? (For example, floods may be harmful in the first days, and then the situation calms down; economic crises may worsen as time passes)
- How is the crisis affecting the general population, with regards to power of purchase, new purchase needs, purchase atmosphere? Is the effect local, regional, global?
- What types of new trends are arising? (For example, online shopping, domestic travel instead of international travel, new ways of advertising).

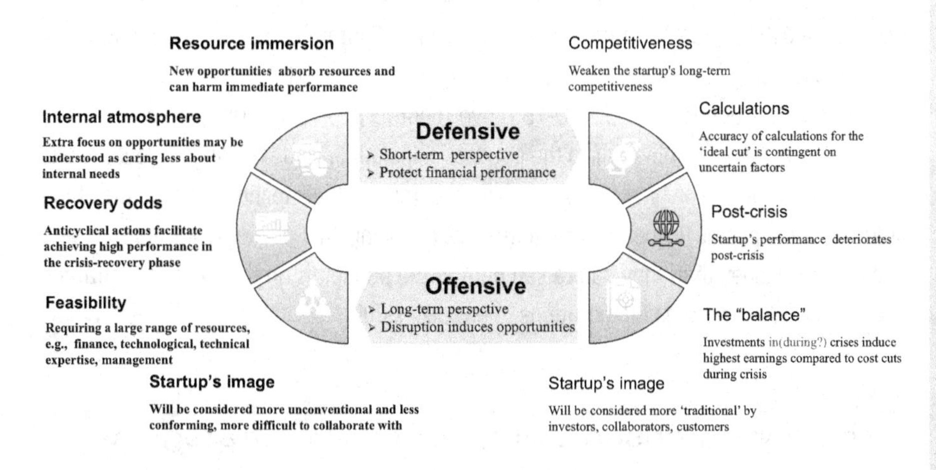

FIGURE 8.4 The entrepreneur's dilemma in managing crisis strategies

The entrepreneur's dilemma in managing crisis strategies is illustrated in Figure 8.4.

Time pressure hinders the ability to reflect on all of these considerations as well as to evaluate them through crisis management methods; in addition, the disruptions already caused by the crisis, even if they do not involve the startup directly, may push startups to employ strategies that have not been planned (i.e., as part of crisis management preparations). Nevertheless, the startup should be prepared with a large array of planned strategies and actual implementation plans: the more strategies detected by the startup, the more information obtained about their value/pitfalls, debates on the crisis are more openly shared, the better the startup's odds of picking a strategy that fits the situation. In the case of Hector, Manuel, and Bruna from Brazil, co-founders of MoneyMe—a smart community that aims to provide 'people-to-people' loans—the crisis pushed them to embrace a defensive approach to managing the disruption; the founders considered the outbreak of COVID-19 as auguring dramatic lowering of their customers' ability to loan money as well as to pay back loans already taken. The three feared that a collapse in the ability to return loans would affect their business' accountability and liability. Therefore, the founders proactively stopped business operations and focused on improving the technology to be prepared with a robust system when the pandemic was over. To date, all three founders are salaried employees in large corporations, and the likelihood of turning MoneyMe back into a thriving startup seems unclear due to the strategy taken by the co-founders aimed at protecting themselves and their business. In another startup from Brazil, co-founders Faren and Yara, two entrepreneurs who met in a university laboratory, created a network for volunteer work (e.g., from painting buildings, repairs, or cooking meals to teaching piano and preparing people for job interviews) provided by students to people residing in deprived regions in Brazil, based on smart AI and machine learning technology. The outbreak of COVID-19 drove them to approach strategic collaborators who had not 'dared' to join prior to the pandemic, including some leading regional public sector associations, for financial support in maintaining their technology and matching students with people in need of volunteer work. Using this strategy, the co-founders raised more money than they had raised prior to the pandemic. In this case, the strategy taken, that is, expanding collaborations, was successful.

Coping with crises using innovative strategies

Academic and professional reports have proven that during crises, innovation flourishes in entrepreneurial businesses, as startups often see crisis effects as an anticipated 'signal' or reason to start innovating. Innovation can be implemented across each of the startup's processes, whereas in times of crisis, it is aimed at protecting the startup from the crisis disruption while exploiting the opportunities raised by the crisis. Innovation is pursued to respond to the crisis differently from the competitors, hence achieving an immediate competitive advantage. The challenge is then to sustain this competitive advantage in the mid- and long term, and to ensure that the innovation is not risking any aspect of the startup that has not yet been uncovered. For example, a startup in the crypto field, initiated by two students—Julia and Julia and their professors in the United

States—ran out of money with the COVID-19 outbreak, and managed the situation by dismissing all internal employees, that is, the crypto experts and technological developers; to fill the positions in the technological department, the founders put out a 'call' for interns to work in their office; to replace the crypto experts, they looked for crypto or blockchain companies that had ceased their activity and scouted their ex-employees, who were out of a job. At this point in time, the experts were looking for new jobs, and were concerned about their odds of finding work during the crisis, as the general assumption was that companies are not hiring. These experts were willing to work for another startup for a lower salary compared to the alternative of being unemployed during a crisis. The startup gained a competitive advantage and is surviving the crisis, although new innovation is required.

Innovation is a promising avenue to tackle a crisis, but it often needs to reinnovate itself, that is, the process that has been innovated, or another business innovation needs to be introduced, that is, in another process that has not yet been innovated. The demand for recurring innovation is risky, as it may transfer the startup's main action from crisis management strategies to innovation. Innovation serves as a means to manage the crisis properly, for a compounded outcome that mitigates the threats, both concurrent and future ones, and creates new avenues to future competitive advantage.

Reviewing business models

Business models are shaped to strategically plan the foundation of the consequent business operations to capture value and competitiveness by planning the How, Who, When, and How Much. Business models hinge on external changes and are modified accordingly; for example, many businesses operated a freemium model prior to the pandemic, such that users only paid for upgraded services. The lockdowns brought on by COVID-19 entailed difficulties for businesses using freemium models, because many people were laid off and were more cautious about money sent for unnecessary services. These businesses therefore began to offer free services, using a model whereby the revenue comes from advertising. Alternatively, with people having to stay at home, often bored and upset due to the social isolation, they spend more time on the web and are more inclined to pay for digital services, providing an opportunity for startups to charge per service costs. These examples show how business models take in the external changes and respond accordingly, not necessarily by constantly changing the business model or its components, but by being aware of the changes and therefore reevaluating and validating the business model on a regular basis.

There are various types of business models, including the traditional pay for product or service model; the freemium model; the razor and blades model, in which the core product is priced for sale and uptake and the revenue comes from the associated consumable (Nestle model for coffee machines, for example); the social 'buy one, give one' model where, for each product sold, the startup gives a product to people in need (see, for example, TOMS shoes); the franchise model—licensed operation of a business by using the trademark, branding, and business model of a franchisor; or the crowdsourcing model, among many others. Some are gradual expansion models, which involve either modifying or pivoting some aspect of existing business models or creating brand new ones; for example, the bundling business model, which is the rethinking of a business model that stresses the key role of packaging together with complementary products, services, product-related knowledge, and so on: these are bundled into a single offering (such as McDonald's Happy Meals, 'combinations' that use product bundles), all for the purpose of navigating the startup to competitiveness under changes, difficulties, and opportunities in the external environment.

These models are sensitive to the customers' attraction to the provided product or service, and to the value customers assign to the startup's offerings; the payment, traction, interest, collaboration, and so forth are based on the customers' perceived need for the startup's offerings. For example, the common assumption that everybody needs basic food, such as bread, and therefore during any disruption, people will still buy bread, no longer holds, as not all people eat 'regular bread' (e.g., gluten intolerance, bread is perceived as a high-calorie food); in addition, bread production has evolved into different kinds of bread, including expensive ones, turning 'bread' into a non-basic food. In a similar vein, users and customers make decisions about the value of a product or service that can be disconnected from reality; for example, during the pandemic, there have been periods during which toilet paper or eggs have been perceived as being in low supply; many startups could leverage these concerns by modifying their business models to seize these opportunities. For example, Wolt,[4] a food delivery company, gained a central position in the market during the lockdowns, and has carefully monitored the customers' changing needs, changing its business model accordingly; the company has done so well that it has been purchased by DoorDash,[5] demonstrating how business models that are directed through a mindful approach, that reconfigure and redeploy their technologies, services, distribution, or prices, among others, according to the customers' expectations and needs, can exploit opportunities in times of crises.

Delving into the pillars of business models

Business model structures and operations, revenue streams, market strategy, leadership, and relationships with the ecosystem and stakeholders—there are multiple creative avenues that can be taken to cope with crises. Each of them lies in the premise that they need to be revised and validated for every new event brought on by the crisis. Tools for managing crises involve agility, creativity, embracing new perspectives on how to achieve the startup's goals, and veering with the changing needs and expectations of all stakeholders involved in the startup, that is, external (customers, users, suppliers, investors, pool of future employees), internal (co-founders, board of directors, management level, permanent and temporary employees), and interns, among others (Egan and Tosanguan 2009; Bullough and Renko 2013; Shepherd and Williams 2014; Davidsson and Gordon 2016; Terjesen, Guedes and Patel 2016; Williams and Shepherd 2016a,b; Doern, Williams and Vorley 2019).

These strategies and practices provide a wide range of avenues to embark on, with the aim of managing the crisis by responding using the four different pillars, often together, referring to both mitigating difficulties and exploiting opportunities. Specifically, the foundation of these practices is to tackle hardship and damages that have either struck or are expected to strike (e.g., if other startups have already been affected by the crisis) by controlling or diminishing the effects on the business; for example, in the case of a financial crisis that leaves customers unable to purchase and pay for the startup's product, a multifaceted effect on the startup is expected, for example, in cash flow, market leadership, potential customer betrayal, and difficulties paying suppliers, among others. The startup responds to these difficulties by retaining the operations that work and are profitable while ceasing all other operations or looking for new opportunities to manage the effects; but in the latter case, a new perspective is required to conquer the crisis' effects: rather than protecting the startup by shielding its operations and resources, they should be unleashed in a controlled fashion. This can be achieved by seizing new opportunities, investing in new areas, and improving the startup's processes, among others, as demonstrated in Figure 8.5.

To execute the coping strategies from the array of discussed practices, entrepreneurs need to embrace an improvisational approach, trust their intuition, take an open-minded attitude to managing the startup and therefore the crisis, and enact an agile mindset and behavior. In addition, external support is a key factor in facilitating crisis management practices; under complex, changing, and distressing circumstances, startups are

TABLE 8.1 Map of crisis management strategies and practices based on business model pillars

Business model	Alternate revenue streams	Market strategy	Startup leadership	Stakeholder
Create an agile strategy and subsequent goals, activities, and projects	Cash burn rate—revisit variable costs, capital investment plans; eliminate unnecessary expenses and if possible, operations	Revise the go-to market strategy or initiate new models of B2B, B2G, B2C, B2B2C, etc.	Innovate—create the novelty now: ways to tackle crises, communities, new venues for digital marketing, etc.	Embrace the ecosystem—share platforms, activities, tools, machinery, personnel, etc. that are less employed due to the crisis
Follow a lean business model—at least in some activities or projects	Extend cash run—leverage bank debts or venture debts; expediate receivables; be creative in new avenues of supply chain financing options	Evaluate sales distribution channels, including difficulties and opportunities	Penetrate new fields—constantly seek new opportunities directly related to your offerings and/or to your consumers' new needs	Contribute to the ecosystem—initiate communities, meetings, virtual conferences, and reunions, engage your stakeholders together
Strengthen the fit between all components by enabling accessibility to and collaboration with the business model	Barter—exchange service, expertise, and even products with other parties in the market instead of using money for payment	Competition: >> Collaborate rather than compete by merging activities/projects >> Share ideas, expertise, tips with your competitors to expand the service platform for your customers	Generosity—show your robustness in the market and in the industry by proposing assistance, providing support, mentoring, advising	Demonstrate value to existing investors and strategic collaborators; focus on exhibiting your response to the crisis rather than your difficulties
Think of the resources existing in the market that can be strategically leveraged for cash injections if needed	Convert fixed to variable costs by delaying payments, regard the suppliers as a source of financing, as they want to maintain the relationship	Anticipate the new customers' needs (due to the crisis) and the competitors' ability to respond to those needs; be the first to respond to them	Communicate changes constantly and ensure that the teams agree with those changes	Ask for professional assistance on financing resources, negotiations with banks, gain a thorough understanding of insurance resources

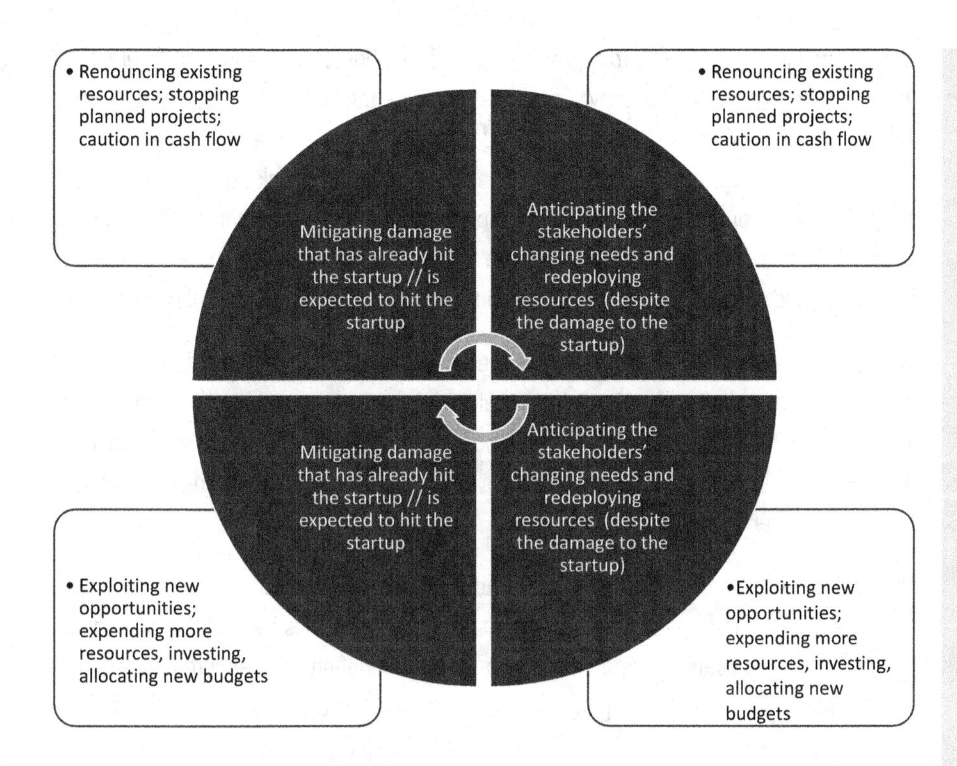

FIGURE 8.5 How to tackle the business models' crisis-related strategies/practices

incapable of reconfiguring and orchestrating the crisis strategies while managing the startup's 'regular' course of action; it is only by engaging other stakeholders' support that an effective response to crises can be mounted (Baker and Miner 2003; Hmieleski and Corbett 2008; Bingham 2009; Hmieleski, Corbet and Baron 2013; Adomako et al. 2018; Charoensukmongkol 2019; Khan et al. 2020; Seetharaman 2020; Wenzel 2021).

Summary

There are multiple ways to respond to a crisis' effects, which embody both risks and opportunities. The strategies and practices used to respond to and manage the crisis' effects should be embedded in the systematic course of the startup's action, and a blueprint of the crisis management strategy should be adjusted from time to time, to echo the changes in the business' capacity, the founders' approach—including the founders' dilemma in deciding on defensive or offensive approaches—and the ecosystem's attraction to the startup's offerings. Such adjustments will enable the startup to operate any crisis management approach more smoothly, as the components of the blueprint are always aligned to the startup's most up-to-date situation.

In fact, crisis management strategies and practices should not be very different from the regular ones, so that whenever they are required, they can be 'naturally' activated. The framework of their activation changes depending on the nature of the crisis and the severity of its fallout for the startup, for example, by fighting back against the damage or dedicating resources to avoid the stressor, among others; retrenchment by reducing costs or complexity; endurance that can be fulfilled by maintaining regular operations, personnel, and strategy; or innovating by courageously challenging the business model.

Innovation is a promising albeit risky avenue for tackling crises, and it includes innovating defensively and offensively, the latter being tightly associated with the opportunities introduced by the crisis. In fact, missing opportunities that arise during crises is destructive; as the crisis effects become more severe, they may prevent future possibilities, which may never come back.

The map of crisis management strategies and practices, based on business model pillars, demonstrates the multiplicity of possible responses to any crisis by focusing on specific pillars or even on specific components of a pillar or bundling several components from the different pillars. Finally, responding to crises requires the entrepreneur's full dedication and self-awareness, an open mind, intuition, and agility.

Reflective questions for class

1. Imagine that in January 2018, Procter & Gamble (P&G) (https://us.pg.com/) opened for business; apart of this imaginary scenario, P&G's evolution is as it has been in reality. In early 2020, as the pandemic broke out and lockdowns were imposed, P&G's activity was severely disrupted. Choose two approaches to managing the crisis based on the model presented in Figure 8.2: Approaches to managing an existing crisis, and discuss their suitability for P&G in coping with the crisis. What are your main conclusions?
2. Provide an example of a business that has tackled a crisis by one of the following processes, discussed in the model presented in Figure 8.5: How to tackle the business models' crisis-related strategies/practices. You may search the web or interview founders that you know. Prior to analyzing its crisis management strategy/practices, provide a brief on the business' main offerings and other relevant characteristics (e.g., location, age, number of employees).

   - Mitigating damage that has already hit the startup/is expected to hit the startup by renouncing existing resources; stopping planned projects; caution in cash flow

- Mitigating damage that has already hit the startup/is expected to hit the startup by exploiting new opportunities; expending more resources, investing, allocating new budgets
- Anticipating the stakeholders' changing needs and redeploying resources (despite the damage to the startup) by renouncing existing resources; stopping planned projects; caution in cash flow
- Anticipating the stakeholders' changing needs and redeploying resources (despite the damage to the startup) by exploiting new opportunities; expending more resources, investing, allocating new budgets

3. Discuss the opportunities and risks of innovation as a strategy to manage a crisis by comparing startups typified as follows:

   - Technological versus traditional
   - Nascent (up to two years) versus advanced (more than five years)
   - Small (up to five permanent employees) versus medium size (more than 30 permanent employees).

   What is your recommendation to startup founders? Explain your answer.
4. Choose one of the following fictional scenarios to discuss the entrepreneur's dilemma in managing a crisis based on points introduced in this chapter:

   - Steve Jobs starting Apple one year before the 9/11 attacks
   - Debbie Fields founding Mrs. Fields cookie stores (https://www.mrsfields.com/) one year before the COVID-19 outbreak
   - Mark Zuckerberg starting Facebook one year before the European debt crisis (2009/2010)
   - Elon Musk founding SpaceX on the same day as the Haiti earthquake in 2010 and the consequent global crisis
5. Search the web for two new startups (started between 2018 and 2020) and generate as much information as you can on them; provide their links and other relevant characteristics. Based on the information gathered, discuss:

   - What are the main challenges for each of these startups imposed by the COVID-19 pandemic?
   - Choose two different crisis management strategies from the map of crisis management strategies and practices based on business model pillars. Explain how you would recommend implementing each of the strategies/practices

you chose; how would it mitigate the fallout of the crisis for each of those businesses?

- Recommend one best strategy/practice for each of these startups. Explain your answer.

Notes

1 See https://help.twitter.com/en/using-twitter/periscope-faq

2 See https://www.forbes.com/sites/saritharai/2015/12/02/in-indias-flood-ravaged-chennai-city-it-is-startups-to-the-rescue/?sh=ce175174463e

3 See "To reinvent itself in telehealth, Wheel lands $150 million." Natasha Mascarenhas@nmasc_ / TechCrunch, January 19, 2022, at https://techcrunch.com/2022/01/19/to-reinvent-itself-in-telehealth-wheel-lands-150-million-series-c/?cx_testId=6&cx_testVariant=cx_undefined&cx_artPos=1#cxrecs_s

4 See https://wolt.com/en

5 See https://www.bloomberg.com/news/articles/2021-11-09/doordash-to-buy-finnish-food-delivery-app-wolt-for-8-billion

References

Adomako, S., Danso, A., Boso, N., & Narteh, B. (2018). Entrepreneurial alertness and new venture performance: Facilitating roles of networking capability. *International Small Business Journal, 36*(5), 453–472.

Baker, T., Miner, A. S., & Eesley, D. T. (2003). Improvising firms: Bricolage, account giving and improvisational competencies in the founding process. *Research Policy, 32*(2), 255–276.

Bennett, D. L., & Nikolaev, B. (2021). Historical disease prevalence, cultural values, and global innovation. *Entrepreneurship Theory and Practice, 45*(1), 145–174.

Bingham, C. B. (2009). Oscillating improvisation: How entrepreneurial firms create success in foreign market entries over time. *Strategic Entrepreneurship Journal, 3*(4), 321–345.

Buchanan, D. A., & Denyer, D. (2013). Researching tomorrow's crisis: Methodological innovations and wider implications. *International Journal of Management Reviews, 15*(2), 205–224.

Bullough, A., & Renko, M. (2013). Entrepreneurial resilience during challenging times. *Business Horizons, 56*(3), 343–350.

Bullough, A., Renko, M., & Myatt, T. (2014). Danger zone entrepreneurs: The importance of resilience and self–efficacy for entrepreneurial intentions. *Entrepreneurship Theory and Practice, 38*(3), 473–499.

Charoensukmongkol, P. (2019). Contributions of mindfulness to improvisational behavior and consequences on business performance and stress of entrepreneurs during economic downturn. *Organization Management Journal, 16*(4), 209–219.

Chattopadhyay, P., Glick, W. H., & Huber, G. P. (2001). Organizational actions in response to threats and opportunities. *Academy of Management Journal, 44*(5), 937–955.

Davidsson, P., & Gordon, S. R. (2016). Much ado about nothing? The surprising persistence of nascent entrepreneurs through macroeconomic crisis. *Entrepreneurship Theory and Practice, 40*(4), 915–941.

Deans, G. K. (2009). Making a key decision in a downturn: Go on the offensive or be defensive? *Strategic Direction,*

Doern, R., Williams, N., & Vorley, T. (2019). Special issue on entrepreneurship and crises: Business as usual? An introduction and review of the literature. *Entrepreneurship & Regional Development, 31*(5–6), 400–412.

Egan, V., & Tosanguan, P. (2009). Coping strategies of entrepreneurs in economic recession: A comparative analysis of Thais and European expatriates in Pattaya, Thailand. *Journal of Asia Entrepreneurship and Sustainability, 5*(3), 17.

Fairlie, R. W. (2013). Entrepreneurship, economic conditions, and the great recession. *Journal of Economics & Management Strategy, 22*(2), 207–231.

Hmieleski, K. M., & Corbett, A. C. (2008). The contrasting interaction effects of improvisational behavior with entrepreneurial self-efficacy on new venture performance and entrepreneur work satisfaction. *Journal of Business Venturing, 23*(4), 482–496.

Hmieleski, K. M., Corbett, A. C., & Baron, R. A. (2013). Entrepreneurs' improvisational behavior and firm performance: A study of dispositional and environmental moderators. *Strategic Entrepreneurship Journal, 7*(2), 138–150.

Khan, Z., Amankwah-Amoah, J., Lew, Y. K., Puthusserry, P., & Czinkota, M. (2020). Strategic ambidexterity and its performance implications for emerging economies multinationals. *International Business Review,* 101762.

Kitching, J., Blackburn, R., Smallbone, D., & Dixon, S. (2009). Business strategies and performance during difficult economic conditions.

Latham, S. (2009). Contrasting strategic response to economic recession in start-up versus established software firms. *Journal of Small Business Management, 47*(2), 180–201.

Martinelli, E., Tagliazucchi, G., & Marchi, G. (2018). The resilient retail entrepreneur: Dynamic capabilities for facing natural disasters. *International Journal of Entrepreneurial Behavior & Research.*

McDonald, R. M., & Eisenhardt, K. M. (2020). Parallel play: Startups, nascent markets, and effective business-model design. *Administrative Science Quarterly, 65*(2), 483–523.

Papaoikonomou, E., Segarra, P., & Li, X. (2012). Entrepreneurship in the context of crisis: Identifying barriers and proposing strategies. *International Advances in Economic Research, 18*(1), 111–119.

Penrose, J. (1995). Essential constructions? The 'cultural bases' of nationalist movements. *Nations and Nationalism, 1*(3), 391–417.

Seetharaman, P. (2020). Business models shifts: Impact of Covid-19. *International Journal of Information Management, 54,* 102173.

Shepherd, D. A., & Williams, T. A. (2014). Local venturing as compassion organizing in the aftermath of a natural disaster: The role of localness and community in reducing suffering. *Journal of Management Studies, 51*(6), 952–994.

Simón-Moya, V., Revuelto-Taboada, L., & Ribeiro-Soriano, D. (2016). Influence of economic crisis on new SME survival: Reality or fiction? *Entrepreneurship & Regional Development, 28*(1–2), 157–176.

Smallbone, D., Deakins, D., Battisti, M., & Kitching, J. (2012). Small business responses to a major economic downturn: Empirical perspectives from New Zealand and the United Kingdom. *International Small Business Journal, 30*(7), 754–777.

Sternad, D. (2012). Adaptive strategies in response to the economic crisis: A cross-cultural study in Austria and Slovenia. *Managing Global Transitions, 10*(3), 257.

Terjesen, S. A., Guedes, M. J., & Patel, P. C. (2016). Founded in adversity: Operations-based survival strategies of ventures founded during a recession. *International Journal of Production Economics, 173*, 161–169.

Thompson, E. R. (2009). Individual entrepreneurial intent: Construct clarification and development of an internationally reliable metric. *Entrepreneurship Theory and Practice, 33*(3), 669–694.

Wenzel, M. (2021). Transcending adaptation: Toward an examination of market-shaping capabilities as a sub-capability of organizational agility. *Journal of Competences, Strategy & Management, 11*, 1–12.

Williams, T. A., & Shepherd, D. A. (2016a). Building resilience or providing sustenance: Different paths of emergent ventures in the aftermath of the Haiti earthquake. *Academy of Management Journal, 59*(6), 2069–2102.

Williams, T. A., & Shepherd, D. A. (2016b). Victim entrepreneurs doing well by doing good: Venture creation and well-being in the aftermath of a resource shock. *Journal of Business Venturing, 31*(4), 365–387.

Chapter Nine

Entrepreneurial psychological capital

- Takeaways
- Psychological distress in times of crises
- Effects of the COVID-19 pandemic on emotional stress
- Stressors
- Emotional representations
- Assessment of stressful events
- Entrepreneurial psychological capital
- Summary
- Reflective questions for class

Takeaways

- Emotional distress commonly accompanies crises; it is a multifaceted reaction that requires attention at the individual, team, and business levels
- Emotional reactions differ in their type, magnitude, and duration, and are reflected in the startup's activity
- Crises stimulate additional work-related stressors that can exhaust the entrepreneur's entrepreneurial psychological capital (EPC), for example, through sleep deprivation, incessant worries about the future, feeling isolated
- Many types of crises induce different appraisals of stressors, which can be classified as negative (in most cases), neutral, or even positive
- There are various criteria for negative appraisals of crises, including damage that has already stemmed from the crisis, and the perceived personal, team, or business resources needed to cope with and mitigate the damage
- Indications of emotional distress can be revealed by self-reports, chats, and talks, which are most important in times of crisis, as well as by physiological, behavioral, and cognitive measures
- EPC is crucial to navigating crisis episodes; it has positive reciprocal effects on the individual, team, and business

DOI: 10.4324/9781003173809-9

Psychological distress in times of crises

Individuals experience stress in response to events that are perceived as threatening, stemming from either outside or inside the business; stress has negative consequences for the stressed individual, that is, the founder, the entrepreneurial team, and the business as a whole; moreover, stressful businesses can create an agitated entrepreneurial ecosystem. Stress is a function of compounded stimuli, such as stressful events, the entrepreneur's personality traits or even mood, and the environment's reaction to external or internal events, among others. Its consequences are multifaceted; stress uses up psychological capital (emotions, thoughts) and can lead to negative outcomes, including exhaustion, apathy, restlessness; however, it can be leveraged into a functional behavior, aimed at deterring the potential outcomes of the stressful situation, such as proactivity, creativity, collaborations, or it can be ignored, as if the stressful event had never occurred, allowing a 'pause'—a moratorium during which the entrepreneur can conduct 'business as usual' until the stressful event is over or its effects have diminished.

Crises stimulate more work-related stressors and concomitantly the general atmosphere during crises is troubled; this may cultivate more uncertainties and distress deriving from the crisis effects or perceived effects.

COVID-19—the pandemic outbreak is considered a 'sudden threat', as it appeared unexpectedly with acute effects very early on, and an impact that was felt throughout the global economy. Many entrepreneurs confronted the crisis with feelings of shock, fear, loss of control and anxiety about the future. In addition, many entrepreneurs felt *loss* because the pandemic took away their 'recognized and known' seemingly overnight. A feeling of loss is often regarded as a bereavement process based on successive stages of 'letting go' of the confining, negative feelings. Building on Bowlby's (1961) theory of attachment and the basic principles of bereavement, this process consists of four main stages:

(i) *Numbness*—represented by shock and its subsequent emotional attributes; research has shown that the pandemic elicited a reaction of shock among many startup founders, which immediately triggered a deliberate sensemaking process for the entrepreneurs with respect to their business' directions; this is mainly because entrepreneurial traits consist of flexibility and an initial 'recovery tendency'

(ii) *Yearning, searching, checking,* and *anger*—a stage typified by a blend of negative emotions, restlessness, and impulsive behavior; many entrepreneurs wonder why this is happening to them, and are enraged about the disruptive situation

Disorganization and *despair*—depicted by a lack of concentration, passiveness, or lack of interest, even in matters that were central to one's life; research has shown that while in non-crisis situations, entrepreneurs maintain a positive state of well-being, entrepreneurship presents extreme contexts in terms of uncertainty, risk, and leaps between unpredictability, ambiguity, and lack of control over activities and their consequent results; hence, the entrepreneurial burden, accompanied by high levels of stress, leads to despair, depression, and other attributes associated with mental disorders along their entrepreneurial journey, which are detrimental to entrepreneurial performance; accordingly, the pandemic may aggravate this stage's typical symptoms (Lin et al. 2003; Cella, Dymond and Cooper 2010; Patzelt and Shepherd 2011; Leignel et al. 2014; Hessels, Rietveld and van der Zwan 2017; Hessels et al. 2018; Lepeley 2019)

(iii) *Reorganization*—which is revealed sequentially; upon reaching this stage, individuals are mentally equipped to let go of the fear, anger, and despair, and devote more space to reorganizing 'what it is' toward recovery (Parkes 1986; Lerner and Keltner 2000; Lerner et al. 2015; Akkermans, Seibert and Mol 2018; Giones et al. 2020; Sassetti 2021)

Entrepreneurial traits, conjoined with entrepreneurs' awareness of their strengths, their higher likelihood to seek external assistance and their frequent experience with disappointments, even failure, are salient factors that elevate entrepreneurs' psychological resources in facing forfeiture due to the pandemic; on the other side, exhaustion of psychological resources, including sleep deprivation, continuous worry about the future, and a feeling of facing problems alone, increases entrepreneurs' vulnerability; some of them will be uncomfortable asking for help, which then prevents them from being proactive and looking for ways to manage the situation, and they may experience symptoms of depression (Morris et al. 2012; Doern and Goss 2013; Delgado García, De Quevedo Puente and Blanco Mazagatos 2015).

Previous crises—classifications of crisis severity[1] include the impact of the crisis, its complexity, its duration, the situation of the people affected by the crisis in both real time and subsequently geographical spread (e.g., regional, national, global), number of crises emerging concurrently, and other aspects that can either independently or together prompt negative emotional reactions among entrepreneurs. These reactions differ in their type (e.g., emotional, cognitive, behavioral), magnitude, and duration, and are often echoed in the startup's concurrent and ongoing activity and its consequences; in some cases, negative emotions will have a substantial negative impact on the business' innovation, new collaborations, relationships with the ecosystem; in addition, the impact can be temporary or last until the crisis' acute effects decrease, whereas in other cases it can be extensive, lasting for longer periods.

While the various types of crises that are continuously being documented worldwide (e.g., the hurricanes in Honduras; the floods in Henan Province, China; the Nicaraguan refugees in Costa Rica; the earthquake in Haiti; or the 'refugee crisis' in Europe) seem to vary widely in their essence, location, or impact, they are similar in that they stimulate multilayered emotional reactions among entrepreneurs who are directly or indirectly connected to them. For example, entrepreneurs who were affected by the hurricanes in Honduras[2] and the 'refugee crisis' in Europe (Ambrosetti and Paparusso 2015; Colucci 2019; Embiricos 2020), clearly two different crises in all respects, reported quite similar psychological effects. Cousins Rodrigo and Hessel Lopez run a startup that provides real-time, location-based information on restaurants, enables making a reservation online, and at times when the restaurant is quiet, sends out alerts on discounts, and more. While their business was not directly (physically) damaged by the hurricanes, many customers were severely affected—restaurants and clients/diners—and the business stopped operations. Rodrigo developed symptoms of depression and cancelled his founder's contract. Two and a half years later, the startup is no longer functional; both co-founders are engaged in other jobs. Bianca,[3] originally from Romania but whose family had moved to Syria for business, is the owner of a family business in Italy that develops smart color sensors; she is still harboring the crisis' effects. "For a short period of time we were treated as illegal immigrants as we had no residence permits; however, some of our family members were well connected, and the problem was resolved in a few months, but the family remained traumatized by the situation. My parents were depressed, and the family situation was grave. My husband and I established our company with members from my husband's side of the family; and for me it was a message of recovery and starting a new life," says Bianca.

Interestingly, though crises may invigorate through adversity in the short and long run, the consequent emotional reactions are often negative and permeate entrepreneurial spheres: the business, the team, and the entrepreneur. This is because the perception of the crisis' severity for one's business, team, or one's own emotional well-being is more consequential than the 'objective' severity of the crisis. Specifically, entrepreneurs are used to encountering crises of various types on a daily basis, which are deemed 'normal' work stressors along the entrepreneurial journey, for example, inability to locate the best technology to implement the business' planned products, unanticipated withdrawal of support, promises of funding that are not kept, and unexpected competitors with similar products/services. Some difficulties are business-centric rather than arising from the outside, such as an inability to allocate time or resources to a unique opportunity; a failed pitch to investors who then refuse to fund the business, among others.

Global crises, such as the COVID-19 pandemic, can inflame some of these 'regular' crises; for example, investors may be more cautious in investing in new businesses or technologies, and entrepreneurs may have stronger feelings about being rejected by stakeholders or being promised funding that then does not materialize. Yet, it is *how* entrepreneurs interpret the crisis situation that will determine the gravity of the crisis for the business, the team, and the entrepreneur. Many threatening aspects of the crisis are still vague and obscure, and may rise at some future time; thus, it is the entrepreneur's perception of the avenues that will minimize the hardship for the business and the team that determines the subsequent action. The accuracy of entrepreneurs' perceptions of the severity of a crisis, for example, how critical it is to their business, its expected duration, the availability of resources to cope with the adversity, etc., craft the emotional stress experienced across all levels of the business, the team, and the entrepreneur (Shepherd 2003; Shepherd, Wiklund and Haynie 2009; Lerman and Williams 2017; Stephan 2018; Lerman, Munyon and Williams 2021). The appraisal of stressors is recapitulated in Figure 9.1.

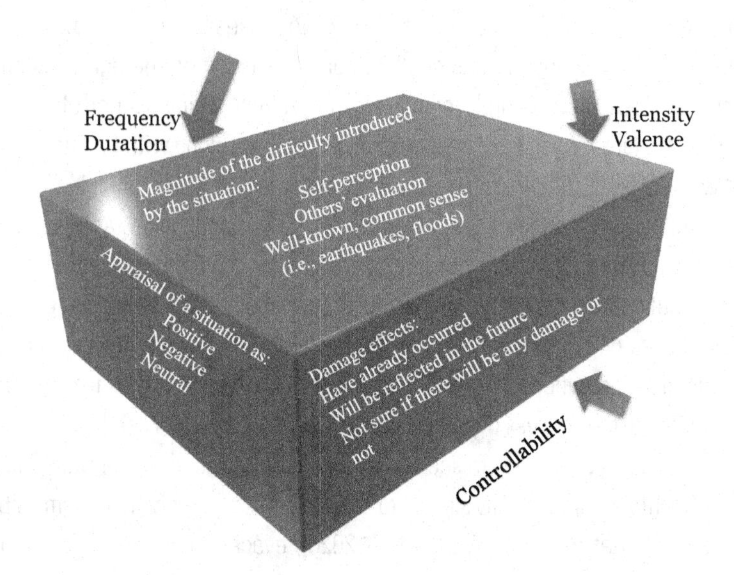

FIGURE 9.1 Crisis evaluation through the appraisal of stressors

Effects of the COVID-19 pandemic on emotional stress

The COVID-19 pandemic is bound to affect entrepreneurs' mental health, as it threatens multiple aspects of entrepreneurial life and taps into various dimensions—personal, family, people in the startup—related to health and the consequent organizational and business aspects, which put the startup at risk. Some concerns are associated with the consequences of lockdowns, quarantines, and in general the economy's unpredictable and unexpected course, and include working from home and the emergence of depression among employees; worries also involve thoughts of downsizing, slowdowns, temporary interruption of the startup's operations, or failure.

The line between 'reality' and 'worries' is blurred, as the crisis is still ongoing; some worries, comprised of perceptions and evaluations of the crisis' severity and consequences, can become real and be either destructive or beneficial for the startup; nevertheless, worrying as it pertains to emotional stress is damaging (Cullen, Gulati and Kelly 2020; Pfefferbaum and North 2020; Yıldırım and Solmaz 2020; Loan et al. 2021; Torrès et al. 2021).

According to the World Health Organization, "Fear, worry, and stress are normal responses to perceived or real threats, and at times when we are faced with uncertainty or the unknown. So it is normal and understandable that people are experiencing fear in the context of the COVID-19 pandemic."[4] However, research shows that interrelations between the distress clusters and combinations consisting of aggregated segments of these clusters breed new grounds for distress; for example, being worried about an elderly parent's illness (area: *health*, subarea: *significant others*), along with finding solutions for absent workers (area: *health*, subarea: *significant others at work*), while learning that the investor can no longer support the startup for personal pandemic-related reasons (area: *uncertainty*, subarea: *the startup*) represent a typical combined 'package' of stressful situations that deepen the entrepreneur's feelings of distress related to the pandemic. As such, and based on research and non-academic reports,[5] distress during this pandemic is not only more prominent than in previous global crises, but it also takes on different forms. Moreover, the distress dynamics parallel those of the virus itself: "the virus is constantly evolving, so we expect to see an accumulation of changes over time"[6] in producing more 'mental variants' that, similar to the virus itself, are highly transmissible (e.g., Anastassopoulou et al. 2021; Wang et al. 2020), evade people's mental or emotional 'immune' response and diminish their psychological well-being. These new mental variants are leading to the new forms of vulnerability experienced by entrepreneurs during

TABLE 9.1 Clusters of distress during COVID-19

Health	Oneself Significant others (family and friends)	• Physical and mental (e.g., being sick, hospitalized, under obligatory quarantine); risk of death • Worries about insufficient medical care/vaccines • Rumors, fake news • Older family members are a source of stress
	Significant others at work (colleagues, main stakeholders)	• Absenteeism (personal illness, family members' illness, taking care of children) • Damage to the startup's operation • Damage to the startup's growth; uncertain prospects • Distress resulting in lack of motivation, depression
Working from home	Being effective at work	• Lack of attention, concentration, enthusiasm • Feelings of loneliness • Restricted meaningful social contact with colleagues and the team • Limited opportunities to 'get together', share, brainstorm
	Organizing home	• Children at home • Organizing a 'suitable' place at home for work • Home-related tasks are neglected • Extended work hours; limited separation between work and home • Lack of privacy
Uncertainty	In oneself and family members	• Physical and mental health • Career advancement • Unexpected changes that require modifications (buying power, entertainment, traveling)
	In the startup	• General or specific departments' slowdown • Risk of shutting down/failure • The best employees quitting • Lack of availability of resources (e.g., funds, investments, experts) • Aggressive competition due to the crisis that will make the startup irrelevant • The solutions are no longer relevant

the COVID-19 pandemic that are ultimately reflected in risk perceptions of both health and economic conditions linked to COVID-19 (Brooks et al. 2020; Dryhurst et al. 2020; Lei et al. 2020; Liu, Yang and Zhang 2020; Shepherd 2020).

Stressors

Startups move through several transition phases that are uniquely stressful. Entrepreneurs are susceptible to three major sources of stress:

- Role-related (e.g., role ambiguity, role conflict, role overload, multivector work, multifaceted work)

- Startup operations (e.g., lack of or insufficient funding, deploying resources, attracting investors, providing solutions for multiple problems concurrently and recurrently, innovating)
- Entrepreneurial life stress (e.g., work-life balance, unpredictable income as an entrepreneur, the need to lead in the ecosystem on a permanent basis, the need to explore, test, and validate as well as iterate, pivot, and change—these are unique entrepreneurial stressors).

According to Selye's general adaptation syndrome, when an individual confronts a stressor, regardless of its type, the physiological response is the same, leading to general adaptation syndrome which consists of three phases when reacting to stressors:

Alarm—the body's first reaction, characterized by arousal of the sympathetic nervous system in a fight-or-flight response, and psychologically, by a primary appraisal process, where the situation is evaluated through a perspective with three dimensions, as demonstrated in Figure 9.2 (Cohen, Kamarck and Mermelstein 1983; Hughes et al. 2004; Lee, Joo and Choi 2013; Ruiz-Fernández et al. 2020).

With respect to the pandemic, these dimensions can be seen in the first appraisal under shock and in an emotion-based evaluation of a catastrophic situation that could considerably harm the business; consequently, entrepreneurs' behavioral response resonates this shock in the form of spontaneous, panicked reactions that have not been thought through, such as ending the business' operation, dismissing the most valuable talent, or

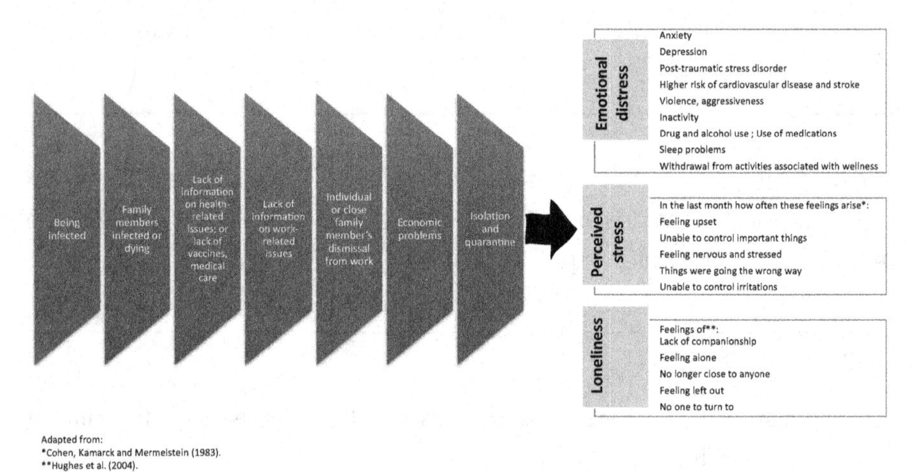

FIGURE 9.2 Stress effects of the pandemic

attracting external money that the founders might then be unable to repay to investors. The pandemic, similar to previous crises, has been typified as initiating panicked, agitated business reactions.

Resistance—this reaction occurs with continued exposure to the threatening situation, and psychologically it is portrayed as a secondary appraisal, which is more concerned with the evolution of one's coping abilities, available resources, needed skills, and relevant networking, among others, to manage or mitigate the threatening situation. This reaction leads to a less panicked and better thought-out response to the enduring threat; and it involves planning and reaching out for assistance while regaining control and recuperating the relevant skills and capabilities to deploy and mobilize the resources needed to adjust to the situation—turning the unusual into the everyday.

During the pandemic, those entrepreneurs who mobilized their existing resources in response to the challenges and adopted an agile mindset and conduct were more successful in fine-tuning their actions to face the difficulties introduced by the situation.

Resistance can be seen as a way of coping with bereavement, as entrepreneurs identify *loss* of the recognized and known and grieve for the 'things' that are no longer relevant or attractive, while being confused by the void arising from this loss. For example, in the case of Anna Bauer and Leon Wolf[7] from Germany, founders of HappyWasserSys, who are developing a smart system for water purification in deprived areas, the pandemic resulted in a dramatic decrease of interest in their system: "it was so unexpected, as the world was turning to better hygiene and more awareness of disinfectants and antiseptics, that we were both shocked. I can say that I was in mourning. I was really depressed, and even removed my name from our business' website, as 'a cry for help'; it was impulsive, and obviously stupid," says Anna. Leon took charge of the situation by strengthening the engagement of the existing customers, while holding back on the strategy of reaching out to new ones, to an indefinite point of time in the future. "In fact, if Leon had not been proactive, I guess we would have lost HappyWasserSys for good. I lay in bed for days, unwilling to do anything, and Leon 'forced' me to work; he connected me with our existing customers in India—a task that was mainly his responsibility pre-corona. My job had been to collect the feedback from our machine learning data analyses to plan the required customization. This is a standard task that we have been performing for almost 2 years, but it is always exciting and stimulating, as we need to think creatively, and make tailor-made adjustments in our system for every customer. Leon's idea to alter my job was the turning point," concluded Anna.

Exhaustion—physiological resources are drained.

Stressors include health-related fears, effects of quarantine and isolation, social distancing and restrictions on crowds, shaking hands, hugging, etc.; boredom; inadequate supplies of food, medication, vaccines; fake news and inaccurate information; financial loss; uncertainty about 'what comes next;' and the fear associated with exposure to conditions that are constantly out of control.

Distress has various symptoms, including exhaustion, detachment from others, lower levels of concentration and attention, and lower work productivity as well as anxiety, irritability, insomnia, and indifference to wellness, good nutrition, sports; such distress can be seen post-crisis as well. For example, studies conducted on Severe Acute Respiratory Syndrome (SARS) showed that people avoided others who were coughing or sneezing, enclosed crowded places, and all public spaces during and after SARS; people showed vigilant handwashing, alcohol abuse, violence, and other atypical behaviors long after the threat of SARS had disappeared (e.g., Cava et al. 2005; Reynolds et al. 2008; Wu et al. 2008).

This provides evidence of higher levels and new contents of distress during and probably after the COVID-19 pandemic. Reports keep showing increased rates of psychiatric and physician visits for anxiety and multiple, complex mental symptoms; higher rates of dispensed antidepressant prescriptions; and higher rates of calls to security forces for violent episodes. One prevailing explanation for this is associated with the widespread uncertainty brought about by the COVID-19 pandemic and a crucial antecedent to anxiety, fears, and depression (e.g., Ettman et al. 2020; Xiong et al. 2020; Fancourt, Steptoe and Bu 2021).

Emotional representations

The emergence of COVID-19 introduced another array of stresses for entrepreneurs, stemming from both the threat of infection and crisis-induced financial difficulties, which have led to various mental health problems among entrepreneurs, including loneliness, fear, confusion, anger, and burnout, among others (Wei et al. 2015; Brooks et al. 2020; Cullen, Gulati and Kelly 2020; Pfefferbaum and North 2020; Rossi et al. 2020; Trnka and Lorencova 2020; White and Gupta 2020; Yıldırım and Solmaz 2020).[8] These can be grouped into general representations as follows:

Emotional distress reflects the individual's subjective evaluation of an objective event (i.e., stressor) as threatening or potentially damaging; such evaluations are associated with individuals' perception of having no, or very limited control, or inadequate resources to deal with the challenge (Lazarus and Folkman 1984) leading to high perceived stress, anxiety, depression, and post-traumatic stress disorder as well as a higher risk of cardiovascular disease and stroke. In addition, studies show higher levels of adverse behavior patterns, in and outside the workplace, such as violence, aggressiveness, inactivity, drug and alcohol use, use of medications, withdrawal from activities associated with wellness— for example, a calm, full night's sleep, sports, good nutrition—that are essential to grappling with the reality, and vigorously dealing with the considerable challenges brought on by the pandemic (Wright et al. 2019; Besharat et al. 2020).

In startups, emotional distress is detrimental through its representation in adverse behaviors, such as an aggressive approach that can be turned inward toward the teams, hence resulting in conflicts and deficient teamwork, or outward toward stakeholders, which can lead to stakeholders' withdrawal and to a bad reputation for the business. Another representation can be found in inactivity and passivity, which are exhibited as reluctant behavior, for instance, overlooking opportunities that arise, neglecting agreements that have been made, or avoiding important stakeholders' needs. In addition, depression and distress are contagious, spreading rapidly inside and outside the startup.

Perceived stress—stress is a complex, negative emotional experience that can be represented in physiological, biochemical, cognitive, and behavioral changes that are directed toward changing the stressful situation or accepting the effects of the stress. Perceived stress is the negative appraisal of an event, mainly deeming it uncontrollable, unpredictable, or exceeding the individual's tolerance of unpleasant situations, hence worse than it really is.

Uncontrollable and unpredictable conditions are mainly associated with 'signs', such as behavioral measures (task performance under stress), physiological measures (aches, increased heart rate, blood pressure), and biochemical markers (elevated catecholamines), and these can draw from external or internal information.

In turn, emergence of perceived stress increases individuals' interpretations of internal or external conditions as undesirable (even those that had not been perceived as undesirable prior to the stress occurrence) and holding negative outcomes for the future, hence further damaging mental wellness.

Perceived stress can be acute, episodic, or chronic and stimulate a pool of negative effects: emotional (e.g., tension, anxiety, depression, irritability, and anger), physical (e.g., headaches, pain, fatigue, and stomach problems), behavioral (e.g., inattentiveness, lack of focus, and motivation), and adverse conduct (e.g., eating and sleeping disorders, abusive behavior, and violence). In the context of COVID-19, stressors that evolve into perceived stress include fear of contamination by the virus, distress from shutdowns and quarantine policies, irritation due to travel restrictions, and worries regarding avoidance of social activities. Perceived stress promotes loneliness, depression, and anxiety which result in an accumulated strain effect and consequent behavioral inactivity that hinders access to corrective experiences. All of these phenomena indicate that the COVID-19 pandemic's impact far exceeds its threat to physical health and is likely to have far-reaching repercussions for people's perceived stress.

Entrepreneurs face additional stressors related to panicked stock markets, sharp curbing of their customers' consumption, economic slowdown, and unemployment. The retention of customers in times of fear of infection coupled with social distancing is another source of stress, as physical visits and meetings at the company have decreased dramatically, hampering the use of entrepreneurs' main assets: transmitting their passion, enthusiasm, and charisma, and convincing their stakeholders of the value that they introduce throughout their process, products, and services.

Loneliness—social distancing, quarantines, shutdowns, and isolation protocols used to combat the virus have led to a new and severe mental health consequence—loneliness. Loneliness is an unpleasant state of sensing a discrepancy between the desired amount and quality of social interactions and that which is available from the person's environment. The social distancing measures that restrict social contact by separating individuals from family, friends, and colleagues, intensify loneliness, perceived as a negative, painful state that can evolve into fears related to social rejection, hence reducing social activity, and revealing increased rumination and worry over experiencing failure in any social interaction, resulting in reluctance to have any social contact. Loneliness is often associated with an array of somatic aches and mental disorders and can deteriorate into suicidal behavior. Continuation of perceived loneliness due to social distancing measures contributes to increased depression and anxiety, which endure after the social distancing measures have been lifted.

The sources of stressors prompting perceived loneliness are tightly linked to work-related situations, such as employee dismissals, which lead to uncertainty about one's job and income; working 'alone' from home, together with intensified exposure to the computer, which mitigate human contact; business shutdowns that can be threating; all of these reinforce the detrimental feeling of 'standing alone' in the face of difficulties. In addition, individuals who perceive loneliness tend to interpret situations as even more severe than they actually are and see the future as hopeless; their reassurance-seeking activities cease, leaving them with limited social capital to deal with the their feeling of loneliness, therefore making it worse.

In the startup's realm, a feeling of loneliness among entrepreneurs and employees is harmful, especially as social interactions are the backbone of startups' activities, that is, teamwork, interactions with stakeholders, customers, investors, market research that requires interaction and gaining insights, or disseminating the startup's offerings. As a social behavior, withdrawal means renouncing one of the salient tools of a startup's activity. Moreover, a pessimistic view, which is a typical consequence of perceived loneliness, is destructive for a startup's course of action (Eriksson, Unden and Elofsson 2001; Parslow et al. 2004; Luthans et al. 2006; Nambisan and Baron 2021); World Health Organization 2019; Ettman et al. 2020; Holmes et al. 2020; Limcaoco et al. 2020; Lin 2020; Tuzovic and Kabadayi 2020;; Liu et al. 2021).

Assessment of stressful events

Crisis situations can be assessed by different measures:

Self-reports—revealed *actively* by reactions to a stressful event, deriving from the entrepreneur's first reports on symptoms of emotional stress or physiological discomforts attached to perceived stress (without asking the entrepreneur) or *reactively* by reacting to questions on emotional distress.

At-a-Glance—the revolution of mental health

Due to the increase in mental health disorders during the COVID-19 pandemic, startups are leveraging technology to transform mental health into a personalized and reachable goal for anyone who needs monitoring and help in coping with difficulties.

One such startup is Circles (https://circlesup.com/), a platform designed to help users overcome life's challenges by matching them based on similar issues or experiences. The relevance of Circles has been proven, as it raised $8 million in the seed round during the pandemic.* According to Irad Eichler, founder and CEO of Circles, "not every challenge requires therapy and, more importantly, sometimes the best way to feel better is to surround yourself with people who actually understand you in a truly empathetic way. This desire to connect with others who are going through the same challenges often means that we wind up on Facebook groups or other unstructured online forums, but those outlets don't enable the types of meaningful connections needed to help people feel better. With Circles, people never have to face their struggles alone."

Mental health is increasingly crucial in times of crisis, especially as the COVID-19 pandemic has generated more stressors, and people are required to limit their physical and social interactions. Thus, fostering human connections is no longer just a 'nice to have' idea, but has become the essence of a healthy society that will be able to recover from the pandemic's effects.

According to Forbes,** Circles' vision is a noble cause in ensuring that nobody feels lonely or emotionally challenged. The pandemic has imposed social isolation across countries, communities, and industries; therefore, the need to connect and realize that 'we are all in the same boat', experiencing loneliness, fear, and worries, requires technological solutions that are accessible to everyone. However, the supply is incomplete and cumbersome. Deriving from robust research on the positive effect of meaningful connections to cope with distressing situations, Circles represents the startups' ability to respond to mental health needs through entrepreneurship.

*"Circles Raises $8 Million for Online Group Support Platform Making Emotional Wellbeing Accessible to All." Business Wire, August, 2021. https://www.businesswire.com/news/home/20210817005201/en/Circles-Raises-8-Million-for-Online-Group-Support-Platform-Making-Emotional-Wellbeing-Accessible-to-All

**"This Startup Just Raised $8 Million To Connect People To Virtual Support Groups." *Forbes.* Jair Hilburn. August, 2021. https://www.forbes.com/sites/jairhilburn/2021/08/17/this-startup-just-raised-8-million-to-connect-people-to-virtual-support-groups/?sh=4ac36d246e75

Behavioral measures—changes in work and task performance under stress; can be generated from observations of significant others, for example, team members, external stakeholders, or family and friends, as well as self-reports.

Cognition-related aspects—decreases in attention span, disorganization, and problems prioritizing; poor time management; trouble focusing on a task; inability to multitask; poor planning.

Physiological measures—such as heart rate, blood pressure, digestive problems, headaches; revealed by the entrepreneur's self-reports on changes or aggravation of symptoms under stress.

Biochemical markers—a biomarker is a characteristic that can be objectively measured as an indicator of a physiological response to stress; it shows which energy-consuming mechanisms are operating inside the body to maintain homeostasis.

These evaluations tend to appear when the negative events are perceived by the entrepreneurs as *uncontrollable* or *unpredictable*.

Entrepreneurs are typified as holding higher levels of job control; they need the freedom to shape their tasks, activities, and timing on their own, and do not tolerate supervision or any other form of control. Classical research has established that entrepreneurs possess high levels of self-confidence based on their omnipotent belief in their ability to control outcomes in the environment, that is, to control and predict what comes next. By encountering conditions that do not align with entrepreneurs' fundamental belief in their capabilities, that is, to control and predict external situations and their effects on the business and the team, entrepreneurs may be even more severely affected (Simon, Houghton and Aquino 2000; Zhao and Seibert 2006; Leutner et al. 2014; Antoncic et al. 2015).

Entrepreneurial psychological capital

EPC refers to the entrepreneur's aggregate capital, derived from his or her trust in being equipped with the relevant skills, knowledge, networking, and resources to manage a crisis. Such self-confidence is tightly related to positive psychological capital; this form of capital is comprised of confidence (self-efficacy), optimism, hope, resilience, and trust.

The elements of EPC, either together or separately, have a significant reciprocal impact on the different levels of the startup; as such, higher levels of EPC at the business level are echoed in the team's vibes and performance as well as in the individual's behavior and well-being. Concurrently, lower levels of EPC at the business level, which can be reflected in disordered performance, result in work delays or commitments that are not

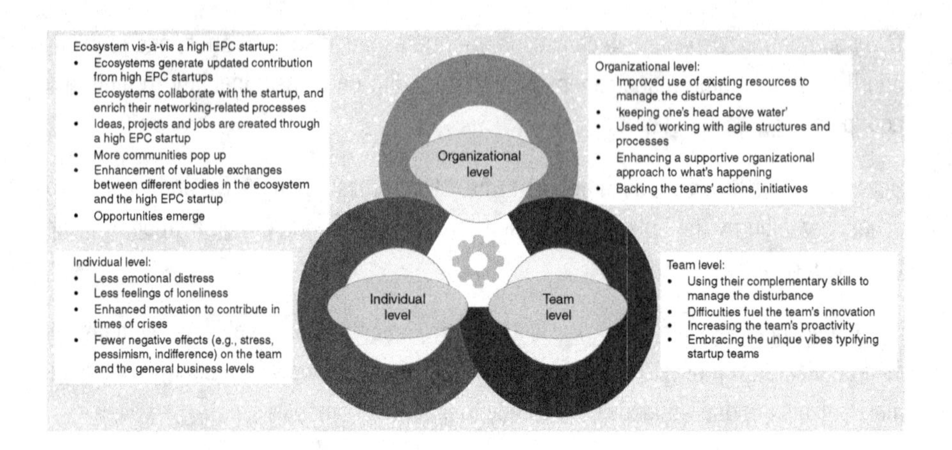

FIGURE 9.3 Effects of higher EPC across startup levels

honored and often reverberate in the team's and individual's lack of passion, boredom, or even apathy. Similar effects can be found bottom-up; a few individuals in the startup who are 'positive' and reflect optimism, hope, or confidence during disruptive situations can elevate the team's and the business' approach to managing the situation, while a group of individuals holding lower levels of EPC can induce higher levels of distress and disorganized performance at the team and business levels (Firkin 2003; Luthans, Luthans and Luthans 2004; Page and Donohue 2004; Luthans, Youssef and Avolio 2007; Baluku, Kikooma and Kibanja 2016).

Figure 9.3 describes the reciprocal effects of higher EPC at individual, team, and business levels.

Summary

The unexpected, uncontrollable COVID-19 pandemic threatens entrepreneurs, who feel not only the loss of the 'recognized and known', but also loss of their control and navigation of the startup. This resembles a bereavement process and raises negative emotions. Though stressful situations may provide the impetus to be functional, thus leading to positive outcomes, the emotions that accompany stressful situations are fundamentally negative. Entrepreneurs represent a 'unique case' in their understanding of and reaction to crises: entrepreneurs are used to crises as well as to their emotional distress when facing adversity; from this perspective, their emotional response to the pandemic would be expected to be similar to that when ordinary crises are faced; yet, emotional distress drains energy and EPC, leaving the entrepreneur with less capacity to emotionally navigate the situation. Moreover, stress effects associated with a crisis, existing or potential, can be manifested in various ways, for example, aggravated perceived stress, feelings of loneliness, and withdrawal, which can lead to unrealistic decisions and subsequent actions that can harm the startup's course and create new crisis layers. Awareness of signs of emotional stress—such as self-reports, behavioral, cognitive, or physiological measures, or biochemical markers—in oneself or in members of the startup is therefore crucial for navigating in times of crisis. Similarly, detecting the EPC at the individual, team, and business levels can regulate the crisis' effects on the startup.

Reflective questions for class

1. Search the internet for a startup that has been severely affected by the pandemic. Learn about the stressors, sources, and current outcomes of the pandemic on the startup's status. Prepare an interview to gauge the founder's emotional reaction to the hardship consisting of eight to ten questions based on this chapter's concepts.
2. Search startups and entrepreneurship newsletters to learn about businesses in times of COVID-19. Choose two to three startups and analyze them based on the main concepts appearing in Figure 9.2: Stress effects of the pandemic. What are your main conclusions?
3. Dafni and Raul from Spain are running a community of experts that provides full coverage of positive psychological attributes, especially in response to the pandemic's effects. The community is operated through innovative drone capacity; it engages experts from around the world and enables optimal updating processes; it is meant to reduce distress anywhere, anytime, and under any circumstances by calling upon the foremost experts. Analyze its effects on the ecosystem based on Figure 9.3: Effects of higher EPC across startup levels.
4. Interview five entrepreneurs that you know/in your local area on the clusters of distress during the COVID-19 pandemic: health, working from home, and uncertainty. What are the most common stressful situations reported by the entrepreneurs? What are your insights based on this mini research?
5. Search the internet for three to four other crises (e.g., natural disasters, economic crises, wars/terrorism, etc.). Investigate them through two aspects of the stressor appraisals, demonstrated in Figure 9.1: Crisis evaluation through the appraisal of stressors. What are your conclusions?

Notes

1 For example, The INFORM Global Crisis Severity Index (GCSI)—an improved, timely way of measuring the severity of humanitarian crises and disasters globally. See https://www.acaps.org/sites/acaps/files/resources/files/gcsi_beta_brochure_spread.pdf; ACAPS is an independent information provider, a nonprofit, nongovernmental project with the aim of conducting independent, groundbreaking humanitarian analyses to help humanitarian workers, influencers, fundraisers, and donors make better-informed decisions (https://www.acaps.org/countries).

2 See https://www.amnesty.org/en/latest/news/2020/12/devastating-impact-hurricanes-eta-iota-honduras/; Hurricane Iota strengthens to 'extremely dangerous' Category 5 storm, takes aim at Central America. John Bacon. *USA Today*. November 2020. https://www.usatoday.com/story/news/nation/2020/11/15/hurricane-iota-honduras-nicaragua-threatened-after-hurricane-eta/6302797002/; battered by back-to-back hurricanes, Honduras braces for a long recovery. Delphine Schrank. *Washington Post*, November 2020. https://www.washingtonpost.com/world/the_americas/hurricane-eta-iota-honduras-central-america/2020/11/25/8cd11e98-2e75-11eb-bae0-50bb17126614_story.html

3 Not all personal details have been revealed as per the interviewee's request.

4 See "Mental health & COVID-19." https://www.who.int/teams/mental-health-and-substance-use/covid-19

5 https://www2.deloitte.com/content/dam/Deloitte/ca/Documents/about-deloitte/ca-covid19-human-impact-pov-en-aoda.pdf; EY (2020) "How COVID-19 reshapes the mental health needs of workers." https://www.ey.com/en_gl/health/how-covid-19-reshapes-the-mental-health-needs-of-workers

6 Quote from Dr. Erik Volz, an epidemiologist who studies the evolution of infectious diseases at Imperial College London in the UK. See Covid-19 variants: Five things to know about how coronavirus is evolving. Richard Gray. Horizon, March 29, 2021. https://ec.europa.eu/research-and-innovation/en/horizon-magazine/covid-19-variants-five-things-know-about-how-coronavirus-evolving

7 Some details have been changed as per the interviewees' request.

8 From Torrès et al. (2021).

References

Akkermans, J., Seibert, S. E., & Mol, S. T. (2018). Tales of the unexpected: Integrating career shocks in the contemporary careers literature. *SA Journal of Industrial Psychology, 44*(1), 1–10.

Ambrosetti, E., & Paparusso, A. (2015). Immigration policies in the EU: Failure or success? Evidences from Italy. In *Italy in a European context* (pp. 28–49). Springer.

Anastassopoulou, C., Siettos, C., Russo, L., Vrioni, G., & Tsakris, A. (2021). Lessons from the devastating impact of the first COVID-19 wave in Italy. *Pathogens and Global Health, 115*(4), 211–212.

Antoncic, B., Bratkovic Kregar, T., Singh, G., & DeNoble, A. F. (2015). The big five personality–entrepreneurship relationship: Evidence from Slovenia. *Journal of Small Business Management, 53*(3), 819–841.

Baluku, M. M., Kikooma, J. F., & Kibanja, G. M. (2016). Psychological capital and the startup capital–entrepreneurial success relationship. *Journal of Small Business & Entrepreneurship, 28*(1), 27–54.

Besharat, M., Khadem, H., Zarei, V., & Momtaz, A. (2020). Mediating role of perceived stress in the relationship between facing existential issues and symptoms of depression and anxiety. *Iranian Journal of Psychiatry, 15*(1), 80.

Bowlby, J. (1961). Separation anxiety: A critical review of the literature. *Journal of Child Psychology & Psychiatry.*

Brooks, S. K., Webster, R. K., Smith, L. E., Woodland, L., Wessely, S., Greenberg, N., & Rubin, G. J. (2020). The psychological impact of quarantine and how to reduce it: Rapid review of the evidence. *The Lancet, 395*(10227), 912–920.

Cava, M. A., Fay, K. E., Beanlands, H. J., McCay, E. A., & Wignall, R. (2005). The experience of quarantine for individuals affected by SARS in Toronto. *Public Health Nursing, 22*(5), 398–406.

Cohen, S., Kamarck, T., & Mermelstein, R. (1983). A global measure of perceived stress. *Journal of Health and Social Behavior,* 385–396.

Colucci, M. (2019). Foreign immigration to Italy: Crisis and the transformation of flows. *Journal of Modern Italian Studies, 24*(3), 427–440.

Cullen, W., Gulati, G., & Kelly, B. D. (2020). Mental health in the COVID-19 pandemic. *QJM: An International Journal of Medicine, 113*(5), 311–312.

Delgado García, J. B., De Quevedo Puente, E., & Blanco Mazagatos, V. (2015). How affect relates to entrepreneurship: A systematic review of the literature and research agenda. *International Journal of Management Reviews, 17*(2), 191–211.

Doern, R., & Goss, D. (2013). From barriers to barring: Why emotion matters for entrepreneurial development. *International Small Business Journal, 31*(5), 496–519.

Dryhurst, S., Schneider, C. R., Kerr, J., Freeman, A. L., Recchia, G., Van Der Bles, Anne Marthe, Spiegelhalter, D., & Van Der Linden, S. (2020). Risk perceptions of COVID-19 around the world. *Journal of Risk Research, 23*(7–8), 994–1006.

Dymond, S., Cella, M., Cooper, A., & Turnbull, O. H. (2010). The contingency-shifting variant Iowa Gambling Task: An investigation with young adults. *Journal of Clinical and Experimental Neuropsychology, 32*(3), 239–248.

Embiricos, A. (2020). From refugee to entrepreneur? Challenges to refugee self-reliance in Berlin, Germany. *Journal of Refugee Studies, 33*(1), 245–267.

Eriksson, I., Undén, A., & Elofsson, S. (2001). Self-rated health. Comparisons between three different measures. Results from a population study. *International Journal of Epidemiology, 30*(2), 326–333.

Ettman, C. K., Abdalla, S. M., Cohen, G. H., Sampson, L., Vivier, P. M., & Galea, S. (2020). Prevalence of depression symptoms in US adults before and during the COVID-19 pandemic. *JAMA Network Open, 3*(9), e2019686.

Fancourt, D., Steptoe, A., & Bu, F. (2021). Trajectories of anxiety and depressive symptoms during enforced isolation due to COVID-19 in England: A longitudinal observational study. *The Lancet Psychiatry, 8*(2), 141–149.

Firkin, P. (2003). *Midwifery as non-standard work: Rebirth of a profession.* Labour Market Dynamics Research Programme, Massey University.

Giones, F., Brem, A., Pollack, J. M., Michaelis, T. L., Klyver, K., & Brinckmann, J. (2020). Revising entrepreneurial action in response to exogenous shocks: Considering the COVID-19 pandemic. *Journal of Business Venturing Insights, 14,* e00186.

Hessels, J., Rietveld, C. A., Thurik, A. R., & Van der Zwan, P. (2018). Depression and entrepreneurial exit. *Academy of Management Perspectives, 32*(3), 323–339.

Hessels, J., Rietveld, C. A., & van der Zwan, P. (2017). Self-employment and work-related stress: The mediating role of job control and job demand. *Journal of Business Venturing, 32*(2), 178–196.

Holmes, E. A., O'Connor, R. C., Perry, V. H., Tracey, I., Wessely, S., Arseneault, L., Ballard, C., Christensen, H., Silver, R. C., & Everall, I. (2020). Multidisciplinary research priorities for the COVID-19 pandemic: A call for action for mental health science. *The Lancet Psychiatry, 7*(6), 547–560.

Hughes, M. E., Waite, L. J., Hawkley, L. C., & Cacioppo, J. T. (2004). A short scale for measuring loneliness in large surveys: Results from two population-based studies. *Research on Aging, 26*(6), 655–672.

Kabadayi, S., O'Connor, G. E., & Tuzovic, S. (2020). The impact of coronavirus on service ecosystems as service mega-disruptions. *Journal of Services Marketing.*

Lazarus, R. S., & Folkman, S. (1984). *Stress, appraisal, and coping.* Springer Publishing Company.

Lee, J., Joo, E., & Choi, K. (2013). Perceived stress and self-esteem mediate the effects of work-related stress on depression. *Stress and Health, 29*(1), 75–81.

Lei, L., Huang, X., Zhang, S., Yang, J., Yang, L., & Xu, M. (2020). Comparison of prevalence and associated factors of anxiety and depression among people affected by versus people unaffected by quarantine during the COVID-19 epidemic in Southwestern China. *Medical Science Monitor: International Medical Journal of Experimental and Clinical Research, 26,* 924609.

Leignel, S., Schuster, J., Hoertel, N., Poulain, X., & Limosin, F. (2014). Mental health and substance use among self-employed lawyers and pharmacists. *Occupational Medicine, 64*(3), 166–171.

Lepeley, M., Kuschel, K., Beutell, N., Pow, N., & Eijdenberg, E. (2019). The wellbeing of women in entrepreneurship. In *A global perspective.* Routledge.

Lerman, M. P., Munyon, T. P., & Williams, D. W. (2021). The (not so) dark side of entrepreneurship: A meta-analysis of the well-being and performance consequences of entrepreneurial stress. *Strategic Entrepreneurship Journal, 15*(3), 377–402.

Lerman, M. P., & Williams, D. W. (2017). Entrepreneurs and stress: A cognitive and dynamic approach. *Frontiers of Entrepreneurship Research, 37.*

Lerner, J. S., & Keltner, D. (2000). Beyond valence: Toward a model of emotion-specific influences on judgement and choice. *Cognition & Emotion, 14*(4), 473–493.

Lerner, J. S., Li, Y., Valdesolo, P., & Kassam, K. S. (2015). Emotion and decision making. *Annual Review of Psychology, 66*, 799–823.

Leutner, F., Ahmetoglu, G., Akhtar, R., & Chamorro-Premuzic, T. (2014). The relationship between the entrepreneurial personality and the Big Five personality traits. *Personality and Individual Differences, 63*, 58–63.

Limcaoco, R. S. G., Mateos, E. M., Fernández, J. M., & Roncero, C. (2020). Anxiety, worry and perceived stress in the world due to the COVID-19 pandemic, March 2020. Preliminary results. MedRxiv.

Lin, C. (2020). Social reaction toward the 2019 novel coronavirus (COVID-19). *Social Health and Behavior, 3*(1), 1.

Lin, S., Lee, C., Pan, C., & Hu, W. (2003). Comparison of the prevalence of substance use and psychiatric disorders between government-and self-employed commercial drivers. *Psychiatry and Clinical Neurosciences, 57*(4), 425–431.

Liu, S., Yang, L., & Zhang, C. (2020). Online mental health services in China during the COVID-19 outbreak. *Lancet Psychiatry, 7*, e17–e18.

Liu, S., Lithopoulos, A., Zhang, C., Garcia-Barrera, M. A., & Rhodes, R. E. (2021). Personality and perceived stress during COVID-19 pandemic: Testing the mediating role of perceived threat and efficacy. *Personality and Individual Differences, 168*, 110351.

Loan, L., Doanh, D. C., Thang, H., Nga, N. T. V., Van, P. T., & Hoa, P. T. (2021). Entrepreneurial behaviour: The effects of the fear and anxiety of Covid-19 and business opportunity recognition. *Entrepreneurial Business and Economics Review, 9*(3), 7–23.

Luthans, F., Avey, J. B., Avolio, B. J., Norman, S. M., & Combs, G. M. (2006). Psychological capital development: Toward a micro-intervention. *Journal of Organizational Behavior: The International Journal of Industrial, Occupational and Organizational Psychology and Behavior, 27*(3), 387–393.

Luthans, F., Luthans, K. W., & Luthans, B. C. (2004). Positive psychological capital: Beyond human and social capital.

Luthans, F., Youssef, C. M., & Avolio, B. J. (2007). *Psychological capital: Developing the human competitive edge.* Oxford University Press.

Morris, M. H., Kuratko, D. F., Schindehutte, M., & Spivack, A. J. (2012). Framing the entrepreneurial experience. *Entrepreneurship Theory and Practice, 36*(1), 11–40.

Nambisan, S., & Baron, R. A. (2021). On the costs of digital entrepreneurship: Role conflict, stress, and venture performance in digital platform-based ecosystems. *Journal of Business Research, 125*, 520–532.

Page, L. F., & Donohue, R. (2004). Positive psychological capital: A preliminary exploration of the construct. *Monash University Department of Management Working Paper Series, 51*(4), 1–10.

Parkes, K. R. (1986). Coping in stressful episodes: The role of individual differences, environmental factors, and situational characteristics. *Journal of Personality and Social Psychology, 51*(6), 1277.

Parslow, R. A., Jorm, A. F., Christensen, H., Rodgers, B., Strazdins, L., & D'Souza, R. M. (2004). The associations between work stress and mental health: A comparison of organizationally employed and self-employed workers. *Work & Stress, 18*(3), 231–244.

Pfefferbaum, B., & North, C. S. (2020). Mental health and the Covid-19 pandemic. *New England Journal of Medicine, 383*(6), 510–512.

Reynolds, D. L., Garay, J. R., Deamond, S. L., Moran, M. K., Gold, W., & Styra, R. (2008). Understanding, compliance and psychological impact of the SARS quarantine experience. *Epidemiology & Infection, 136*(7), 997–1007.

Rossi, R., Socci, V., Talevi, D., Mensi, S., Niolu, C., Pacitti, F., Di Marco, A., Rossi, A., Siracusano, A., & Di Lorenzo, G. (2020). COVID-19 pandemic and lockdown measures impact on mental health among the general population in Italy. *Frontiers in Psychiatry*, 790.

Ruiz-Fernández, M. D., Ramos-Pichardo, J. D., Ibáñez-Masero, O., Cabrera-Troya, J., Carmona-Rega, M. I., & Ortega-Galán, Á. M. (2020). Compassion fatigue, burnout, compassion satisfaction and perceived stress in healthcare professionals during the COVID-19 health crisis in Spain. *Journal of Clinical Nursing, 29*(21–22), 4321–4330.

Sassetti, S. (2021). *Entrepreneurship and emotions: Insights on venture performance*. Emerald Group Publishing.

Shepherd, D. A. (2003). Learning from business failure: Propositions of grief recovery for the self-employed. *Academy of Management Review, 28*(2), 318–328.

Shepherd, D. A. (2020). COVID 19 and entrepreneurship: Time to pivot? *Journal of Management Studies*.

Shepherd, D. A., & Patzelt, H. (2011). The new field of sustainable entrepreneurship: Studying entrepreneurial action linking "what is to be sustained" with "what is to be developed". *Entrepreneurship Theory and Practice, 35*(1), 137–163.

Shepherd, D. A., Wiklund, J., & Haynie, J. M. (2009). Moving forward: Balancing the financial and emotional costs of business failure. *Journal of Business Venturing, 24*(2), 134–148.

Simon, M., Houghton, S. M., & Aquino, K. (2000). Cognitive biases, risk perception, and venture formation: How individuals decide to start companies. *Journal of Business Venturing, 15*(2), 113–134.

Stephan, U. (2018). Entrepreneurs' mental health and well-being: A review and research agenda. *Academy of Management Perspectives, 32*(3), 290–322.

Torrès, O., Benzari, A., Fisch, C., Mukerjee, J., Swalhi, A., & Thurik, R. (2021). Risk of burnout in French entrepreneurs during the COVID-19 crisis. *Small Business Economics*, 1–23.

Trnka, R., & Lorencova, R. (2020). Fear, anger, and media-induced trauma during the outbreak of COVID-19 in the Czech Republic. *Psychological Trauma: Theory, Research, Practice, and Policy, 12*(5), 546.

Wang, Y., Wang, Y., Chen, Y., & Qin, Q. (2020). Unique epidemiological and clinical features of the emerging 2019 novel coronavirus pneumonia (COVID-19) implicate special control measures. *Journal of Medical Virology, 92*(6), 568–576.

Wei, Y., McGrath, P. J., Hayden, J., & Kutcher, S. (2015). Mental health literacy measures evaluating knowledge, attitudes and help-seeking: A scoping review. *BMC Psychiatry, 15*(1), 1–20.

White, J. V., & Gupta, V. K. (2020). Stress and well-being in entrepreneurship: A critical review and future research agenda. In *Entrepreneurial and small business stressors, experienced stress, and well-being.*

World Health Organization. (2019a). *WHO global report on traditional and complementary medicine 2019.* World Health Organization.

World Health Organization. (2019b). *The WHO special initiative for mental health (2019–2023): Universal health coverage for mental health.* World Health Organization. Retrieved from http://apps.who.int/iris/; WHO IRIS https://apps.who.int/iris/handle/10665/310981

World Health Organization. (2021). *Global antimicrobial resistance and use surveillance system (GLASS) report: 2021.* World Health Organization.

Wright, E. N., Hanlon, A., Lozano, A., & Teitelman, A. M. (2019). The impact of intimate partner violence, depressive symptoms, alcohol dependence, and perceived stress on 30-year cardiovascular disease risk among young adult women: A multiple mediation analysis. *Preventive Medicine, 121*, 47–54.

Wu, P., Liu, X., Fang, Y., Fan, B., Fuller, C. J., Guan, Z., Yao, Z., Kong, J., Lu, J., & Litvak, I. J. (2008). Alcohol abuse/dependence symptoms among hospital employees exposed to a SARS outbreak. *Alcohol & Alcoholism, 43*(6), 706–712.

Xiong, J., Lipsitz, O., Nasri, F., Lui, L. M., Gill, H., Phan, L., Chen-Li, D., Iacobucci, M., Ho, R., & Majeed, A. (2020). Impact of COVID-19 pandemic on mental health in the general population: A systematic review. *Journal of Affective Disorders, 277*, 55–64.

Yıldırım, M., & Solmaz, F. (2020). COVID-19 burnout, COVID-19 stress and resilience: Initial psychometric properties of COVID-19 Burnout Scale. *Death Studies, 46*(3), 524–532.

Zhao, H., & Seibert, S. E. (2006). The big five personality dimensions and entrepreneurial status: A meta-analytical review. *Journal of Applied Psychology, 91*(2), 259.

Chapter Ten

Female entrepreneurship in crises

- Takeaways
- Female entrepreneurship: a general overview of its uniqueness and challenges
- Female entrepreneurship and crises: identification and exploitation
- Entrepreneurial emotions—a gendered look
- Strategic orientation from a female entrepreneurship point of view
- Women's psychological capital
- Summary
- Reflective questions for class

Takeaways

- Noting that women-led startups are unique entities
- Observing that COVID-19 has a negative impact on some components of startups (e.g., purchase power, sales, liquidity, attracting investors) which is more pronounced among female entrepreneurs
- Recognizing that the course of action of identifying and then deciding on how to navigate a crisis is exclusive among female founders of startups
- Understanding that the business areas affected by crises and disturbances in women-led startups are diverse and involve areas that women are more vulnerable to, such as finance, turnovers, partnerships, relations with investors
- Recognizing that female entrepreneurs are well equipped with abilities and characteristics that enable them to identify changes that can predict potential crises; their openness to the emotional aspects of entrepreneurship, including awareness, feelings, intuition, and acceptance of sensemaking, allow them to take in the full range of the situation
- Exploring the notion that emotional intelligence is a key driver in identifying changes and actions and is most beneficial in times of crisis for gaining an understanding from a variety of analyses that compound perceptions, appraisal, emotional knowledge, etc.

DOI: 10.4324/9781003173809-10

- Being alert to the dark side of the startup's intensified work, competition, and ongoing rivalry for resources, experts, funds, etc. during crises
- Using entrepreneurial psychological capital to identify potential crises and to deploy resources in preparation for managing the crisis

Female entrepreneurship: a general overview of its uniqueness and challenges

Crises and turbulent times have a severe negative impact on both women and men's employment, including job loss, decreased salaries, reduced opportunities to find new jobs; such effects are exhibited in the entrepreneurial dynamics. While COVID-19 has impacted all entrepreneurs worldwide, its effects show some disparity between the genders. In fact, in clinical and academic studies, more women than men reported that the pandemic poses a real threat to their entrepreneurial undertakings, although their perceptions of concern and threat did not progress to closures.

Female entrepreneurs run smaller startups, and as such are more vulnerable to economic impacts due to lower average firm age and size; moreover, they are concentrated in the industrial sectors (e.g., wholesale/retail trade, health, education, and social service sectors) that are hit hardest by economic shutdowns; in addition, these sectors' lower entry barriers and higher competition at the outset make them among the most vulnerable in most economies. Women's startups have less capital and attract lower levels of investment; moreover, during the pandemic, many women have had to carry the brunt of the caregiving as a result of school closures and support of aging parents through social distancing. Although many women entrepreneurs feel that they are barely able to keep their startups afloat, many also trust that they will not 'shut their doors'; instead, they will pivot and concentrate on internal and neglected processes such as reorganization, documentation, and training. Overall, they feel that they can navigate the situation.

This resilient, vigorous spirit among female entrepreneurs is more typical to founders of startups than to founders of entrepreneurial businesses in general, particularly because they work in specialized teams, are deeply involved in innovation—mainly technology—and most of them have attracted external funds, to which they are accountable; hence, they have more to lose in 'shutting their doors' on the one hand, and have more to introduce with their expertise, innovation, and invested money on the other.

The general picture of the effects of COVID-19 on female startup founders is still puzzling; there is some evidence of a more pronounced negative impact on men, whereas others show that women have been more strongly affected by the crisis. Most statistics and narratives stemming from global reports show that female startup founders have pivoted their business activity and models in response to the effects of the crisis, albeit not immediately; rather, they have strategically 'paused' to reorganize their opportunities, resources, and needs while 'keeping the wheels in motion' in practice (Kalnins and Williams 2014; McManus 2017; Diallo, Qayum and Staab 2020; Manolova et al. 2020[1]; World Economic Forum 2020[2]; Kariv, Baldegger and Kashy-Rosenbaum 2022). According to the comprehensive research from Diana International Research Institute surveys conducted by Manolova and her colleagues (2020), the COVID-19 pandemic has presented the following three major challenges for female entrepreneurs: (1) the industries in which most women operate are disproportionately affected by recessions; (2) women are more likely to run many of the youngest, smallest, most vulnerable businesses; and (3) with schools closed and elderly family members at risk, women are more likely to be juggling primary caregiving and homemaking while they scramble to save their businesses. More recent statistics show that although opportunities for women seemed daunting, new avenues began to open up for some women-led startups in digital and creative industries, where female founders have adapted relatively rapidly by exploiting opportunities directly associated with the pandemic's needs. Among other worldwide organizations, the World Bank[3] and the OECD[4] have thoroughly investigated female entrepreneurs' navigation through the pandemic, including in tapping opportunities to enable their businesses to survive; in the typical women-based sectors, the COVID-19 pandemic has unevenly impacted their businesses and their recovery activity has not yet fully materialized.

In comparison to past crises, the COVID-19 pandemic has prompted different patterns of impact on employment and entrepreneurship. The sharpest deviation from the historical norm is the disproportionate impact of the pandemic on working women. According to world reports and research,[5] rates of job loss are much higher for women; moreover, while the actual rate of business creation during crises declines, this drop is more noticeable among women entrepreneurs. Global statistics show that new businesses are more likely to be started by men, although it should be noted that the gender gap has been narrowing in recent years. Regardless, the COVID-19 pandemic seems to be having an amplified impact on women's readiness to start new businesses (Paulson and Townsend 2004; Klapper and Love 2011; Elam et al. 2019; Dattani 2020; Fairlie 2020; Kariv, Elisha and Schwartz 2021).

While crises present stressors with negative effects on the workforce, these are more pronounced among women than men, because the former tend to be more negatively affected in terms of physical and mental health than the latter. These effects are further reflected in gender differences in entrepreneurial intentions, perceptions, and attitudes as well as in women's engagement in low-quality entrepreneurial endeavors compared to men due to limited income choices and difficulties accessing funding (Arenius and Minniti 2005; Pines, Lerner and Schwartz 2010; Paul and Sarma 2013; Giorgi, Lockwood and Glynn 2015; Zampetakis et al. 2017).

What makes female entrepreneurship an exclusive aspect of entrepreneurship?

Female entrepreneurship can be defined by three perspectives, as demonstrated in Figure 10.1. The human capital perspective addresses female entrepreneurship through the inner business lens by looking into gender, seniority, and quantity; as such, a female entrepreneurial business is a company with at least one woman on the founding team and higher rates of women in apex management as employees, on the board of directors, and as other stakeholders directly related to the business. Some studies deriving from this perspective go 'beyond the numbers' to the traits that are most cited in the literature as representing female or male social capital, such as motivation (e.g., the need for achievement, autonomy and independence, risk-taking, and locus of control). The underlying premise is that a higher number of women in a business with higher seniority will be related to women-driven social capital.

The sector or vertical perspective considers the following attributes as associated to women-based or men-based sectors:

- Labor intensive—requires high specialization/expertise
- Crowded with competitors
- Offering opportunities for growth
- Introducing high profitability
- Traditional/non-traditional, entailing innovation and R&D (e.g., technology, construction, manufacturing)
- Attractive to the ecosystem, 'trendy'

Women are portrayed as more concentrated in sectors/verticals that are less promising with regard to offering opportunities or growth prospects or are less attractive to the ecosystem; for example, the technology sector is perceived to be male-dominated, though actually it has a strong female presence; yet, unlike the human capital perspective, the sector attributes are what count here.

The third perspective can be considered a result of the two former perspectives and looks at the orientation toward how to lead the business' processes; some orientations are attributed to a man's approach and others to a woman's. For example, research on female entrepreneurs' management and leadership style, termed 'feminine mode' of management, associates it with being risk-averse, unstructured, and not growth-oriented, while concurrently values building strong relationships with employees, nurturing a less hierarchical organizational structure, promoting a work-family business culture, and overall is aligned with women's values in taking care of people's needs and well-being; these, in turn, align with the business' goals and therefore the pursuit of social goals (Chaganti 1986; Brush 1992; Greene et al. 2003; Eddleston and Powell 2008; Fenwick 2008; Moore, Moore and Moore 2011; Adkins et al. 2013; Kariv 2013; Bamiatzi et al. 2015; Galloway, Kapasi and Sang 2015; Henry et al. 2015; Harrison, Leitch and McAdam 2018; Dean et al. 2019; McAdam, Harrison and Leitch 2019). Consequently, startups led by women are portrayed as employing less organizational and business strategies that target higher financial profits, growth strategies such as 'exits', IPOs, and exponential development in market dominance or global exposure; instead, women founders tend to 'keep' their startups, nurture their companies, and are less liable to sell them; they are more engaged

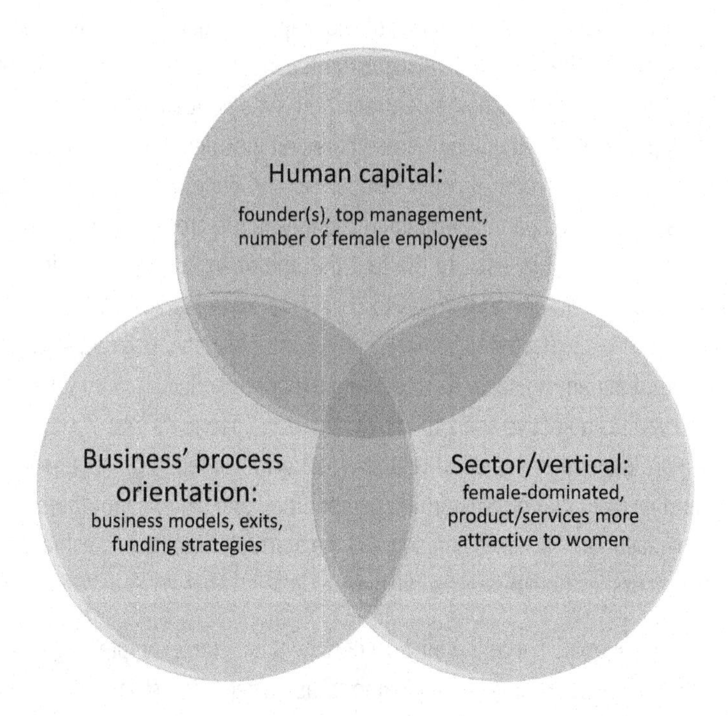

FIGURE 10.1 Perspectives in demarcating female entrepreneurship

in social values, although financial factors are prominent in their business' decisions and implementation; they are dedicated to the community—and human—aspects of their businesses, which may sometimes slow their financial potential (Coleman and Kariv 2013; Kariv and Coleman 2015).

Business interpretations and perceptions

Startups aim for success, contribution, and sustainability, but the operational definition of these concepts varies between the genders. The notion of success is a subjective and relative evaluation; the view of a business as a successful undertaking is often formed relative to the initial expectations regarding its outcomes and dynamics, to competitors, and to significant others' feedback. Sensemaking is therefore critical in observing, analyzing, and deciding upon situations or episodes that are unpredictable and unplanned, consisting of the metaphors, mental models, and language used (Hill and Levenhagen 1995; Nicholson and Anderson 2005; Weick, Sutcliffe and Obstfeld 2005).

Business success can also be determined by its outcomes, which is probably the most frequently used measure of success; yet, inputs or processes can be successful, even if they do not lead to a successful outcome, hence emphasizing the incompleteness of considering outcomes as the main and most substantial measure of success. For example, in the case of Sylvie, a French Canadian entrepreneur who co-founded a food tech startup that is developing smart technology to match human nutritional needs with customized daily diets in partnership with grocery companies, the penetration of new, larger, and global food and retail companies, reflecting changes in the process, is perceived by Sylvie as an achievement; this, despite the fact that the financial outcomes, including the business' financial state decreased due to costs related to marketing. Sylvie feels that such partnerships are expected to be financially profitable in the long run, to enhance the startup's reputation, and to serve as a learning experience. Success can thus be judged according to various objective and subjective factors; components that are specific to the startup or more general or expected relative to effort invested (e.g., engagement, commitment, and investment on the startup), competitors, and significant others' feedback. In addition, measures of success can address the startup's outputs and achievements as well as its process, as demonstrated in Figure 10.2.

A woman's measure of success can be contingent on, for example, significant others' expectations about women's employment, as entrepreneurship is perceived to be male-dominated; hence, 'just' being a startup's founder may be perceived as success

Evaluated by:	Contingent on:	Founder's engagement	Startup's VRIN; stage of development; exponential growth	Startup's investments	Competitors' status	Significant others' feedback
Quantitative data:						
Numbers & facts on the startup itself						
Statistics of the ecosystem						
Research: Measures, outcomes, opportunities						
Qualitative data:						
Founder's expectations						
Team evaluations						
Blogs, social media, posts						
Qualitative research: interviews, narratives						

FIGURE 10.2 A startup's success: what it is contingent on and its evaluation

by some women, while men would be less apt to consider such aspects in evaluating success. Making a contribution is frequently seen as a situation or achievement that can be attributed to promoting or changing 'something' or 'someone', an approach associated with doing good in the world, contributing to the community. This can be achieved through the startup's offerings; for example, Antonella and Sofia from Chili are developing sustainable solutions using solar energy for renewable energy, and thus combating climate change, or Mimi Chan, who is the founder and CEO of Littlefund,[6] a way for family and friends to gift savings to a fund dedicated to a child's future goals and dreams. It can also be achieved through the startup's processes, such as hiring people with disabilities; for example, Himari, originally from Japan, who is developing, as part of her doctoral studies in the United States, a smart device to monitor medication usage in hospitals; she is hiring people with disabilities for documentation and reporting. Finally, it can be achieved by contributing to the business' profits or by self-actualization through starting a business (i.e., the founder's perspective), among others. Women and men tend to 'see' contribution differently; women are more focused on promoting causes and are more engaged in the values that they advance. Sustainability is associated with the determination to 'keep the wheels in motion' by nurturing and cultivating the business. This approach is attributed to women founders more than to men, due to their family-driven—rather than business-driven—approach, termed the 'motherhood' factor. Women are depicted as more prone to keeping their business, its employees, and its loyal customers, even when little profit is generated.

Gender differences prevail in the startup realm, and thus in the identification of situations as disruptive, and in the avenues taken to manage the opportunities and inhibitors that such situations entail.

Female entrepreneurship and crises: identification and exploitation

Crises embody a multifaceted construct that has prompted various conceptual models to define and demarcate them. These models have generated a variety of criteria to delineate crises based on different premises: hard versus soft data, qualitative versus quantitative assessments, and external versus internal factors, among others, which are contingent upon interpretation. Combining women's unique mindset, entrepreneurial style, and operation with the complex construct of 'crisis', the sensemaking and meaning of crisis differ between the genders, which is attributed to women's interpretation of the 'facts' that comprise the crisis.

Defining a 'collection of factors interacting with each other' as a *crisis* may draw on financial aspects of the business and can include analyses related to the here and now or prospective financial attributes; different time periods (e.g., daily, monthly, annual

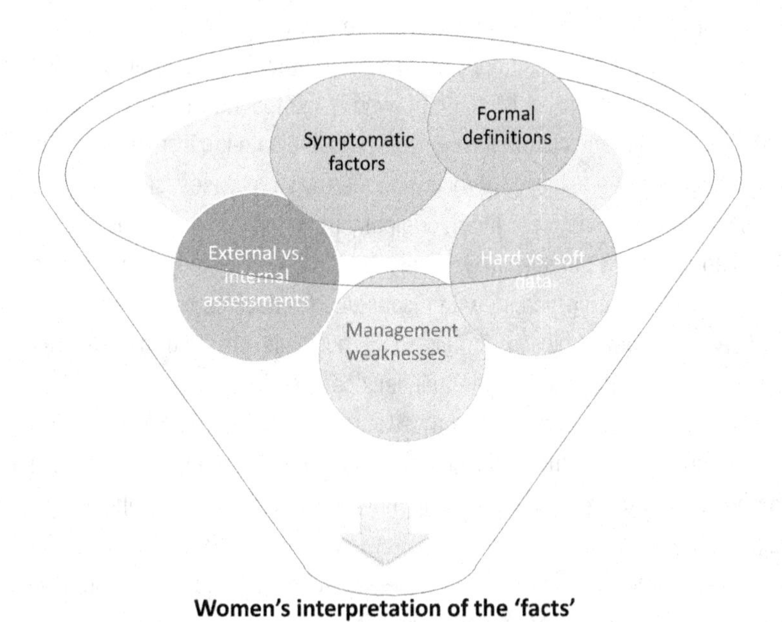

FIGURE 10.3 Premises of crisis definition

analyses); and different approaches to 'money' gained, such as liquidity, expenses, revenues, profits, permanent versus temporary financial assets, a company's capitalization and liabilities, bankruptcy diagnostics, and funding debt and equity ratios, among many other measures (Altman 1968, 2000; Taffler and Tisshaw 1977; Springate 1978; Zavgren 1985).

Among the other measures, which are not directly connected to financial components, crises draw on the following areas:

Areas	
• ***Sales***	Purchasing power, offerings' attractiveness
• ***Competition***	Based on sectors, geographical location, business' stage of development
• ***Turnover***	Of board members, management, employees as well as partners, customers
• ***Attraction of investors***	Viability and feasibility of financial support; financial dependence/independence
• ***Partnerships***	Leading companies' interest in M&A,[7] financial support, strategic alliances, barter formulas
• ***Relations with shareholders***	Viable interest in and an ongoing attraction to the startup's action by stakeholders and shareholders; reliable and valuable networking
• ***Globalization***	Global interest in the startup; global potential of the startup's offerings, technology, expertise, etc.
• ***Business' robustness***	Level of the management's control; role of the board of directors; pace of reaction to changes; agility
• ***Leadership***	Sustainable leadership, trust, and contribution to the business' community
• ***Agility and crisis management***	Openness to pivot, change, let go, or amend ideas, processes, projects, or products based on pressures, disruptions, or turbulent episodes; resilience

The identification of a startup's crisis is thus complicated and relies on different areas, methods of assessment, and approaches.

Entrepreneurial emotions—a gendered look

Adaptability and agility are key virtues for startup founders in order to consolidate the multidimensional pressures that are continually bombarding their companies, which can evolve into potential crises. Entrepreneurial emotions embody the array of mindsets, approaches, feelings, and consequent thoughts, planning processes, and actions that promote higher adaptability and agility. Research has established that emotions precede both cognition, represented by thoughts and consciousness, and behavior, represented by performance and actions, as emotions 'run fast' and manipulate the brain's functional and cognitive abilities; as an example, while being stressed or afraid (emotions), it is very difficult to learn new material and concentrate (cognitive, thought) and therefore complete an exam on the new material (behavior). Emotional resources often dictate the way people think, perceive (cognitive), and, consequently, act. Startup founders are generally deemed to be more attached to their emotional side and thus more open to detecting, intuiting, and empathizing with others, which creates a competitive advantage in providing a quicker and fuller sense of the situation. Higher levels of entrepreneurial emotions enable adapting, altering, or pivoting the startup's action to manage disruptions. Cardon and colleagues (2012, p. 1) define entrepreneurial emotion as "the affect, emotions, moods, and/or feelings—of individuals or a collective—that are antecedent to, concurrent with, and/or a consequence of, the entrepreneurial process, meaning the recognition/creation, evaluation, reformulation, and/or the exploitation of a possible opportunity." Entrepreneurial emotions run the gamut from passion, joy, happiness, or feeling of full engagement to fear, including fear of failure and fear of taking risks, anger, FOMO,[8] reluctance to act, and more.

A stronger emotional orientation and its consequent cognitive and behavioral representations are attributed to female as compared to male founders. Women founders tend to consider feelings, moods, meanings, and interpretations as significant components 'that matter' and as embedded in identifying situations, decision-making processes, and action. As such, the insights obtained from situations by female founders are rich and span the full range of 'understanding' a situation by harmonizing objective and subjective perspectives into a more complete conception of the situation that is being faced.

Entrepreneurs in general are exposed to emotional volatility, with the negative and positive emotional components playing a dominant role in their entrepreneurial journey. These emotions are strongly influenced by the circumstances and context, which are recognized as dynamic and fluctuating in the startup realm. Concurrently, contextual factors and situational processes are interpreted through the individual's range of emotions, from fear (i.e., negative emotions) to enthusiasm (embracing a challenge or treating it as an opportunity, i.e., positive emotions).

Female founders tend to interpret situations through an emotional filter, which enables them to be more alert and to more quickly distinguish any internal or external changes that imply a potential crisis, and they can plan their actions accordingly. Moreover, they have the advantage of being able to turn these disruptive factors, processes, or relationships into opportunities that can be leveraged and promote their business (Baron 2008; Foo, Uy and Baron 2009; Breugst et al. 2012; Welpe et al. 2012; Audretsch and Lehmann 2016; Audretsch 2017; Bernoster et al. 2018; Stuetzer et al. 2018; Stroe et al. 2020). The example of Eliza Blank, founder of The Sill, a thriving brand that sells plants,[9] demonstrates this advantage. She encountered a severe setback with the outbreak of the COVID-19 pandemic; she had to temporarily close all of her stores, and she lost money across her five shuttered locations. According to Blank, "It was terrifying at first"; yet, by being open to her entrepreneurial emotions, she was able to see more clearly and quickly how she could turn the situation into an opportunity:

> We had solicited feedback from our retail team at the beginning of January 2020, and many of them felt that they did not have enough time to train before being put in front of the customer, and they didn't have clarity concerning their career trajectory and growth paths. So we used those 12 weeks when we were shut down to go back to the drawing board and redo things, like training and process and education.

Blank spent the time well by pivoting her actions to training and education, strategically foreseeing what would be required to manage the crisis ahead.

Women's emotional proclivity allows them to be alert to and aware of settings and relationships in their startups, such as recruitment of new experts who can change the status quo, new competition from the outside, or unplanned costs that require reorganization of priorities. By being open to reacting emotionally and broadening their reactions to the full range, women gain the advantage of 'having dibs'; they are the first to identify any changes, and have the privilege of serving as 'gatekeepers' and deciding whether to approve the changes or prevent them from entering the business.

At-a-Glance—the pandemic's effect on a female startup freeing cattle from medication*

A startup based on smart technology introduced a novel monitoring system for cattle's body measurements to predict mammary infections as a preventive approach to managing diseases and optimizing milk that is free of preventive antibiotics. The founders negotiated the second round of investment with a network of local investing angels and a university fund. The purpose was mainly to market the system to farms, laboratories, and 'kibbutz' areas. The outbreak of the pandemic changed the investing angels' priorities, and they decided to shelve their endowment. Consequently, the heads of the university fund decided to postpone their support. The five co-founders, all female graduate students, met in a biology laboratory at a prestigious university in India and started developing the system; they panicked from the unexpected lack of financial support. In fact, the startup still had some resources that allowed it to proceed with the technological development of the system; it also had some ongoing contracts with some kibbutzes in Israel and with a laboratory in India. Factually, there was no reason to panic. Yet, three co-founders foresaw a catastrophic scenario for the startup, and consequently, their performance decreased. For example, one of the co-founders contacted their existing clients to inform them of the postponement of the next investing round, which immediately led to misunderstandings and trust issues with these clients. The other co-founder, responsible for the patenting process, decided to withdraw from the application process; she was the only expert in the biological and scientific aspects of the system, hence her exit from the process was a most detrimental act. The five had many conflicts inside the team and with stakeholders. Eventually, only the two co-founders continued developing the system; it has been pivoted to censor microorganisms in public objects, and the first object was public escalators in malls; it attracted some financial support from local governmental associations, which enabled technological refinement of the system. The startup is still struggling to form a community around its vision and technology and to attract clients.

*Some details have been changed by the interviewees' request.

The dark side of the startup—disruptors

Along with the passion and enthusiasm involved in startups' intense and unplanned dynamic rise, intensified work has some negative impacts on the founders and teams. The startup is subjected to potential crises stemming from inside and outside the firm, while concurrently, it can stimulate such crises; both directions can have severe effects on the startup's founders and teams, and these effects are recognized as more pronounced among female founders due to their high levels of entrepreneurial emotions. *Forbes* published an article "The Emotional Cost of Being a Female Millennial Startup Founder"[10] (Loubier 2017), listing the emotional effects of successful startups and the cost of the mantra 'fake it till you make it' in terms of elevated stress and burnout, unrealistic expectations from the founder to demonstrate constant improvement and exponential achievements, and loss of work-life balance. Concurrently, female founders are among those who create such crises by pushing for constant improvement, intensified competitive advantage, and leadership in their ecosystem. This is then resonated in the requirements that they impose on their teams: working tirelessly for hours on end, obtaining diverse information, being constantly on the alert and ready to act in the face of challenges, unplanned situations, needs or expectations with which they are bombarded, and continuously improving their technological and professional capabilities to maintain leadership in this ongoing up-to-date field. Such requirements, though inherent to the startup's activity, cultivate layers of disturbance at both the founder and employee levels. Women experience emotional distress from outside or inside the startup at high volume. The effects can be at the individual level (e.g., emotional, cognitive), collective level (e.g., team conflicts, unhealthy competition among employees), organizational level (e.g., shifts from the core activity of the firm to manage the disruptions), or business level, including negative competition for experts, investors, or customers' attention, as exhibited in Table 10.1.

TABLE 10.1 Startups induce disruptions

	In the company Impact on founders and employees	Outside the company
Long working hours	• Fatigue • Emotional distress • Loss of work–life balance	• Setting unfavorable standards for other startups • Exhausting the ecosystem
Pressures to lead professionally; be #1! Be exclusive	• Constant stressful environment • Unrealistic requirements to be professionally, business- wise, globally, etc., updated on a daily basis • Feeling unaccomplished; never feeling fulfilled • Internal conflicts; damaging competition	• Constant competition • Lack of measures to assess professional leadership can create hostility in an unfair race • Unethical/dishonorable ways to gain customers' attention
Competing to attract the best experts	• Internal (negative) competition for dominance of expertise and knowledge • Frustration due to search for experts outside the firm • Social and cultural disputes due to recruitment of experts and new entrants	• Lower negotiable status vis-à-vis experts (e.g., salaries, working conditions) • Conflicts with companies in the ecosystem • Irrelevant(?) pressures in recruitment
Continual financial constraints	• Constant emotional stress and pressures • Conflicts on the ways to attract more funds, reduce costs, etc. • Giving up on projects due to lack of resources • Shifts from plans and goals to attract money • Instructing employees across the firm to resolve financial constraints	• Competition on resources • Racing to attract investors

The case of Ayanthi[11] from Sri Lanka exemplifies some perspectives of the disruptive aspects of startups. For her, as a co-founder of a business based on a smart online platform that connects, through machine-learning, micro-business founders with the best-matched job leads in Sri Lanka, the COVID-19 pandemic opened the way to expanding globally. Ayanthi and her colleagues garnered interest from some investors and global companies who were outsourcing recruitment of remote workforces, but the co-founders knew that some budding startups were working intensively on developing platforms that provided similar services, leveraged by the restrictions imposed during the pandemic; and when a national competition was announced, the 'race' began. According to Ayanthi:

> It felt like a race against the time. Our company started to work intensively, for long hours, under stress and very rigid requirements, in our attempt to develop the platform before the competition. It was unrealistic considering the time framework.

In their attempt to hasten the development of the platform, the company used a head-hunting method to hire an expert. "This was the last straw in our company's craziness," says Ayanthi; they invested a lot of financial resources to recruit the expert, and the employees complained about being unappreciated for the excessive work that they had invested while the founders recruited an external (costly) expert. The startup eventually won the prize at the competition, but some team members left the company. Ayanthi concludes that she and her co-founders had "to recalculate our roadmap, to show our teams our respect and trust."

Emotional intelligence

Research has already established that women entrepreneurs possess a high level of emotional intelligence, identified by Salovey and Mayer (1990) as "the ability to monitor one's own and others' feelings and emotions, to discriminate among them and to use this information to guide one's thinking and actions" (p. 189), which includes four dimensions (Mayer and Salovey 1997):

- Perception, appraisal, and expression of emotions
- Emotional facilitation of thinking
- Understanding and analyzing emotional information, employing emotional knowledge
- Regulation of emotions

The relevance of emotional intelligence for female founders encountering disruptions can be broken down as follows.

TABLE 10.2 Emotional intelligence-related reactions

	Emotional intelligence-related reactions			
	Perception and expression of emotions	*Emotional facilitation of thinking*	*Analyzing emotional information*	*Regulation of emotions*
Crisis reactions				
Identification	Identifying potential disruption through an in-depth alert to peoples' intuitions, fears, excitement, emotions	Seeking opportunities within the hardship	Using any type of information to filter the disruption	Testing figures, numbers, statistics; investigating by talking to people
Orchestrating the startup's activity	Being attentive to people's emotional expressions, conducting meetings, encouraging people to share, to capture the general vibe, mood and energy	Planning action—ad hoc and strategically—through evaluations based on people's inputs	Conducting personal and team meetings, providing a safe place to share and plan	Analyzing input, insights, feedback, and narratives obtained from the startup's internal and external stakeholders

Emotional features that have been recognized to contribute to emotional intelligence are self-awareness, self-regulation, motivation, empathy and social skills; each of these features of emotional intelligence and the accumulated construct is critical to crisis identification and to the impetus to find a direct solution to either mitigate the damaging effects of such existing or potential crises, or avoid them in advance. For example, self-regulation embodies the ability to control or redirect disruptive impulses and moods, and suspend judgment and think before acting, which are relevant to crises; empathy captures the area of networking and partnerships, and addresses the ability to create, maintain, and leverage relationships; these are important factors in managing disruptive situations, and coupled with social skills and the ability to navigate an activity, these features are key factors in crisis identification and planning for its management. Hence, people with emotional intelligence are prone to identify in the early stages the changes and processes that could result in a crisis (Goleman 1998, 2000; Calás, Smircich and Bourne 2009; Cardon et al. 2012; Nixon, Harrington and Parker 2012).

Taken together, female founders draw on their emotional resources to promptly identify disturbances that can progress to a crisis and at the same time they can be severely affected by crises, while as startup founders, they work to create disruptive situations. Their high levels of emotional intelligence enable them to dampen the flames of existing or potential eruptions, and thus contribute to avoiding their development into a crisis and paving the way to effectively orchestrating the factors that can potentially evolve into a crisis.

The use of emotional intelligence through the following actions is effective for alleviating disruptive situations and enabling the thorough and systematic identification of such situations:

- Establishing an open culture in the startup; building a safe environment
- Maintaining positive and satisfying relationships in the startup teams
- Conducting regular individual conversations, including uncomfortable ones, by being aware of others' emotional state
- Striving to settle conflicts in the company
- Forming and managing teams that psychologically complement and can provide a multidimensional perspective on changes, gaps, irregularities, etc.

Strategic orientation from a female entrepreneurship point of view

Women are more prone to identifying changes across their business, and consequently, they are alert to the emergence of factors that can evolve into potential crises; in a similar vein, women are more likely to take a drill-down approach and tap into the activity in each department or team meticulously to verify the trends, numbers, and figures, along with interviewing the people involved, to gain a more comprehensive picture of what is different or changing and can break out into a crisis.

Strategic entrepreneurship draws on the premise of opportunity identification—opportunities to create a competitive advantage by developing and diffusing innovation, establishing a clear vision, and being surrounded by a supportive ecosystem to develop a profitable startup. At the same time, strategic management involves avenues to ascertain agility, creativity, and risk-taking in the startup to respond effectively and in a timely manner to changes or factors that can be 'threatening'. Strategic thinking, planning, and management require a smart combination of a detailed awareness of the fundamentals of the startup, for example, relationships with clients, social media activity, or recruitment of new people, and an open view to generate information from words, expressions, conversations, and collaborations that can give indications of enthusiasm versus reluctance toward innovation, happiness versus discontent at work, engagement versus withdrawal from teammates, and more. Women's strategic aptitude enables them to anticipate such factors and changes promptly and through a large scope of objective and subjective information.

The strategic actions that female startup leaders tend to engage start with applying emotional intelligence, to feel and sense, and then through sensemaking, they intuit some alternative scenarios on the sources of the changes as well as on how to treat those changes; this information is generated by multiple sources, with an emphasis on people's feedback regarding the changes; the existing resources are then strategically orchestrated by enhancing the opportunities and gauging their potential production value. The input captured from people's insights and experiences while emanating from personal points of view—intuitive and biased—provide a richer understanding of the existing and potential situation and a quite resolute signal of the startup's preparedness to manage the potential disruptors (Ndemo and Maina 2007; Kyrgidou and Hughes 2010; Hughes et al. 2012; Bianchi, Parisi and Salvatore 2016; Bernat, Lambardi and Palacios 2017; Cabrera and Mauricio 2017; Raghuvanshi, Agrawal and Ghosh 2017; Nikoulaou, Tasopoulou and Tsagarakis 2018; Allahar 2019).

Women's psychological capital

Entrepreneurial psychological capital is defined as entrepreneurs' broad foundation of aggregate capital—including confidence (self-efficacy), optimism, hope, resilience, and trust—which empowers them by allowing them to trust that they possess the abilities and capabilities to initiate and lead a successful startup. *Self-efficacy* represents confidence in the actual exertion of efforts to deploy the required resources to exploit the available opportunities and to reduce risks or the perceptions of risk and fear of failure. Studies show that while encountering conflicts, higher levels of self-efficacy enhance the feeling of security and ability to address such challenges (Krueger and Dickson 1994; Firkin 2003; Luthans, Luthans and Luthans 2004; Page and Donohue 2004; Goel and Karri 2006; Luthans, Youssef and Avolio 2007; McGee et al. 2009; Dimov 2010; Zou et al. 2019). Whereas in research, women are found to hold relatively lower levels of self-efficacy as compared to men, female founders—by having already shown their ability to deploy resources and start a business—hold higher levels of self-efficacy. Research demonstrates that while high self-efficacy is beneficial for business growth, extremely high levels of entrepreneurial self-efficacy can be counterproductive and detrimental to the business, particularly when deciding how to respond to setbacks; overconfidence is an antecedent to venture failure. Women are depicted as possessing moderate levels of self-efficacy, hence they can benefit from this psychological capability in managing crises (Trevelyan 2008; Jain and Ali 2013; Artinger and Powell 2016). *Optimism* is defined as a psychological force that motivates action, resilience, and commitment by building confidence in the prospect of positive outcomes, that is, the expectation of an eventual payoff, though not rationally justified or verified. Optimism can be advantageous in crisis situations, and women tend to be optimistic, hence can leverage their optimism to minimize crisis episodes (Fraser and Greene 2006; Trevelyan 2008; Hmieleski and Baron 2009; Storey 2011). *Hope* is described as a motivational state of persistence toward goals and, when necessary, changing the path to the goal to attain success. Entrepreneurs who score high on measures of hope are more likely to find alternative ways to address business pressures and challenges. In addition, people who score high on indicators of hope are more positive about their success via their focus on goal attainment and on the different ways of reaching it and have lower levels of stress. Women are found to hold high levels of hope, though concurrent levels of stress are also high, as reflected in the ways women tackle crises and manage them (Snyder 2002; DiPietro et al. 2007; Luthans, Avolio and Avey 2007; Baron, Franklin and Hmieleski 2013). *Resilience* addresses the acts of coping with and adapting to risk or adversity and is directly associated with crises and disturbances; it enables individuals to keep moving toward their desired goal, bounce back from negative and positive challenging events, and adapt to positive change, progress, and increased responsibility (Luthans, Avolio and Avey 2007; Hanson and Blake 2009; Brandt, Gomes and Boyanova 2011; Bullough, Renko and Myatt 2014). Finally, *trust* is derived from the perception that probabilities will behave as expected. It is related to fairness, openness, honesty, and commitment to relationships, hence critical to managing crises, though it can be risky in identifying them (Paine 2003; Goel and Karri 2006; Zhao, Seibert and Lumpkin 2010; Welter 2012; Panda and Dash 2013).

Overall, research has shown that the genders react differently to disruptive situations due to their differences in preparedness, responsiveness, and use of the benefits provided to entrepreneurs during crisis episodes (Bradshaw 2013; Kalnins and Williams 2014; Marshall et al. 2015; McManus 2017; Elam et al. 2019; Grözinger et al. 2022).

Summary

One striking aspect of the COVID-19 pandemic has been its impact on female startup founders. This chapter tapped into this phenomenon by outlining both the female startup realm and women's inclination as entrepreneurs. Combining the startup's unique processes, involving cutting-edge professional teamwork and expertise, continual creation of innovation, and technology, among others, with entrepreneurial capabilities and mindsets typifying female entrepreneurs—such as openness to emotional perspectives and strategic thinking and action—enable women to identify changes, movements, factors, and processes that can lead to potential crises. Women tend to cull information from various sources; they are aware of the ways in which information is gathered and shape their understanding of the situation by drawing on a full range of clues. As such, women are quick to identify potential crises, although the generated information can be intuitive and stem from emotional grounds, thus leading to the deployment of resources to navigate a crisis that has not yet emerged. Unlike women in SMEs, female startup founders possess higher levels of entrepreneurial psychological capital, which is useful for the identification and exploitation of crises. In this chapter, we discussed the benefits of female startup founders' moderately higher levels of self-efficacy/confidence, optimism, hope, resilience, and trust compared to their male counterparts; the value of these traits in the recovery phase will be further discussed in the next chapters.

Reflective questions for class

1. Search the internet for a company that was founded and is led by men (e.g., Facebook, Apple, LinkedIn) and that tackled a crisis. Briefly describe the crisis. List two to three entrepreneurial psychological capabilities that *could have* served to avoid or minimize the crisis. Explain your answer.
2. Beyond Health (https://beyondthehealth.com/), founded by Jurgita Budraityte, is providing tools and strategies for people who are looking to improve their health and wellness lifestyle. Based on the components of emotional intelligence, how did Budraityte leverage the opportunities embodied in the COVID-19 crisis?
3. Search for a woman-led startup on the web; provide the startup's link. Analyze if and in what sense this startup matches the female entrepreneurship characteristics.
4. Fiona Canning from the UK is co-founder of Pollinate (https://www.pollinate.co.uk/), which develops software aimed at improving merchant acquisition for banks, while providing merchants with digital tools and insights into their businesses. Pollinate has raised (https://www.eu-startups.com/2021/03/british-fintech-startup-pollinate-announces-e42-million-to-further-global-expansion) €42 million to further global expansion.

   Suppose you were Canning's mentor, what would you suggest that she be aware of, based on the components in Table 10.1: Startups induce disruptions.
5. According to *Forbes*,[12] *Harvard Business Review* released a new report claiming that in the United States, "17% of Black women are in the process of starting or running new businesses, compared to just 10% of white women, and 15% of white men." However, there's a catch: though Black female entrepreneurs take the

lead early on, only 3% continue to run mature businesses. Based on the chapter section 'Female entrepreneurship and crises: identification and exploitation', what are the reasons for this dropout of female entrepreneurs and how do you anticipate the effect of the crisis on women's "tendency" to drop out?

Notes

1 See https://www.oecd.org/cfe/smes/inclusive-entrepreneurship/womensentrepreneurshipandcovid-19ensuringthegapdoesntgrow.htm
2 See https://www3.weforum.org/docs/WEF_Unleashing_the_power_of_Europes_women_entrepreneurs.pdf
3 See https://live.worldbank.org/pivoting-pandemic-women-entrepreneurs-tap-regional-opportunities
4 See https://www.oecd.org/cfe/smes/inclusive-entrepreneurship/womensentrepreneurshipandcovid-19ensuringthegapdoesntgrow.htm
5 See Elam et al. 2019; Fairlie 2020; Naudé 2020; OECD SME and Entrepreneurship Outlook 2021, https://www.oecd-ilibrary.org/sites/97a5bbfe-en/index.html?itemId=/content/publication/97a5bbfe-en; SIGI 2020 Regional Report for Latin America and the Caribbean https://www.oecd-ilibrary.org/sites/cb7d45d1-en/index.html?itemId=/content/publication/cb7d45d1-en
6 See https://www.littlefund.co/
7 M&A—mergers and acquisitions.
8 FOMO—fear of missing out.
9 See athttps://www.thesill.com/?sscid=71k5_qwose&utm_source=shareasale.com&utm_medium=affiliate_link&utm_campaign=314743; see also: https://www.entrepreneur.com/slideshow/356977
10 See https://www.forbes.com/sites/andrealoubier/2017/10/12/the-emotional-cost-of-being-a-female-millennial-startup-founder/?sh=23bb13b8485d
11 Some details have been changed as per the interviewee's request.
12 Black Female Entrepreneurs Are Launching More Businesses Than Ever: Here's What They Need To Help Them Mature. Forbes. May 2021. https://www.forbes.com/sites/shelleyzalis/2021/05/25/black-female-entrepreneurs-are-launching-more-businesses-than-ever-heres-what-they-need-to-help-them-mature/?sh=28a5a28b6bc0

References

Adkins, C. L., Samaras, S. A., Gilfillan, S. W., & McWee, W. E. (2013). The relationship between owner characteristics, company size, and the work–family culture and policies of women-owned businesses. *Journal of Small Business Management, 51*(2), 196–214.

Allahar, H. (2019). An innovative entrepreneurial ecosystem-based model for supporting female entrepreneurship. *Innovation, 5.*

Altman, E. I. (1968). Financial ratios, discriminant analysis and the prediction of corporate bankruptcy. *The Journal of Finance, 23*(4), 589–609.

Altman, M. (2000). A behavioral model of path dependency: The economics of profitable inefficiency and market failure. *The Journal of Socio-Economics, 29*(2), 127–145.

Arenius, P., & Minniti, M. (2005). Perceptual variables and nascent entrepreneurship. *Small Business Economics, 24*(3), 233–247.

Artinger, S., & Powell, T. C. (2016). Entrepreneurial failure: Statistical and psychological explanations. *Strategic Management Journal, 37*(6), 1047–1064.

Audretsch, D. B. (2017). Entrepreneurship and universities. *International Journal of Entrepreneurship and Small Business, 31*(1), 4–11.

Audretsch, D. B., & Lehmann, E. (2016). *The seven secrets of Germany: Economic resilience in an era of global turbulence.* Oxford University Press.

Bamiatzi, V., Jones, S., Mitchelmore, S., & Nikolopoulos, K. (2015). The role of competencies in shaping the leadership style of female entrepreneurs: The case of North West of England, Yorkshire, and North Wales. *Journal of Small Business Management, 53*(3), 627–644.

Baron, R. A. (2008). The role of affect in the entrepreneurial process. *Academy of Management Review, 33*(2), 328–340.

Baron, R. A., Franklin, R. J., & Hmieleski, K. M. (2013). *Why entrepreneurs often experience low. Not high.*

Bernat, L. F., Lambardi, G., & Palacios, P. (2017). Determinants of the entrepreneurial gender gap in Latin America. *Small Business Economics, 48*(3), 727–752.

Bernoster, I., Rietveld, C. A., Thurik, A. R., & Torrès, O. (2018). Overconfidence, optimism and entrepreneurship. *Sustainability, 10*(7), 2233.

Bianchi, M., Parisi, V., & Salvatore, R. (2016). Female entrepreneurs: Motivations and constraints. An Italian regional study. *International Journal of Gender and Entrepreneurship.*

Bradshaw, D. (2013). *Bringing learning to life: The learning revolution, the economy and the individual.* Routledge.

Brandt, T., Gomes, J. F., & Boyanova, D. (2011). Personality and psychological capital as indicators of future job success? *Liiketaloudellinen Aikakauskirja,* (3).

Breugst, N., Domurath, A., Patzelt, H., & Klaukien, A. (2012). Perceptions of entrepreneurial passion and employees' commitment to entrepreneurial ventures. *Entrepreneurship Theory and Practice, 36*(1), 171–192.

Brush, C. G. (1992). Research on women business owners: Past trends, a new perspective and future directions. *Entrepreneurship Theory and Practice, 16*(4), 5–30.

Bullough, A., Renko, M., & Myatt, T. (2014). Danger zone entrepreneurs: The importance of resilience and self–efficacy for entrepreneurial intentions. *Entrepreneurship Theory and Practice, 38*(3), 473–499.

Cabrera, E. M., & Mauricio, D. (2017). Factors affecting the success of women's entrepreneurship: A review of literature. *International Journal of Gender and Entrepreneurship.*

Calás, M. B., Smircich, L., & Bourne, K. A. (2009). Extending the boundaries: Reframing "entrepreneurship as social change" through feminist perspectives. *Academy of Management Review, 34*(3), 552–569.

Cardon, M. S., Foo, M., Shepherd, D., & Wiklund, J. (2012). Exploring the heart: Entrepreneurial emotion is a hot topic. *Entrepreneurship Theory and Practice, 36*(1), 1–10.

Chaganti, R. (1986). Management in women-owned enterprises. *Journal of Small Business Management, 24*(4), 18–29.

Dattani, K. (2020). Rethinking social reproduction in the time of COVID-19. *Journal of Australian Political Economy,* (85), 51–56.

Dean, H., Larsen, G., Ford, J., & Akram, M. (2019). Female entrepreneurship and the metanarrative of economic growth: A critical review of underlying assumptions. *International Journal of Management Reviews, 21*(1), 24–49.

Diallo, B., Qayum, S., & Staab, S. (2020). COVID-19 and the care economy: Immediate action and structural transformation for a gender-responsive recovery. *Gender and COVID-19 Policy Brief Series.* UN Women, New York.

Dimov, D. (2010). Nascent entrepreneurs and venture emergence: Opportunity confidence, human capital, and early planning. *Journal of Management Studies, 47*(6), 1123–1153.

DiPietro, R. B., Welsh, D. H., Raven, P. V., & Severt, D. (2007). A measure of hope in franchise systems: Assessing franchisees, top executives, and franchisors. *Journal of Leadership & Organizational Studies, 13*(3), 59–66.

Eddleston, K. A., & Powell, G. N. (2008). The role of gender identity in explaining sex differences in business owners' career satisfier preferences. *Journal of Business Venturing, 23*(2), 244–256.

Elam, A. B., Brush, C. G., Greene, P. G., Baumer, B., Dean, M., Heavlow, R., & Global Entrepreneurship Research Association. (2019). Women's Entrepreneurship Report 2018/2019.

Fairlie, R. (2020). The impact of COVID-19 on small business owners: Evidence from the first three months after widespread social-distancing restrictions. *Journal of Economics & Management Strategy, 29*(4), 727–740.

Fenwick, T. (2008). Workplace learning: Emerging trends and new perspectives. *New Directions for Adult and Continuing Education, 2008*(119), 17–26.

Firkin, P. (2003). *Midwifery as non-standard work: Rebirth of a profession.* Labour Market Dynamics Research Programme, Massey University.

Foo, M., Uy, M. A., & Baron, R. A. (2009). How do feelings influence effort? An empirical study of entrepreneurs' affect and venture effort. *Journal of Applied Psychology, 94*(4), 1086.

Fraser, S., & Greene, F. J. (2006). The effects of experience on entrepreneurial optimism and uncertainty. *Economica, 73*(290), 169–192.

Galloway, L., Kapasi, I., & Sang, K. (2015). Entrepreneurship, leadership, and the value of feminist approaches to understanding them. *Journal of Small Business Management, 53*(3), 683–692.

Giorgi, S., Lockwood, C., & Glynn, M. A. (2015). The many faces of culture: Making sense of 30 years of research on culture in organization studies. *Academy of Management Annals, 9*(1), 1–54.

Goel, S., & Karri, R. (2006). Entrepreneurs, effectual logic, and over–trust. *Entrepreneurship Theory and Practice, 30*(4), 477–493.

Goleman, D. (1998). The emotionally competent leader. Paper presented at *The Healthcare Forum Journal, 41*(2), 36, 38, 76.

Goleman, D. (2000). *Emotional Intelligence, terj.* Gramedia.

Greene, P. G., Hart, M. M., Gatewood, E. J., Brush, C. G., & Carter, N. M. (2003). Women entrepreneurs: Moving front and center: An overview of research and theory. *Coleman White Paper Series, 3*(1), 1–47.

Grözinger, A. C., Wolff, S., Ruf, P. J., & Moog, P. (2022). The power of shared positivity: Organizational psychological capital and firm performance during exogenous crises. *Small Business Economics, 58*(2), 689–716.

Hanson, S., & Blake, M. (2009). Gender and entrepreneurial networks. *Regional Studies, 43*(1), 135–149.

Harrison, R. T., Leitch, C. M., & McAdam, M. (2018). Breaking glass: Towards a gendered analysis of entrepreneurial leadership. In *Research handbook on entrepreneurship and leadership.* Edward Elgar Publishing.

Henry, C., Foss, L., Fayolle, A., Walker, E., & Duffy, S. (2015). Entrepreneurial leadership and gender: Exploring theory and practice in global contexts. *Journal of Small Business Management, 53*(3), 581–586.

Hill, R. C., & Levenhagen, M. (1995). Metaphors and mental models: Sensemaking and sensegiving in innovative and entrepreneurial activities. *Journal of Management, 21*(6), 1057–1074.

Hmieleski, K. M., & Baron, R. A. (2009). Entrepreneurs' optimism and new venture performance: A social cognitive perspective. *Academy of Management Journal, 52*(3), 473–488.

Hughes, K. D., Jennings, J. E., Brush, C., Carter, S., & Welter, F. (2012). Extending women's entrepreneurship research in new directions. *Entrepreneurship Theory and Practice, 36*(3), 429–442.

Jain, R., & Ali, S. W. (2013). A review of facilitators, barriers and gateways to entrepreneurship: Directions for future research. *South Asian Journal of Management, 20*(3), 122.

Kalnins, A., & Williams, M. (2014). When do female-owned businesses out-survive male-owned businesses? A disaggregated approach by industry and geography. *Journal of Business Venturing, 29*(6), 822–835.

Kariv, D. (2013). *Female entrepreneurship and the new venture creation: An international overview.* Routledge.

Kariv, D., Baldegger, R. J., & Kashy-Rosenbaum, G. (2022). 'All you need is… entrepreneurial attitudes': A deeper look into the propensity to start a business during the COVID-19 through a gender comparison (GEM data). *World Review of Entrepreneurship, Management and Sustainable Development, 18*(1–2), 195–226.

Kariv, D., & Coleman, S. (2015). Toward a theory of financial bricolage: The impact of small loans on new businesses. *Journal of Small Business and Enterprise Development.*

Kariv, D., Elisha, D., & Schwartz, D. (2021). Financial capabilities, entrepreneurial self-belief and motivations among Israeli female and male entrepreneurs. In *Entrepreneurial finance, innovation and development* (pp. 303–331). Routledge.

Klapper, L., & Love, I. (2011). The impact of the financial crisis on new firm registration. *Economics Letters, 113*(1), 1–4.

Krueger Jr, N., & Dickson, P. R. (1994). How believing in ourselves increases risk taking: Perceived self-efficacy and opportunity recognition. *Decision Sciences, 25*(3), 385–400.

Kyrgidou, L. P., & Hughes, M. (2010). Strategic entrepreneurship: Origins, core elements and research directions. *European Business Review.*

Loubier, A. (2017). *How working remotely is helping women close the gender gap.*

Luthans, F., Luthans, K. W., & Luthans, B. C. (2004). Positive psychological capital: Beyond human and social capital.

Luthans, F., Youssef, C. M., & Avolio, B. J. (2007). *Psychological capital: Developing the human competitive edge.* Oxford University Press.

Manolova, T. S., Brush, C. G., Edelman, L. F., & Elam, A. (2020). Pivoting to stay the course: How women entrepreneurs take advantage of opportunities created by the COVID-19 pandemic. *International Small Business Journal, 38*(6), 481–491.

Marshall, M. I., Niehm, L. S., Sydnor, S. B., & Schrank, H. L. (2015). Predicting small business demise after a natural disaster: An analysis of pre-existing conditions. *Natural Hazards, 79*(1), 331–354.

Mayer, J. D., & Salovey, P. (1997). What is emotional intelligence. *Emotional Development and Emotional Intelligence: Educational Implications, 3,* 31.

McAdam, M., Harrison, R. T., & Leitch, C. M. (2019). Stories from the field: Women's networking as gender capital in entrepreneurial ecosystems. *Small Business Economics, 53*(2), 459–474.

McGee, J. E., Peterson, M., Mueller, S. L., & Sequeira, J. M. (2009). Entrepreneurial self–efficacy: Refining the measure. *Entrepreneurship Theory and Practice, 33*(4), 965–988.

McManus, M. J. (2017). Women's business ownership: Data from the 2012 survey of business owners. *US Small Business Administration Office of Advocacy, 13*(1), 1–17.

Moore, D. P., Moore, J. L., & Moore, J. W. (2011). How women entrepreneurs lead and why they manage that way. *Gender in Management: An International Journal*

Ndemo, B., & Maina, F. W. (2007). Women entrepreneurs and strategic decision making. *Management Decision.*

Nicholson, L., & Anderson, A. R. (2005). News and nuances of the entrepreneurial myth and metaphor: Linguistic games in entrepreneurial sense–making and sense–giving. *Entrepreneurship Theory and Practice, 29*(2), 153–172.

Nikolaou, I. E., Tasopoulou, K., & Tsagarakis, K. (2018). A typology of green entrepreneurs based on institutional and resource-based views. *The Journal of Entrepreneurship, 27*(1), 111–132.

Nixon, P., Harrington, M., & Parker, D. (2012). Leadership performance is significant to project success or failure: A critical analysis. *International Journal of Productivity and Performance Management.*

Page, L. F., & Donohue, R. (2004). Positive psychological capital: A preliminary exploration of the construct. *Monash University Department of Management Working Paper Series, 51*(4), 1–10.

Paine, K. D. (2003). Guidelines for measuring trust in organizations. *The Institute for Public Relations, 2003*, 9–10.

Panda, S., & Dash, S. (2013). Trust and reputation in new ventures: Insights from an Indian venture capital firm. *Development and Learning in Organizations: An International Journal.*

Paul, S., & Sarma, V. (2013). *Economic crisis and female entrepreneurship: Evidence from countries in Eastern Europe and Central Asia.*

Paulson, A. L., & Townsend, R. (2004). Entrepreneurship and financial constraints in Thailand. *Journal of Corporate Finance, 10*(2), 229–262.

Pines, A. M., Lerner, M., & Schwartz, D. (2010). Gender differences in entrepreneurship: Equality, diversity and inclusion in times of global crisis. *Equality, Diversity and Inclusion: An International Journal.*

Raghuvanshi, J., Agrawal, R., & Ghosh, P. K. (2017). Analysis of barriers to women entrepreneurship: The DEMATEL approach. *The Journal of Entrepreneurship, 26*(2), 220–238.

Salovey, P., & Mayer, J. D. (1990). Emotional intelligence. *Imagination, Cognition and Personality, 9*(3), 185–211.

Snyder, L. S. (2002). The glass boardroom ceiling. Women have the know-how to solve corporate crises but aren't getting the chance. *Modern Healthcare, 32*(39), 21.

Springate, G. L. (1978). *Predicting the possibility of failure in a Canadian firm: A discriminant analysis.*

Storey, D. J. (2011). Optimism and chance: The elephants in the entrepreneurship room. *International Small Business Journal, 29*(4), 303–321.

Stroe, S., Sirén, C., Shepherd, D., & Wincent, J. (2020). The dualistic regulatory effect of passion on the relationship between fear of failure and negative affect: Insights from facial expression analysis. *Journal of Business Venturing, 35*(4), 105948.

Stuetzer, M., Audretsch, D. B., Obschonka, M., Gosling, S. D., Rentfrow, P. J., & Potter, J. (2018). Entrepreneurship culture, knowledge spillovers and the growth of regions. *Regional Studies, 52*(5), 608–618.

Taffler, R. J., & Tisshaw, H. (1977). Going, going, gone–four factors which predict. *Accountancy, 88*(1003), 50–54.

Trevelyan, R. (2008). Optimism, overconfidence and entrepreneurial activity. *Management Decision*

Weick, K. E., Sutcliffe, K. M., & Obstfeld, D. (2005). Organizing and the process of sensemaking. *Organization Science, 16*(4), 409–421.

Welpe, I. M., Spörrle, M., Grichnik, D., Michl, T., & Audretsch, D. B. (2012). Emotions and opportunities: The interplay of opportunity evaluation, fear, joy, and anger as antecedent of entrepreneurial exploitation. *Entrepreneurship Theory and Practice, 36*(1), 69–96.

Welter, F. (2012). All you need is trust? A critical review of the trust and entrepreneurship literature. *International Small Business Journal, 30*(3), 193–212.

Zampetakis, L. A., Bakatsaki, M., Litos, C., Kafetsios, K. G., & Moustakis, V. (2017). Gender-based differential item functioning in the application of the theory of planned behavior for the study of entrepreneurial intentions. *Frontiers in Psychology, 8*, 451.

Zavgren, C. V. (1985). Assessing the vulnerability to failure of American industrial firms: A logistic analysis. *Journal of Business Finance & Accounting, 12*(1), 19–45.

Zhao, H., Seibert, S. E., & Lumpkin, G. T. (2010). The relationship of personality to entrepreneurial intentions and performance: A meta-analytic review. *Journal of Management, 36*(2), 381–404.

Zou, B., Guo, J., Guo, F., Shi, Y., & Li, Y. (2019). Who am I? The influence of social identification on academic entrepreneurs' role conflict. *International Entrepreneurship and Management Journal, 15*(2), 363–384.

Chapter Eleven

Beyond the pandemic

The path to the new normal through case studies

- Introduction
- Case 1 The pandemic's role in stimulating startup creation: Asem
- Case 2 A startup that failed due to the crisis: Valeries
- Case 3 "Put a ding in the universe"[1] (Steve Jobs): Papaya Global
- Case 4 "Against all odds"—A story of resilience, trust, and sustainability: Guesty
- Case 5 "A pivot is a change in strategy without a change in vision"[2] (Eric Ries): Bizzabo
- Case 6 Ecosystem stakeholders embrace startups: Startup México and Dux Capital
- Case 7 Reciprocity is the name of the game: JetztInvest (JI)—the open innovation platform
- Case 8 Forging the future: Co-Creation Network Universities (CCNU)

Introduction

This chapter introduces different angles of crisis fallout and management through the perspective of various startups and stakeholders. It includes new startups, such as the case of a startup that evolved during the COVID-19 pandemic by touching on the emergent and newest needs introduced by the crisis, and the opposite experience of a startup whose core business involved an area that seemed to no longer exist, hence had to take decisions on how to manage the situation; another case embodies the role of the pivot as a coping strategy; other cases include existing startups that have experienced growth during the pandemic and have gained extraordinary achievements, including one that became a unicorn; a startup that had to cease its activity due to the crisis; the perspective of accelerators on supporting startups; and the perspective of an investor on promoting entrepreneurship during the crisis and guaranteeing the startup ecosystem's sustainability. All of these case studies are based on personal interviews, conducted with the founders and managers of the businesses by the author of this book and/or interviews in the media, reports, or research, among others. At the end of this chapter, I include questions pertaining to each chapter of the book that can be used for several case studies for comparison—to broaden the scope of the different avenues taken by the companies—employing the models discussed in the chapters and providing a wider foundation to

DOI: 10.4324/9781003173809-11

reflect on the practical implementation of the models introduced in various companies. The cases focus on the interviewees' experiences during the COVID-19 pandemic, and include both startups and stakeholders, the latter dedicated to supporting startups and the entrepreneurial ecosystem. The assortment of companies for the case studies provides a diverse range of responses to the pandemic. The case studies are categorized as follows:

Startups	
Born	Case 1 ASEM—Startup born out of the crisis
Failed	Case 2 Valeries—Startup failed due to the crisis
Succeeded	Case 3 Papaya Global—Startup in the 'right' niche that exploited opportunities that were scaled by the crisis
	Case 4 Guesty—Startup that scaled against all odds during the crisis
	Case 5 Bizzabo—Startup that pivoted in the face of the crisis and 'made it'
Stakeholders	
Accelerator	Case 6 Startup México and Dux Capital—accelerator and venture capital fund that embrace startups during the crisis
Financial company	Case 7 JI—Startup outreach in a global, financial company
Academic institution	Case 8 CCNU—Entrepreneurial academia

To facilitate the reflection and debate using the questions, the cases that best suit each question are suggested. Cases 1, 2, 3, 4, and 5 are indicated as 'Startup' and cases 6, 7, and 8 as 'Stakeholder'. It is possible to use a question to reflect on one or more of the suggested cases concurrently, but it is not necessary to cover all recommended cases for each question. When comparisons between cases are called for, this is specifically indicated, for example, 'cases 3 and 4', the 'and' signaling that both cases must be addressed in the question.

Case studies

Case 1
The pandemic's role in stimulating startup creation: ASEM

"I saw it coming, but still could not believe it," says Amara Kaya from South Africa, who, with three co-founders, launched ASEM in January 2021, a startup that is drawing on Pura Fresh technology to develop a smart device that can sense and measure the smallest inhalable particles and volatile organic compounds, and can detect bacteria and viruses, including COVID-19. Upon sensing the quality of the indoor air in real time, it sends signals to other devices that will purify the room. Kaya moved to the United States in 2015 for her university studies in microbiology, where she received a grant for her project to develop a sensor that measures air quality. She met three colleagues in the laboratory, her future co-founders; in 2017, they decided to commercialize the invention and turn the technology into a real business. Prior to deploying their resources, the four co-founders signed a strategic collaboration with a hospital and were supported by the university to test their technology; concurrently, they established a strategic partnership with a design company that developed their device—the sensor—and were searching for financial support from the government. But then the hospital decided to cancel the contract with the co-founders, and at that point, disappointed by the hospital's sudden move, the co-founders decided to drop the idea of commercialization. Kaya applied for a research position at the university laboratory and her colleagues got jobs elsewhere. More than two years, in March 2020, the coronavirus pandemic became a fact, lock-downs were announced in the United States, and there was general concern regarding contamination via the respiratory tract. As the numbers of infected people increased and hospitals became overloaded, Kaya contacted her colleagues and urged them to join her to work intensively on the technology they had already created. She was thinking about 'doing good' and not commercializing the technology, as she was engaged in her laboratory job, and they had all had a bad experience in their prior effort to bring their product to market. "I could not abandon my dream to launch a business for our device, but I lost faith after our first attempt," explains Kaya.

> When the COVID-19 pandemic broke out, I felt a deep responsibility to make use of our sensor; I was convinced that it could be of huge value for hospitals, schools, workplaces and buses. So I swallowed my pride and contacted the hospital that had ended the contract with us 2 years before, to provide it with our technology, for free; the management quickly approved it. I felt like I was 'saving the world', and contacted other hospitals as well to provide them with our technology for free. They all agreed and began operating it, even though the product was not finalized—there was no device yet, and the hospitals used a beta version of our technology. Kelechi, one of the co-founders who identified the swift approval of our technology in hospitals came up with the idea of actually testing the technology by 'doing good'; so we distributed it and measured the experiences of these de facto early users, to make the needed modifications and develop the technology accordingly. Uvo, another co-founder, took the technology to his relatives at the headquarters of Nigeria's train system. We detected the need. We partnered with engineering students from my university who worked on developing our technology based on the

> feedback we received. We attracted eight hospitals and a train company in the United States and Nigeria.

says Kaya. In January 2021, the four co-founders launched ASEM, having developed a device for the technology.

> We are working through strategic collaborations, especially during the pandemic, as most of the companies we approach are eager to work with an innovative startup, so it makes it easier to attract partners. Michael, one of the co-founders, is an expert in crafting strategic collaborations in and outside the United States; these collaborations are not only beneficial for exchanging expertise, knowledge and technological platforms, but they also constitute our safety net. I know that we can sustain our activity now that we are not dependent on one hospital as we experienced in the first trial

concludes Kaya. She shares her tips in urging enthused entrepreneurs to try, dare, take risks, and be grateful for failures in order to learn from them. She sees the pandemic as a turning point, enabling ASEM to grab at opportunities and explore them.

Case 2
A startup that failed due to the crisis: Valeries

Chantal Garnier is the CTO and co-founder of Valeries, a startup that aims to monitor fitness training loads by measuring strength, jumping, and sprinting capacity and duration through the physiological responses before and after the training by connecting various measures, such as heartbeat, camera information, and transpiration, among others, to a smartphone. It provides valuable information on the best training program for the 'regular' trainer, including the required load, duration, and state of rest as well as for people who are recovering from accidents and for rehabilitation. "In my case," says Garnier,

> I lost a third of my weight at the age of 27, after 2 years of strict sports workout programs. I was content with my weight but it was clear to me that I depended on my daily workouts; once I overloaded on my workout and in 2 minutes, felt paralyzed. I spent some time in the hospital until I could regain my movements, and the diagnosis was that I had overtraining syndrome. The doctors and physiotherapists recommended that I stop all sporting activities for 6 months. I started to gain back my weight and I panicked, so I decided to work on an application for cases such as mine.

The name Valeries has a meaning with a connotation of power, and Garnier felt that it fits both the physiological and mental power she had to garner to recover from her situation. Valeries was initiated in 2017 and was contingent on two business models from its initial stages: the marketplace for any businesses involved with sports, from personal trainers and sport psychologists to sportswear brands; this was Valeries' 'bread and butter' in terms of revenue; and its main focus, though still less profitable: an application for smartphones. The Valeries team was unusually structured; it was comprised of five francophones, experienced entrepreneurs from countries in Europe, Canada, and Africa. Garnier was the main co-founder (50%) and the four others were equal investors in the remaining 50%. Some of them franchised the business in their native countries, depending on the best fit with the local market. The five co-founders deeply believed in strategic collaborations for any development in the business, for example, developing the application, designing it, marketing it, and attracting the new markets that they expected would use and pay for the app; they targeted both businesses (B2B model) and customers (B2C). Garnier explains:

> we worked day and night, in different time zones, traveling to different places worldwide. We were all thrilled with the gradual achievements of the marketplace model in our startup, and were most encouraged by the feedback we were receiving from our partners. We managed to engage one of the leading companies to develop some features of our app, we worked with a leading American hospital on adjustments and tests for the physiological measurements' accuracy, reliability, validity and stability, we collaborated with a leading American university through a government grant on data accumulation and research. Donna, one of our team members, managed to attract leading European wholesale sports companies to channel and advertise our business. In 2019, we opened our second office in the United States; while the European office was our R&D center, the American office became our marketing hub.

In August 2019, Garnier was invited to a government council aimed at fighting obesity among children in deprived areas, where she presented their app. As a consequence, more than ten organizations approached her to purchase it. "As we had not anticipated the future, only a few months later," says Garnier,

> we were convinced at this point that it would be better to strengthen our product, include more features and introduce it to the market in its final, most complete form, so without any hesitation, we refused the offers we received in September, October and December 2019, and verbally agreed to be in touch in April–May 2020. In fact, at this point, we were only depending on our partners,

> who supported our business' development, marketing and operations. Since these were all large, global and stable companies, we felt secure and trusted the situation. I was in the airport in Nairobi when I received a call about lockdowns in neighboring countries; this was after a successful meeting with African health-related governmental associations that supported us in developing the app. I did not realize the meaning of the COVID-19 pandemic. I was laid back, and convinced that since the lockdown had not been imposed on areas in which we were operating, it would not affect us. So we all continued with our search for new collaborations but not yet for customers; Jean-Sébastien, one of our co-founders, had rejected a potentially huge deal on that day with a gym chain in North America, after consulting all of us, as we were still eager to introduce the 'perfect product' to the market and we all truly believed that the COVID-19 pandemic would soon pass. I remember saying that we have one shot; if we sell an app that is 'half-baked' now, we will suffer from this in the future, so we have to refuse all offers.

says Garnier. Valeries was open to opportunities and decided to develop a tangible small device that monitors, takes photos, videos, and communicates with the smartphone, including during sleep and rest periods; this development was a turning point for Valeries. The co-founders encountered for the first time many refusals to collaborate from existing and new stakeholders; then, one of them received a breach of contract from two European wholesale sports companies with which Valeries was engaged, saying that they had pivoted their business focus due to the pandemic and that they were no longer interested in marketing Valeries' app; then the American partners began dragging their feet, eventually stopped communicating with Valeries' co-founders, and failed to deliver the agreed-upon services. The marketplace eventually dried up and revenues dropped dramatically; as the business was well-managed financially, the co-founders did not go bankrupt, but the atmosphere was troubled and fraught with anxiety.

> One of the co-founders decided to step back; he no longer believed in Valeries and had a bad feeling about our denial of the situation being the initial stages of a pandemic. He was the owner of a large company associated with agriculture in Africa and faced severe difficulties in the business there as well. His departure split the co-founders' unity and damaged their trust.

Garnier continues:

> the four of us who were left were most dedicated and we truly believed in our product, Jean-Sébastien had even produced a prototype of the mini-device that

> looked like the perfect fit for the markets we were targeting, but the conditions worsened. Donna received an offer from one of the global companies that was collaborating with us to be their global marketing chair, so she accepted, and the others were upset by these departures of our co-founders. The zeal we had dwindled.

Valeries still exists, but it is not active; the co-founders are still hoping for its recovery, yet the company is not being updated and the marketplace is operating only sporadically. The mini device is only a prototype, and the only process that is still ongoing is the research with the hospital and the grant with the university, giving hope to Garnier and her colleagues. "In fact," says Garnier,

> we did not dare to announce that we had failed. We are no longer in contact, except in cases connected to Valeries that arise from time to time, some formalities and declarations. Of the five co-founders, the only person that I am in contact with is Jean-Sébastien, who is also family. I am still looking for opportunities, but something has disappeared: the enthusiasm, the trust, the entrepreneurial vibe. Several weeks ago I was approached by one of the government associations supporting Africa, and this gave me a ray of hope. If it works, I am going to start the business differently, by first looking for the right employees, not 'managers' and co-founders, but people who are eager to work hard, and will be dedicated and loyal in difficult times. I am also determined to set rules, to plan, to monitor progress and most importantly, to create an open atmosphere, so that everything is communicated and known, and no more 'surprises' arise among the staff.

concludes Garnier. Her main message is that the pandemic broke the trust among the colleagues; operations did not cease due to financial constraints.

Papaya's mission is to help your company grow. As one of the fastest growing startups in Israel, Papaya Global, which has recently become a unicorn with a valuation of over $3 billion with 400+ employees currently around the globe, is aiming to solve the complex process of managing an international workforce across labor laws, time zones, and languages. Its global people management platform covers all employment needs. Papaya was founded by Eynat Guez, Ruben Drong, and Ofer Herman, three highly experienced entrepreneurs in both working with startups and managing global operations.

Forbes article that at least shows the stats at round D: https://www.forbes.com/sites/gilpress/2021/09/11/raising-250-million-the-leading-future-of-work-startup-has-increased-valuation-10x-in-one-year/?sh=12bd77707837

Case 3
"Put a ding in the universe"[1] (Steve Jobs): Papaya Global

Eynat Guez, CEO and co-founder of Papaya Global, has been on a long entrepreneurial journey: in 2009, she founded Relocation Source, a DSP and Global Mobility Solutions provider that served hundreds of multinational companies, followed by another startup, Expert Source, an Asian PEO organization helping United States corporates expand their business into Asia, and in 2016, she founded Papaya Global.

"COVID-19 confronted us with a new reality, and it is here to last," says Guez.

> I hope to return to working physically with the team, and not strictly in a remote setting, where we never really meet. I can see the distress of people that have to be isolated, either in lockdowns or because they, or a family member, have been infected. I remember being in New York when public schools were instructed to close, and saw teaching teams collapse emotionally. I see Papaya Global as a response to the remote situation, which is no longer 'just' passing through countries and continents, but has become the reality and will apparently be the new normal once the COVID-19 threat is mitigated. In fact, I work hard to enable my teams to have a social experience, albeit virtually; for example, we have initiated Zoom challenges, including sports and other things, we have established daily one-on-one Zoom coffee sessions to meet new people in our offices (in Israel, the United States, Australia and Ukraine).

I interviewed Guez only a few days before she went into labor; the pandemic was severe and Guez, realistic and pragmatic, yet self-confident and reassuring, said:

> We are in the remote HR industry, and the new conditions were already known and clear to us; we had the exact tools, strategies, mindsets and orientation to tackle such situations. Yet, we remained humble; we listened closely to our customers' new needs, and addressed them carefully. We detected our customers' urge to make swift decisions related to their remote employees, which could be two blocks away from the workplace; the whole flow of needs had to be modified in their case. While remote work seemed to be the exclusive niche of the growing, global companies, the reality changed, and consequently, priorities changed and our customers were eager to automate all of their HR-related processes. We were there for these changing needs.

During 2020, Papaya Global launched many new features to accompany both the company and the employees through different organizational phases; more and more companies were adopting remote work models and were keen to recruit from the global talent pool and therefore to go through the entire selection process remotely as well as the following steps, including the development of a global management payroll system for both contracted and subcontracted employees and suppliers. Since the start of 2021, Papaya Global has increased its roster of employees; then, with the company onboarding 100 new customers from the beginning of the year, it acquired *Mensch, a startup that aims to collect* employee data from within the organization and create a digital HR portfolio that includes all of the necessary documentation, feedback, and other information to allow HR to make accurate decisions about employees. Through the money it has raised, Papaya Global has become one of the Israeli unicorn companies, which has increased its valuation during the COVID-19 pandemic. According to Guez:

> For a long time now, the world has perceived Israelis as selling cheap, claiming that we don't know how to build market leaders. A lot of money is being invested here, and many new technologies are coming out of the ecosystem. And that's amazing!

Along with these amazing achievements, Guez admits that:

> when the pandemic broke out, I would not say that Papaya immediately benefited from the new conditions like Zoom; we anticipated to end the year according to our financial predictions. We didn't thrive from day pone! Initially, the startup scene, in Israel and around the world, was in shock, and activities and processes were only routinely operated; however, quite rapidly, startups got back on their feet. In Papaya's case, we were looking meticulously at the new, gradually emerging trends in our industry, and figured out that we should deeply engage in developing our product, the customer experience, and the customization of our offerings. We also observed a new 'escapism' trend relevant to our core activity, in which people were searching for peaceful, uncrowded places to relocate, at least temporarily, and to work remotely from. We followed this trend to fully understand it and prepared our platform to accommodate it.

Guez anticipated the trends; even in early 2020, she could see the opportunities in both raising money from external investors and expanding her offerings' presence through acquisition; she also saw the avenues to recruit more employees. She analyzed the situation back in 2020 as follows:

> Every player in the ecosystem needs to show accountability; startups have to raise money, and investors have to invest. COVID-19 slowed down the investment process for both sides, startups and investors. However, while very young or novice startups faced difficulties in attracting investors, and more mature startups who had promising metrics were able to locate the right financial sources, it was, in fact, startups that focused on the most saliently emerging needs, such as remote work, communication and engagement, who were exposed to more opportunities, including in raising money for a higher company valuation. Ultimately, investors would favor engaging in the less risky startup.

While Guez and her partners have accumulated achievements, she openly speaks about the challenges they face:

> We still have not decoded the 'secret sauce' of integrating the new employee remotely. It is a complex process, and physical encounters promote successful integration and engagement. I truly believe that remote work will become firmly rooted in our daily employment processes, and we are therefore preparing for this new reality; we are working on employees' engagement, we are listening to our employees and empowering them. We have also observed the employees' need for flexibility, and we are making room for it.

concludes Guez.

Guesty is the largest short-term rental property management platform in the world. It is used by property managers and hosts to manage short-term rentals listed on Airbnb, Expedia, Vrbo, Booking.com, and more—all from one unified platform.

CEO and co-founder Amiad Soto started the company in 2013 after renting out properties on Airbnb and spending excessive time dealing with guest-related issues.

Originally launched as a service for homeowners to get their properties ready for listing on Airbnb, it now helps property managers automatically deal with everything from guest communication and check-ins, cleaning and laundry, accounting, channel, and task management—while allowing customers to easily track their revenue from each property.

The company is a Y Combinator graduate, has made several acquisitions, and raised a total of $110 million in funding from investors such as Apax Digital Fund, Viola Growth, Buran VC, Magma Venture Partners, TLV Partners, and Vertex Ventures Israel.

Case 4
"Against all odds"—A story of resilience, trust, and sustainability: Guesty

Vered Raviv Schwarz is the President and COO of Guesty (https://www.guesty.com/), a software management platform for short-term rentals. "Pre-COVID-19, we were very fortunate," explains Raviv Schwarz. "We were operating eight offices worldwide, with the largest one in Israel, but there were also offices in the United States, Europe and APAC." As a most experienced and leading figure in the tech community, who managed the 2008 crisis extremely successfully at a previous company (followed by taking that company public and selling it), Raviv Schwarz:

> noticed a slowdown in February 2020; I recall that I talked with our American customers who were still not experiencing the pandemic, and they pushed us to proceed normally with our business. However, we acted responsibly. We leveraged the fact that we were global and we started preparing ourselves for a new reality. Then, mid-March came, and it was traumatic for the entire travel tech industry, and for the travel and hospitality industries as a whole. Many companies panicked, and it affected the whole travel tech ecosystem. So in a way, it was a lot about taking a deep breath and making the right decisions.

Employees are our main asset: we protect them and help them develop—the outbreak of COVID-19 was accompanied by deep concern about the future and relevance of the travel industry as dramatic changes in traveling customs and behaviors were anticipated; people avoided travel and vacations and generally used travel for urgent situations rather than for leisure and relaxation. Although the crisis consequences were striking swiftly, a strategic response had to be employed. Raviv Schwarz had a rule of thumb: her employees are her first priority. Any crisis, in her view, can be weathered with a resilient, dedicated, and happy team. Guesty's teams were disseminated in offices around the world, and the pursuit of engaging and protecting the teams from the crisis' effects was challenging and called for creative strategies. Raviv Schwarz and the management team thoroughly analyzed the situation and determined that they needed to start coping with the crisis situation by strategically reconfiguring the human factor, drawing on the premise that "our employees are our asset." First, an in-depth focus was directed to operational efficiencies, followed by direct and indirect redeployment of internal resources, processes, and costs, including cuts in the management's salaries and certain employee positions, internal changes in team formations, roles, and structures, and reanalyzing employees' status, such as permanent or temporary, among others. Then, the Management Team exercised what Raviv Schwarz regards as the second-most important rule:

communication. Any change must be openly communicated to the employees in a direct, respectful, and clear conversation, where people are heard and their voices are then transformed into real actions and improvements. This approach to communication turned out to be one of the most successful crisis management strategies at Guesty. The challenges and the new conditions confronting Guesty were communicated to the employees up-front while concurrently introducing the coping strategies, so that the employees would not be overwhelmed with problems but with solutions to the problems. Raviv Schwarz explains:

> We worked tightly with our milestones to monitor and adjust our budget, with transparency to our board, employees, customers and partners; this included weekly open Company meetings in which we discussed the changing global travel trends, and shared ideas about our position in the changing reality.

The foundation for success, according to Raviv Schwarz, is team unity and engagement, and therefore building resilience and trust among her employees took precedence. Guesty's management was aware of the employees' concerns about the travel industry's relevance and sustainability in a world with COVID-19, perceiving it as a tenuous situation, and they therefore tackled the conditions through a multifaceted perspective, where every aspect of the crisis fallout was sought and analyzed with respect to all other aspects. As such, the process rested on communicating each challenge, debating its existing and potential effects, listening to all employees, and in some cases implementing their ideas. This was quite a challenge because the employees were in multiple offices worldwide. Raviv Schwarz explains:

> On top of the threat to our industry, and our concerns about losing our best people who may choose other, more stable industries, we had to manage our staff remotely, dispersed in different countries, where each one of our offices was experiencing the same pandemic-related difficulties, such as lockdowns, isolation, sickness, children being at home instead of at school, but at different times. We were lucky as we were already spread out in eight offices prior to the COVID-19 pandemic, so we were used to working and communicating remotely. Yet, we strived to keep our employees secure and happy. As a result, a new team atmosphere emerged, with employees appearing to 'fight for the travel industry'. Our teams from the different offices started to communicate more, raising most creative ideas on how to save the travel industry. It seemed that our staff developed confidence in their contributions to Guesty; they felt that they had a real voice' and that it mattered. In addition, work was both

> more challenging and more motivating, as the employees encountered new situations and difficulties in their daily jobs that were unusual or that they had never tackled before the pandemic, so a stimulating atmosphere developed; everybody was excited to raise solutions for the new difficulties being faced. One such idea was to dedicate the time to improving internal processes, across all departments and venues; to establish more training and learning processes.

adds Raviv Schwarz.

"Our customers are our partners"—it was natural for Guesty to empathize with its customers and partners. According to Raviv Schwarz:

> We had a lot of customers coming to us early on saying 'listen, my business has dropped so and so percentage points and I can't pay you right now, it's very difficult for me'; we listened very carefully and gave a lot of payment relief and discounts. We did everything we could to help our customers push through. And it's not just the right thing to do, morally, I think it also makes business sense, because when you are a good partner during bad times, your customers will remember that during the good times and we believe that eventually, we got better retention as a result of being understanding and forthcoming to our customers during their difficult time.

At this point, Guesty decided to accelerate its contribution to the ecosystem.

> We were thinking, how can we really help our customers, not just with payment relief, how can we help them succeed? We created an information center on our website with plenty of resources, tips and ideas on how to manage through COVID-19. It was very reassuring for our customers and partners.

says Raviv Schwarz.

Strategy and innovation—Guesty carefully followed the trends and realized that the changes created an opportunity in domestic travel.

> While there was more domestic travel than international travel, people were still looking for rentals, but near their homes; people needed short-term rentals for different purposes, including frontline staff at hospitals who were working 24/7 and needed to be close to their workplace, or people who were isolated or in quarantine and needed some space. So Guesty decided to assist its customers in finding those new prospective clients who are looking for short-term rentals.

explained Raviv Schwarz. Through such support, Guesty conveyed its knowledge of the new travel personas, the best channels to attract them, the new marketing campaigns to target customers with new habits.

> Since we had data from many sources, across 80 countries, we strengthened our position as the go-to resource and voice of the industry, providing property management companies, hosts, and even guests with the valuable data-driven insights and advice that empowered them to navigate the uncertainty gripping the ecosystem – and thrive in a new reality.
>
> We found we could contribute a lot of value to our customers, provide suggestions on new directions and trends and make recommendations to our customers and partners, and actually to the entire ecosystem. We were determined at that point of the need to work together; it doesn't matter if you're my customer or not, it doesn't matter if you're competing with me day to day or not, now is the time for the industry to stand together , this is how we can all survive and come out stronger.

according to Raviv Schwarz. Bringing the ecosystem together played an important role in coping with the COVID-19 crisis; Guesty initiated many educational initiatives through virtual events and timely content, and had to shift its marketing department's focus. This enabled Guesty to gain insights, knowledge, and expertise, and it became an expert and thought leader in both the travel industry and in operating virtual professional events. It constantly updated data and was leading the whole spectrum, from new personas to global trends, on what customers are looking for and how the ecosystem is responding to it. Eventually, a year-and-a-half into COVID-19, Guesty managed to secure a significant funding round, acquire competitors, launch new products, break out from the pack to emerge as the clear industry leader, and demonstrate staggering year-over-year growth.

Raviv Schwarz sums up her tips for managing a global crisis:

> The first thing is not to panic; whatever happens, take a deep breath, think and plan ahead for different scenarios, in detail; don't assume the worst, don't assume the best, but be prepared. Plan different actions for those different scenarios by involving all of your stakeholders, from your employees to your investors, to your community; communicate and make sure that everybody knows and understands your plans. Empathize with your employees, partners, customers, community; show them that you care, that you understand what they're going through, that you're thinking about ways to help them. Exploit

> opportunities. Don't say that 'everything's terrible', rather, make lemonade out of the lemons given to you. And finally, it is a good solution to pivot, but it is also costly, so give it a second thought; instead of turning 180 degrees, can I take a 20 degree or 30 degree turn? So for example, we would keep our main business but complement it with additional personnel, features and products that are crafted step by step to respond to both the current situation and the anticipated needs in the future.

Bizzabo https://www.bizzabo.com/

Bizzabo provides customers with a new era of event platforms to plan and run both virtual and in-person conferences, from conception and handling sponsorships through to managing attendees and provisioning the conference itself. By unlocking the most important data, event organizers can measure returns on events in a virtual setting, while concurrently treating every event as an amazing opportunity to build a sustainable community.

Case 5
"A pivot is a change in strategy without a change in vision"[2] (Eric Ries): Bizzabo

Eran Ben-Shushan, Co-Founder and CEO along with Alon Alroy and Boaz Katz, founded Bizzabo in 2011, a platform to combine the fundamental elements of a successful event: registration system, payment collection from attendees, breakout rooms, advanced technology to help exhibitors, sponsors, and attendees to connect with each other during the event, a customized event website and mobile application for the event, and collection of data. Ben-Shushan recounts:

> I was an officer in the Israeli Air Force for nine years and then nine more years in the reserves; this journey shaped my entrepreneurial and leadership capabilities. I was in Elbit Systems for four years, where I got good perspective for an enterprise organization/corporate environment and product development. Then, I was a CEO of an event production company, where I gained insights into the complexities and anxieties related to running conferences and events as a whole.
>
> Only then did I join the Zell Entrepreneurship Program in 2010 at Reichman University and met Katz and Alroy. We enjoyed working together and

> vigorously believed that we could create a very strong and sustainable team. We were extremely passionate about the events industry, as we are all 'people persons' and believe in the power of events to bring people together and build relationships.
>
> We felt the event industry was antiquated, cumbersome, and years behind where technology was already at that time, with a gap that is only expected to grow exponentially, and we could make them so much better and efficient, and data-driven by using technology. However, we figured out that nobody was really doing it the right way and we said, we're going to do it and make things much better for event organizors and revolutionize this industry. And with that, we embarked on our journey. We started with something that was relatively niche-driven—a mobile networking app for events, and then we realized—after about a year and a half, two years—that while it was great, it wasn't sufficient to build a sustainable business based on that offering.

Bizzabo has established itself as a smart integration of measurable tools for productivity and communication that an event organizer might use. The idea is to provide a platform to combine these tools and give organizers a way of using apps and online services to extend touchpoints in-between and with attendees.

The power of core values—the development of Bizzabo's idea and product and the fit with its customers were carefully, vigorously, and smartly formed while listening to specific customers' needs and being open to opportunities. Bizzabo faced challenges that required pivoting before the COVID-19 pandemic. Ben-Shushan recounts:

> Our first pivot was back in 2014–2015, about two years after starting the company; I believe that is one of the things that has helped us succeed over the years is our ability to identify our core values as an organization and stay very loyal to them, as well as the ability to look inside and admit failure or deficiencies that we might have as an organization, or as part of our product offering. This is actually something that I attribute to the organizational culture that all three of us came from—the Air Force. One of the things that the Israeli Air Force is very well-known for is the ability to constantly improve and remain agile, embrace the lean startup mentality where building and learning are entwined. From day one we put a lot of emphasis on our culture and values; at some point, when we started growing and realized we need to articulate our values in words so everyone who's joining or part of the team has the required level of clarity about our culture and values, we identified eight core values;

> one of them was humility, and embracing the recognition that you don't know it all and that you need to keep an open mind and welcome change; this is actually intertwined with another core value that we have – we dare – which speaks for the desire to "swing for the fences", to go really big, even when facing adversity or failure, while being able to get back up each and every time you're knocked down, resulting in a resilient business and employees. Embracing change and feeling comfortable stepping out of your comfort zone is tightly combined with those core values. I think these helped us tremendously in our first meaningful pivot back in 2015 and then again during the pandemic.

Bizzabo ranks among its core values grit, resilience, and unique organizational culture, and dissemination of the values of "we care, we dare, we own it, we are humble, we are better together, we choose excellence, we are honest, we smile" (https://www.bizzabo.com/our-team). According to Ben-Shushan:

> we had a quite a significant pivot, transforming our entire offering strategy and vision to develop a successful event platform that provides all of the tools needed to manage the event, help our customers craft unique experiences, and measure the ROI, i.e., the return that you can get on an event that you are organizing through our platform compared to others. The journey to this platform was a pretty substantial and meaningful pivot for us that turned out to be a successful one.

Bizzabo strives to grow and scale up by introducing more offerings that are more tightly aligned with customers' needs and expectations, and its ability to really listen to the customer and craft optimal events has resulted in great success; Bizzabo powers on average hundreds of conferences a week. It has garnered positive reviews from leading international organizations on its solutions, technology, user experience, team support, and engagement with the customers.

Tackling change through core values—the COVID-19 outbreak halted Bizzabo's core business, as conferences and events became non-existent. It was even more challenging to tackle such a dramatic change when success was just around the corner. "March is a very strong month in a very strong period of the year in terms of events taking place, and we have literally hundreds of events lined up, thousands for the entire quarter," says Ben-Shushan.

> Suddenly, the first event was canceled, followed by a domino effect of cancellations due to social distancing. In a matter of days, our entire industry was

flipped upside down. And the first thing we did was to focus a lot of attention on our employees because they are the ones who make everything else happen. The second most important thing that we did is to put 'a blanket of love on our customers'. Our customers were going through hell during the first weeks of the pandemic, and we needed to be empathetic, to realize that for event marketers and planners who sometimes begin planning events nine months or a year prior to the event, suddenly everything collapsed overnight. Then we went into a high operational mode which was almost like running a military operation. We built a task force to deal with the day-to-day management of the situation. We stressed the importance of quickly understanding what's happening at the macro level; while focusing on our customers, employees, and establishing an efficient communication structure, while everyone is operating remotely. So, we had a leadership task force to deal with that. We built contingency plans and mapping scenarios for different levels of uncertainty and started mapping out (reasonable) financial and operational scenarios for the company. Then we quickly started thinking about making sure that from a financial standpoint, we have enough longevity to make it through this crisis. We had to make an incredibly tough decision to downsize the company by approximately 25% at the end of March 2020. This was one of the most challenging and painful moments for me personally in my career and as a leader. As an entrepreneur, you're so focused on building and building and building and suddenly you find yourself "breaking" and "ruining" and downsizing, which is a very unnatural and non-intuitive thing to do. You need to stop being the typical overly optimistic entrepreneur and you need to look reality in the face and make tough decisions. That's what is expected from you as a leader. At the same time, we were trying to gather a lot of knowledge about crisis management; I was reading a lot and communicating with whoever we thought could add value; I was leaning on board members, advisors, and experienced entrepreneurs, and looking for advice on the best lessons learned for crisis management. One of the things I remember very clearly is when you need to make tough decisions, they need to be deep and to be put into effect only once, and not in the "salami-slicing style" of multiple waves or downsizing cycles; just do it once and in a substantial enough way that will put you in what you believe is the required place to power through the crisis ahead of you. It was a very emotionally difficult decision for me and for us as the founders and executive team, but we made what back then felt like the right decision based on the information that we had.

Ben-Shushan goes on to say that "the COVID-19 outbreak forced us to acknowledge that everything had completely changed. We were thinking, let's recognize that and look at reality. We reevaluated basically everything that we could think of in a very positive, rather than defeatist, mindset."

The opportunity to drill down—the COVID-19 crisis confronted Bizzabo with the understanding that virtual events were thoroughly recognized, in fact, by everyone in the industry. According to Ben-Shushan:

> a virtual event is not a big Zoom meeting or a Webinar. Similar to the in-person world where you were going to make business connections, acquire knowledge and have new experiences—all of the reasons that we would attend a physical event, were suddenly also the expectation for virtual events. Personally, I never went to a true 'virtual event' and, in fact, nobody I spoke to ever had either; thus we had to recognize that there's a chance that actually no one knows better than we do what a virtual event is, or what it could and should be. This gave us the confidence to take a leadership stand in the market and tell our customers that this is what we believe a virtual event needed to look like. We were curious to hear our customers' opinions and offered them to work together on crafting and designing those events. As a strategy, we remained very attentive and attuned to the market, to our competitors, and based on those continued learnings, we shaped those experiences and redefined our vision, strategy, product roadmap, and operational plans. What quickly happened was that we suddenly found ourselves being a meaningful resource to our customers and the entire market. We ran a virtual event in early May 2020; we called it 'almost in-person' and we opened the virtual gates to the 6,500 people who registered for this event. We realized that this was a different ballgame and we needed to take it at the most serious level. Only at that event, we truly started to understand the complexities of virtual events, what the video-streaming element and production elements of an event looked like, what were the possible pitfalls and risks, and so forth. Running the event virtually and experiencing those challenges and complexities firsthand was a transformational moment for us that helped us, again, evolve over time to become industry subject matter experts and then help our customers rely on us. In other words - it was not only 'talk the talk' but also 'walk the walk'. This helped us gain a lot of confidence and understand all of the difficulties, what works and what doesn't at the product level and technology level.

He emphasized a second important crisis management strategy followed at Bizzabo:

> to build a multidisciplinary task force. The military background of my co-founder and I helped us tremendously in the ability to move into 'emergency mode' and manage it effectively. I even remember us using these specific words at an all-hands meeting with the entire company: 'There is peacetime management of a company, and there is wartime management. This is war-time,' and our multidisciplinary task force had representatives from technology, product marketing, sales operations, client services, the people team, finance, etc. and we carefully selected the right people in the organization to be part of this taskforce. This taskforce continues for five months and was extremely efficient as a way to manage all of the information flow and effectively transition the company and pivot through a very unpredictable period with constant changes. I think the combination of all those actions is what helped us pivot gracefully at such a turbulent and challenging moment in time at the macro and micro levels.

The turning point—The lockdowns, health concerns, and isolation halted all in-person conferences and events; however, event organizers started considering shifting the event experience online, which brought a whole new set of needs from event organizers and participants, both technically, such as how to create roundtable formats or register and split participants efficiently to different virtual workshops, how to create a unique and branded experience to your virtual event. Another meaningful challenge was how to facilitate networking in those virtual events. An unexpected challenge and dilemma was how to charge participants and sponsors or exhibitors for virtual conferences.

> We were realizing what virtual events meant and added that to our agenda to change the product offering; very quickly we were able to launch a solution to the market. I'm talking about three and a half, four weeks after the COVID-19 pandemic had started, we already had our first PR announcement that we have a virtual solution. It was not yet fully functional, but it was already something that we could show to customers and test with them. We were amazed by the influx of demand for the introduction of a virtual offering to the market. Most of the work was still ahead of us, because it's a super dynamic environment and we believe that a new era—of hybrid events—is approaching. Aside from continuing to scale up and grow, we truly believed that we needed to remain agile and super innovative in times of continuous change and paradigm shifts
>
> shares Ben-Shushan.

Bizzabo identified a new demand for tools that they had already developed to provide the communication foundation, such as streaming, which had not been used as a core part of its platform before COVID, but was quickly built and integrated into Bizzabo's offering as a live streaming service. In December 2021, Bizzabo announced one of the largest rounds of funding recorded for that year—$138 million.

According to Matt Gatto, a managing director at Insight Partners who joined the Bizzabo board of directors:

> COVID-19 has permanently transformed the professional events category. Bizzabo's impressive growth and momentum began pre-pandemic and accelerated during the pandemic, as they launched the industry's first end-to-end event technology solution. Their pedigree in both in-person and virtual events and their impressive execution capabilities have them well-positioned to lead this rapidly evolving space. We are excited to partner with their leadership team and to support them in this new phase of growth.

Cody Crnkovich, Head of Platform Partners and Strategy for Adobe Partner Programs, adds:

> The coronavirus has fundamentally changed the way B2B marketers engage prospects and customers through professional events. Bizzabo's platform helps them meet the moment, empowering marketers to run personalized virtual or hybrid events, while also making it possible to activate event data across the customer journey. We look forward to continuing our work with Bizzabo.

Bizzabo's co-founders anticipated the power of hybrid events, combining virtual and in-person communication. Virtual events are attractive in providing a longer reach and lower production costs, yet Ben-Shushan and his team detected event organizers' and attendees' strong desire to (re)meet in person and consequently marked a new era in the event industry—the hybrid era that integrates participants' remote and live experiences.

Startup México (https://www.startupmexico.com/) provides incubation programs, acceleration programs, boot camps, startup weekends, and various programs that embrace entrepreneurs and their teams, aimed at equipping them with the best tools to realize their ideas into successful startups. The programs cover a full range of topics relevant to entrepreneurs, including identification of areas to achieve substantial growth and opportunities; strategic growth plans; sales, marketing, finance, and human capital; tools for presentations to potential suppliers and strategic partners; and mentorship to overcome challenges faced by entrepreneurs, among others.

Dux Capital (https://www.duxcapital.vc/) is a venture capital fund based in Austin, Texas, and Mexico City, committed to investing in early stage startups across Latin America and the United States, mainly innovating in the Consumer and Retail, Technology, and Impact industries. It provides support, mentoring, advice, and various tools to turn any entrepreneurial, innovative idea into a real, sustainable new venture.

Case 6
Ecosystem stakeholders embrace startups: Startup México and Dux Capital

Marcus Dantus[3] (https://www.marcusdantus.com/), a well-known 'shark' on the popular television show in Mexico *Shark Tank*, is the founder of the successful Startup México, aimed at promoting innovation, entrepreneurial culture, and economic development in Latin America and bridging between Latin American and North American startups. He is also the managing partner at Dux Capital, a seed capital fund. "I care about the Mexican entrepreneurial ecosystem," says Dantus,

> and my enthusiasm is focused there. From 2012 and 2018 in Mexico, there was an organization called the National Institute of Entrepreneurship. It was the first time Mexico had an independent institution funded by the government to support the creation of startups. I founded Startup México, supported by a grant, and worked intensively to promote and encourage entrepreneurship in our ecosystem. The outcome was evident and most inspiring; during that time, the ecosystem in Mexico flourished like never before; we created around 500 incubators in universities, private organizations; there was an incredible explosion in the number of funds for startup creation, increasing from 2 in 2008, to 14 in around 2012, and by 2017, there were over 60 funds, and we were intensively striving to double and triple the investments every year. The ecosystem matured, though it is still operated as a novice entrepreneurial ecosystem.

For Dantus, a typical entrepreneurial figure who is targeting a field to change, promote, and grow, and consequently is generating the means, tools, and best expertise around to realize those goals, investments 'alone' are not sufficient to create a thriving, entrepreneurial ecosystem. Dantus thinks big!:

> I was aiming to create the entrepreneurial culture in Mexico, so that entrepreneurship would be sought after, and be perceived as the best opportunity, especially in such times as the COVID-19 pandemic, when entrepreneurship

can be the best prospect for anyone tackling lockdowns, isolation, dismissals, and so on.

According to Dantus, "the foundation of a thriving entrepreneurial ecosystem is the country's entrepreneurial culture, which is open to innovation, daring and risking." However, political and country-related events have dramatically changed the governmental support in startups and the SMB[4] industry. "There was a state of confusion in the ecosystem when the government stopped funding programs for entrepreneurs, which was echoed in the state of the ecosystem in 2019 and 2020," explains Dantus.

> COVID-19 hit Mexico severely, with the highest percentage of infected people, and one of the lowest rates of testing and vaccinations. Under such conditions, entrepreneurship should be fortified to prevail. But the situation was destitute, and I focused on it with all of my energy, out of frustration and a deep eagerness to turn our ecosystem into a vibrant and successful one.

says Dantus.

> In 2020, we faced the biggest downfall in the economy, we lost 8.5 percentage points, the size of our economy decreased by 8.5%, the biggest shrinkage in the economy since the Great Depression in 1930, and I anticipate that recovery will take about 3 to 4 years. The funds are still there, they're still trying to fund new, innovative companies, there are still a lot of startups being born every day; but SMEs[5] are suffering in Mexico, and numbers show that of 4.8 million SMEs, around 1 million went bankrupt. We encounter unemployment; a lot of people have dropped into poverty; more and more people are unbanked, so they live day to day, they don't have insurance, they have no savings. As an involved individual, I put all of my effort into gathering the ecosystem's four helices, encouraging a practical collaboration of industry, academia, government and environment/ecosystem to advance innovation and entrepreneurial zeal; opening economic dynamics in the country without government intervention, which can resolve some cultural and systemic problems; for example, Latin Americans in general and Mexicans in particular, are very, very intolerant of failure, even venture capital is translated (in Spanish) into 'entrepreneur capital' instead of the correct translation ´risk capital´. At the same time, we punish success; then you are creating mediocrity.

says Dantus. The effort put into improving the ecosystem from this premise, by orchestrating the various associations and organizations that may bring about change, is fundamental for Dantus; the COVID-19 pandemic is deemed an opportunity to rebuild and redeploy resources, including reconfiguring mindsets and perceived constraints, so that people will dare to initiate and create the next cutting-edge innovation. Dantus does not give up, even when change seems impossible, and he is doing his utmost to revolutionize the ecosystem by stimulating various areas through the invigoration of entrepreneurship. He truly believes that such changes can stimulate stock market dynamics, accelerate mergers and acquisitions, exits and unicorns, and overall promote the general blossoming of startups in Mexico in particular and Latin America in general. "Mexico is a beautiful place," says Dantus.

> The weather, the natural resources, geographically, we are next to the largest market in the world and we connect Latin America with the Anglo-Saxon world; we also have a 'demographic bonus' in that over half of the population is under 30 years of age. We are becoming more and more educated—the number of college graduates has tripled in the last 15 years; we are ranked something like eighth in the world in the number of engineers and scientists produced. There are so many good things going on that there is the evident potential to create a culture of collaboration.

Dantus has undergone a vibrant journey, from launching his first tech startup in 1993, then founding a telecommunications company, acting as CEO of a medical device business, being central to the founding team of Wayra Mexico, launching Startup México where he acts as CEO, and becoming managing partner in Dux Capital, hence, switching from the entrepreneurial position to the investor position while still holding and even strengthening his entrepreneurial capabilities. Dantus is fueled by the entrepreneurial vision, and vision pushed him to create what he calls "Disneyland for Entrepreneurs" by transforming a warehouse in Mexico City, supported by the Mexican government, into an incubator program that provides support, resources, and mentorship for early stage startups. Dantus is confident that technologies such as blockchain, big data, automation, and IoT will change Mexico's future. Dux Capital invests in clean energy, retail, and tech innovation to help bring those disruptive technologies to Mexico. According to Dantus:

> Startup México has positioned itself as entrepreneurship and innovation experts; we've created over 900 companies, we've expanded to several cities in Mexico, we are currently opening two dozen offices in Latin America, and right now, I have an initiative to open an accelerator in Miami, Camp 4, where we

> would send 20 companies every year to open new avenues and opportunities for Latin American entrepreneurial businesses.

Dantus' main message for turbulent times such as the pandemic is:

> startups should equip themselves *now,* with mindsets, strategies, networking or anything that you can give them as food for thought about what should be done next. They should pursue practical steps, such as engaging in a program of maintaining cash flow, renegotiating new contracts as well as existing, unfavorable ones; they need to accelerate sales cycles, including being open to change, and create a couple of smaller products that can maintain the cash flow. Another important complement to managing crises in the long term is to expand the digital presence; they need to have a website, a digital marketing campaign, social networks, a remote customer service system, so that during the pandemic's shutdowns they can communicate with their customers, and retain their loyalty. We advise startups to install technology in their offices, to thoroughly prepare for the reopening, and most importantly, use the present chaotic situation to reorder the company, to learn, to research, to be able to recover later by establishing the competitiveness now.

concludes Dantus.

Case 7
Reciprocity is the name of the game: JetztInvest (JI)—the open innovation platform

Susanne Roth is the senior executive for startup outreach in a global financial company JetztInvest (JI) responsible for locating startups in various fields that are innovative, are developing cutting-edge products, use frontline technologies, and are comprised of a team that is engaged and dedicated. These startups are sought to develop a technological solution for JI customers, based on those customers' long-term needs. JI provides support, resources, and expertise, and shares platforms, processes, and advice.

Roth and her team approach startups directly and individually through a smart scouting process; around 25–30 startups are selected from all over Europe and matched to JI customers who need technological solutions. The customers themselves are consulted and mentored by JI to determine the innovative technological needs that they can integrate, once developed by the startup, providing solutions that can, according to JI analysts, greatly accelerate and expand the customers' revenues in two, four, and six years. This exclusive process is provided to a limited number of private companies (i.e., JI customers). "It's a W-W-W- situation," explains Roth.

> Our elite customers gain the cutting-edge solutions that are expected to galvanize their competitiveness, JI gains through its customers, and the customers' gratitude for our unique services grows. The startups are provided the rare opportunity of a 'beta site' to test their unique technologies, and since they provide such solutions only to our elite customers—who are market leaders, these startups gain an amazing referral from a most prestigious company. We at JI orchestrate the whole operation, learn about the startups' technologies, recruit the expertise, tools and platforms required for such technological developments; we engage the startups in our core activity at JI, and maintain our elite customers' loyalty. In fact, one member of my team revealed that there is a secret competition between JI customers, to be selected for this process.

says Roth. One of many successful examples of the process is a British startup in the blockchain industry, which has developed a brand-new smart platform for buying and reselling items through non-fungible token transactions. The startup was selected by JI and matched with a diamond company that was interested in this technological expertise, albeit for a completely different use. The match turned out to be successful, as the diamond company gained, in a short time, a competitive technology that enabled it to open a new line of lab diamonds, while the startup launched a professional branch for diamonds.

"When COVID-19 started," says Roth,

> we encountered the unique threat of a L-L-L situation. Our team approached multiple startups, which turned us down, mainly because until the pandemic struck, the chosen startups had been asked to be physically present at our venues, to enjoy our many resources. On the other side, our various elite companies all seemed to put any activity that was outside their core business on hold, including technological developments for future competitiveness, and they were therefore hesitant to enroll in our unique open innovation platform. In addition, we had some internal disagreements; some of our board members preferred keeping JI resources for its core business, rather than invest them toward increasing our customers' competitiveness.

discloses Roth. In this challenging time, Roth and her team were asked to take a leave of absence for up to six months, so that JI could reconsider its priorities. However, two to three months into the leave, Roth was being approached by more and more elite customers to open the process, as they realized that this was the perfect time to inaugurate the 'next innovation', which would be introduced when things went back to normal. Roth was invited back to JI, but with fewer employees on her team, less financial support from JI, and fewer resources to be provided to the elite customers. Regardless, JI expected swift wins for these top customers. "It was stressful and seemed impossible to produce such wins in 2–3 weeks," says Roth.

> We were lacking the best startups, as well as the team members who used to scout for such startups. So we opened the scope of our dual clients, from only JI elite customers and the best tech startups to JI customers' clients and our portfolio startup partners (which were also startups). I was terrified as we took this different path, congruent with the changing conditions and difficulties, yet not entirely approved by the entire management ladder. Surprisingly, the more we risked by widening the search for our 'dual' clients, the more I was approached by leading companies as well as startups in Europe to be included in this process; so we reached out to the seemingly 'lower-ranking' clients in terms of branding, wealth or industry leadership, but generated requirements from more higher-ranking clients.

says Roth. The team worked day and night to extract the customers' needs, anticipate through analysts the best solutions for competitiveness, and locate the best startup to develop such technological solutions. In one case, Roth received a request from one of the leading technological companies asking for a creative solution to money collection in a very specific niche in its services, but Roth could not find a matching startup:

> We understood that a success story in this case would be a game changer. So we accumulated experts from startups that we had worked with in the past, as well as from our community, and formed a highly professional task force that we called the JI startup; we shared technological platforms with this leading company, and in 3 weeks' time, the perfect solution was developed for testing. We garnered rave reviews and feedback from this leading company, which then became a JI customer, in our core business. The members of our JI startup returned to their original startups equipped with more knowledge, networks and a new potential industry-leading customer.

says Roth. By detecting this new need of mainly established companies to collaborate with startups for their technology, innovation, and customized solutions while being monitored by JI analysts, Roth and her team expanded to scouting, which was still executed directly, confidentially, and privately, but for a large range of companies, industries, and countries. "While the pandemic nearly abolished our unique business for JI customers and the startup ecosystem, it also introduced an opportunity," claims Roth.

> I was attentive to its potential, and took the risk to activate it, though this ran against the expectations of the board of directors for my role at that time. As a lawyer, I tend to avoid risks, but the opportunity was there, and I could anticipate its potential for JI in terms of attracting more top customers for its core business, generating more knowledge on new technologies, and expanding its community. We could also identify startups' intensive search for such opportunities; they were coming up against companies' reluctance to collaborate with them to test technologies, as all members of the ecosystem were endeavoring to avoid risk. In the startups' case, their investment resources dwindled because in the early stages of the pandemic, investors were cautious about investing in new startups, leaving fertile ground for our business. Luckily I was right.

concludes Roth.

Case 8
Forging the future: Co-Creation Network Universities (CCNU)

"Companies should be located close to the talent, and 'creating' talent is our expertise," says Raahi Ng, the COO and driving force of Co-Creation Network Universities (CCNU), a consortium of universities from different regions across Asia. The idea of opening such a unique academic institution came from Ng's wife Binita, after a long search for the right job. Binita was number 1 in academic achievements at the faculty of chemical engineering, but faced difficulties finding a job, as she was either overqualified or being offered positions that, aside from the job title (e.g., chemical engineer, process safety engineer, technical sales person), had nothing to do with her training, which meant that she would have to take courses to become certified for the job being offered. CCNU is dedicated to preparing students for the exact expectations of their dream job as well as co-creating with the industry the required knowledge, expertise, mindsets, networks, and skills.

"The premise of CCNU rests on co-creation," explains Ng.

> We build customized academic projects that we introduce as elective curricula, added to our basic requirements as an academic institution. These projects can be courses, workshops, internships, mentoring sessions, competitions, visits, peer-to-peer sessions, and more, that are shaped jointly by our company partners. Our community is vast. It is comprised of the many companies that are gradually joining us, and it is expanding exponentially. Our partner companies, either individually or as a vertical net, provide us with their expectations, needs and challenges, and we develop the academic curricula to meet those requirements, by involving the partner company. We work with the most specialized content developers to create this program and ensure its customized practical focus, while maintaining high academic and research standards

says Ng. For now, this unique method has only been developed for the fields of entrepreneurship and innovation. The decision to initiate this educational method in areas that are tolerant to innovation was deliberate; with practice and experience, it will be modified and implemented in other fields. Moreover, the fields of entrepreneurship and innovation have high industry involvement, and they are also 'contagious'. Companies in the ecosystem observe the fit between the talent hired for the partner company's needs, and they join the CCNU network to co-create curricula from which they themselves can benefit.

The elective program is dynamic and changes every year, based on the companies' requirements. To facilitate the process, the additional offerings can serve several companies. As Ng exemplifies:

> One of our partner companies is a large retail chain. It brought challenges related to sales during the pandemic, as people began losing their jobs and were less prone to spending their money on unnecessary merchandise. We built a cutting-edge program for 15 students who were interested in these areas of expertise, and planned their careers in the retail field. Then an American net of stationery manufacturers and suppliers expressed interest in our offerings; they preferred to join existing courses and workshops rather than co-creating new ones. We are flexible.

says Ng. "We meet our partner companies at least once per semester to review the program, achievements and student-satisfaction rates, and to evaluate the fit between the partner company's requirements and the program courses, workshops, etc." Ng continues:

> We create, with our partner companies and our students jointly—and these are mandatory for each student—'executive committees' and 'boards of controllers' where we evaluate the fit between the students and the partner companies' levels of satisfaction from the value gained, the fit between the expertise acquired and the industry needs, lessons to learn and consequently use to modify the program components. We keep our partners active, engaged and content.

he concludes.

It is quite an expensive model: the partner companies pay to participate and for unique program development, and the students' tuition is relatively high, hence attracting only those who can afford it. However, during the pandemic, many students and their families lost their incomes, especially those from the tourism and food sectors, and CCNU management took a proactive stance by asking its partner companies to hire students in this program for temporary positions to enable them to manage the crisis. "In one case," says Ng,

> one of our students, originally from Japan, was hired by an American partner company for a student position, and she was so brilliant that she saved the company approximately 1 million dollars by detecting a bug in the system. She was then offered a position in the partner-company offices in New York City; we approved her relocation, and enabled her to complete the program virtually. We are very attentive to both the partner companies' and students' changing and dynamic needs, and we respond to them swiftly. In another case, unfortunately, we witnessed a financial crisis in one of our partner companies, a leading manufacturer of restaurant equipment, recognized for its focus on improving safety in restaurant kitchens. We encouraged the company to stay in our network, free of charge, and jointly with other universities, we developed, in less than a month, a 'student advisory atelier' aimed at providing practical means for the manufacturer's company to recover, and it worked!

exclaims Ng, presenting a letter from one of the students participating in the atelier. The student, Rajesh, wrote:

> I came back to school after many years in startups in India and was a bit cynical about the value I could obtain from academic studies, as 'I had seen it all' in the startups, as a programmer, team manager and the CTO of a startup company.

But the way CCNU managed the case [of the manufacturer, D.K.] showed me what universities should look like. CCNU's commitment to the community has prevailed. CCNU detected the pandemic's disruptive effect on a manufacturing company that lost its business as restaurants were, and still are, closed. It established an advisory atelier of students from different universities of our consortium, with the highest ranked CEOs of partner companies here in Asia, aimed at rescuing the manufacturer's company. Now I know that I am equipped with everything I need for my next dream job. More importantly, I know that I will be safe and secure in any future crisis, because CCNU is there for me, as a (future) alumnus and (future) entrepreneur.

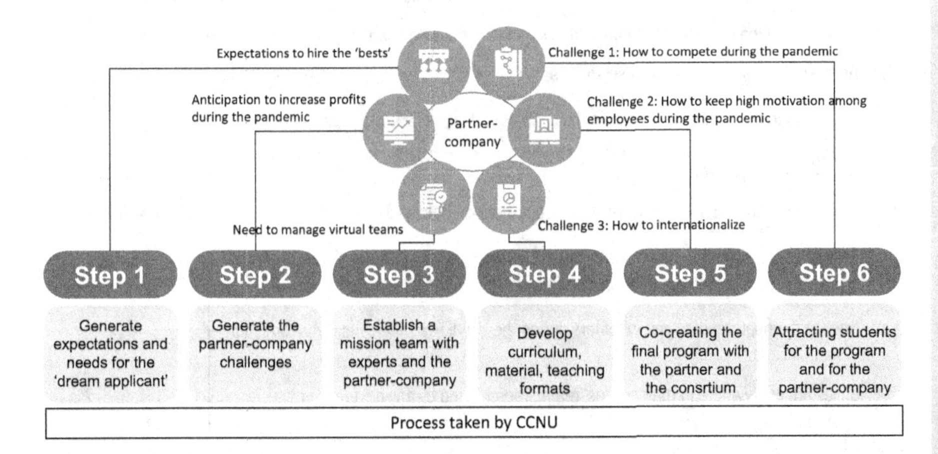

FIGURE 11.1 CCNU process

Questions for the cases:

Questions for discussion	Best used for cases
Chapter 1 Paving the way for the 'new normal': an introduction to the field	
Fill in Table 1.1: The minimum optimal actions required in crisis events for all of the cases introduced	1, 2, 3, 4, 5, 6, 7, and 8
Chapter 2 Startup dynamics	
1. According to Kariv (2020), startups are typified by value creation, competitive advantage, innovation, stages of development, and entrepreneurs' characteristics and mindsets. Analyze the startup through these characteristics. Address one startup from the case studies • Is it a typical startup? What are its salient characteristics? • In your view, which of these characteristics (choose one or several) can reduce or even prevent the crisis' destructive effects on the startup? Explain.	1, 2, 3, 4, and 5

(Continued)

Case studies

Questions for discussion	Best used for cases
2. Look at the components of startups' distinctiveness presented in this chapter. Address one startup from the case studies • Which component(s) differentiates this startup from any other type of business? • In your view, does the startup's distinctiveness contribute to or inhibit its navigation through crises? Explain.	1, 3, 4, and 5
3. Let's explore the external perspective of the startup's operation through its relevant environment. Address one stakeholder from the case studies • Based on this chapter's content, what is the stakeholder's main role(s) in any startup's creation and survival and in mitigating crisis fallout?	6, 7, and 8
4. According to the chapter, what makes this stakeholder company an ecosystem?	6, 7, and 8
5. Address one startup from the case studies According to the model introduced in the chapter and Figure 2.1: Startups' imperative 'challenging existing business' settings, how does the startup challenge other businesses? Explain.	1, 2, 3, 4, and 5
6. Address one startup and one stakeholder from the case studies Choose two elements from the model introduced in Figure 2.2: Startups' unique internal operation elements as opportunities and inhibitors. Decode the opportunities and inhibitors during the COVID-19 pandemic. What are your main insights?	1, 2, 3, 4, 5, 6, 7, and 8
7. Crises are everywhere in the startups' realm, represented by any adversity or gap tackled. Address a startup or stakeholder from the case studies: Relative to this startup/stakeholder, is COVID-19 more than just 'another' crisis, and if so, in what way?	1, 2, 3, 4, 5, 6, 7, and 8
8. Address one startup from the case studies Evaluate the startup through the agile-driven approach shown in this chapter and Figure 2.3: Use of unique elements in startups: an agile-driven approach. In your opinion, what are the main components employed by the startup that contributed to its success during the pandemic? Explain.	3, 4, and 5
9. Search the web for a startup that has scaled during the pandemic. Describe it and provide the link to its website. To investigate the internal perspective discussed in this chapter, chose one component from the model in Figure 2.2: Startups' unique internal-operation elements as opportunities and inhibitors. Address one startup from the case studies • Investigate this component in the startup from the case studies and in the one that you found on the internet. How does this component function in each of them? • In your opinion, which way of functioning would be more effective in managing the pandemic effects? Explain.	1, 3, 4, and 5

Question	Case studies
10. Address one stakeholder from the case studies What are the main reasons for this stakeholder's success during the pandemic?	6, 7, and 8
Chapter 3 Types of crises	
1. Address one startup from the case studies Choose one case study and two measures from the chapter's list of measures that can prompt the outbreak of a crisis (e.g., topic, who is affected by the event, timing). Compare the startup that you have chosen to case number 2 (a startup that failed due to the crisis: Valeries) through these measures. What are your conclusions on the successful and unsuccessful navigation of the investigated startups?	1, 3, 4, 5 (choose one), and 2
2. Address one stakeholder from the case studies Choose one case study and two measures from the chapter's list of measures that can prompt the outbreak of a crisis (e.g., topic, who is affected by the event, timing); the measures should be different from those chosen for question number 1. Based on this stakeholder's activity in fostering entrepreneurship, indicate which measures this company should be aware of. Suggest one to two ways to be used by this company to protect startups from the measures you have selected.	6, 7, and 8
3. Address one startup from the case studies Investigate the case of the startup through two different models introduced in Figure 3.2: Models of relationships among crisis topics. Indicate one to two ways that the startup could avoid the multiplicity of topics.	1, 4, and 5
4. Address one startup from the case studies Suggest practical methods for a startup to detect the subjective components of a crisis, based on Figure 3.1: The nexus of objective and subjective components of a crisis.	1, 2, 3, 4, and 5
5. Address one stakeholder from the case studies Suggest practical methods for the stakeholder to teach startups how to detect the objective components of the crisis, based on Figure 3.1: The nexus of objective and subjective components of a crisis. How can the stakeholder apply this method?	6, 7, and 8
6. Address one startup from the case studies Search the web for a startup in the same industry as the case study that you selected, but from a different location. Address the components introduced in the chapter that affect the severity of crises' effects on startups: • Regional perspective • Industry • Political power of the 'event' participants • Recurrence of the same 'event' • Culture • Timing and focus Compare the startup from the web to the one from the case studies through these components. According to your investigation, which components are most important in explaining the severity of crises on startups?	1, 2, 3, 4, and 5

(Continued)

Questions for discussion	Best used for cases
7. Address one stakeholder from the case studies What are the main roles of the stakeholder in preparing startups to avoid/reduce the effects that a crisis will have on them? Base your answer on the crisis indicators introduced in the chapter.	6, 7, and 8
8. Address one startup from the case studies How do startups create crises?	1, 3, and 5
9. Read the *New York Times* article: "Is a pandemic the right time to start a business? It just might be." November 2021 https://www.nytimes.com/2020/05/20/business/coronavirus-small-business-startup.html Suppose you were asked by the startup for your advice on opening a spin-off of Guesty. Write a report to Guesty's management laying out the pros and cons.	3
10. Should academia promote startups' preparation for crisis management by addressing each type of crisis or should it address crises as a general concept? Base your answer on the prevailing models discussed in this chapter vis-à-vis CCNU's academic vision.	8
Chapter 4 Born into crises	
1. Address one stakeholder from the case studies Startups base their coping abilities on the following: • Strong management • Vision, hope, and self and team efficacy • Shared and well-embedded values • Team trust • An ongoing learning culture How can the stakeholder assist startups in equipping themselves to enhance their coping abilities?	6, 7, and 8
2. Address one startup from the case studies Search the web for a startup in your country, describe this startup briefly, and provide the link to its website. Explore Seymour and Moore's (2000) two crisis concepts—the Python and the Cobra—by comparing one case study to the startup found on the web. What are your main conclusions?	1, 3, 4, and 5
3. Address two startups from the case studies You are requested to advise these two startups on how to manage the crisis through preventive and constructive approaches. Choose one model for each case study (e.g., escaping, solving, interacting, provoking). Describe your advice to the startup.	1, 2, 3, 4, and 5
4. Address one startup from the case studies You are hired by the startup to advice on information flow during a crisis. Base your advice on the relevant components introduced in the chapter (e.g., consistency, body language and tone, bad news, vision, what's next). What are your main suggestions?	1, 3, 4, and 5

5. You are hired by an accelerator to advice on the critical factors that startups should consider in a crisis, as these may determine how the crisis will be perceived. Address the individual, organizational, and ecosystem levels. Address the required resources, ways, and skills needed in the accelerator to develop the relevant tools to detect these factors and to respond to them.	6
6. Read the TechCrunch article: "Accelerators embrace change forced by pandemic," from November 2020 at https://techcrunch.com/2020/11/10/accelerators-embrace-change-forced-by-pandemic/ You are hired as an evaluator of the stakeholders' roles in assisting startups during crises. Write a short report on the role of the accelerator (case 6). In your opinion, does academia have an additional role (case 8) in such assistance? Explain your answer based on the chapter's concepts.	6 and 8
7. Imagine that hypothetically, the COVID-19 pandemic erupted at each of the startup's stages of evolution. Analyze the startup stages through the model introduced in Figure 4.1: Evolution of crisis and startup stages—perceptions of crisis severity, considering the 'Immediate period of the crisis'. In your opinion, would Bizzabo look different today if it had encountered COVID-19 at a different stage of development?	5
8. Address one startup from the case studies Ask ten colleagues, friends, or family members to rank the three most critical areas for founders in times of crisis, as described in the chapter: • Information flow • Preparation • Trust • Influence • Communication • Authenticity and accuracy Based on your data, advice the startup founders on how to manage the next crisis.	2, 3, and 5
9. Address the three startups from the case studies Compare the founders' leadership styles in depicting crises.	3, 4, and 5
10. Startups are born into crises. How can academia prepare students for the next crisis, based on the chapter's models?	8
Chapter 5 External effects of crises	
1. Address two startups from the case studies Choose two factors from the model introduced in Figure 5.1: Reciprocal relationships between external forces and startups—first tier. Analyze each startup's relationship with the external forces you have selected. Based on your analysis, what is each startup's forte? How did it help the startup manage the crisis?	1, 3, 4, and 5
2. Investigate the various roles of JI through the model introduced in Figure 5.2: Reciprocal relationships between external forces and startups—second tier. What are you main conclusions?	7

(Continued)

Questions for discussion	Best used for cases
3. Which is the more prevalent role of the accelerator and venture capital to detect, reduce, or recover crisis effects on startups and the ecosystem? Base your answer on the model introduced in Figure 5.3: Crisis effects through bottom-up and top-down views. Discuss the roles through each of the views. What are your conclusions?	6
4. Some industries or sectors become irrelevant in a specific crisis period (e.g., tourism during the COVID-19 pandemic). How should a startup in an irrelevant sector act during a crisis? Which stakeholders should it engage to cope with the crisis fallouts and which types of reciprocal relationships should it create with external bodies?	4
5. How can financial stakeholders assist startups in irrelevant sectors without risking their turnover and profits?	6 and 7
6. Organize the following stakeholders through the ecosystem constituents: organizations, processes, and capabilities, based on the concepts introduced in this chapter. Accordingly, what are the main roles of each stakeholder in crisis management? Do startups approach the 'right' stakeholder in assisting them to navigate the crisis?	6, 7, and 8
7. Observe the grid in Table 5.2: Ecosystem components and viability in the face of crises' external effects—a crisis management perspective. Discuss the function of the accelerator versus that of academia in keeping the startups and entrepreneurial ecosystem viable, even in times of crisis. What are your conclusions?	6 and 8
8. Address one stakeholder from the case studies. Investigate the role of stakeholder as connector. Refer to the concepts discussed in the chapter (e.g., robust networking processes between established and nascent businesses; diverse vertical representation rather than focusing only on the highly ranked vertical; a diversity of entities with fair representation of the genders, ethnicity, age, socioeconomic status; connectors; and dynamic and agile embracing of change).	6, 7, and 8
9. Discuss the value of the stakeholder's feedback. Draw on the concepts discussed in this chapter.	6 and 7
10. Which stakeholder do you think is responsible for managing and monitoring the chaotic situation brought on by a crisis? If you choose more, then categorize the responsibilities, roles, and functions of each of those stakeholders.	6, 7, and 8
Chapter 6 Effects of crises on startups—a micro-perspective	
1. Address two startups and stakeholders from the case studies. Pick one topic from Table 6.1: Emerging changes—opportunities and threats, which details the opportunities and threats to the business that the selected change brings about. Investigate how the selected topic 'acts' in each of these cases. What are your conclusions on opportunities and threats brought by crises?	1, 2, 3, 4, 5, 6, 7, and 8

2. Address two startups from the case studies You are hired by the two startups for advice on how each can leverage the changes produced by a crisis to grow and succeed. Provide three to four ways to leverage the business. Refer to Table 6.2: Leveraging the changes caused by crises, in your answer. What are the main implications?	1, 3, 4, and 5
3. Address a startup from the case studies Reflect on the effect of the 'new normal' on this startup by: • Inspecting the current situation in the startup. Has the startup already applied some components of the 'new normal' or can you detect the seeds of the 'new normal' in this startup's operation? • Anticipate how the 'new normal' is going to affect this startup in the next year, in two years.	1, 2, 3, 4, and 5
4. Address a stakeholder from the case studies Reflect on the effect of the 'new normal' on this stakeholder by: • Inspecting the current situation of this stakeholder's activity and operation vis-à-vis startups. How is this stakeholder applying the 'new normal' components in embracing the startup's operation? • Anticipating how the 'new normal' is going to affect this stakeholder's approach to assisting and recuperating startups and the entrepreneurial ecosystem.	6, 7, and 8
5. Address a startup from the case studies Search the web for a startup in the same industry as the one in the case study. You are hired as a mentor to assist these two startups (the one extracted from the web and the one selected from the case studies) in merging their operations to raise their odds of surviving the crisis. Your approach as a mentor relies on making the exception routine. Provide three to four ways to manage this merger by routinizing the changes and expectations. Accordingly, do you anticipate that the merger will assist both startups in surviving and thriving as one unit?	1, 2, 3, 4, and 5
6. Address a startup from the case studies • You are asked to evaluate the level of digitalization in a successful startup compared to that in one that failed. With respect to digitalization, why did one startup thrive and the other fail? • Provide two new practical suggestions on additional digitalization for the thriving startup, based on Figure 6.1: The digitalized startup: functions and sections. • Provide Valeries with three to four practical suggestions for additional digitalization which could save it from failure, basing your answer on Figure 6.1.	1, 3, 4, 5 (choose one), and 2

(Continued)

Questions for discussion	Best used for cases
7. The pandemic has highlighted the need for better work-life balance, and many companies have implemented a four-day work week. As a 'new normal', suppose that ASEM wishes to implement a four-day work week. Design a plan for ASEM, including a hybrid work model, which can facilitate its shift to a four-day work week. Explain your design.	1
8. Explore two cases from the nine startup failures in the UK's high-growth ecosystem in 2021, published at Beauhurst, October 2021, https://www.beauhurst.com/blog/top-startup-failures-uk/; search for more information from the web on the cases that you have chosen. In your opinion and based on the chapter's concepts and models, what are the similarities of these cases to Valeries? What are the differences?	2
9. Address a stakeholder from the case studies Design a plan for the stakeholder company to train entrepreneurs, startups, entrepreneurial teams. Base your design on the concepts presented in Table 6.4: Negative and positive effects of digitalization on various levels of the startup. Detail how, in practice, the stakeholder company can convey the planned activities to the startups.	6, 7, and 8
10. According to Euractiv.com (February 2021): "Over 20% of digital healthcare startups emerged during the pandemic" (https://www.euractiv.com/section/coronavirus/news/over-20-of-digital-healthcare-startups-emerged-during-the-pandemic/). As a consequence of this new trend, you are hired to advise an academic institution on the avenues to prepare entrepreneurs and startups for this 'new normal'. Write a short report to the academic management specifying the rationale for the changes you are recommending and four to five practical suggestions. Base your report on the chapter's concepts and models.	8
Chapter 7 Strategy, preparation, and design	
1. Compare the startups' approaches to the COVID-19 crisis based on Table 7.1: Startups' approaches to disruptive events. Categorize the startups in the grid below and explain why you placed the startup in the specific cell.	1, 2, 3, 4, and 5

Maintaining the routine	Business as usual Cases: Explanations:	Embrace the routine Cases: Explanations:
Strategies for adjusting to the crisis	Misery likes company Cases: Explanations:	Stay awake, remain Cases: Explanations:

2. Compare the startups' reactions to the crisis based on Table 7.2: Exploiting the crisis from a startup's point of view.

   Categorize the startups in the grid below and explain why you placed the startup in the specific cell.

Threat	Close to the vest Cases: Explanations:	Lower engagement Cases: Explanations:
Opportunity	Innovating and initiating Cases: Explanations:	Vision to scale Cases: Explanations:

   1, 2, 3, 4, and 5

3. You are hired as a mentor by Guesty to prepare the startup for the next crisis. You have read the Harvard Business Review article from October 2020 on "Mentoring during a crisis" (https://hbr.org/2020/10/mentoring-during-a-crisis).

   Describe how you would prepare yourself, as a mentor, to train Guesty teams for the next crisis. Why is it important for Guesty?

   4

4. You are hired as an adviser for crisis management, and as part of the training, you start by presenting JI's management with the roadmap for the startup's preparations for the crisis, exhibited in Figure 7.3: Startups' preparation to maintain their resources—a roadmap. The management of JI does not see the need to prepare their portfolio startups for the next crisis.

   Write a proposal to JI's management convincing them of the imperative need for their startups to follow the roadmap. Explain to JI management why JI needs to convey the roadmap to the startups in its portfolio.

   7

5. In your opinion, which heuristics and biases were prevalent in Valeries' strategy and understanding of the crisis consequences and the need to prepare in advance?

   2

6. Address a startup from the case studies

   Pick two elements (e.g., technology, production, finance) of the coping design, exhibited in Figure 7.4: Designing the coping strategy: functions and strategies. Sketch a plan designed to prepare for the next crisis. Be specific (e.g., under 'Technology, R&D' detail exactly what is required, such as digitalizing the payment system, improving the UX/UI of the product, training employees at home on a new automatic system for customer retention).

   1, 3, 4, and 5

7. As part of the preparation for a crisis, it is important to detect the decision-making processes of entrepreneurs.

   Discuss the decision-making of Bizzabo's founder while tackling the COVID-19 pandemic and, based on his background, by addressing the concepts and models discussed in the chapter (e.g., rational/intuitive/improvisational approach; programmed versus non-programmed; tactical versus operational; routine versus strategic; and organizational versus personal).

   5

(*Continued*)

Questions for discussion	Best used for cases
8. Address a startup from the case studies Provide four to five recommendations on how to ensure the startup's crisis preparedness; refer to the concepts discussed in the chapter, including risk mapping, responsibility plan, the 'Go!', communication, emergency contacts, and 'hands-on'.	1, 2, 3, 4, and 5
9. • Refer to the McKinsey article published in May 2020 on "Helping start-ups overcome inevitable challenges and crises" (https://www.mckinsey.com/~/media/McKinsey/Business%20Functions/McKinsey%20Digital/Our%20Insights/Helping%20start%20ups%20overcome%20inevitable%20challenges%20and%20crises/helping-start-ups-overcome-inevitable-challenges-and-crises.pdf). • Extract the five main insights and describe them as practical recommendations. • Prepare a short presentation for the management of the Startup México accelerator and Dux Capital aimed at convincing them to use your five insights in their acceleration program.	
10. Write a two-page transcript of a discussion between the founders of ASEM and Valeries on the need to prepare for the next crisis.	1 and 2
Chapter 8 Managing crises	
1. Sketch the blueprint of a mentoring plan: list five to six steps for a mentoring plan for the accelerator (case six) to support the portfolio companies in Latin America in times of crisis. Base your plan on the chapter's contents and on the model in Figure 8.1: When does acute coping happen?	6
2. Address two startups from the case studies • Categorize the startups according to their approaches to managing an existing crisis. • Are there differences between these two startups, and if so, explain why in your view they exist.	1, 2, 3, 4, and 5
3. Address three startups from the case studies Suppose you are recruited to the startup during the pandemic as the Communications Manager and your responsibility is to be the voice of the startup for stakeholders, social media, and others. • List three to four main messages for each startup analyzed that you would communicate to the outside. Draw on the chapter's concepts and on Figure 8.3: Startup's comprehensive view in coping with an acute crisis. • What are the similarities and differences in these messages among the three startups? Explain your answer.	1, 2, 3, 4, and 5
4. Discuss application of the two coping strategies—restructuring and resizing—in the two startups; indicate which components of each coping strategy have been applied and in which way (e.g., in marketing, contact with the ecosystem).	4 and 5
5. Suppose that prior to its closure, the management of Valeries invited you to advise the startup on how to cope with the pandemic effects through innovation and development strategies. • List four to five recommendations for Valeries. • Accordingly, in your opinion, could such coping strategies have prevented Valeries' closure? Explain your answer.	2

6.	• Choose four elements of the 'entrepreneur's dilemma': two included in the business' perspective and two included in the crisis perspective. • Write a two-page transcript of a Zoom meeting between Susanne Roth—the senior executive for startup outreach at JI—and the executive director of JI's board of directors that describes the views of each regarding these four elements in the 'entrepreneur's dilemma'. • In your view, which element in the 'entrepreneur's dilemma' is more critical in times of crisis? Explain your answer.	7
7.	Address a startup from the case studies Now, tackle the 'entrepreneur's dilemma' through a different view; refer to the model in Figure 8.4: The entrepreneur's dilemma in managing crisis strategies. Advise the startup on how to cope with the pandemic through this model's concepts; write a one-page report that explains the rationale and practical steps to be implemented.	1, 2, 3, 4, and 5
8.	Address two startups from the case studies • Choose four strategies from the tables displaying the map of crisis management strategies and practices based on business model pillars. • Discuss the two startups' coping strategies accordingly. • Do you think that different crisis types require different coping strategies? And if so, specify which.	1, 3, 4, and 5
9.	What would you recommend that these startups change in their coping strategies to ensure their company's success? Explain your answer.	1 and 3
10.	What would you recommend that academia add/change to prepare its students to cope with crises? Explain.	8
Chapter 9 Entrepreneurial psychological capital		
1.	Address two startups from the case studies Analyze the four main stages of Bowlby's (1961) theory of attachment vis-à-vis the COVID-19 pandemic for each of these startups. Are there differences in these startups' bereavement? Why, in your opinion, did such differences emerge?	1, 2, 3, 4, and 5
2.	How can psychological distress in times of crisis affect financial stakeholders? Base your answer on the chapter's concepts.	6 and 7
3.	In your view, how can stakeholders reduce startups' distress during crises? Refer to the concepts and ideas discussed in the chapter.	6, 7, and 8
4.	Provide three to four different ways for these startups to measure their employees' distress during a crisis. Base your answer on the ways suggested in the concepts and models introduced in this chapter.	1 and 3
5.	According to Reuters, December 2020, "Mental health tech startups fetch record investments with COVID-19" (https://www.reuters.com/business/mental-health-tech-startups-fetch-record-investments-with-covid-19-2020-12-15/). This presents an interesting opportunity to scale the startup's activity and potential profits. Suppose you were hired to advise one of the startups to expand their activity and open a spin-off for mental health technology. Which of the startups would you advise to do so? Explain your answer based on the startup's robustness, resilience, and EPC discussed in this chapter.	1, 3, 4, and 5

(*Continued*)

Questions for discussion	Best used for cases
6. From an ecosystem perspective, how can a financial entity propel EPC among startups in times of crisis? Relate to the concepts in Figure 9.3: Effects of higher EPC across startup levels.	6 and 7
7. Address a startup from the case studies Give its management recommendations on how to strengthen their EPC at both the organizational level and team level (separately). Relate to the concepts Figure 9.3: Effects of higher EPC across startup levels.	1, 3, 4, and 5
8. Address a startup from the case studies Read the *Forbes* article, February 2021: "How to build resilience as a startup founder" at: https://www.forbes.com/sites/forbescoachescouncil/2021/02/16/how-to-build-resilience-as-a-startup-founder/?sh=4a7bc98c662d Write a two-page transcript of a hypothetical management meeting in which one founder is against the recommendations in the *Forbes* article and the other one is for adopting them. Address the potential gains and costs in implementing these recommendations. What are your conclusions on the value of these recommendations?	3, 4, and 5
9. Describe how academia can foster EPC in the entrepreneurial ecosystem (e.g., students, active entrepreneurs, entrepreneurs whose startups failed, and wanna-preneurs, among others).	8
10. Address a stakeholder from the case studies Write six to eight points for stakeholders that support startups in times of crisis on the pros (three to four points) and cons (three to four points) of recognizing the startups' psychological distress in advance, while supporting them during a crisis.	6, 7, and 8
Chapter 10 Female entrepreneurship in crises	
1. Address a startup from the case studies Search the web for a female-led startup. Describe the startup and provide the link to its website. Refer to the model demarcating female startups in Figure 10.1: Perspectives in demarcating female entrepreneurship. Demarcate one of the startups described in the case studies. Discuss the similarities and differences between these two startups with reference to the pandemic's effects on them. What are your main conclusions?	1, 3, and 4
2. Suppose Valeries has asked for your mentorship to prevent its failure. • How would you tackle the mentorship? • Refer to the template in Figure 10.2: A startup's success: what it is contingent on, and its evaluation. Which factor(s) would you stress in your mentoring? Explain why these are important and how you see them saving Valeries from failure.	2
3. Ask ten women in your surroundings what they think are the most emergent challenges for female entrepreneurs during the pandemic. Accordingly, write a two-page recommendation for JI on how to attract female startups and how to grow those startups in their portfolio. What are your main messages? Explain.	7

4.	• Compare the female founders' interpretations of the 'facts' of the crisis effects. • Do you find an association between the interpretation and the startup's success? If so, explain.	1, 2, 3, and 4
5.	Address a startup from the case studies Search the web for a startup headed by a male founder. Describe it and provide the link to its website. Write the transcript of a hypothetical Zoom session between the female (i.e., from the case studies) and the male (i.e., from the web) founders that emphasizes the premises of their definitions of the crisis and its effects on their businesses. What are your main insights? Explain.	1,2, 3, 4, and 7
6.	• Explain the success of the two female startups (Papaya and Guesty) based on the chapter's main concepts and models. • Compare the different ways of tackling the crisis in these female-led startups. Explain your answer.	3 and 4
7.	Suppose Startup México and Dux Capital are asking for your advice on how to encourage female entrepreneurship in crisis episodes. Write six to seven recommendations. What are your main insights?	6
8.	Suppose Bizzabo is considering a merger with a female-led startup during the pandemic, and they hire you to advice on the best workflow to guarantee a successful merger. Write a one-page rationalization and five to six practical suggestions for Bizzabo that will facilitate the merger. Take Bizzabo's attributes in terms of flexibility, agility, and awareness to the environment into account.	5
9.	Search Papaya Global's website (https://papayaglobal.com/about/; https://papayaglobal.com/). Indicate its uniqueness in relation to female entrepreneurship. In your view, what is the effect of inclusion and diversity on the startup's success in times of crisis?	3
10.	Compare the strategic orientation of startups—a female-led versus a male-led—in facing the crisis' effects. • What are your main conclusions? • Accordingly, should stakeholders treat female- and male-led startups differently when supporting them in times of crisis? If so, explain how.	1, 2, 3, 4, and 5

Notes

1 See discussion on the quote at Quora, https://www.quora.com/What-did-Steve-Jobs-mean-when-he-said-I-want-to-put-a-ding-in-the-universe
2 See "Advantages" May 2021, https://www.advantages.net/unleash-the-power-of-the-pivot/
3 Mr. Dantus confirmed sharing his story
4 SMB = small and medium-sized businesses.
5 SME(s) = small and medium-sized enterprise(s).

Index

Note: **Bold** page numbers refer to tables; *italic* page numbers refer to figures and page numbers followed by "n" denote endnotes.

Printed in the United States
by Baker & Taylor Publisher Services